AMIABLE AUTOCRAT

A BIOGRAPHY OF DR. OLIVER WENDELL HOLMES

Dr. Holmes in his study, 296 Beacon St.—c. 1894

Amiable Autocrat

A BIOGRAPHY OF

DR. OLIVER WENDELL HOLMES

By Eleanor M. Tilton

NEW YORK

HENRY SCHUMAN

Table of Contents

Half-tone Plates

Acknowledgments

Like any writer of a biography, I am so far in debt that no amount of gratitude could be adequate payment. The kindness and generosity of my creditors, however, can be recalled with such pleasure that the state of bankruptcy seems altogether agreeable.

It goes without saying that this work could not have been carried through without the co-operation of the grandson of Dr. Holmes. Mr. Edward Jackson Holmes has kindly allowed me access to material and given me permission to quote freely from manuscripts. Of his friendly interest and that of Mrs. Holmes, and of their hospitality I have the most pleasant memories.

To my sorrow, two of my largest debts must be acknowledged posthumously. The late Thomas Franklin Currier's gifts of information and leads to sources of material were innumerable. Moreover, he allowed me free access to his notes for his bibliography of Holmes—a courtesy his family continued to extend to me. Those who are familiar with the thoroughness and accuracy of his bibliography of Whittier can appreciate how helpful such generosity would be. In dozens of ways Mr. Currier made the task of research easier and more comfortable than it would have been without his help. I shall long remember with affection and gratitude the co-operative spirit with which he offered all this assistance.

Another of my creditors, Mr. Carroll A. Wilson, had so often before opened his excellent private library to students that the vocabulary of thanks has been pretty much exhausted on his name. Like the others, I have to thank him not only for the use of his library and permission to print from his manuscripts, but also for advice and encouragement, to say nothing of his practical help in locating material. As liberal with his time as with his possessions, he was also kind enough to read the entire manuscript.

For the same helpful service and criticism I am happy to thank Miss Miriam Small of Wells College, who is collecting and editing the letters of Holmes. She, too, has generously shared her discoveries and allowed me access to her notes. This book is dependent upon her work as it is upon that of Mr. Currier.

From the very beginning, Professor Ralph Leslie Rusk of Columbia University has been ready with his help and encouragement. I am grateful for his valuable guidance and criticism, for his sound advice, and for his readiness to give it when needed. Needless to say, he has patiently read my manuscript several times.

The most recent but most indefatigable reader of the manuscript is Mr. Henry Schuman, for whose knowledge of medical history I have reason to be thankful. His meticulous criticism has lightened the work of revision. I am also very thankful for Mr. Lewis Thompson's careful copy-reading.

To three busy doctors I am grateful for their gift of time and suggestions: Dr. George Rosen read the chapters on Holmes's medical study in Paris; Dr. Claude E. Heaton, the puerperal fever material; and Dr. Gregory Zilboorg, the sections on psychiatry.

My indebtedness to the authors of books and articles about Holmes cannot be adequately acknowledged in this brief space, but two names I wish to mention here. Mr. M. A. DeWolfe Howe, author of *Holmes of the Breakfast-Table,* has given me kindly encouragement. More than that, he has been good enough to read my manuscript. His son, editor of *Touched with Fire,* the Civil War diaries and letters of the younger Holmes, has generously shared manuscript material.

Other individuals whose names I recall here with much gratitude for their acts of kindness are Mrs. Frederick Winslow, Miss Clara Barnes, Miss Marion Barnes, Mr. Kenneth Porter, Dr. Henry Viets, Mr. James E. Ballard, Mr. Cecil Barnes, Mr. William A. Jackson, Mr. Wilfred Barnes, and Mr.

Clifford P. Monahon. I shall not try to list by name the personal friends whose sympathy and interest were constant sources of encouragement. Nor shall I try to express my gratitude to my parents for their help and, above all, for their patience, which was, I know, sometimes sorely tried.

For practical aid, I am indebted to MacMurray College for a leave of absence, to Columbia University for a fellowship, and to the American Association of University Women for their Fellowship Crusade National Fellowship.

For allowing me to use manuscripts and letters, my thanks are due to Mrs. Ward Thoron, Mr. Henry Lee Shattuck, Mr. John T. Winterich, Mr. H. W. L. Dana, Mr. Edward W. Forbes, and Comdr. John A. Brownell, USNR. The institutions which have allowed me to use manuscripts and pictures in their possession are Houghton Library, Harvard University Archives, Harvard Medical School, Massachusetts Historical Society, Boston Public Library, Boston Medical Library, Boston Athenaeum, Boston Dispensary, Phillips Academy at Andover, Springfield Public Library, Middlebury College, Connecticut Historical Society, New York Public Library, Library Company of Philadelphia, American Philosophical Society, Library of Congress, Duke University, Henry E. Huntington Library, and King's Chapel.

Houghton, Mifflin Company has kindly given me permission to quote extensively from *The Writings of Oliver Wendell Holmes,* Riverside Edition; *The Complete Poetical Works,* Cambridge Edition; John T. Morse, Jr., *The Life and Letters of Oliver Wendell Holmes*; and Horace E. Scudder, *James Russell Lowell.* I owe my thanks, too, to the *Springfield Republican* for access to their files of the paper.

I should like to add here my appreciation of the courtesy and helpfulness of the librarians in these institutions and in the Louisville Public Library, the Enoch Pratt Library in Baltimore, the American Antiquarian Society, the Historical and Philosophical Society of Ohio, the Connecticut Valley Historical Society, the Berkshire Athenaeum, and Widener Library.

Minister's Son

*His initiation into the Christian Church was
not delayed.**

In the early spring of 1801, a young woman of Cambridge, Massachusetts, sat down to get her mother up to date on the gossip of the town.

> Now, Mamma, I am going to surprise you. Mr. Abiel Holmes, whom we so kindly chalked out for Miss N. W. is going to be married, and of all folks in the world, guess who to. Miss Sally Wendell. I am sure you will not believe it; however, it is an absolute fact. . . . I could not believe it for some time, and scarcely can now; however, it is a fact they say.[1]

The writer had her news straight from the Jackson girls, who had it from a friend.

It was a fact. On March 26, the handsome minister of the First Church, aged thirty-eight and a childless widower, married Sarah Wendell, thirty-three-year-old daughter of the Honorable Oliver Wendell.

Eight years later, on the last Sunday in August, the Reverend Abiel Holmes, after rounding off his sermon, asked his parishioners to take home with them the psalmbooks and the cushions, to clear the meeting-house for the ceremonies of Wednesday morning, Harvard College commencement day. On Monday and Tuesday, the small children of Cambridge excitedly watched the hoisting of boards and poles and old

---

* The quotations are all taken from Boswell's *Life of Johnson,* which Dr. Holmes read annually. Johnson, born in 1709, became a kind of ghostly companion for Holmes, born a hundred years later.

sails that turned the College Yard and the Common into a carnival ground. To the west of the tents, rows of stands tempted children and adults with candy, toys, and soft drinks. In Captain Stimson's house, traveling showmen set up their stands—a Punch and Judy show, a few freaks. Cartloads of watermelons and peaches drew into the market place.

On Wednesday morning, attended by a troop of Light-horse, the Governor and his retinue paraded into the town to the blare of trumpets. The meeting-house was already crowded at nine o'clock when the procession of professors and students marched in to take their places for the commencement ceremonies.

"I remember that week well," wrote an old man many years later, "for something happened to me once at that time, namely I was born." [2]

The sounds of trumpets, the strains of processional marches, and the hullabaloo of a circus marked the first day in the life of the son of the minister of the First Church. Perhaps the pressure of events, private and public (for the minister was an overseer of the college), or perhaps natural restraint kept Abiel Holmes from taking special notice of the birth of the first son in a houseful of three daughters. Opposite the date August 29 in his almanac, he wrote in his neat hand "Son b." On September 10, the minister entered in the parish records a note of the baptism of Oliver Wendell Holmes.

The house in which Holmes was born stood just north of the Harvard Yard, across the street from Stoughton and Hol-worthy, on the present site of the Littauer building. Less pretentious than the mansions on Tory Row, the gambrel-roofed house was not set back from the road like Elmwood, where Lowell was born, or Craigie House, to which Longfellow brought his beautiful wife. The Holmes house crowded close upon the street, its small front yard a little too thick with syringa bushes, its south windows shaded by a row of elm trees. Another row of elms led up to the west door; and along the west wall, a stiff line of Lombardy poplars had something of a funereal aspect. To the north were the out-buildings, the

4

garden, and the neighboring houses; to the east—riverwards—was an open field.[3]

Although it was simple, "genteel" rather than aristocratic, it had historical associations of importance. It was perhaps for these associations that Judge Wendell had bought the place for himself, his daughter, and her family. The judge had known it well in the days when he and the other patriots who were members of the Massachusetts Committee of Safety had used it as their meeting place. The dents in the floor of the southeast room were not really made by militiamen's rifles, but an imaginative boy liked to think so, as he heard his mother and grandfather tell stories of the Revolution, of which his scholarly father had written in a less personal way in his *Annals of America*. From the west windows, the Washington elm was visible, making with two others the pattern of a coral fan. From such surroundings a boy could not help absorbing something of provincial patriotism—of the Federalist variety, to be sure, but under sufficient stimulus likely to be fired with revolutionary zeal.

The house itself was full of ghosts, a few too many for a small boy afraid of the dark. It had all the proper accommodations for them: a damp cellar with cold brick pillars and sepulchral arches, and an attic which was in part "a realm of darkness and thick dust, and shroud-like cobwebs and dead things they wrap in their gray folds." [4] Grandfather Wendell's chamber, with its great mirror and dim portraits, left its sharp impression to be recalled later for literary purposes and recollected in personal nostalgia:

The room where the aged owner, whom I just remember, died was a kind of Bluebeard chamber to my imagination. A tall mirror—the one of a pair which had survived the British occupancy of the house in Boston where they belonged—showed me to myself in my entire personality. Two portraits—a young man with handsome features and flowing locks, a young woman of much beauty in a cloud of floating drapery, showed dimly through the gauze that covered them. A third hung on the opposite wall. It was a young girl in antique costume, which made her look at first sight almost like a grown woman. The frame was old, massive, carved, gilded—the canvas had been stabbed by a sword-thrust—the British officer had aimed at the right eye and just missed it. The young lady was Dorothy Quincy, aunt of the young patriot known as Josiah Quincy Junior.[5]

In spite of his fear of midnight visitors, his uneasy feeling as he passed the garret door, and his suspicion that there might be something besides unmended furniture in one of the outhouses, the boy did not entirely believe in ghosts. The phantoms, moreover, were respectable, not at all the kind of spectres that haunted another boy, born in the same year across the river in Boston. Holmes's ghosts, unlike Poe's, added up in the end to something like the "first-rate fit-out" Holmes has the Autocrat give in his description of the ideal ancestry, even to a colonial governor. "Above all things," he insisted, going on about his man of family, "as a child, he should have tumbled about a library." [6]

The library of the Reverend Abiel Holmes had certain deficiencies. "It was very largely theological so that I was walled in by solemn folios making the shelves bend under the load of sacred learning," [7] wrote Holmes. When his brother John began raiding the Harvard Library, he came away with armloads of fiction—novels not to be found on his father's shelves.[8] Wendell Holmes could later recall having found only one piece of secular fiction among his father's books. The censor's hand was there, too, tearing some leaves from Dryden's poems and entering in the margin a Latin note declaring that the hiatus was not one to be lamented.[9] Even the mother, with intentions protective rather than moral, "crossed out with deep black marks something awful, probably about BEARS." [10]

In the library and the book-hospital in the southeast chamber of the otherwise terrifying garret there were nearly two thousand books, among them, history, biography, and the classics of English literature. From the sermons, the histories, the biographies, Rees's *Encyclopedia,* and periodicals like the *Annual Register,* the boy nosed out the narratives, skipping the moral, and sampled the biographical sketches "if the subjects of them were not too exemplary to have adventures." He was ready to read "everything but what tasted too strong of

'Thou shall' and 'Thou shalt not'—'Be good and you will be happy.' " [11]

The minister, whose choice of books for his church library ran to such cheerful items as *A Friendly Visit to the House of Mourning* and who considered Saurin's sermons proper food for children, offered to his son lugubrious tracts with melancholy frontispiece portraits of unhealthy children. The boy sampled these tales of prayerful children "buzzed round by ghostly comforters, or discomforters," and turned away in sharp distaste. Foraging for himself, he turned up some not exactly light-hearted stories in such volumes as Foxe's *Actes and Monuments*; here at least was action and adventure along with an horrendous diet of blood and torture. The heroes and heroines in Foxe died quickly, at least, and dramatically, not slowly and boringly amid their tears and prayers.

Pilgrim's Progress was naturally on the shelves, but the moral of the story was either unavoidable or made too plainly manifest to the son of a Puritan, for "it seemed . . . more like the hunting of sinners with a pack of demons for the amusement of the Lord of the terrestrial manor than like the care of a father for his tender offspring." Perhaps the task of sidestepping the theology and moralizing, of finding some "green patches among the deserts" in many of his father's books, got him into the habit of reading "*in* books rather than *through* them." There were a few compulsory deserts to get through, sermons not his own choice and Scott's commentary on the Bible. The latter Holmes describes as "one of the books that most influenced me, but not in the direction which the author intended." [12]

A prejudice of a different kind was firmly fixed by a book discovered in the book-hospital—*The Negro Plot,* a volume which "helped to implant a feeling . . . which it took Mr. Garrison a good many years to root out." The minister had spent seven years in a pastorate in Midway, Georgia, and the notions he there acquired helped out the impression his son had got from this volume. Holmes's later reluctance to accept the arguments of the abolitionists, like his cousin Wendell

7

Phillips or William Lloyd Garrison, seems to have had its origin here.

Other treasures of the attic room were less pernicious in their effects. There was that curious volume *Palladium Spagyricum,* by Peter John Faber, the first of a series of volumes "accidentally" thrown his way and later turned to account for his fight against scientific charlatans. The young boy went at the ragged volume with a practical purpose, searching for some lucid directions for turning "lead sinkers and the weights of the kitchen clock into good yellow gold." [13] For all its mysterious jargon peculiar to the alchemist jealously guarding his secret, the volume was better reading than *The Saint's Rest.*

There is nowhere a hint that he turned with any unnatural avidity to the volumes of poetry on his father's shelves, but he absorbed enough of Dryden, Pope, and Goldsmith to fall into making up heroic lines of his own, reciting them to himself, but not going to the trouble of writing them down. Perhaps he knew then that they were "not as good as those on the duck which Sam. Johnson trod on." [14] One day when an accident kept him home from school, his father set for him the theme: " 'Perdidi diem.' Tiberias." [*sic*] and was proud and pleased, if not discriminating, when the boy turned up a short time later with eight lines of verse which the father carefully copied. Coming upon the lines many years later, the abashed author scrawled a note: "Not very bright for a boy nearly 13 years old in my private opinion." The lines were:

> "I've lost a day," old Tibby said,
> Then sighed and groaned, and went to bed.
> This monarch, as they said of old,
> Knew time was worth much more than gold.
> I'm of this sage opinion too,
> And think this man judged pretty true.
> But now my friends, I'll bid good-bye,
> For you are tired—and so am I.[15]

The minister himself had written a little poetry in his youth, correct, uninspired verses in the style popular among the Yale poets, among the Connecticut Wits. With his first

8

wife Maria Stiles, her sisters, and apparently another young friend he had, in 1795, compiled a book, *The Family Tablet*. The preface describes the book as "designed for the eye of friendship" and fashionably quotes Ossian.[16] Far from Ossianic, however, the most ambitious piece is a Popeian mock epic called "Yaratilda," by "Myron," the minister's pseudonym. The poem is not too bad for what it is supposed to be— "a winter's evening entertainment" [17]—and reveals a gentleness in the author's nature, a Dr. Primrose cast of thought. The poems are not unpleasantly sentimental; some of them show a decorous but thoroughly secular wit. The hallmark of them all is eighteenth-century correctness. It was this fondness for verse that made the minister substitute in his church Watt's hymns for those of Tate and Brady and include in his library the works of Milton and the English Augustans, whom he quoted liberally in his sermons.

Not all the verse to which he exposed his son was as sound as that of Milton, Dryden, and Pope; the boy encountered a good deal of the arid and commonplace verse of the lesser eighteenth-century poets and not a little plain doggerel. The tuneless specimens in the *New England Primer* had some affecting tales, particularly the verses attributed to John Rogers, the Smithfield Martyr, and illustrated with an ugly woodcut showing "his wife with nine small children following him to the stake" and reporting that with this "sorrowful sight he was not in the least daunted." The youthful reader seems to have been daunted, however; he admits to having shed a tear or two over the lines the martyr supposedly addressed to his offspring.

Such poems as Cowper's "The Rose has been washed, just washed in a shower" were presented to my youthful appetite,—literary confections not favorable to the growth of a sound and wholesome taste; but I had Gray's "Elegy" and "The Spacious Firmament on High" and, by and by, *The Galaxy of American Poets*, Bryant shining among them. . . . But my favorite reading was Pope's Homer; to the present time the grand couplets ring in my ears and stimulate my imagination, in spite of their formal symmetry, which makes them hateful to the lawless versificators

9

who find anthems in the clash of blacksmith's hammers, and fugues in the jangle of sleigh bells.

> "Aurora now, fair daughter of the dawn
> Sprinkled with rosy light the dewy lawn"

thrills me with [its] splendid resonance. . . .[18]

On the whole the books in Abiel Holmes's library, especially the folio volumes on the lower shelves, were more useful as blocks for the erection of fortresses and bridges than they were for reading. Holmes's schoolmates might have written of him as he makes the fashionable schoolmates report of a character in one of his novels: "We have the oddest girl here . . . she hasn't read any book that isn't a thousand years old." [19]

Life in the Holmes household was likely to be rather old-fashioned, for it took some of its tone from the minister, who came from Woodstock, Connecticut, a village "more favorable to the growth of an hereditary faith than of inquiry." [20] Abiel Holmes had been brought up in the Calvinist faith and educated at Yale University, fortress of the orthodox Puritans. The difference between the atmosphere of Yale and that of Harvard is suggested in the nice provincial distinction one of Abiel Holmes's Cambridge parishioners made. He described the minister as "liberal—for a Connecticut man." [21]

In the minister's puritan home, Sunday was usually a day of unrelieved gloom. The observance of the Sabbath, from sundown to sundown, was rigidly enforced, requiring a decorum, a silence, an inactivity very trying to a nervous and talkative boy. Even studying was forbidden so that the minister's son, calling on another boy, was shocked to find his host doing his lessons on the Sabbath. Nor were two long sermons, even the agreeable and melodious ones of his father, exactly what he desired. As the minister's son he had to pay attention. There were always callers, too, some of them delightful people, but too many of them were men "smitten with the Sabbath paralysis which came from the rod of Moses and killed out their natural spirits. . . ." One leader of the fire and brimstone faith provoked young Wendell Holmes to laugh aloud in church and to contrive to knock over the preacher's inkstand, antics possibly taken as evidence of youthful corruption.[22] Another with a whining voice and lugubrious words had a particularly nagging way of attacking small boys. He "did more in one day to make the boy a heathen than he had ever done in a month to make a Christian out of an infant Hottentot." [23] None of these purveyors of horror and gloom were likely to impress a boy with the beauties of the faith.

The father himself did not insist too unpleasantly, as some of his colleagues did, on the natural wickedness of children and the probability of their eternal damnation, but he did believe in giving children a thoroughly orthodox training. In paying his parochial calls, "he was wont . . . to distribute catechisms and hymn books and to question the children on religious matters and duties." [24] The five children in the Holmes family learned that they were "a set of little fallen wretches, exposed to the wrath of God by the fact of that existence which [they] could not help." [25]

Even the garden provided the boy's father with a puritan text now and then. Just to the left of the door was "that remarkable moral pear tree. . . . Its fruit never ripened, but always rotted at the core just before it began to grow mellow." The boy believed that the tree had been planted on purpose to "preach its annual sermon." Abiel Holmes was just enough of a poet to find illustrations of his doctrines even in his vegetable garden; the lowly radish suggested the notion of "total depravity, a prey to every evil emissary of the powers of darkness." [26] Yet the father's teaching was not always austere. He could not forbear the moral lesson, but he might make it amusing.

Among the books of my father's library was the *Histoire ecclésiastique* of the Abbé Fleury, in some twenty or thirty volumes. A book-worm, one of the literal kind, had bored his way straight through the leaves—every one of them—of the first volume from cover to cover. My father, who wrote verses now and then, drew a lesson from the book-worm for my benefit, beginning

"See here, my son, what industry can do. . . ."[27]

The *New England Primer,* however, with its crude wood-cuts and its iteration of the doctrine of original sin, was still the textbook of the orthodox New England household. From it, the puritan boy learned the shorter Westminster catechism with its 107 questions and their answers. John Cotton's "Spiritual Milk for Babes," another catechism, required the young answerer to declare that he "was conceived in sin, & born in iniquity" and that his "corrupt nature is empty of grace, bent into sin, and that continually." [28] The two girls in the household were apparently amenable to this teaching, being properly converted and becoming members of the church.[29] Neither of the boys, however, could reach that state of acceptance. The doubts and questions that troubled young Wendell made part of his childhood an ordeal. "To grow up in a narrow creed and to grow out of it is a tremendous trial of one's nature." [30] Beginning early to revolt and not being a silent boy, he apparently attacked his father with questions for which there were no satisfactory answers in the minister's heavy theological volumes.[31]

The father was not a hard man or an unkind one, being a scholarly rather than a militant Calvinist, but his calling, his faith, and his background would tend to make him a much more sober companion to his children than their mother. For Holmes, as for William Cullen Bryant, whose experience he felt to be like his own, the "important point was not his father's creed but his mother's character." [32]

Entrusted with the task of hearing the children recite the responses of the harsh catechism, Sarah Wendell Holmes had to assume a sober face, although she was by nature a smiling and cheerful woman, a sharp contrast to the minister's first wife, pale, poetical, and consumptive Maria Stiles. The Cambridge gossip who had been surprised at the minister's choice of Sarah Wendell may have realized that he had chosen a woman "bred in an entirely different atmosphere from that of straight-laced Puritanism." [33] Her home, Boston and Cambridge, had begun to diverge from Woodstock and New Haven before the turn of the century. The coast city, center of mercantile interests, and its neighbor across the Charles were already getting some reputation as the home of infidels and characters suspiciously liberal in their religious, if not in their political, thinking. Although she was no bluestocking, Sarah Wendell was an intelligent woman, and she could not have escaped being in some measure affected by this environment.

It is no accident that in later life Holmes could write "of my paternal ancestors I know little compared with what I know of those on my mother's side." [34] The Wendells were men of property, landowners and merchants, Dutchmen who reversed the procedure described by Irving in Knickerbocker's history, for they invaded the homeland of the Yankee. It was a Wendell who owned the land that is now part of the town of Pittsfield, Massachusetts, and the name of the original patroon is still preserved in the city's most attractive street. Annually during his childhood, young Holmes had the excitement of seeing his parents off on a visit of inspection of the Wendell property in the western part of the state. An expedition of 150 miles was a large undertaking in those days, one to leave an impression on a small boy's mind.[35] It was Grandfather Wendell who occupied the great chamber upstairs; of Dr. David Holmes, the boy heard little. Years later he would hold in his hands David Holmes's copy of the works of Sydenham, the great seventeenth-century physician, and possess the orderly books of this grandfather, who had been a surgeon in Washington's army; but it was, however, the doctor in his mother's family, great-grandfather James Oliver, whom the boy heard most about; the name was constantly before him in an inherited remedy—a plaster of mysterious ingredients, known as a "Dr. Oliver" and applied for toothaches.[36] Great-grandfather Holmes was an obscure citizen of a Connecticut village, sufficiently important to be a church deacon but leaving no other record of his activities. Great-grandfather Wendell had owned a sizable lot of business property in Boston. Tales of his Wendell ancestors Holmes must have often heard from the grandfather for whom he was named and from his mother. His father's imagination was busy working on a much larger canvas; he was getting his history of the country, *Annals of America,* up to date. The scholarship and theology of Abiel Holmes would necessarily be less attractive to a small boy than the sociability and personal chatter of Sarah Wendell.

Lightheartedness came to her more easily than to her husband and infected her children. Her daughters turned into village belles; her sons, into wits. Abiel Holmes might worry about the "light and unhallowed airs" [37] to which some hymns were set, but his wife had no misgivings about music. Probably it was in response to her desire that the minister invested $250 in a pianoforte.[38] When the London-made Clementi was installed in the south parlor, the house was full of noisy excitement as the pushing children crowded each other to see the new instrument. The noise, so the poem says, did not stop at the father's request for quiet, but the mother hushed the tumult with the words, "Now, Mary, play." [39] They sang the songs of Tom Moore, whose lyrics sounded more agreeably in the ears of young Wendell than the grim words of Calvinist hymns.

Music lessons were probably not unheard of in puritan households, but dancing lessons were another matter.

Some of the mothers in our small town, who meant that their children should know what was what as well as other people's children, laid their heads together and got a dancing-master to come out from the city and give instruction at a few dollars a quarter to the young folks of condition in the village. Some of their husbands were ministers and some were deacons, but the mothers knew what they were about, and they didn't see any reason why ministers' and deacons' wives' children shouldn't have as easy manners as the sons and daughters of Belial.

That Sarah Holmes was one of these enterprising mothers her husband's account-book bears witness. The minister's children learned to do country dances, the cotillon, and "something called a 'gavotte' from a lively little gentleman" who "cocked his hat a little too much on one side" and used to "spring up in the air and 'cross his feet.' " At the exhibition ball at the end of each term:

He used to bring out a number of hoops wreathed with roses, of the perennial kind, by the aid of which a number of amazingly complicated and startling evolutions were exhibited; and also his two daughters, who figured largely in these evolution, and whose . . . performances . . . were something . . . surpassing the natural possibilities of human beings.[40]

The Cambridge Turveydrop could help to turn the minister's children into models of unpuritanical fashion. Whatever puritan gloom there may have been in the minister's house would be in part dispelled by a smiling mother, who helped bring dancing-masters to town and pianofortes to the house.

Schoolboy

1815–1825

*Now, Sir, if a boy could answer every question,
there would be no need of a master to teach him.*

THE BOY, who was fond of reading stories and adroit at untangling adventure from theology, could also have adventures of his own. Of course, there were some terrors to be encountered in the outside world. The country boys, who helped in the house and grounds, had alarming tales to tell of "death-signs,—of apparitions," of contracts written in blood and left out over night "to fall into the hands of the devil on his nightly rounds." That the Devil was abroad in the world was evident; his footprints were plainly outlined in bare sandy patches below the orchard. The dark crevice high up in the wall of one of the Harvard dormitories marked the place where some students once engaged to their damnation in profane practices the nature of which was never quite clear.[1]

Always small for his years, Wendell Holmes had his private fears of tall, towering things like the skeleton forest of masts at the foot of the West Boston bridge. Nevertheless, he hoped that "O.T.," one of the country boys who worked in the kitchen, would not forget to bring him the promised toy ship. The glove-maker's clutching, wooden sign never did snatch him up in spite of its threatening look; and there was, after all, a huckleberry pasture beyond the devil's stalking ground.[2]

On the whole the pleasures of the outer world outnumbered the mysteries and dangers. He could leave the house by passing the sweet-scented spice cupboard and, going through the kitchen, come out in the garden.

We had peaches, lovely nectarines, and sweet white grapes. . . . As for the garden-beds . . . hyacinths, pushing their green beaks through as soon as the snow was gone, or earlier; tulips, coming up in the shape of sugar "cockles," or cornucopiae . . . peonies, butting their way bluntly through the loosened earth . . . lillies, roses, damask, white, blush, cinnamon; larkspur, lupins, and gorgeous hollyhocks. With these upper class plants were blended in republican fellowship, the useful vegetables of the working sort—beets, handsome with dark red leaves; carrots, with their elegant filigree foliage; parsnips that cling to the earth like mandrakes . . . onions, never easy until they are out of bed, so to speak . . . squash-vines with their generous fruits. . . .[3]

The moralizing pear tree was, happily, flanked by sunflowers that attracted bright troops of goldfinches. He remembered them, "flitting about, golden in the golden light, over the golden flowers, as if they were flakes of curdled sunshine." [4] The boy might be given to poetic notions, but somehow in the dim remembrances of childhood, apples were linked with flowers; the garden and orchard had their practical uses, ministering to senses less romantic than the eye.

Beyond the garden lay the world. To the east the view was "widely open," with "sunlit sails gliding along as if through level fields, for no water was visible." [5] Even toward the center of town, the prospect was open, the distant hills glimmering.

Beyond, as I looked round, were the Colleges, the meeting-house, the little square market-house . . . the burial ground where the dead Presidents stretched their weary bones under epitaphs stretched out as full length as their subjects; the pretty church where the gouty tories used to kneel on their hassocks; the district school-house, and hard by it Ma'am Hancock's cottage, never so called in those days, but rather "tenfooter"; then houses scattered near and far, open spaces, shadowy elms, round hilltops in the distance, and over all the great bowl of the sky . . . this was the WORLD as I first knew it.[6]

And in a measure this was the world as Holmes always knew it—the Harvard Yard, the Cambridge Common, the Charles River, the elm trees.

A large, infirm old lady ruled his first schoolroom. Ma'am Prentiss's age and bulk made it hard for her to move, but a long willow rod reached easily across the small room to "stimulate the sluggish faculties or check the mischievous sallies of the child most distant from her ample chair." [7] The minister's son was "an inveterate whisperer," [8] unusually garrulous even at six. The willow rod probably moved often enough in his direction to indicate that he was not too good a boy. On hot summer days, the low-studded room was not the most comfortable place; a small boy's eye very naturally wandered in the direction of "one particular pailful of water, flavored with the white-pine of which the pail was made, and the brown mug out of which . . . a boy was averred to have bitten a fragment in his haste to drink." [9]

But adventures outside the Dame school were more likely to stick in his memory, especially the exciting day when the War of 1812 came to an end and New Englanders, who had opposed the war in the first place, celebrated the Peace with particular fervor.

I remember well coming from the Dame school, throwing up my "jocky" as the other boys did, and shouting "Hooray for Ameriky," looking at the blazing college windows, and revelling in the thought that I had permission to stay up as long as I wanted to. I lasted until eight o'clock, and then struck my colors, and was conveyed by my guardian and handmaidens from the brilliant spectacle to darkness and slumber.[10]

In the fall of the same year, 1815, a "gale" struck the town, a wind not to be matched for 118 years; for what was called a "gale" in 1815 was a hurricane in 1938.

The wind caught up the waters of the bay and of the river Charles, as mad shrews tear the hair from each other's heads. The salt spray was carried far inland, and left its crystals on the windows of farm-houses and villas. . . . There was a mighty howling, roaring, and banging, and crashing, with much running about, and loud screaming of orders for sudden taking in of all sail about the premises, and battening down of everything that could flap or fly away. The top-railing of our old gambrel-roofed house could not be taken in, and it tried an aeronautic excursion as I remember.

Travelers, full of wild tales, took refuge in the minister's parlor. "There was an awful story of somebody taken up by the wind, and slammed against something with the effect of staving in his ribs." [11]

At least, that's the way he remembered the event, although

somehow the sharpest detail was the ground strewn with Rhode Island greenings in generous and appetizing profusion. The Sunday breeches lamented in the poem "September Gale" were a bright young man's invention; the minister's son most surely appeared in church on the following day, and he was certainly suitably clad.

To a small boy, adventure was adventure however it came about, but parents have a way of making a distinction between those that just happen and the kind a boy might engineer. Holmes was seven years old when he ran away from school, and, taking his five-year-old brother with him, set out for Jones's Hill. There on the outskirts of town stood the engine of old-fashioned justice—the gallows. There the two small sons of the minister watched the last hanging in Cambridge.

Justice of the parental sort was undoubtedly administered later. Whatever its form, the minister's punishment was not violent enough to prevent other expeditions. What were the charms of school compared to those of the race-course? Watching a good horse was a better occupation than filling an exercise book with words like "emoluments" or "amanuensis" or moral adages like "Procrastination is the thief of time." [12] One could safely procrastinate learning if there were a chance to see Revenge or Peacemaker in action.

Whenever he could get a ride behind a good horse, or any horse at all, he would take it. Thomas Dowse, the leather-dresser, was usually willing to give him a ride in his wagon. The puritan Sunday was a grim enough day, but it could be exciting when the minister drove away to preach in neighboring villages and took his son with him, although he did not go quite fast enough to suit his young passenger.

The eccentrics of Cambridge offered amusement. Old Dr. Benjamin Waterhouse, a neighbor, was never known for his pleasant disposition, and since his dismissal from the Harvard Medical School, he had become more irascible than ever. He was a famous man, however, responsible for introducing the practice of vaccination for smallpox to America, advertising himself truthfully as the American Jenner. Although no longer an active practitioner, the old doctor performed the service of vaccinating children, among them the son of his minister.[13] He was a frequent caller, regarding Abiel Holmes as his friend and helping him to set up a Humane Society for the town.

As a visitor to the Holmes's house, Dr. Waterhouse was less alarming to children than the regular family doctor, before whom "came a soul-subduing whiff of ipecacuanha, and after [whom] lingered a shuddering consciousness of rhubarb. He had lived so long among his medicaments that he had at last become a drug himself. . . ." [14] If Dr. Waterhouse was less threatening in a personal way than Dr. Gamage, he was still rather eerie. Near the Holmes house, a shallow brook ran under the dirt path, bridged with a patch of brick pavement; on this bridge, the old doctor used to stop in the course of his daily walks, tap the hollow pavement with his cane, and call, "Tom! Tom!" as if he supposed he might conjure his dead nephew up from the brook.[15]

One of the few "foreigners" in town was a Scotsman, somewhat given to drink, and not often approved by adults, but fascinating to boys, for he had, or was said to have, two complete sets of teeth in his head. And besides, he had been, according to his own account of it, a great warrior in his day and could engage the attention of a large audience with recitals of his achievements in battle. The town barber, a Dutchman, was not attractive in himself, but his shop was apparently all things to all boys, being a combination of museum and zoo. There was a ship model—perhaps such a boat as "O.T." had promised to bring—and a bright cockatoo. There were canaries and Indian relics. There were pictures of battles and generals.

For the annual event of his birthday, Wendell Holmes had always a circus to count on. If his curious taste for side-show freaks developed early, commencement day always provided a few—a Canadian Giant; Siamese twins; Columbus, the largest horse in the world; the Flying Horses; Dwarfs; the Fat Boy. And once, according to James Russell Lowell, the town pump flaunted a Mermaid.

Even the old yellow meeting-house took on a new face from

the majestic presence of the two town constables who flanked the doorway, "propped by long staves of blue and red." [16] For those who cared, six hours of sustenance for the intellect were offered within, but in the tents and stands outside the meeting-house there were offerings more satisfying to boys:

mountainous hams, thick-starred with cloves all over their powdery surface; the round of beef . . . the pie of various contents, the satisfying doughnut . . . the ginger-cake, hot in the mouth.[17]

Lewis, the negro vendor of spruce and ginger beer, displayed his stock in a white-roofed handcart under a sign of tipped bottles pouring into a tumbler. Even the flat tombstones in the churchyard were turned into picnic tables.

There were parades and music and dancing. There might even be a scrap with the Charlestown boys, who were obliged by unwritten law to fight their way into Cambridge if they wished to share in the academic carnival. Altogether it was quite as good an affair as election day in Boston.

Election day, however, had its special attractions: military parades and a lethal kind of bun which boys of Holmes's generation ate with the same reckless appetite that boys of later generations applied to popcorn and hot dogs. In Boston, too, was a quartet of cousins, who lived in a pleasant house on the corner of Walnut and Beacon Streets. One of the four, George, would be in Wendell Holmes's class at Harvard, famous in his own way for his extraordinary good looks. Another of the four bore the same name, Wendell. Of what the cousins argued as boys there is no record, but in the forties and fifties, the slavery question would keep them at friendly odds, the younger, Wendell Phillips, laboring to change the older one's mind.

With the years ticked off by a circus, and the weeks by Sunday's brace of sermons, the ordinary days went by with no special marks to distinguish them save initials and curlycues cut in schoolroom desks. Whittling is a proper Yankee pastime; and Wendell Holmes, always a "contriver," made up in imagination for what he lacked in skill. "Other boys were neater with their jackknives," [18] but not so ambitious. He

21

made his first attempts at skating on a wooden skate of his own
making. He cut a ball in a cage with chain attached, all from a
single piece of wood. He rigged up a perpetual motion machine. None of his "great absurdities" were carefully finished;
all of them were too hastily done, but they were somehow
satisfying to the contriver, who for the rest of his life enjoyed
fiddling about a carpenter's bench, making his own improved
stands for his microscopes and crude models of his stereoscope.
The habit of doing too many things too easily and quickly was
one that stuck.

He was quick and clever enough in school to have his first
master tap him on the head with a pencil in what was meant
to be a gesture of approval. William Biglow was a rather queer
schoolmaster in some ways, given to punning and writing
macaronic verses. He had some reputation as a scholar, but
to his students he seemed as strange as Rip Van Winkle.

A much ink-splashed exercise book survives to indicate the
kind of busy-work to which Master Biglow set the eight-year-
olds. The ink blotches on the cover may be a youthful expression of distaste for the mean countenance of the gentleman
whose picture illustrates it; the inside pages are neat enough.
The teacher set his students to filling their books with odd
words like "sacramental" and "recanter"; adages like "Good
manners procure respect," and bits of geographical lore:
"Olympus a mountain of Turkey in the Lesser Asia." At least
one supposes that the teacher set the exercises, although such
items as "Canary Point, Canary Isles, Atlantic Ocean," suggesting a boy's fondness for the complete address, may have
been the laboring schoolboy's invention.[19]

Young Holmes did not remain long under the guidance of
Biglow. With other town leaders, Abiel Holmes co-operated
to start a select private academy, known as the "Port School,"
located somewhat inconveniently a mile or more from the
Harvard Yard in the settlement of Cambridgeport. There
were certain hazards involved in getting to school. The local
residents of Cambridgeport—all those who could properly be
called boys—were known as Port-Chucks and looked upon the

too well-dressed academicians from Cambridge as interlopers. Wendell Holmes learned quickly that a wide-brimmed leghorn hat might lay him open to remarks damaging to his ten-year-old dignity.[20] He and his fellow academicians, however, presented a solid front and led by their champion, Richard Henry Dana, Jr., established their right to enter the domain of the Port-Chucks. By means of more or less regular battles, a certain equilibrium was maintained. In such battles, the small Holmes could not make much of a showing, but if his fists were useless, his tongue was not. "He dominated us all by his superior gift of speech," [21] achieving with wit victories he could not win on any battlefield.

In school, a succession of masters found in young Holmes a "moderately studious boy, very fond of reading stories" and likely to read them in school hours. He could not, however, stop talking, and "was apt for this reason to have a visitation from the ferrule when that implement was in use. A Gunter's scale got the worst of it in one of these collisions, flying to pieces as it came down on his palm." [22]

The schoolwork itself offered no special difficulties except for mathematics. He was going to Harvard College, however, and had to be "well versed in . . . vulgar and decimal fractions; proportion, simple and compound; single and double fellowship; alligation, medial and alternate," [23] not to mention algebra. Parsing Cicero, mastering the intricacies of Greek verbs, and learning the facts of ancient and modern geography were easy enough; and writing fluent and facile compositions was a pleasure.

A letter to his sister Mary, recently married to Dr. Usher Parsons of Providence, suggests something of his style. He was thirteen when he wrote: "Our family is now made smaller, and less lively by your absence and Cambridge is deprived of one whom it will be long before she can forget—Yet we cannot say, deprived, for we still keep up a communication which lights up the gloom which we feel, and is the means of driving away the absence of her who was the life of all our enjoyments." He wrote his letter in the midst of a familiar family

23

scene in the little back parlor. His mother and father were planning a trip to Providence; his sister Ann was "enjoying a fine tete a tete" with a visiting Harvard student, William H. Furness,[24] present friend of Ralph Waldo Emerson and future Unitarian minister. Young Furness was so often closeted tête-à-tête with Ann Holmes that the family was fearful lest he turn out to be a dangerous rival to her chief suitor, Charles Wentworth Upham, of Salem. He came to the Holmes house, in fact, to gossip with Ann of his own secret engagement to a Salem girl; he enjoyed too the flattering attention of young Wendell, who admired the college man's verses and laughed at his jokes. If Furness thought Wendell a "very bright boy," [25] sister Mary, much loved for her charm and admired for her learning, was apparently a less indulgent judge, for Wendell ended his letter: "I . . . beg you not to be too critical remembering that it comes from your loving Brother O.W.H." [26]

Perhaps he had good reason to expect criticism, for he was not inclined to be a thorough student; indeed, with more than average conceit, he supposed himself to be among those who "had drawn a prize, say a five-dollar one, at least, in the grand intellectual life-lottery." His self-satisfaction was shaken somewhat by a strange tall girl with a disconcertingly aloof manner. Margaret Fuller with "a watery, aqua-marine lustre in her light eyes" and a "long, flexible neck, arching and undulating in strange sinuous movements" was not pretty like the golden blonde" who bewitched half the school, but she was supposed to be smart and she talked about "nah-vels." When some themes were sent home from the school one day for his father's literary judgment, Wendell got a look at Margaret's. It began: "It is a trite remark . . ." The reader went no further; he did not know what trite meant.[27] He did not like the girl and could not like the woman she grew to be—learned, intellectual, and given to philosophy. He came to suspect that he had always been jealous of her.

He was something of a student because of his quickness rather than industry; but he bore no resemblance to the pale-faced, praying children of the tracts. He scattered his enthusiasms with a fine disregard of his father's moral lesson about the bookworm. The jackknife would be laid aside for the magnifying glass his father had brought home from Salem; the glass be put aside for a flute; and all be abandoned for the old King's Arm, a revolutionary flintlock from the storecloset. With this formidable weapon he "popped away at everything that stirred, pretty nearly, except the housecat." He owned a pistol, too, which did double duty. Revealing what might very well have been taken as evidence of original sin, he bought cigars and smoked them by installments. The pistol barrel in the meantime served as a quite safe storage place, "for no maternal or other female eyes would explore the cavity of that dread implement in search of contraband commodities." [28]

Possibly the cigars had something to do with Abiel Holmes's decision to send his son to Andover for a year. Boys did enter Harvard at fifteen, but the minister may have thought his clever, quick-talking son needed the sobering atmosphere of Andover, where a strictly orthodox theological seminary set the tone of the town and the preparatory school. Cambridge was running over with infidels, and whatever its merits as an academic institution, Harvard was more than suspect in its religion. In Cambridge, genial President Kirkland and liberal Henry Ware, Professor of Divinity, set the tone.

The Holmes house itself had been fairly regularly invaded by Harvard men, for Mary and Ann, especially Mary, were powerful attractions. Upon Cambridge boys, the college students exercised a fascination likely to be thought dangerous by an orthodox clergyman. Did Abiel Holmes know that his son's admiring eyes had fallen upon such showy figures as that of John Gaillard Keith Gourdin of South Carolina? The southerners "were the reigning *elegans* of that time. . . . Their swallow-tail coats tapered to an arrow-point angle, and the prints of their little delicate calf-skin boots in the snow were objects of great admiration." [29] In 1823, J. G. K. Gourdin's ex-roommate Ralph Waldo Emerson, had been teaching school in Cambridge; John Holmes was one of his students. The tall, thin young man was too soberly dressed and too quiet to attract attention, but his thoughts were symptomatic of the times and the place and were actually as alarming, from the orthodox point of view, as the spectacular elegance of Gourdin.

In a setting predominantly liberal and Unitarian, Abiel Holmes was an anomaly, but because his interests were anti-quarian, scholarly rather than theological, he had not yet be-gun to feel any particular discomfort in his position. He was not disposed to quarrel with those whose theology differed from his own; he agreeably exchanged pulpits not only with men of his own faith but with preachers suspected of leaning toward Unitarian heresy, even with such men as William Ellery Channing. He simultaneously served as trustee of An-dover Seminary, and as overseer and teacher of ecclesiastical history at Harvard, hotbed of liberalism.

"The prevailing character of his preaching was practical." [30] His neatly constructed sermons, rhetorical in an old-fashioned style, were lucid, scholarly—academic rather than evangelical, shot through with quotations from poets and classical authors. They reflected the tastes of a man of letters and the patriotism of the historian and the New England Federalist more often than the religious zeal of the Calvinist. A listener described one of his sermons as being as placid as the preacher looked.[31]

In his historical writing he shows himself to be reasonably free from prejudice about matters with which his religious beliefs might be expected to be in conflict. Throughout, the Annals show the author carefully maintaining his equilibrium between prejudice and scholarly tolerance when confronted with such dark passages of history as the witchcraft trials, such "singular" individuals as Roger Williams, such problems—to the Orthodox minister—as the Quakers. The bias, political and theological, is plainly there, but so also is an earnest de-sire for truth and a good leaven of eighteenth-century ra-tionalism. The latter leads the annalist to quote Addison and Sir William Temple and to observe of the witchcraft episode:

This part of the history of our country furnishes an affecting proof of the imbecility of the human mind, and of the powerful influence of the pas-

26

sions. The culture of sound philosophy, the dissemination of useful knowledge, have a happy tendency to repress chimerical effects.[32]

He had none of the conservative theologian's suspicion of science. To his record of the comet of 1680, he adds a long footnote expressing similar rationalistic views, and, further, his respect for scientists as correctors of superstition. In such passages, Abiel Holmes sounds like a layman and a Deist rather than a Calvinist preacher.

Altogether, the Reverend Abiel Holmes, in his scholarly love for history, his devotion to charitable and educational projects, his avoidance of evangelical or polemic theology, appears as a rather mild kind of Puritan, a lukewarm Calvinist. But the militant members of his sect were already on the march; the *Boston Recorder,* orthodox paper, was urging its subscribers to act against the rapidly growing heresy of the Unitarians. In a few years Cambridge would be the scene of one engagement in the battle, and Abiel Holmes would be the principal actor and victim.

Whether or not he sent his son to Andover to have him inoculated with orthodoxy before complete exposure to Harvard heresies, the minister's action was bound to have the opposite effect. Already in revolt from Calvinism, young Wendell could have encountered no influence in Cambridge to check that rebellion. At Andover he would meet his enemy in forms more formidable than his father offered, and the effect would be to drive him further away from a creed already repellent.

But his thoughts as he rode toward Andover with his father and mother were probably not on religion. Wendell had visited the school often with his father; the twenty-mile drive was a familiar pleasure; but that trip in August 1824 was different from the start. Even the company of his affectionate mother did not make it any less painful. Before the carriage drew up before the two-story white house opposite Lock's Tavern on the outskirts of Andover, he was thoroughly homesick. He was being delivered up to all kinds of mysteries. Doubtless the thought that his father would soon be taking his sister Ann on a long jaunt to visit sister Mary in Providence, attend the Yale commencement, and see Lafayette did not make the situation any happier, especially as it meant that he had to be left at his new school before the term began.[33]

A great boulder on Dr. Murdock's front lawn looked excessively cold and hard; the plainly furnished north room, which he would share with some strange boy, was bare and unfamiliar. He had met the Murdocks and old Persis, the "worthy gentlewoman of the poor relation variety" who looked after the boys, but on that day they might as well have been strangers. Sarah Holmes stayed long enough to settle his possessions and to make certain that he would have hot water for bathing carried to his room every Saturday night, but she had to leave him at last. He watched the carriage down one hill and up the next "until the window in the back of it disappeared like an eye that shuts."

Persis, who had succumbed to Sarah Holmes's charm, tried to comfort the boy who looked so much like his mother, but she seemed to think that homesickness was like a stomach-ache and administered a dose of soda. "The *fiz* was a mockery and the saline refrigerant struck a deeper chill to my despondent heart." [34]

The bare old academy building had nothing cheering in its aspect. Its long main room was doubly governed, presided over by the principal and his assistant. On a side wall was a large clock-dial bearing these words:

YOUTH IS THE SEED-TIME OF LIFE

I had indulged in a prejudice, up to that hour, that youth was the budding time of life, and this clock-dial perpetually twitting me with its seedy moral had a forbidding look to my vernal imagination.

He was assigned a seat beside a dark, scowling youth, very much bigger and older than he. This young man's favorite occupation was to kick his small neighbor's shins with all his might, "not as an act of hostility, but as a gratifying and harmless pastime." [35] There was nothing in these circumstances to make him feel less wretched, but he managed not to disgrace himself.

Before too long he had recovered, and was cracking nuts on the great rock that at first had seemed so forbidding, laughing at Persis's "high-sounding big words," [36] and succumbing to the antics and jests of little Tom Clark, his first acquaintance. If long-faced seminarians and grim doctors of Puritan theology set the tone of the adult world of Andover, the boys took their cue from the "imp of all mischief," Tom, who could never, in spite of a sober face, put on solemnity. An agreeable roommate, Nathaniel Dodge, put in an appearance and Holmes became acquainted with the daughters of the household. By the time the first affectionate letter came from home, he was reasonably settled, although not so pleased with his situation as his parents hoped.

He wrote his mother that he was "contented" and that he and his roommate had "good times." With a show of courage, he declared, "I admire the independence of my position." He expected, nevertheless, to see his parents at the examination of the seminary, and wanted to see his father very much.

I shall depend on your coming up to see how I keep house. I wish if you go into town you would get me some burnt almonds. Quite a childish request for an *Academician!* But you must remember that just as I was going to buy some the horse started & I forgot all about it—I have taxed your patience too long and to end with a tax on your purse is rather hard, but you can do as you choose about it.[37]

The letter is plainly that of a homesick boy putting on a brave front.

He did not attend to his studies with the devotion his father urged upon him. There was more pleasure, and quite likely more profit, in wandering the woods and hills of the countryside with his particular friend, fourteen-year-old Phinehas Barnes, from Maine. Climbing to the top of Indian Ridge, swimming in the Shawshine River, airing one's thoughts upon an admiring companion were more attractive occupations than sitting under the scowl of old John Adams or of being the victim of the hair-trigger temper of Jonathan Clement. What young Wendell did to provoke the teacher was never recorded; but Clement, whose deceptive smile and wit con-

cealed his temper, was provoked to give Holmes so unmerci-
ful a beating that the boy's hand turned black from the
bruises. His schoolmates and the Murdock children, with
whom he lived, gave the boy all their sympathy, but it was
not enough to efface the memory of the event which both
teacher and pupil remembered for years afterwards. Clement
was the only man Wendell Holmes wholeheartedly hated.
The teacher's conscience nagged him for many years, until
one day he came in person to apologize for his injustice.[38]

At Andover, however, there was no long-necked girl to
rival his rhetoric, and there was one teacher, at least, Samuel
Stearns, who detected a poetical quality in the boy's not
inept, if imitative, verse translation of some lines from the
Aeneid.[39] The treasured praise was not enough to offset the
total effect of Andover, but it was some help. Wendell
Holmes was not one of the two great men of the school about
whose probable destiny the boys debated. Among his own
friends, he had rivals. Tom Clark and Francis Crocker were
nearly his equals in wit, and Barnes could beat him out in
a rational argument; but young Holmes could turn out impressive sentences.

A member of the Social Fraternity, a literary club, Holmes
distinguished himself in speaking-contests. The leader of
his group in these combats, he had the satisfaction of seeing
his crew the victor. The secretary's terse notes leave only
tantalizing hints of the Club's activities, but suggest that its
meetings were serious. Declamations, compositions, criticisms, and debates were the staples of each meeting; the speaking-contests were apparently special affairs. Young Holmes
contributed to all these literary displays, but there is no hint
of the subjects he chose for his compositions. Of the debates,
Francis Crocker, the secretary, has a little more to say. He
and Holmes, for instance, argued the classical question of
whether the poet or the orator was the more worthy of admiration. The topics for debate were not always literary;
Holmes upheld the negative in an argument on the tariff;
but since the precise question remains a mystery, there is no

way of knowing whether or not young Holmes here forsook
the Federalist position of his father. Of the debate with his
friend Barnes on the question of the justice of Queen Elizabeth's treatment of Queen Mary, Holmes has left his own
record. Of the two contestants he was the more sentimental
and rhetorical, his friend Barnes being more logical than he.[40]

Apparently the literary masterpiece of the year was his
essay prepared for the final public exhibition on August 23.
The subject, "Fancy" was one of which young Holmes was undoubtedly qualified to speak; he had a sufficient quantity of
it, although it was likely to run out in a watery kind of sentiment. Much later, raking "Cinders from the Ashes," he described the composition:

Treatment, brief but comprehensive, illustrating the magic power of
that brilliant faculty in charming life into forgetfulness of all the ills that
flesh is heir to—the gift of Heaven to every condition and every clime,
from the captive in his dungeon to the monarch on his throne; from the
burning sands of the desert to the frozen icebergs of the poles, from—
but I forget myself.[41]

Was it suspicion of the true quality of the work that made
him angry with his friend Barnes when the latter begged a
copy of it? The younger boy wanted it as a remembrance of
the "mind" he admired; perhaps the owner of that mind,
for all his conceit, had fewer illusions about it than his
friend.[42]

Scribbling, wandering through the country, playing the
flute, talking sentiment and schoolboy philosophy with
Barnes and riotous nonsense with Tom Clark—all these pleasures offset to some extent the pervasive orthodox grimness
of Andover. Some of the preachers cut fine figures in the
Seminary Chapel; Moses Stuart had a Roman look and a
flair for oratory a boy could admire; the scholarly Dr. Murdock, in whose house Holmes lived, was a temperate Calvinist
like his own father; but for the most part Andover was, in
the words of Dr. Murdock's young daughter, Ann, "all swimming in Orthodoxy." [43] Dr. Leonard Woods looked too much
like his "rectilinear theology" [44] and, in manner, was "aristo-

31

cratic and overbearing." [45] Or so, at least, he appeared to two critical boys.

Along with a few others, Holmes came outwardly unscathed through a great revival that hit the town while he was there. If some boys were eager to spend their Sundays with a pious woman who invited them to pray with her and be prayed for, Wendell and his friends preferred less sober doings.[46]

But all Holmes's subsequent writing, particularly his letters to another offspring of orthodoxy, Harriet Beecher Stowe, indicate that his religious struggles reached a climax here. Recalling his Andover days many years later, Holmes promised himself "to be amiable";[47] but a few years out and writing to Barnes, he did not bother to subdue his language.

In my own opinion [Adams] is one of the most bigoted, narrow-minded, uncivilized old brutes that ever had the honor of licking into shape the minds of two such promising youths as P.B. and O.W.H.[48]

The "very dove's nest of Puritan faith" [49] hatched a few rebels.

But Abiel Holmes had not sent his son to Andover to make a preacher out of him; he wished that his son "be fitted . . . for admission into college" and then that he "be virtuous & happy." For the first, Wendell seems to have had no misgivings; he blithely sold his books at auction having apparently no further need for them. For the second, he had, within reason, obeyed his father's injunction to "associate, voluntarily, with none but the virtuous & good" and to maintain his standing in his class. He was outwardly happy enough, although not so happy that he did not need a warning from his father:

Your dear Mother has been some time intending to run up to Andover and see you—and this is the first day that unites all the good points that we desired. She has been too unwell for a week past for such a ride, but now I hope it will do her good. The morning opens finely for her, and I trust she will reach Andover in such season that she can pass an hour or two with you, and return in good time. You know the old English precept.
"Welcome the coming, speed the going guest."
Do not detain your Mother after 11 o'clock; for I wish her to be at home by sunset or before.[50]

When it finally came time for him to leave, Holmes was probably more than glad to go. He had made a good friend in Barnes, and he had not a few pleasures and triumphs, but the year at Andover was not his happiest. He was, however, prepared for college.

Being of good moral character and "well versed" in the classics, geography, and mathematics, he appeared before the examiners of Harvard College on August 29, 1825, his sixteenth birthday, about to exchange the "doctrinal boiler" of Andover for the "rational ice-chest" [51] of Harvard.

ℋarvard 𝒮tudent

1825–1829

He might perhaps have studied more assiduously.

Two days later, having gone easily through the examinations, Oliver Wendell Holmes was admitted to Harvard College, and on September 30 he signed his name in the Subscription Book, pledging himself to obey the laws of the college. He assumed the uniform dress required of the collegers—a single breasted, black mixed suit. The waistcoat had to match, unless he chose to wear one of white linen. He could not have more than two capes on his surtout; all his buttons had to be plain and flat, and he could not have more than eight or fewer than six. The rules were relaxed a little before December; if he wished, he might sport a plaid overcoat and wear a cap of Oxford mixed cloth, "of a form and price to be approved by the Committee on Dress." [1]

Presumably Holmes, although he lived at home, was under the surveillance of this busy committee which not only attended to the students' dress but also inquired into all cases of extravagance, going out of town without leave, going to Public Houses, parties and theaters. It was rather difficult for even the most properly behaved young man to escape discipline of some sort. Even the supposed model of rectitude, Charles Sumner, got caught going to the theater and was obliged to report to the vigilant committee on all evenings when theatrical performances were going on.[2] Young Holmes's unblemished record is probably accounted for by the fact that he lived outside the college walls for all but his senior year.

The college was careful to keep its students busy from morning until night; even before the half-hour for breakfast they had to attend morning prayers and wait upon Dr. Popkin for a lesson in Greek. Two years later the Committee on Prayers came to the conclusion that this arrangement was not satisfactory; it was important not only that students should be "roused from their beds" but also that they be "called to some intellectual exertions at an early hour; and, above all, a recitation immediately after rising in the morning is the best security for the proper employment of the evening." [3]

The young student's mornings were devoted to "intellectual exertion" until one o'clock when he could eat and kick a football around the Yard until a bell at two called him to afternoon study and recitation. Evening prayers, supper, and a little more exercise wound up the day at eight o'clock, when the boys living in the dormitories were required to be in their rooms. Saturday varied the schedule a trifle. One got Grotius and a little extra exercise. Benjamin Peirce, future mathematician, wrote home rather unhappily that he had to study a great deal.[4]

The students were not altogether pleased with their academic life; the teaching seemed too often uninspired and the curriculum too rigid. "To get above the others was the sole aim presented to me by every other teacher," [5] wrote Henry I. Bowditch, excepting only Charles Follen, instructor in German, from his indictment. James Freeman Clarke, finding Homer ruined by Dr. Popkin, and stirred by only one teacher, John Farrar, Professor of Mathematics and Natural Philosophy, turned with others of his class to the "new" books for inspiration. Holmes, coming into Clarke's room one day, was greeted with a burst of quotation—from Coleridge.[6] It was perhaps enthusiasm for Farrar and distaste for the Professor of Greek, as well as scientific curiosity, that led thirty-six members of the class of '29 to petition in their junior year to study Good's *Book of Nature* or Smellie's *Philosophy of Natural History* instead of Griesbach's Greek

35

Testament. The signers included Clarke and O. W. Holmes.[7]

The class of '29 had a particular grievance. They were the victims of a new scheme of instruction in which subjects rather than books were to be taught to students arranged in graded sections. According to the critical Smith Professor of Modern Languages, George Ticknor, the first part of this program was not carried out except by himself and his department; but his examination reports suggest that the Professor had little reason for self-congratulation. It was the policy of graded sections, however, which the students resented. The seventy-seven members of the class considered the shifting and labeling obnoxious and unrepublican.[8] They threatened a rebellion, and one anxious mamma hurried to Cambridge to take her son away from the temptation of becoming a revolutionary. A future Justice of the Supreme Court (to become famous for his dissenting decision in the Dred Scott case), Benjamin Curtis showed his judicious character even at sixteen and calmly refused to have anything to do with his mother's scheme.[9]

There was no open rebellion, after all, but there was considerable dissatisfaction. According to Samuel May, who entered the class in the sophomore year, the effect upon its members was vicious,[10] and he hints at the existence of factions more serious than the division of the class into "Puffs" or "Aristocrats"—the smokers of whom Holmes was one—"Anti-Puffs" and "Neutrals." Holmes seems to have moved happily through the opposing groups, having among his acquaintances men who did not speak to each other.

For all the divisions, the class—the whole student body, for that matter—was really homogeneous, made up largely of sons of the Brahmin caste and of the well-to-do merchants of New England. The factions were not political, at any rate. "We are almost all Adams men except the Southrons, and consequently rather down in the mouth," [11] Holmes wrote Phinehas Barnes after the election of Andrew Jackson in 1828. He might have added that one of the southerners, Isaac Morse of Louisiana, had just collected a small fortune in election bets. The elegant Morse was a future Congressman, but at the moment he was merely "Beau Collins" and a lively friend for Holmes, who could not become much exercised over politics.

Although Holmes never wearied of talking of some of the episodes of his youth, he never had much to say of these four years; even the annual poem for his classmates was rarely reminiscent. Allusions to Professor Sales's characteristic "py Shorge!" and to Professor Popkin's menacing "The Next!," and an immense retrospective pity for the sad life of the poor tutor are about as far as he goes toward recalling the academic part of these four years.

He seems to have been a fairly diligent student. When Phinehas Barnes, his Andover friend, opened a correspondence, he wrote of having heard that Holmes was "a good scholar." [12] As a sophomore, Holmes was one of the twenty listed for *Deturs,* a scholastic honor, and was duly presented with a handsomely bound copy of *The Poems of James Graham, John Logan, and William Falconer.* [13] The rank lists show him at first in the upper ten of his class. In the spring term of his junior year he dropped down to fifteenth place, falling off in languages, apparently Spanish, and in the second term of his senior year, recovering his good grade in Language, he came a cropper in, curiously enough, declamation. [14] To his Andover schoolmate, he confessed:

With regard to moral qualities, I am rather lazy than otherwise, and certainly do not study as hard as I ought to. . . .[15]

Barnes, at Bowdoin, had apparently dug into his books, but he complained that his college was conducted like a school. [16] He longed for a solid intellectual correspondence, which was not forthcoming from his blasé friend, for the undergraduate Holmes was something of a pseudo-sophisticate, more than slightly touched with affectation. Still, a student does not maintain a decent place on the rank lists, as Holmes did, and become a member of Phi Beta Kappa without some application to his work. He was perhaps not quite so lazy as he pretended.

In its rigid curriculum, Harvard allowed its students almost no electives; in 1827, however, a little leeway was allowed upperclassmen who could substitute a modern language for an ancient one or for mathematics. The recognition of modern languages as a legitimate academic subject was relatively new; except for the University of Virginia, carrying out the progressive ideas of Thomas Jefferson, no college had until recently provided for its students any subjects touching in any way upon contemporary life. With the appointment of George Ticknor at Harvard, the teaching of modern languages began, and now in 1827, Ticknor's department offered Italian, German, and Spanish as well as French; Ticknor himself gave a series of polite lectures on European literature.

Taking advantage of the modern languages offered by the college, Holmes began with French. At the end of the winter term of his sophomore year he was among those described by Ticknor as "the more gifted members of the class" [17] and was reported as ready for examination. The group, described as deficient in pronunciation but good in reading and writing, was examined upon Wanostrocht's *Grammar,* Voltaire's *Charles XII* and *Henriade,* La Fontaine's *Fables,* and Molière's *L'Avare, Le Bourgeois gentilhomme,* and *Tartuffe.* Six years later Holmes would see these plays in Paris and attempt to correct the deficiency in pronunciation by attending to the precise diction of Mlle Mars.

Holmes made the most of Harvard's language offerings. He may perhaps have elected Italian and Spanish to escape from the hated mathematics and from any more of Professor Popkin's dreary training in the classics. His father was not likely to discourage him in such choices, for Abiel Holmes had provided even for his daughters private lessons in French and Spanish.

When Holmes elected to take Italian, Ticknor had already begun the practice of having the language taught by a native instructor, Pietro Bacchi. As Longfellow had to do when he began to teach at Bowdoin, Bacchi had to provide his own elementary text. At the end of three terms, the class came up for examination on Bacchi's *Grammar*, Goldoni's *Aventuriere*, Alfieri's *Antigone* and *Oreste*, seven books of Tasso's *Gerusalemme liberata*, and Dante's *Inferno*, Holmes appears to have done well with Italian as with French, coming out with a top twenty.[18] Spanish, however, which he began at the end of his junior year, gave him enough trouble to bring his grade down to an ignominious six.[19] Neglecting German Holmes found himself in his middle age struggling to teach himself German after it had become the language of science.

The Harvard undergraduate of Holmes's generation, of many generations to come, for that matter, got his most severe training in rhetoric. "We have themes once a fortnight, forensics once a month, and declamation every week." [20] The theme-writing began in the sophomore year and continued until graduation; the oral work was added for juniors and seniors. Henry Adams belonged to the generation of Holmes's son, but his observation on this part of a Harvard education applies well enough to the whole period before Charles William Eliot came to turn the University upside down.

If Harvard College gave nothing else, it gave calm. . . . Self-possession was the strongest part of Harvard College, which certainly taught men to stand alone, so that nothing seemed stranger to its graduates than the paroxysm of terror before the public which often overcame graduates of European Universities. . . . He was ready to stand up before any audience in America and Europe, with nerves rather steadier for the excitement, but whether he should ever have anything to say, remained to be proved.[21]

Successive generations of Harvard boys brought down the house in a Cambridge gravel pit, where they practiced delivering a solemn variety of oratorical forms: dissertation, discussions, disquisitions, and disputations as well as conferences, translations, essays, original poems, dialogues and orations in Latin and Greek. Every Thursday in Holden Chapel, the efforts rehearsed in the gravel pit were heard by a highly critical audience. The college attached considerable importance to this part of its training; failure to prepare a forensic, was equal to cutting six recitations.[22]

The training culminated each term with a public exhibition in which the chosen few demonstrated their powers. Holmes twice appeared at an exhibition; as a junior he offered a translation from Catullus as his part of the fall exhibition; in his senior year, at the spring exhibition, he appeared with an original poem. The eighteenth-century echoes plainly in the subjects assigned to those who took part: a colloquial discussion on "The Pleasures and Pains of a Life of Study,," a forensic disputation on "Whether a Life of Retirement have a Tendency to diminish the Force of the Passions," an oration in English on "The Influence of an Enthusiastic Spirit upon the Happiness and Glory of Man."

Yet Edward Tyrell Channing, Professor of Rhetoric, was not entirely behind the times. Some of his students, perhaps Holmes among them, may have been introduced to the wonders of the novel for the first time. Along with exercises in translation from the classics and philosophical subjects of the kind already noted, Channing asked for themes on "Irving's foreign tales compared with his domestic," "Cooper's character of Leather-Stocking," "The alleged want of variety in Scott's principal characters," "Of novels formed upon sea-life or upon domestic incidents and character." Quotations from Scott, Cervantes, Sterne, and others provided some of the subjects.

Holmes here would have to fill in the gaps in his reading and sample the fiction banned from his father's bookshelves, but available in the libraries of the literary clubs to which he belonged. He discovered Fielding and favored a classmate with a critical monologue.[23] Possibly John Holmes's raid on the college library was prompted by the older boy. Occasionally the assignments allowed for free creation, such as "Impressions of a New England Village," a subject Holmes develops in considerable detail in his novels. In spite of his recognition of fiction, and American fiction at that, if Channing had ever heard of Coleridge and Wordsworth, as his students certainly had, there is no indication of it in his theme subjects. A comparison of Pope's versification and Milton's was the only poetical subject he touched. Such themes as "Great intellectual powers without moral and religious principle," for which Hume, Voltaire, and Bolingbroke were given as examples, were the most common type.[24]

Although he used Blair's *Rhetoric* as a text, Channing's own standards and tastes were for something less ornate than the style represented in Blair. His review of Dana's *Two Years Before the Mast* expresses his admiration for the author's perfection of style which he describes as follows:

to some extent it will always be found in an intelligent writer, who, without thinking much of himself, or of making a sensation, says honestly how things were, and how they affected him.

The perfect style is one that "is content with doing its work." [25]

Channing's practice was to read the themes aloud with acid critical comment as the accompaniment. A member of Holmes's class, apologetically presenting some verses for a class reunion, prefaced his lines with a recollection of Channing.

On one of these occasions, taking up a paper and addressing one of our number, he said in his dry way

"Why you begin all your lines with a capital letter."

"Yes, sir," stammered our crestfallen brother, "It is poetry." [26]

Channing need not be blamed for the sophomoric effusions of which his famous students from Emerson on were too often guilty in their youth. The discipline of translations from the classical prose writers and sharp criticism from a teacher with austere tastes in style were not likely to offset the young men's natural taste for something high-sounding, for a style which might make up for its lack of content with a superfluity of verbiage.

Holmes tells a story which neatly illustrates the undergraduate taste. In the class of '28, the rival scholars were George Stillman Hillard and Charles Chauncy Emerson, brother of Ralph Waldo, looked upon with awe and admiration by the students. Holmes, gossiping with Hillard about one of the college exhibitions, heard the upperclassman refer to one student as "the Post." "Why call him the Post?" Holmes asked. "He is a wooden creature," answered Hillard. "Hear him and Charles Emerson translating from the Latin *Domus tota inflammata erat*. The Post will render the words, 'The whole house was on fire.' Charles Emerson will translate the sentence, 'The entire edifice was wrapped in flames.' " As Holmes observed, when he reported this anecdote at a much later date, it was natural for Hillard to prefer "the Bernini drapery of Charles Emerson's version to the simple nudity of 'the Post's' rendering." [27]

Holmes's own contributions to the declamations and the themes were probably respectable; and if he submitted verse to the Professor's caustic comment, it was likely to be too correct, in good Popeian fashion, to have been the subject of Channing's sarcasm. He was not averse to displaying his literary talents publicly, and there is not much doubt that the sound of his own voice and the scratching of his pen gave him considerable pleasure. But with all his self-satisfaction he assumed a half-apologetic attitude toward the things he wrote. There was something else about which he could get excited.

He was a junior when he signed the petition to substitute science for Greek. He was a senior when he asked Barnes if he ever went "mineralizing," referred admiringly to Bowdoin's Professor Cleaveland, and expressed a wish to "give a good knock about the rocks in Maine." "I have paid considerable attention to Chemistry and Mineralogy, and think them both very interesting studies." [28] But even before he began to study chemistry with Professor John Webster, in fact only a few months after he entered college, he had drawn from the college library three volumes on the subject,[29] old books, to be sure, but none the less indicative of his interests.

That the chemistry taught by Webster in 1827 was probably not much more than a twentieth-century small boy can discover for himself need not be taken to belittle Holmes's interest. If he did not then realize the limits of man's knowledge of chemistry, he soon found out. More than half a century later, in an introductory lecture for the Harvard medical students, he recalled the "alluring" face the subject of chemistry had presented to him in his academic days.

A course of chemical lectures was one of the most agreeable of entertainments. To redden a vegetable blue, to precipitate a cloud of some carbonate or sulphate; to burn iron into oxygen; to inflate bubbles with hydrogen; on great occasions to solidify carbonic acid; to make light with electricity or phosphorus which should blind everybody with its intensity; to make a smell with sulphurated hydrogen which should cause all to hold their noses; such was a specimen of chemical teaching as I remember it.[30]

The odor of phosphorus came later to be a stimulus to sentimental reflection.

During a year or two of adolescence I used to be dabbling in chemistry a good deal, and as about that time I had my little aspirations and passions like another, some of these things got mixed up with each other: orange-colored fumes of nitrous acid, and visions as bright and transient; reddening litmus-paper, and blushing cheeks. . . .[31]

Nevertheless, in spite of the conflicting attractions of young ladies who doted on poets, the young man's interest in science was genuine, spontaneous, and apparently intense. At any rate, he studied it hard enough to come out always with a straight top, twenty, in the subject.

Mineralogy and chemistry—the two would later play into the hands of a man who was bent on destroying an "inorganic" faith and anxious to expose pseudo-scientific follies. The small boy who had contrived gadgets with a jackknife, played with a magnifying glass, and sought a way to turn the weights of the kitchen clock into gold, but who had also made up lines of heroic verse for amusement was on the edge of making a choice between a sober interest and a pleasing talent.

Meanwhile a drama was going forward to which young Wendell Holmes could not be indifferent. He was living at home on July 20, 1827, when his father received a letter from

43

his parishioners. On July 9 the parishioners of the First Church in Cambridge had drawn up a memorial addressed to their minister. After ten days of hesitation, the memorialists had handed him their petition, and a week later Abiel Holmes presented his answer.[32] This exchange between the parish and the minister was the opening move in an engagement which caught the minister between the two opposing forces of orthodoxy and liberalism, now everywhere engaged in conflict.

The headquarters of the orthodox party was Yale University, but it had its champions in Boston and its environs. One Boston minister, Lyman Beecher, pastor of the Hanover Street Church from 1826 to 1832, was a formidable warrior for the orthodox party. With such a campaigner and with a widely circulated newspaper, the *Boston Recorder,* the orthodox party was in a position to make itself heard, if not felt in quite the way it intended. Increasingly from 1826 on, the *Recorder* attacked the common practice among clergymen of exchanging pulpits with their neighbors with no particular regard for their doctrinal beliefs. One weapon for the defense of the orthodox faith was what was called the "exclusive" practice, the exchange of pulpits only with those of orthodox belief. Abiel Holmes followed the lead given him by his Calvinist brethren and by the newspaper which came daily to his house. He adopted the "exclusive" practice and himself began to preach frequently upon doctrinal matters. Among the embattled Calvinists with whom he exchanged was Lyman Beecher who exhorted the First Church parishioners to a "Change of Heart" and used all his eloquence to warn them that with the growing heresy a "moral desolation shall sweep over the land." [33]

For about a year Abiel Holmes's parishioners, growing increasingly restive under the fire of a succession of Calvinist divines, had endured their minister's new practice. The memorial which they presented to him on July 20, asked that he return to "that liberal system of professional exchanges" which he had formerly practiced. The minister refused to comply with the request and the battle was on, growing in bitterness until

"the town of Cambridge . . . can be called the peaceful little village no longer, as husband is against wife and mother is against daughter as it were." [34]

In Cambridge the liberal or parish party outnumbered the orthodox or church party by about two to one. The parish group was led by Abraham Hilliard and William Whipple; the church, by Deacons William Hilliard and James Munroe. Where the minister himself was mild in temper and averse to controversy, his principal deacon, the bookseller Hilliard, was apparently a Christian warrior of the old-fashioned type. If the minister had at any point been tempted to modify his practice, the militant deacon was there to stiffen his resolve. The *Boston Recorder*, meanwhile, was growing more and more eloquent upon the subject of faithless ministers and the dangerous Unitarian heresy.

During the Cambridge phase of the battle, there was never any question of Abiel Holmes's compromising with his faith, and the parish party, respecting his integrity, never asked that he do so. It was not *his* preaching, except as he had changed his tune, to which they principally objected, but the preaching of Beecher and others like him with whom Abiel Holmes exchanged his pulpit to the exclusion of the liberal ministers they used to hear and desired to hear again. They did ask for one innovation; the substitution of the Harvard College Hymnbook for Watts.

As the affair progressed, both parties behaved badly; the hymnbook part of the controversy was apparently lugged in to fill out the slim bill of indictment against the minister. The comment of Edmund Dana suggests the rational point of view of the few who did not become hot-headed in the course of the quarrel. The calm detachment of Edmund Dana was the exception even in his own family, which like other families was itself split into opposing camps: Richard Dana for the orthodox—Francis for the liberals. Lucinda

Willard, writing to her brother Joseph, gave this account of behind the scenes activity.

Have you heard that Mr. Abram Hilliard called upon Mr. Edmund Dana to see what part he would take in Parish affairs; Mr. Dana answered that he had no concern with Dr. Holmes as a preacher but thought him a good man; that for himself, he read his Bible for himself; it seems to be against his principles to hear preaching; he thinks his freedom is violated in listening, but his brother Richard and sisters make up, I cannot say atone, for his deficiencies in this respect. Mr. Hilliard found fault with Dr. Holmes for introducing Watts; Edmund Dana said if one wanted poetry there was a good deal in Watts, more he thought than in any other version.[35]

Eleven years had passed since Abiel Holmes had introduced Watts's hymns; the College Chapel had been separated from the First Church for fourteen years. Under the circumstances the parish's complaint was a little absurd.

The quarrel, carried on at first with some dignity on both sides and by means of open parish meetings at which both parties were represented, finally went into committees, who badgered each other and the minister with letters, memorials, petitions, protests, and remonstrances. At first the parish party addressed its communications directly to the minister and received direct replies; later a church committee became increasingly active, and there began a bewildering three-way exchange of documents more and more bitter in tone, and, in matter, further and further away from the initial subject.

The point at issue late in 1828 was the selection of a Mutual Ecclesiastical Council to which the whole problem might be submitted for arbitration. Before this proposal, made in an open parish meeting, could be submitted to the minister, the church group had held a separate meeting, chosen its committee and drawn up a memorial declaring that it wished this committee to represent it on any Council called. This move on the part of those of his own faith had put the minister in an awkward position from which there was no escape. He was caught in the cross-fire.

For five months, the three-way negotiations continued; the parish committee moved slowly in its attempts to get the

46

minister to agree to the selection of a Mutual Ecclesiastical Council, and the church committee clung to its blockading position. Failing to move the church group and unable to deal with the minister alone, the parish party finally called an *Ex Parte* Council. The Council met in May 1829, and on the 19th came to the only conclusion to which under the circumstances it could come, namely, that the parish had sufficient cause to terminate its contract with its minister.

The feeling that Abiel Holmes had been victimized by his own people is implied in contemporary comment by liberals not connected with the parish. Even when allowances are made for the kind of expression convention might require of the members of the council which removed the minister from his pulpit, the concluding paragraphs of the council's report are suggestive.

This Council wish it to be distinctly understood that the service to which we have been called, is one of the most painful services of our life. We do not arraign or condemn the motives of the Rev. Dr. Holmes. We are happy to testify, that our impressions of his course during the peaceful state of his society are associated with the most interesting and honorable views of his ministerial character and the Christian spirit. We sympathize with him under his trials. . . .

We lament with the parish, that the principles and practice of the times on which we have fallen have in any degree interrupted the quiet and blighted the prospects of a society, which, from the earliest period of its existence, has known how good and how joyful it is for Christians to dwell together in unity.[36]

On June 7, 1829, Abiel Holmes preached his last sermon in the meeting-house on the text: "I have no greater joy than to hear that my children walk in truth." Yet he must have known that his own son could not accept that truth. On the following Sunday, he preached to the orthodox party in the town courthouse; his text was "Beloved, think it not strange concerning the fiery trial among you, which cometh upon you, as though a strange thing happened unto you." [37]

Ousted from the meeting-house, the orthodox deacons William Hilliard and James Munroe formed the Second Con-

47

gregational Church with Abiel Holmes as the minister. One might suppose the fiery trial to be over, but one more strange thing awaited the minister. Within a year his orthodox congregation provided Abiel Holmes with an assistant, the Reverend Nehemiah Adams. The *Christian Register,* a liberal paper, took notice of the ordination and showed itself as bewildered as the council had been, confused by respect and liking for Abiel Holmes and distaste for his theology. The *Register* observes:

We have been accustomed to look on Dr. Holmes with respect and confidence. We do not believe he has followed the impulses of his heart, which we know to be full of kindness. Others must have blinded his judgment, when they could not pervert his feelings, and having accomplished their ends, they are now willing to require the cooperation they urged upon him, as a matter of duty, with empty praise, and real neglect. If our words are strong, our feelings restrain them, for they rise almost to indignation, when we see such an abuse of the privileges of friendship, and the conscientiousness of old age.[38]

But the minister himself showed no resentment, although the text of his sermon for the Reverend Adams's ordination may have been ironic: "Now, if Timoetheus come, see that he be with you without fear, for he worketh the work of the Lord as I also do." [39] The minister was generous; Nehemiah Adams's way of doing the Lord's work was very different from his own, for Adams was a militant, old-fashioned Calvinist.

What the Harvard senior thought of all this at the moment there is no record; he did not answer his friend Barnes's query about the "persecution" of his father. The only indication of the state of his feelings during this time is the admission, "I am cross as a wild-cat sometimes." [40] As well he might be. His father's "fiery trial" had come as the climax to a series of unsettling experiences: the normal religious doubts of his adolescence, the souring encounters with orthodoxy at Andover, the liberal pressures of his "heretic [he crosses out "Godless"] college." [41] And now, in his senior year, brought into conflict with family loyalties and affections, he suffered an experience not easily endured or soon

48

forgotten. As the son of the central figure in this church struggle, he was condemned to silence at a time when to speak out might have been better for him; but, during all this period, the outward record of Wendell Holmes's life is as noncommittal as his remark to Barnes.

Poet of the Class of '29

Sir, we are a nest of singing birds!

WHILE THIS DRAMA went on in the background, young
Holmes did not study as much as he should, but, continuing
his confession to Barnes, "I am not dissipated and I am not
sedate." It would be a little difficult to be sedate if one
measured only "five feet three inches when standing in a
pair of substantial boots. . . ." [1] Even without his schoolboy
treble, he still looked more like a small boy than a college
student. There was no possibility of his cutting a fine military
figure in the Harvard Washington Corps or measuring off
against the champion of the college heavyweights, whose "six
feet and trimmings" were sufficiently impressive to be recalled years later.

But a sociable spirit and a talent for verse-writing could
compensate for missing inches. If he did not have an "angel
voice" like the class tenor, Joseph Angier, he was willing to
"sing most unmusically" verses of his own making.[2] The
future laureate of the class of '29 found himself unofficial
Master of the Revels, who could be counted on for his "willingness to promote our festivities." [3] In all the clubs to which
he belonged, his liveliness and wit were a source of pleasure
to his friends.

Holmes belonged to several clubs, some of them private
affairs founded by himself and his friends, and others the
established clubs of the college. In 1827, Sam May and
Holmes, with six other fellow "Puffs," formed a club where
they might indulge their taste for smoking, a luxury for-

bidden by some of the large organizations like the Hasty Pudding Club. At seven every Thursday evening, the eight members of the Coffee Club gathered for "Coffee, Chocolate, Toast, and Cigars." The amusements of the evening were whist, backgammon, and chess. "Charitable Ann" Hunt of the Holmes household was under strict instructions to provide six quarts of the best Mocha or Batavia coffee, with loaf sugar and *good* cream, fifty slices of toast—two kinds: buttered and milk-dipped. The bread must be home-made and toasted on both sides, slightly.[4] If these young men put on adult sophistication with their cards and cigars, they were plainly boys when it came to their stomachs. Describing the pattern of his life to the curious Barnes, Holmes wrote, "I read a little, study a little, smoke a little, and eat a great deal!"[5] And Holmes, living at home, had not the excuse of being underfed at the College Commons.

Naturally he found many of his good companions among those who liked to write. Park Benjamin was never known for his pleasant disposition, but he scribbled as Holmes did, and besides he had a brace of extremely pretty sisters. Mary, especially, was something of a belle and attracted among her admirers the little Holmes with his album verses and the handsome John Lothrop Motley, who subsequently won her from her other suitors. With Benjamin and John O. Sargent, of the Class of '30, Holmes later made his first literary ventures.

In his own class, the rival poet was James Freeman Clarke. With Benjamin Curtis the two belonged to a club (possibly their own invention) magnificently named *Diaphemizomenoi*.[6] Where Clarke's mind ran to Coleridge and metaphysics, Holmes's imagination was likely to turn on Pope and science and sentiment; but the two spent pleasant evenings together. Clarke remembered the chess, the apples from the Reverend Abiel Holmes's orchard, and the talk. Always a chatterbox, Holmes was likely to do a little more than to keep up his end in the conversation. Clarke never forgot an epigram Holmes turned out. "I'll tell you, James, what I think metaphysics is like. It is like a man splitting a log. When it is done, he has two more to split." [7]

The secretaries' reports of Hasty Pudding Club meetings suggest that Brother Holmes was irrepressible. He joined this convivial group in the fall term of his junior year and was promptly called upon to produce a poem for the Washington's birthday celebration. In April, becoming secretary of the club, Holmes kept the minutes with more enjoyment of the chance to display his wit than fidelity to his job as reporter.[8] The quality of his undergraduate humor can probably be anticipated, but in the midst of verbal posing, fancy Latin, and ornate conceits, there are signs of something a little better than sophomoric. The following effort is, however, typical with its self-conscious introduction and its fusillade of puns.

I cannot refrain from untying the pinions of my muse for a few seconds.

> For soon appeared the smiling pot
> Brimful of pudding, smoking hot
> With ready step and joyful faces
> The glad providers took their places
> Soon as their bowls and spoons they found
> To make all *square* they helped us *round*
> Two different ways their footsteps tend
> For one *began* at either *end*
> And therefore these providers seem
> To *carry things* to *the extreme* [9]

Another of the secretary's reports is in his most flamboyant manner. The "honest reader" apostrophized recognizes the justice of the confession "I am a little given to prosing."

There are certain seasons when a flow of happiness almost too great for the soul to bear comes rushing over it like a mountain torrent. Such are those blissful evenings when the lovers of Ceres and her gifts repair to the room where her altar is erected to pay their vows and homage. No matter where her temporary shrine is raised, whether beneath the venerable shade of Massachusetts or the splendid roof of Holworthy, whether in the lap of Stoughton or under the sheltering wing of Hollis it is alike the common resort of the intellectual sitentophagi. . . .

To proceed with the business of the evening, after an energetic appeal to the pots we resolved ourselves into a court of equity and proceeded to try the Mayor of Boston for prohibiting the sale of spiritous liquors more especially of egg pop* upon the common upon election day. . . .

* Egg-pop or popp probably derived from the Greek—*popoi* and *ego*—See Worcester's, Walker's, Todd's, Johnson's dictionary.10

Holmes's successor in office was his friend Clarke, who, with a style less peppered with the first person singular, managed to tell a little more of what went on in the club meetings. A gloomy meeting at the beginning of the senior year was brightened considerably when Ned Sohier made proposals for a library committee and suggested that:

Brother Brigham be chosen to inquire into the state of matters on the upper shelves & Brother Holmes the lower partitions, the former being (to you Posterity do I speak) several inches above seven feet in height, the latter not ascending above four of the same.11

Whether a properly constituted participant in the mock trials that were the main business of the club meetings or an unofficial commentator, Holmes, now known for lively imagination and wit, was quick, in Charles Sumner's words, with "his usual fluency and readiness of language." 12 When the club reviewed the case of Miss Fanny Wright, advocate of free love, Holmes was there to unsettle the dignity of the trial with the kind of punning the occasion allowed, saying "something about mis-taking the thing in hand &c. &c." 13 As attorney-general in the case against opera-dancers, Holmes opened for the prosecution:

with all the ingenuity of man who grasped his subject as by intuition, who penetrated [the] matter with the eye of a philosopher and graced it with all the imaginings of Poetry. He thought it was turning this pure land into a sink of misery. It was not the unbaring of their elegant ankles that he complained [of], it was the "ne plus ultra" which they showed, deserving, as he said, our heartiest execrations.14

Then as now Hasty Pudding Club entertained the public; but the tone of these public meetings was in those days deceptively solemn. The habits established by the fortnightly session of declamations and by the public exhibitions were not lightly broken; an oration and a poem were the customary wares offered to the faculty and students who gathered for the occasion in Dr. Popkin's recitation room. A favorite subject for the oration of the day was the future of American literature, that question which teased the minds of all young Americans with admitted or concealed leanings toward authorship. No record of Holmes's poem for one of these occasions survives; since he never saw fit to be unduly solemn even for such occasions as commencement day, it is probably safe to assume that his offering added a little more to his growing reputation as a poet and a wit.[15]

All these public appearances, whether put on by students or by the college, were good excuses for celebration. Hasty Pudding Club members usually adjourned to Porter's Tavern, where that gentleman's famous flip was part of the supper. "Our Exhibition days," wrote Holmes to Barnes, "are very pleasant."

In defiance of or rather evading injunctions of the government, we contrive to have what they call "festive entertainments" and we call "blows." A fine body of academic militia, denominated the "Harvard Washington Corps," parades before the ladies in the afternoon and there is eating and drinking and smoking and making merry.[16]

Holmes's first appearance at an exhibition had given him no chance for a display of talent, but for the spring exhibition on April 28, 1829, he produced rather too many rocking-horse couplets on the subject "Forgotten Ages." His reflections on this familiar theme were the usual stereotypes, phrased smoothly enough but otherwise dull. In the two passages where he speaks of the moment directly to his audience, the accents of his master, Pope, are audible, but the tone of the whole is his own. After a prolix opening in which he gets himself from his room to the platform, he turns his attention to the ladies in the audience to "meet the radiance of those brighter eyes."

> What various beauties crowd upon my sight
> Flash from the left and sparkle from the right.
> The matron's sweetness and the maiden's bloom—
> The flaunting ribband and the waving plume—
> Blushes the saucers never owned before
> And locks unpurchased from the fancy-store—

> In queenly pride the lofty head-dress towers
> And bonnets blossom with unfading flowers—
> Their different charms the smiling sisters blend
> All nature gives, and all that Art can lend.

He again takes too much time to get himself off the platform, but in the process turns out a few more lines that show the same sense of the courteous recognition due to an audience on such an occasion.

> If our young Muse has managed to beguile
> Her fairer sisters of one favoring smile—
> If hard-heeled students and if booted boys
> Will aid her exist with their flattering noise—
> If sterner age will spare the humble lays
> And kindly pardon what it cannot praise,
> Though e'er tomorrow it shall be forgot,
> That she has hovered round this little spot,
> Without a murmur that her feeble wings
> Must share the fate of empires and of kings,
> No longer fluttering in your wearied sight,
> She folds her mantle and she takes her flight.[17]

Presumably he got the "flattering noise" for which he asked; it would have been a little difficult for his audience to refuse. The occasion was not immediately forgotten, for the poet's room (he was now living in a dormitory) "was for several days the seat of continuous revelry." Only a cynic would suggest that the callers in his room in Holworthy came only to sample some of the considerable stock of wine the poet had laid in. Holmes had his parents' consent, of course, for this splurge of hospitality. The minister could not very well refuse, for his own mother, Temperance Holmes, had sent him off to Yale "with a Dutch liquor case containing six large bottles filled with various kinds of strong waters, probably brandy, rum, gin, whiskey, doubtless enough to craze a whole class of young bacchanalians." [18]

A part in an exhibition was dignified recognition from the college government; recognition from his fellow students came in another form. He had received a degree from the "Medical Faculty" whose triennial catalogue he sent to Barnes.

This will require some explanation. It is a mock society among the students, which meets twice a year in disguise, and, after admitting members from the junior class, distributes honorary degrees to distinguished men. The room where they meet is hung round with sheets and garnished with bones. They burn alcohol in their lamps, and examine very curiously and facetiously the candidates for admission. Every three years they publish a catalogue in exact imitation of the Triennial Catalogue published by the college. The degrees are given with all due solemnity to all the lions of the day.[19]

The responsibilities of his fame kept him busy during the last months of his college days, for besides the exhibition poem, he had to turn out some verses for the class valedictory exercises on July 14. His class-day poem, which was too short according to Sam May, told the sad tale of his "hapless amour with too tall a maid." [20] A member of the audience on the occasion describes the poet and his verses.

He is both young and small in distinction from most others, and on these circumstances, he contrived to cut some good jokes. His poem was very happy and abounded in wit.[21]

Meanwhile there was another poem to write; the college government had assigned him a commencement part and asked for a poem. The habit of commandeering his muse for all possible occasions was well established before he was out of college, and he was never after able to break others of asking for verses, or himself of saying "yes."

Commencement morning, August 26, was clear and cool as October. In President Quincy's house, everything was in an uproar. The student's degrees were strewn over Susan Quincy's bed. The names were still to be written in, the scrolls tied.[22] Somehow things were got ready; the president's daughters scurried to dress, Maria in blue "with blonde gauze handkerchief and cameo comb"; Abby in white "and her hat"; Susan in "a beautiful yellow dress for this day." [23]

They were later, with the other girls who crowded the meeting-house, to be described by the poet of the day as:

> Fair creatures kindling with a starlike glow
> The Hallowed precincts of the lofty row.[24]

He must have seen the "fair creatures" piling into the meeting-house on similar occasions, but he chose to ignore the facts in a gentlemanly way. According to Maria Quincy, the feminine part of the audience was anything but decorous.

As soon as the doors opened [we] caught up our frocks and ran. The rush of ladies was very great, and as they uplifted their voices and screamed as they ran, it was really frightful.[25]

By her own admission, Maria got in first and "flew" into the king's box, where she perched on a music-stool in the most conspicuous place. The galleries, reports Maria, were filled with ladies "dressed with great elegance and in the most showy style." [26] There was an immense amount of chattering which presumably quieted down when the band began playing for the procession—the Governor's aides in full uniform, followed by the academic dignitaries. Dr. Porter gave the prayer; President Quincy took his place in the pulpit, and at 10:30 the long program began with Charles Fay presenting the salutatory oration.

More than two hours later, Oliver Wendell Holmes faced his audience. The audience had already attended to an "Essay," and a "Philosophical Discussion." It had heard something about dueling, something about Lord Bacon, and been mildly disturbed by the queer utterances of the class eccentric, Albert Locke. It had been asked to reflect upon the subject of "Natural, Civil, Ecclesiastical, and Literary History, Considered in Relation to the Tendency of Each to Improve and Elevate the Intellectual Faculty." The speaker who had just left the platform was William Brigham, tallest man in the class. It was, moreover, nearly one o'clock and the poet knew very well that his audience was weary and hungry. Young Holmes did not have an enviable spot on this program.

Critical members of the audience were ready to annotate their programs with their comments on the performance. One listener carefully wrote in the time, 12:52, when the poet came forward and as carefully noted that the poem took eight minutes. Then he marked the speaker's name with his symbol of highest approval, "GGG.," a distinction only one other performer received. Another listener chalked up an "excellent," one of four he was willing to bestow.[27] The lyrical reporter for the *New England Palladium* went into details.

Holmes of Cambridge, has a very youthful appearance, & came forward with modesty and childlike innocence to beguile the audience with song. He has the elements of poetry in his nature, and his production, on this occasion, though of a light and sarcastic character was received with much applause.

There were eight minutes of applause if the time-keeping listener's watch can be relied upon. The *Palladium* reporter goes on:

The muse complained that, on commencement day, the whole array of beauty was in arms against the trembling candidate for a degree—under the keen glances of a thousand eyes scanning the angles of his outward man the poet felt trepidation from crown to heel—and by way of reprisal, and to carry the war into the enemies' camp, made the ladies the subject of his song. The ladies were pleased, and the poet, if every laugh draws a nail from a coffin, made a good business.[28]

One may take the note of Holmes's "modesty and childlike innocence" with a grain of salt; but there is no doubt that he "made a good business," with the following lines:

> And this dread moment is at last our own,
> And we are left unpitied and alone
> With beating heart and trembling hands to dare
> The idle glance—the stern unwavering stare,
> The sneers of youth—the darker frown of age,
> The schoolboy critic and the solemn sage,
> The pensive miss who listens as she sighs
> For 'golden ringlets' and for 'sunny skies,'
> The nameless being whose existence fills
> What would be vacuum in his faultless gills,
> The sober people who consult the time
> And think of dinner in despite of rhyme
> And those that crowd around the sacred door
> To see the place they never saw before. . . .

Softening his satire with complimentary phrases and dulling its edge with verbiage, the poet hits off the fashions and foibles of his subject and once touches upon a feminine type which he knew only too well, the "female monster" who teases poets into contributing verses to her autograph album. He warns:

> Trust not the light of her insidious smile
> 'Tis but the splendor of your funeral pile
> Though all the graces in her pout appear
> That pinkleaved album follows in the rear.

On the whole it was fortunate that the poet might "not stay to raise the idle paeans of unneeded praise," for he was in these couplets likely to be carried away by Popeian "resonance" and to offer too many neatly metrical lines in proportion to his actual content. Still the verses were the kind that would go over well in oral delivery for which some redundancy was necessary. The poet finally brought his poem to the ladies to an end with a promise:

> One classic tribute shall at least be thine
> The deepest bumper of the brightest wine.[29]

No doubt the ladies, thus teased and flattered, repaid the poet in kind when students and guests met later for dancing and frivolity. His vanity, which Holmes came later to recognize as a dangerous weakness, probably received the praise it thrived on. With nothing in his outward appearance likely to make an impression, Holmes had to use his wits and his tongue to get the attention taller and handsomer men than he could get without trying. In the delicate art of carrying on a flirtation, Holmes had disadvantages to overcome.

The toast the poet promised was drunk by the Class of '29 at their evening supper at Mr. Wyeth's Fresh Pond Hotel. The young men had claret, Madeira, and champagne to choose from. The celebration finally came to an end; the class secretary records this suggestive note: "We broke up in pretty good order and returned to Cambridge without the occurrence of any accident." [30]

Three days later, Oliver Wendell Holmes, A. B. Harvard College, was twenty years old, and it behooved him to settle upon a profession.

In March 1829 he had written to his friend Barnes:

I am totally undecided what to study; it will be law or physick, for I cannot say that I think the trade of authorship quite adapted to this meridian.[31]

There was no danger of his choosing the ministry. Literature was very much to his taste, but if Barnes thought "the profession of an author is the best that can be followed at present in this country," [32] Holmes had other notions.

October found him in his own room in his father's house, with the books of his chosen profession "intermingled in exquisite confusion" [33] with his carpenter's tools. The books were Blackstone and Rawle; but, before the winter was out, he found himself as bored with the law as Longfellow and Irving had been before him. He was "sick at heart of this place and almost everything connected with it . . . the temple of the law . . . seems very cold and cheerless about the threshold." The notion of doing the country à la Goldsmith would attract him, if he had thought his countrymen liked music well enough to pay for it. No doubt the situation at home contributed to his melancholy, especially if he were obliged for form's sake to attend to the sermons of his father's assistant.

Besides there were no pretty girls.

If there was a girl in the neighborhood whose blood ever rose above the freezing point who ever dreamed of such a thing as opening her lips without having her father and mother and all her little impish brothers & sisters for her audience—nay if there was even a cherry-cheeked kitchen girl to romance with occasionally it might possibly be endurable. Nothing but vinegar-faced old maids and drawing-room sentimentalists—nothing that would do to write poetry to but the sylph of the confectioner's counter and she—sweet little Fanny has left us to weep when we think of her departed smiles and her too fleeting icecreams. I do believe that I shall never be contented till I get the undisputed mastery of a petticoat.

Not surprisingly he forgot all the philosophy of contentment he had meant to give his friend. Perhaps he was a little vexed that the Cambridge ladies did not appreciate his talents as much as the girls who used to tell him that he wrote "very pretty verses in their good for nothing albums." He was writing a little verse. There were some pathetic lines "about a frail sister of the chemise . . . it is whispered that a Platonic intimacy between this fair philosopher and another disciple of the same master has resulted as Malthus says it should not." Barnes was favored, too, with some doggerel stanzas giving the gossip of Cambridge from the college president's ball to his own tumble from a horse. The poem includes this skeptical quatrain:

> The undergraduates have made
>   Proposals for a monthly paper,
> Which I am very much afraid
>   Will end in something worse than vapor.[34]

The undergraduates thus lampooned proved a blessing to the bored law student. Their monthly paper materialized, and the first issue, appearing in February 1830, printed three poems by the doubting alumnus.

The *Spectator* papers still had imitators at this late date; the *Collegian* was put out by three seniors and two juniors who assumed fanciful names and pretended to be members of a club. The probable instigator of the venture was John O. Sargent, who assumed a double role as "Charles Sherry" and "Francis Hock." His colleagues were disguised as "Luke Lockfast," "Frank Airy," "Arthur Templeton," and "Geoffrey La Touche." Sargent's brother Epes produced an occasional verse, and John Lothrop Motley made his literary debut with a prose contribution: the only outsider contributing generously to the magazine's six issues was the disgruntled law student.[35]

His three contributions to the February issue were "Runaway Ballads," a pair of elopement songs, one grave and the other gay; "Enigma," a verse riddle; and the familiar "Toadstool." The newspapers picked up the ballads and reprinted them with approval; to the self-critical author, only "Toadstool" was worth saving. So apparently thought the mysterious "W." who gave the magazine its first—rather backhanded— "puff" in the *New England Galaxy* for February 5.

Then followed some stanzas, entitled the "Toad-stool"—a low subject, and the stanzas themselves good for but very little. They contain one delicate poetical image about the stars weeping dew; but the metal of

61

that was stolen from Byron, and has not been improved by the coinage of the author. We may say, in general, of the original poetry throughout the volume that it is rather indifferent.

This is scarcely complimentary to the author of all the original poetry in the number.

Two weeks later the editor of the *Galaxy* denied all responsibility for the puff, declared he had not laid eyes on the magazine, and alluded to the rumor that the author of the review was someone connected with the magazine. For himself he had to take his copy of "Runaway Ballads" from a New York paper.[36] When, finally, the editor had a copy of the third number in his hands, he was pleased to observe that "the *Collegian* is sprightly, without frivolity: witty, without vulgarity; and sensible, without pedantic affectation. Some of its poetry is very good. . . ."[37] To prove his contention, he reprinted Holmes's "Dorchester Giant" and "Scene from an Unpublished Play."

By the time four issues of the *Collegian*, containing fifteen poems by the anonymous contributor, had appeared, the poet's winter melancholy had disappeared. Scribbling had become a fine antidote for Blackstone, and the girls had become less chilly and perhaps more appreciative now that Wendell Holmes was getting his poems in print. By May, he was a little giddy with an excitement he tried to cover up with mock eloquence.

I have been very busy for some time past with one kind of nonsense and another, and you must know the laxity that always follows this tension of a man's sinews— In the first place I have been writing poetry like a madman, and then I have been talking sentiment like a turtledove and gadding about among the sweet faces and doing all the silly things that spoil you for anything else— And now I have subsided into that lethargy of soul which with us men of talent come as periodically as calms upon the ocean. This month of May is too good for anything but love—the air whispers of sighs and the blue sky looks down upon you like a great blue eye and the motion of every leaf is as soft as the step of a barefoot beauty, and our pulse begins to beat with all the warmth and more than all the freshness of summer— If that had been put into an ode it would have rung from Maine to New Orleans, but I cannot take the trouble to string my pearls.

He had been doing nothing else but stringing his pearls; and it was an odd lethargy of soul that produced over fifty poems before the year was out. He tossed aside the serious Barnes's worried allusions to his bump of amativeness, and chattered on about his verses. Later in the year his lines would ring from Maine to New Orleans, and even now the poetry he had written so "fiercely" for the *Collegian* had been copied. "It was silly stuff I suppose but the papers have quoted some of it about as if they really thought it respectable." [38]

The last number of the *Collegian* came out early in July with a "Tail-Piece" by Holmes and five other poems, among them "The Height of the Ridiculous." The twenty-year-old poet, who does not dare to write as funny as he can, is acclaimed by the editor of the *Galaxy*. "Its admirable comic poetry has been one of its most conspicuous characteristics." It is "surpassed by the broad humor of Hood alone." [39]

Either the editor of the *Galaxy*, Frederick Hill, had known a good thing when he saw it and sought out the law student or Holmes had been made bold by praise; whatever the cause, he was now a contributor to both of Hill's literary newspapers —the *Galaxy* and the newly founded *Amateur*. When the undergraduate editors of the *Collegian* brought their venture to an end, Holmes and John O. Sargent were both sure of publication in the columns of Hill's papers. The two young men scribbled away, "shoulder to shoulder, and quill to quill," as Holmes later described it. [40]

They were neglecting their academic occupations for the exciting job of being Mr. Hill's "obliging" correspondents; their special feature was a series of "Illustrations of the Athenaeum Gallery of Paintings." For the past four years the Boston Athenaeum had put on an annual exhibition of paintings by artists, old and new, foreign and American; for a month and a half, the readers of the *Galaxy* and the *Amateur* were favored with versified impressions of the landscapes and portraits on view in 1830. The painters, it is true, might have had some difficulty in recognizing their work from the poetic reports; but Hill was apparently satisfied. Toward the end of

July, he collected the series in a now very rare, paper-bound pamphlet nowhere mentioning the authors' names. Nine of the poems were by Holmes.[41]

This anonymity seemed to suit Holmes's purpose. He was somewhat skeptical of his newspaper popularity, however much he may have been flattered by having his verses re-printed. In "To a Blank Sheet of Paper," which appeared in the *Amateur* about the same time that the "book" came out, Holmes expressed his doubts:

> The weekly press shall gladly stoop
> To bind thee up among its sheaves;
> The Daily steal thy shining ore,
> To gild its leaden leaves. . . .

> Take, then, this treasure to thy trust,
> To win some idle reader's smile,
> Then fade and moulder in the dust,
> Or swell some bonfire's pile.[42]

The idle readers, however, were numerous enough and de-lighted enough to keep in circulation "barbarisms" the poet wanted to forget; "The Ballad of the Oysterman," [43] for in-stance, was unsuppressible; set to music, it was sung by popu-lar entertainers and even by his own classmates until the poet wished that he had never written it. Other verses, of which he had no reason to be ashamed, were copied and recopied in newspapers all over the country, but outside of Boston no one knew who wrote them. As late as 1848, a Kentuckian wrote to a magazine to confess that he had carried around in his hat for years newspaper clippings of some of Holmes's poems, hop-ing that some day he would find the author.[44]

While Sargent ran to pen names, Holmes cautiously kept his anonymity. The *Collegian* verses had been unsigned; even the index to the final volume did not reveal the authorship of his twenty-six contributions; an asterisk identified the titles as being all by the same author. It was not until the July 30 issue of the *Galaxy* that Holmes signed a timid "H." to the first of the "State Prison Melodies," the uncollected "Gallows Bird's Last Song," verses probably evoked by the recollection of his youthful escapade on Jones's Hill. He would have done better to sign a poem which had appeared a few weeks before (July 2)—"September Gale." As his letters to Barnes suggest, he was not indifferent to the popularity of his verses, but he was not overeager to claim them by signing them with the distinctive initials "O. W. H." until after he had written lines which actually did ring from Maine to New Orleans.

In the *Boston Daily Advertiser* on the morning of September 14, he found a short paragraph copied from a New York paper. The New York editors expressed regret that the Secretary of the Navy should consider dismantling a famous ship, the frigate *Constitution*. In the long white chamber of the gambrel-roofed house, itself the scene of revolutionary drama, the historian's son was shaken with instant feeling. His responsive imagination turned out the three rousing stanzas of "Old Ironsides"; he did not even wait to sit down to his desk, nor trouble to provide his lines "with a complete rhyming outfit" [45] of the sort his eighteenth-century taste approved.

The next morning, the subscribers to the *Advertiser* read the indignant lines by "H."; before the week was out, the poem was going the rounds of the country's newspapers. The story that broadside printings were handed about the streets of Washington is apparently a legend; just as the assumption that the lines alone saved the ship from being dismantled is probably an exaggeration. The protests came from all quarters. The poem, however, did keep some of Secretary Branch's successors from destroying the ship.

During the rest of the year Holmes published only five more poems, two in the *Amateur,* signed H., and the others between the less ephemeral covers of two giftbooks, *Youth's Keepsake* and the *Token*.[46] These three poems he acknowledged with the signature O. W. H. He would not use these initials in a magazine until the end of March 1831. He did not sign his name to a poem until "The Wasp and the Hornet" appeared in the *Token* for 1833.

While the best of his early poems went unacknowledged into ephemeral newspapers, a few were given some kind of permanence in such giftbooks as the *Token*. In such volumes, too, he was in good company. Any young man who bought a copy of the *Token* for 1831 as a Christmas present for his girl was getting more for his money than he supposed. Between the fancy, tooled-leather covers of this handsome volume with its "embellishments by native artists" appeared, besides Holmes's "Lost Boy," two prose pieces by an unknown young man from Salem—"The Haunted Quack" and "Sights from a Steeple," by Nathaniel Hawthorne. In the *Gleaner,* which, as its name implies, gathered its material from newspapers, Holmes appeared in the company of another poet who would make a name for himself, a young newspaper editor, John Greenleaf Whittier. Yet even if Holmes had been less reluctant to put his name to his verses and make it known beyond the small literary circle of Boston and Cambridge, such "fame" as he might have had in the 1830's did not carry with it the assurance of a living and the respect of his fellowmen, and both Holmes desired.

Nothing had happened in the short interval between his letter to Barnes in March 1829, and the fall of 1830 to change his mind about the prospects of a literary career in America. His own description of the period, written years later, is accurate for the moment:

Dana, Halleck, Drake, had all done their best work. Longfellow was not yet conspicuous. Lowell was a schoolboy. Emerson was unheard of. Whittier was beginning to make his way against the writers with better educational advantages whom he was destined to outdo and outlive. . . . Our schoolbooks depended, so far as American authors were concerned, on extracts from the orations of Webster and Everett, on Bryant's Thanatopsis . . . To a Waterfowl . . . on Drake's American Flag, and Percival's Coral Grove, and his Genius Sleeping and Genius Waking—and not getting very wide awake either.

A year later in 1831, William Joseph Snelling would apply to a host of now-forgotten names a "tomahawk sort of satire" in his *Truth, A Gift for Scribblers*. With considerable justice on his side, Snelling would massacre the reputations of the embryonic poets of the day, very few of whom were ever able to prove him wrong. In it, Holmes himself "escaped with a love-pat as the youngest son of the muse." [47]

With genius half asleep and a love pat the best he could hope for, Holmes was not wrong in thinking the times out of joint for a literary life; a prose writer like Irving or Cooper or John Neal had a chance, but a poet was handicapped, however gifted he might be. That Holmes had talent beyond the ordinary is obvious when his juvenilia is set beside that of two of his contemporaries. His early verse is far superior in finish and grace to that of either Longfellow or Whittier; nothing either of them produced among their early verse can equal "The Height of the Ridiculous," "Old Ironsides," and "The Last Leaf" (1831). All three of these poems have, besides finish, originality. All three spring from direct experience about which the poet has his own thoughts and feelings; they are not imitations of other poets, fuzzily informed by bookish sentiments supposed to be appropriate for verse. And in one of them—"The Last Leaf"—the form is the poet's own creation, good enough to merit the praise of the best craftsman and critic among the American poets of the first half of the century, Edgar Allan Poe.

It is useless to speculate on what might have happened if— if Holmes had chosen any profession except the one he is in 1830 about to choose. But his fellow-poets were all to earn their livings in fields having close connections with literature; that Holmes made the choice he did make helped, I think, to condemn him to be one of those whom he later described in "The Voiceless," one of those "who die with all their music in them."

In 1830, although he had "tasted the intoxicating pleasure of authorship" and discovered that "there is no form of lead-poisoning which more rapidly and thoroughly pervades the blood and bones and marrow than that which reaches the young author through mental contact with type metal," [48] he did not mean to let the disease affect his choice of profession. If he never did recover from author's lead-poisoning, he did begin almost at once to put up a fight against it. He got through the winter of 1830-31 without an outbreak of the disease, but it was not the chilling effects of a Boston winter that reduced the poetic fever.

He had left the Harvard Law School and his father's house in Cambridge. He was living in a boarding-house at 2 Central Court, Boston. The book on his desk was Wistar's *Anatomy;* a scalpel and a stethoscope had replaced Blackstone and the lathe and awl.

Medical Student

I have enjoyed many instructive hours . . . with Dr. James whose skill in physick will be long remembered.

In MARCH 1831 Holmes resumed his neglected correspondence with Barnes.

I suppose now that whenever you take the trouble to think about me your fancy sketches a twofold picture. In the front ground stands myself, on one side sparkle the fountains of Castalia and on the other stand open the portals of Nemesis. . . .

My most excellent romancer it is not so. I must announce to you the startling position that I have been a medical student for more than six months and am sitting with Wistar's anatomy beneath my quiescent arm with a stethoscope on my desk and blood-stained implements of my ungracious profession around me. . . . I know I might have made an indifferent lawyer—I think I may make a tolerable physician—I do not like the one and I do like the other. And so you must know that for the last several months I have been quietly occupying a room in Boston attending medical lectures, going to the Massachusetts Hospital and slicing and slivering the carcasses of better men and women than I ever was myself or am like to be. It is a sin for a puny little fellow like me to mutilate one of your six foot men as if he was a sheep. . . .

If you would die fagged to death like a crow with the king birds after him, be a schoolmaster—if you would wax thin and savage like a half-fed spider, be a lawyer—if you would go off like an opium-eater in love with your starving delusion, be a Doctor. . . .

To change the subject—I have just now a ruse in my head which I am in hopes to put in execution this summer— You must be aware then that there is a young lady, or what sounds sweeter a girl in Maine. . . . Well perhaps I am in love with her and perhaps she is in love with me. At any rate I made a strapping fellow bite his nails, who had the impertinence to think she was pretty. I quizzed the caitiff in his remarks, anticipated his gallantries and plagued him till he went about his business.

Now I have a sneaking notion of coming down to Maine to see you as I shall tell the folks, and take a cross-cut over to her log house [if] I can find it. She had so much the air of a human-[be]ing while she was here that I have a curiosity to see her wild. . . .

By the way if you find any floating scraps with O.W.H. to the tail of them set them down to the owner and I believe the only one of those preposterous initials.[1]

The preposterous initials appeared the next day, March 26, in the *Amateur* at the tail of lines the poet could own without misgivings—"The Last Leaf."

Medicine, scribbling, and love—these three made the pattern of his life for the next two years. He traveled a little but not Down East, going instead to Providence to visit his doctor brother-in-law. He did not get engaged, perhaps the girl did not like being told that to write a letter every two weeks was to write too often. Besides it was wise to wait a little, to be established before becoming a husband; "a man who has to swim without a cork jacket had better not put lead into his breeches' pocket." [2] There were girls in Boston silly enough to hold hands with a poet. He settled down in his boarding-house and went to work, the intervals between writing-jags becoming longer and longer, as he became more and more in love with his starving delusion.

The apothecary Brown and his wife were accustomed to the curious habits of medical students and doctors of whom there were always one or two among their boarders. They were used to scribblers, too; besides O. W. H., now a contributor to the very respectable *New England Magazine,* there was an energetic widow who wrote verses and articles with unladylike zeal —Sarah Josepha Hale. The new boarder was not so much different from the others except that perhaps he talked too much, and there might be some question of his ever being a real doctor if he went on writing verses.

His companions now were not only the bright young men who haunted the Benjamin house and talked schemes for new magazines. They were young men of different ambitions who crowded about a table "with a skeleton hanging over, and bones lying about." The new medical student had been somewhat shocked at first and "disposed to moralize upon mortality" [3] and not immediately eager to learn the mysteries of osteology. The pale faces of the sick in the hospital wards stirred at first more pity than careful attention. In the operating-theater the block and tackle rigged from the ceiling suggested only too well the terror and suffering in these days before the use of anesthetics. He did not, however, faint as some of his fellows did at the dreadful scenes there enacted.

The first lessons were anatomy. Dr. Winslow Lewis, who presided over the dissecting-tables and taught Holmes to slice and sliver carcasses, was a man who loved his subject and enjoyed teaching. He mixed medical history and talk of old books with anatomical puzzles. And in his classes, the nearest thing to a laboratory which medical education had then to offer, the students learned to handle their instruments with some skill. Holmes himself later had some reputation as a dextrous and careful workman in the art of preparing complicated dissections.

Holmes had begun his study of medicine several months before the Massachusetts Anatomy Act made legal the use of the human body for dissection. Neither the law nor popular feeling had sanctioned the work in which these young men were engaged; but their teachers, Lewis in the private school and John Collins Warren of Harvard, had not let public superstition stand in the way of their own education or that of their students. Laboring for years to push through the passage of the Anatomy Act, the first of its kind in the United States—in the English-speaking world for that matter—Warren had been in his youth an accomplished robber of graves.

The most honorable men among these physicians had not caviled at the ghoulish crime of body-snatching. Warren, trying to build up a collection of anatomical specimens, healthy and morbid, which he was later to present to Harvard, had often been indignant at the shifts to which he was obliged to resort. On one occasion, unable to bear the thought that the body of an Indian, illustrating a particularly nice point in morbid anatomy, should be lost to science, Warren had managed to steal the cadaver. He happily carried off his specimen to his museum while the undertakers, complaining of the unnatural weight of the coffin, carried away and buried with due propriety—a log of wood. The doctor had been very careful to choose a log that would fit tightly in the coffin. An honorable and thoroughly religious man, Warren tells the story himself without the slightest trace of even macabre humor, but rather with a grim anger that the deed had been necessary.[4] Even with the passage of the Anatomy Act, which allowed physicians to requisition unclaimed bodies from state institutions, popular feeling of superstitious horror put limits upon the number of subjects available, made necessary the softening of the act in 1850, and, as late as 1883, was easily aroused to active expression against the school. The prejudice operated also to prevent any adequate study of pathology; families would rarely permit autopsies; in medical schools, the subject was not given separate attention but was taught along with surgery, itself limited by the lack of any knowledge of anesthesia.

The narrow curriculum of the medical schools suggests the limited medical knowledge of the day. The subjects then taught were five in number: Theory and Practice of Medicine, Anatomy and Surgery, Obstetrics and Medical Jurisprudence, Chemistry, and Materia Medica. A staff of five professors of these subjects was the normal one for a medical school of the time; Harvard had recently added Winslow Lewis as Demonstrator of Anatomy. There was no such subject as physiology, except the little that got mixed in with anatomy. Although the achromatic microscope had recently been invented, it was not being used in medical schools, which consequently did not teach any kind of histology or embryology.

Any student could enter a medical school with or without a college education if he gave evidence of a knowledge of Latin and elementary physics. He was required to attend two terms of lectures; at the most the school term lasted four months, usually only three—November through January. The greater part of his training he received as an apprentice to some busy general practitioner in his home town. After he had had three years of such apprenticeship and if he were twenty-one, he submitted a thesis and took a perfunctory oral examination. In the state of Massachusetts, the Harvard degree alone entitled the student to practice in the state; graduates of other institutions were examined by the state medical society.[5]

Holmes's own notes of the cases he observed at the Massachusetts General Hospital give revealing and dramatic evidence of the state of medical knowledge. The twentieth-century reader, following young Holmes with his notebook through the hospital wards, cannot help wondering how any of the patients escaped alive.

There were a number of influenza patients, a few with pneumonia, a few with typhoid or typhus—the distinction between the two was not very clear in 1832. And there was the coach-driver with sciatica but suffering just then from an overdose of cathartics; and there, the syphilitic sailor and the diabetic fisherman. In the same ward with patients down with influenza were twelve-year-old Thomas Young and Amos Drury with clinical pictures alarmingly like that of infantile paralysis. There seemed to be nothing much wrong with Theodosia who thought she had a liver complaint but was apparently just hysterical; Priscilla's greenish color proclaimed her anemic state and she was given iron. But in the woman's ward, too, were Sally Sparrow with scarlet fever and Clarissa Child who had either chickenpox or smallpox, just which had not yet been decided.[6] In the 1830's, many physicians denied that there was such a thing as contagion; and the possibility of taking preventive measures did not occur even to men who, like those under whom Holmes was studying, recognized the possibility of contagion.

The fever patients who filled up the wards every fall were considered to be victims of something called "miasmata," a mysterious and deadly force welling up from stagnant water, perhaps, and borne on the night air. Such were the vague notions of the etiology of diseases. Sporadic study of morbid anatomy did not help to clear away the uncertainties. Just what, for instance, the visiting celebrity, Dr. Spurzheim, died of, no one at the Massachusetts General Hospital was very certain. An autopsy was performed, and the inside of the famous phrenologist's cranium was examined as he himself had examined the outsides of the crania of others. The brain wasn't entirely healthy; neither was the peritoneum, but still the distinguished gentleman's interior showed nothing to account for his dying. He had had a "fever." [7]

Spurzheim, himself, was a good example of the "psychology" of the day, especially the popular variety. The phrenologist professed to be able to analyze character by studying the contours of the skull; the assumption was that character traits were located in specific parts of the brain and manifested themselves outwardly in the irregularities of the individual skull. A citizen of the twentieth century can still have his "bumps" read somewhat after the manner of Spurzheim, for the "science" he undertook to study passed quickly into the hands of charlatans and superstitious laymen, some of whom can be found today, along with teacup readers, and astrologers. Spurzheim himself was a serious student, as his master, Franz Joseph Gall, had been before him; if the errors of these two men gave rise in one direction to a brand of quackery, in another direction they led to further study of the anatomy of the brain and ultimately to modern psychology. Many of the young men who had sat in on the autopsy performed on Spurzheim had also attended his public lectures on the subject of phrenology, among them young Holmes, whose later speculations on psychological themes had their origin here.

Considering the amount of medical ignorance, it is not surprising to find that methods of treatment were often of a kind to fill the mind with horror. These were the days of "heroic" measures. Potentially poisonous drugs like antimony and the various mercurials were handed out in terrifying quantities by followers of the antiphlogistic method of treatment. From such doctors a patient might expect to be bled, blistered, and dosed to his grave; or, if not quite to his grave, at least to a state of misery that might persuade him that the sufferings of disease were preferable to the sore mouth and violently disrupted stomach induced by his doctor's treatment. There were, of course, patients who liked such treatment and felt themselves neglected if they were not abused.

The men under whom Holmes was studying, however, had begun to doubt the efficacy of the heroic measures they had learned in the medical schools of England and Scotland, to recognize the fact of medical ignorance, and to rely upon careful observation after the manner of the French clinicians. Men like Dr. Warren and James Jackson who had sons following their profession sent them to Paris to complete their studies, and traveled there themselves to see the new work being done in the French hospitals. And they had also begun to alter a little their program of medical education. One such innovation was the private school which Holmes told Barnes he was attending.

When Holmes put aside Blackstone for Wistar, he did not need to apprentice himself to a single busy practitioner; for Walter Channing and James Jackson of Harvard had joined forces with three other Boston physicians, Winslow Lewis, George Otis, and John Ware, to provide an organized course of training better than a single overworked doctor could possibly give. Dr. Warren had a similar co-operative arrangement with another group of local doctors. These private schools using the facilities, such as they were, of the medical college and pooling their libraries and illustrative material, were in effect extensions of the Harvard Medical School, and what they had to offer was certainly superior to the training a single busy doctor could give the two or three young men who might follow him on his rounds.

In putting himself under the tutelage of the physicians of this school and in Harvard, Holmes was providing himself with the best medical education his country had then to offer. The fame of these doctors was not so monumental as the insular Bostonians liked to think, but they were men who had the courage and force to introduce new discoveries and practices. While John Collins Warren, Professor of Surgery and Anatomy, had worked for the Anatomy Act, Walter Channing, Professor of Obstetrics and Dean of the medical college, had worked for the establishment of the Boston Lying-In Hospital. Thirteen years later the two men were to make courageous use of ether and, by publishing their cases, help to make the use of the anesthestic universal. It was Warren who at the age of seventy-three performed the first public operation on a patient anesthetized with ether. On the Harvard staff, too, was Jacob Bigelow, Professor of Materia Medica, an ingenious and versatile man. Bigelow's particular field was botany, and his volume on New England flora is still a classic. He dabbled a little also in physics and on his own initiative gave a special course in mechanics to Harvard undergraduates. His ideas on education emphasized practical and scientific subjects, modern history, and modern languages and minimized classical studies; he there anticipated the technological schools and educational reforms of the last half of the century, reforms which today we seem to be regretting.

Bigelow would soon (1835) publish his essay on *Self-Limited Diseases*. The recognition that some diseases were self-limiting made it plain that many supposed cures were natural recoveries after a disease had run its course. This observation threw the whole system of drugging in doubt; and even before the book was published, he and his colleagues on the faculty of the Harvard Medical School (then called the Massachusetts Medical College) began to employ the "expectant" method of treatment, in which remedies were directed to the relief of symptoms and not assumed to have curative powers.

Of all his teachers in the college and the private school, Dr. James Jackson, Sr., was to Holmes the most important. Quite literally Holmes carried out the Hippocratic Oath—"to reckon him who taught me this Art equally dear to me as my parents." Nor was he being sentimental when he claimed Jackson as a second father.[8]

From Jackson the students of the private school and of

Harvard received their clinical training. For three years Holmes was in and out of the doctor's house. Among his fellow-students was the doctor's brilliant son. There is no reason to believe that Holmes was in any way alienated from his own father, but there is some suggestion that he envied those young men like Jonathan Mason Warren and James Jackson, Jr., who were bound to their fathers by the same professional interest, or like Henry I. Bowditch, son of the famous author of *The New American Practical Navigator* and translator of Laplace, who had a concern for science as a bond between him and his father.

To some extent his brother-in-law, Dr. Usher Parsons, filled in this lack for Holmes. The young man could not write to Barnes about his studies, but he could write to Parsons, whose varied experiences included teaching and military surgery as well as general practice. He could not talk to his father about his work; it would certainly be natural for him to turn to the teacher with whom he was most closely associated and whose ideas he absorbed so thoroughly that in much of his later medical writing the thoughts are Jackson's although the language is Holmes's. The only notes the student preserved from these first years of study are those of Jackson's lectures.

Jackson was first and last a ministering physician who "truly loved his profession. He had no intellectual ambitions outside of it, literary, scientific or political." In his practice and teaching, he seems to have carried out the Oath with rare exactness. The first tenet of his creed was his insistence that a doctor does not so much cure his patients as care for them.[9] In expressing to his students considerable skepticism about so-called cures and putting his emphasis on the value of fresh air, sensible clothing, exercise, and cleanliness, not only for general good health but as helps toward recovery from disease, he was well in advance of the common practice of his day. At a time when tuberculous patients were commonly shut up in airless, dark rooms and dosed with laudanum, Jackson was recommending sunlight and fresh air and teaching his students the truth that there was no known cure for this disease.

In an early stage of the disease a change to a warm climate will be useful not because its air is healing—this will do for poets—but because the patient will be able to exercise in the open air.[10]

The poet in the class absorbed the "fresh air and exercise" doctrine thoroughly as his own casebooks show.

For all diseases which experience had shown him were self-limiting, Jackson used the expectant treatment, teaching his students that "as the disease is fixed, remedies can do nothing." [11] Of an autumnal fever, he taught:

I have seldom seen any good effects produced by active treatment. You must learn this from your own experience. When I began practice, calomel was given . . . but after trying it, I have relinquished its use.[12]

On the whole, Jackson went in for very little dosing, discontinuing remedies when his patient showed no benefit, keeping to those tested by experience, and sometimes giving harmless concoctions solely to satisfy the imagination of patients "who think they must take physic." [13] Bleeding and the application of leeches he resorted to for certain kinds of inflammation; he seemed particularly fond of venesection in the early stages of pneumonia. "His materia medica was a simple one," [14] said Holmes; and his notes bear out the statement; Jackson used opium, quinine, calomel, senna, and antimony, if the patient did not have a horror of the drug.

"We must," he exhorted his class, "attend also to every circumstance relating to the patient's comfort." [15] Nor was he thinking only of the patient's bodily comfort. When he speaks of the "Passions of the Mind" in his lectures on disorders of the digestive functions, his language is not that of modern psychosomatic medicine, but his thought is.

The state of mind should be carefully observed, and such means employed as will overcome the depressing passion.[16]

His favorite treatment, exercise, is called for, but "amusement of the mind is also beneficial," not, however, to the exclusion of "consideration of the primary disease." [17]

His students particularly admired the way Dr. Jackson kept the patient's comfort in mind when he came to examine him.

Miss Rebecca Taylor, much respected chief nurse of the Massachusetts General, might be subjected to questioning as "good as one would be like to hear outside the courtroom" [18]— the doctor would have a straight story and nothing else—but with patients the cross-examiner gave way to the solicitous friend. From Jackson, Holmes learned the precept he later turned into rhyme for "The Morning Visit":

> So of your questions; don't in mercy try
> To pump your patient absolutely dry;
> He's not a mollusk squirming in a dish,
> You're not Agassiz, and he's not a fish.

When using the methods of direct exploration and employing the new instrument, the stethoscope, Holmes was taught by Jackson's example to consider the patient's comfort, mental and physical. In the same poem, the poet-doctor advises:

> If the poor victim needs must be percussed,
> Don't make an anvil of his aching bust;
> (Doctors exist within a hundred miles
> Who thump a thorax as they'd hammer piles;)
> If you must listen to his doubtful chest,
> Catch the essentials and ignore the rest.[19]

Under the stimulus of Jackson's teaching, Holmes worked hard both in the dispensary, where he served as chemist, and in the wards of the hospital, which he visited at odd hours to take a second look at the cases Dr. Jackson was discussing in the morning clinical lectures. He brought materials to his room for dissection, a practice which his landlady managed to put up with as she endured having her breakfast-table appear in print. For he was still writing now and then and had already invented the Autocrat who rambled on in two issues of the *New England Magazine*. But he had been working too hard to write a great deal; where one year of law had produced more than fifty verses, more than two years of medicine left him time for only half as many titles. Besides, although he was not tired of studying, he was weary of following a routine and of writing "trash." He could not promise to be much of a host if his friend Barnes should take it into his head to visit Boston.

I cannot promise you much, but I will give you a good dinner, and a glass of wine somewhere or other, and some good cigars if you smoke, and say "Come in" when you knock at the door of my attic. But I must go to the Hospital and to the Eye Infirmary, and I must dissect, if you bring the Governor and Senate with you.[20]

The same letter reports him ready to leave for Providence to cut up a cadaver. He was willing enough to travel for work, if not for love.

The young man who liked light chatter and puns and who got his name in print attached to funny verses was bent on making himself a thorough-going doctor; he expected "to trot off to Europe some of these days" he had written casually in 1832, thinking of his friends, Jackson, Warren, and Bowditch who had already gone to Paris.

By the end of his second year at Harvard, he had made up his mind to postpone taking his degree and to follow his friends to France. Ambitious for professional distinction and aware of the advantages and prestige of a French medical education, young Holmes naturally turned his thoughts toward Europe. The expense of the undertaking was probably somewhat greater than his parents could easily afford. The Wendell property in Cambridge, Boston, and Pittsfield did not yield a large income, but Abiel Holmes had always provided generously for his children's education and was willing to make the sacrifice now required of him by his son. On March 29, 1833, Wendell Holmes was in New York ready to sail for France. That night his teacher, James Jackson, sat down to write a letter to his son.

Many of my cases have been interesting and instructive—to me at least. Students do not seem to me so eager to acquire the knowledge which cases afford, as I could wish. Holmes knows more of my cases this winter than anyone—he spent three or four months in the hospital as apothecary. If you see him, he can tell you much that is interesting. Do not mind his apparent frivolity and you will soon find that he is intelligent and well-informed. *He has the true zeal.*[21]

Traveler in Europe·

> *Nor is that curiosity ever more agreeably or use-*
> *fully employed, than in examining the laws and*
> *customs of foreign nations.*

On March 27, 1833, Holmes left the boarding-house behind him, done for a time at least with too familiar faces and disagreeable people, with Francis Dana's incessant monologues on the remarkable character of Scylla.[1] The companions who traveled with him by stage to Providence and by steamboat to New York were an unexpected delight. Charles Amory's pretty wife was "a transparent Magdaleine blonde" with a sweet voice and kind smile. Traveling with the honeymoon pair was Mary Benjamin, as usual "gathering beaux about her like a snowball."

In New York at the American Hotel he found that half Boston was going out on the packet *Philadelphia*. Half Boston included the gay Tom Appleton and Bob Hooper, a fellow medical student. Holmes was to share a stateroom with Bob, "one of the pleasantest fellows." Dr. Jacob Bigelow and his wife were in the group. A bare two hundred miles from home, the traveler wrote his parents, "You cannot imagine the pleasure which my falling into this little party has given me." The son of the Calvinist minister spent his first night in New York at the theater where he saw that "very fine affair," Fanny Kemble, playing with her father in *The Hunchback*.[2]

On the morning of April 1, "an enchanting day," the passengers for the *Philadelphia*, Captain Christopher H. Camplin, assembled on board the steamship *Hercules* which would carry them out to The Narrows where the packet lay at anchor. The steamboat had then to tug the packet out to Sandy Hook. They looked, the *Hercules* and the *Philadelphia*, like a Beacon street couple they all knew said Holmes: "she all paddle and steam and smoke, he all dignified inertness."

The cry of "man overboard" caused a furor; someone tossed a plank over the side and the floundering sailor was speedily hauled up. At Sandy Hook, "a collation having been served," the passengers' friends were taken off and carried back to shore on the efficient steamboat. The travelers were really under way. The journey promised to be a delightful one; Tom Appleton already had his eye on a Mlle Victorine, who was inclined to be flirtatious.[3]

In a twenty-four-day voyage the travelers did not always escape boredom, and sometimes the diarists, Appleton and Hooper, had nothing to record except that a hen was lost overboard or that the hymn was "Greenland's Icy Mountains." Ten days out, Appleton wrote:

What an odd, good-for-nothing life we lead! A prolonged morning nap, jokes, and a wire-drawn breakfast; a turn on the deck, a sluggish conversation, a book held in the hand an hour or two, another turn on the deck—we dash to dinner; three courses, laughter, candles, tea, and the moon.[4]

There was plenty of laughter. Holmes, Hooper, and Appleton kept up a cannonade of puns; one of the steerage passengers with "an admirable voice" entertained with ballads; two of the ladies were glad to play for the company.[5] Tom Appleton seems to have done enough flirting for the three of them, but all amused the French girl with imitations of a menagerie. And once the captain put up a light for a passing ship that turned out to be the moon! Perhaps he was wise to be over-cautious; the last packet had struck a field of floating ice.[6] There was enough suggestion of danger to give some excitement to the journey, although the only trouble the *Philadelphia* encountered was a storm which kept the passengers below decks for a day and a "fresh breeze that split the main topsail." [7]

The big event of the journey was the mid-ocean meeting with the brig *Economist*, sixty-six days out of Sierra Leone and short of provisions. The two ships were becalmed side by side. When the mate of the Portuguese vessel came aboard the *Philadelphia* to get supplies, he found himself loaded down with luxuries by the excited passengers of the American vessel.[8]

And once Appleton saw or thought he saw a nautilus— "that most poetical of ocean-rovers."

It was spinning around in the foam, in shape like a sculpin, with a many-colored and semi-transparent body, and two beautiful azure, gauze-like wings or sails. I saw no oars. It was whirled instantly out of sight.[9]

Perhaps Holmes saw it too, or only heard Appleton's romantic and traditional description when the two talked sentiment.[10]

At the end of the long voyage, the Boston travelers were inclined to agree with Holmes who said that the worst part of the journey was the ride to Providence.[11] On the 24th of April the ship took on a pilot and the next day they landed at Portsmouth.

While waiting for the boat to Havre, Holmes and his friend Hooper became earnest tourists, admiring the garden-like landscape of the western downs, the cottages of "quaint but infinitely varied and almost always pleasing form," the neat White Hart Inn at Salisbury, the elegant coaches "like models for a parlour," and the coachmen dressed like kings. But England was expensive, and Holmes, although he could never complain of any lack of parental generosity, did not have so much to spend as his wealthy companions. Old England was comfortable enough, but "for these comforts you must feed with gold and silver a set of lying, cringing, and shameless extortioners." [12]

Nevertheless, one went sight-seeing. With the Quebec Hotel as their base the young men made raids into the surrounding territory and saw everything from Stonehenge to Nelson's flagship. They took in a pair of castles and admired Salisbury Cathedral. Of all that he saw in these few hurried days, the spire of the cathedral remained clearest in his memory. He wrote of it later: "As one drives away from the town the roofs of the houses drop out of the landscape, the lesser spires disappear one by one, until the great shaft is left standing alone—solitary as the broken statue of Ozymandias in the desert. . . ." [13] They were taken to call upon the son of Mr. McAdam—the "Colossus of Roads," Holmes called him, the punning instinct irrepressible. Their host showed them about the estate of the Earl of Pembroke. The Earl, reported Holmes, was "a scapegrace—married to an Italian actress—will not live at home &c." [14] They saw statues and pictures and some of "Queen Elizabeth's duds" and King William's yacht. With his taste formed by the pictures in the Athenaeum Gallery, Holmes found himself admiring the Claude Lorraïne landscapes and ignoring paintings he would notice on his second visit fifty years later.[15]

In an enterprising mood, the young travelers posed as Englishmen and explored the Portsmouth docks. Energetically, they rowed out to inspect the Isle of Wight. And at Salisbury in a theater that looked like a barn, they saw Mr. Angel and the beautiful Mrs. Shields in *The Illustrious Stranger*.[16] They had crowded a good deal into their lay-over in England, even squeezing in another play, when their boat was held over a day.[17] Perhaps it was just as well that they had received the benediction of a Lord Bishop who got £15,000 a year.[18]

The morning of May 4 found them at Havre. "By giving the custom house officers a hint that we were Americans our baggage was passed over lightly; our passports were made out and having secured our passages in the diligence we slept quietly for the first time in France." The next day they set out for Paris.

The young American, who liked a smart turn-out, was startled and amused by the "odd vehicle" in which he had taken passage. It was all too disorderly and the conductor was dressed up like a jackanapes.

Another fellow called the postillion rides upon one of the horses. These are harnessed to the diligence partly with leather and partly with ropes with about as much order as a flock of sheep. On the bad parts of the route they tied on extra horses to the first place a rope will hold by, so that I counted nine at one time scampering along in such a fashion that I laughed right heartily.

Even though the passengers had to get out and walk on the hills between Rouen and Paris, this equipage brought them finally to the outskirts of Paris in the early hours of May 6. Holmes awoke, observed the unbecoming attitudes of his still sleeping fellow-travelers and caught a glimpse of great cathedral walls. The diligence rode into the city with the marketers, "some on asses with panniers and some in great carts." [19]

On their arrival, Holmes and Hooper bravely trusted themselves to a cabdriver, fortunately a kind one, for the Harvard graduates discovered that they could not after all speak French. The deficiencies in pronunciation Professor Ticknor had observed in his students were now a handicap. The hotel to which Hooper directed the driver would have nothing to do with the foreigners, but the pitying driver took them back to an establishment near the office of the diligence where "we were treated very kindly till we could find our friends." [20] The Boston boys turned up shortly and took the new arrivals off to breakfast.

It was in the Place de la Bourse, on a beautiful sunshiny morning. The coffee was nectar, the *flûte* was ambrosia, the *brioche* was more than good enough for the Olympians.[21]

—or so it seemed in retrospect, thirty-three years later. The recollected idyll is likely a translation of the comfort of finding friends, the elegant Jonathan Mason Warren, the studious James Jackson, Jr., and the extremely earnest Henry I. Bowditch.

There were as usual too many Americans in Paris; one was tempted to talk too much English. Although within a week of his arrival Holmes was cheerfully bragging to his parents that he was "almost naturalized," [22] he had to admit there were imperfections.

You will wonder, I suppose how I make out to talk French enough to keep out of fire and water. The truth [is] that I am rather deficient. . . .[23]

Before the first month was out, Hooper and Holmes put themselves in the hands of a French master, M. Delaraux,[24] and
took to dining at Mme. Morel's pension where nothing but
French was spoken.[25] The pension had served a similar function for other helpless Americans, but its claim to historical
distinction rested upon its more remote past. It was there that
Charlotte Corday murdered the revolutionary Marat, as he
lay soaking in his bath.[26] It still sheltered ardent republicans,
one of whom was hauled off to jail during Holmes's stay in
Paris.

Meanwhile Holmes had settled himself in lodgings at 55
rue Monsieur-le-Prince, with the Luxembourg Gardens half-a-
dozen rods from his door. His family were invited to imagine
they had come to call.

We have come to a small green door in a narrow house 5 stories high.
I ring the bell; and you expect somebody to come: no—the latch is
lifted by an invisible hand and we go in. We walk up one flight of
stairs and we have come to the porter's room—I ask for the key of
No. 6—my room—he gives it to me and we proceed to what we should
call the 4th floor story but what is the 3d of the Parisians who never
think of living below stairs. We walk in and having looked around for
a while, you have seen what I am going to tell you; and I suppose this
is about a fair specimen of the common chambers of respectable people.
The room is about as large as the study at Cambridge and has two
windows parallel with one street—Rue M. le Prince, and heading another, Rue Vaugirard. . . . These windows like all the others in Paris
open inward like folding doors. The floor is of hexagonal tiles—the
walls are papered after our fashion. There is a recess for a bed with
ample white curtains hanging from a very handsomely gilded pole. . . .
The floor has a very nice green carpet laid upon it, and the windows have
double sets of white curtains and blinds that are raised by pullies [sic].
My furniture is the following: A large mahogany bureau with a marble
slab covering it—a mahogany table with two large drawers—a small
round table covered with white marble—2 looking glasses each about
5 feet by 3—2 arm chairs covered with yellow velvet—four landscapes
on proof paper in gilt frames—(which I believe are respectable, for I
never looked at them) and a sentimental picture which makes me laugh
—besides washing table and things—more chairs than I can manage—
and an inkstand.[27]

For this luxury M. Bertrand, his landlord, asked about eight dollars a month, and for a little extra, the porter would wake him up, make his bed, brush his clothes, and clean his boots. It was always of some importance to young Holmes to live as "respectable people do"; he might have gone through his two years in Europe at slightly less expense to his generous parents if he had been willing to stint himself, but he made a point of living decently.

He had scarcely settled in his quarters when he showed the zeal which his teacher had recognized beneath his frivolous manner. Every morning at seven-thirty he turned up at the Pitié, where until ten he followed Pierre Charles Alexandre Louis through the crowded wards, attending the pathologist's analysis of cases as well as his slight hold on the language would allow. Ten-thirty found him with his compatriots in the Café Procope, ready for his long-delayed breakfast.[28] For almost a century and a half, the café had served its famous customers: Voltaire, Rousseau—when he could afford it. Now Bowditch, who knew everyone of consequence, could point out among the frequenters of the café the physicist Arago, the philosopher Jouffroy, and the mathematician Poisson. The restaurant was the favorite rendezvous of students, scientists, poets, and revolutionaries in these days when Louis-Phillipe was showing himself in his true and unrepublican colors.[29]

The young Americans liked the excellent coffee, took quickly to sipping sugar and water. From this late breakfast until five "we study or go to lectures, or do what we choose, and at five we dine. These two meals are all that anybody pretends to take in Paris," [30] reported Holmes. On weekdays he dined faithfully at his French boarding-house, but on Sundays the Boston boys splurged, dining at famous establishments to which they, as old hands, proudly took travelers like Ralph Waldo Emerson, Isaac Morse, and Tom Appleton when they turned up in Paris. In the evenings, there were French lessons, or "sometimes some amusement or other," the *Combats des Animaux,* for instance, to which Mason Warren introduced him a few days after his arrival.[31]

87

He was settled, he had friends, he was getting hold of the language, he had begun his work. By the end of June he felt as if he had known Paris from his childhood.

I live at Paris just as if I had been there all my life, and indeed I can hardly conceive of anybody's living in any other way so completely have I naturalized myself. It seems hideous to think of more than two meals a day, how could I ever have dined at two o'clock? How could I have put anything to mouth but a silver fork? How could I have survived dinner without a napkin? [32]

And not so many weeks later, he was practically a Frenchman. "I love to talk French, to eat French, to drink French every now and then." And he added a soothing parenthesis—"these wines are superb, and nobody gets drunk, except as an experiment in physiology." [33] He was so thoroughly at home that Boston might be only thirty miles away. There was only one source of anxiety; he had had no letters at all. He made a resolution not to worry, wrote by every packet, and tried hard to keep his feelings under control, but they came out in words of restrained complaint, in a certain stiffness of tone. Fortunately he was very busy. There was no time to torment himself; there was too much to see and too much to do. Visitors from home were always turning up; July was a month of holidays. In some ways the first months in Paris were like one continual college commencement on a royal scale.

The Americans who came to France showed, even as early as the 1830's, a characteristic astonishment at finding noticeable traces of civilization in the Old World. What seemed to strike these students most were the free institutions—the public gardens, the art galleries, the museums—places like the Botanical Gardens which so moved Emerson when he visited Paris in this same year. The serious-minded Bowditch had given his parents an enthusiastic account of the opportunities of Paris and expressed a patriotic wish to see something of the same kind at home.[34] The bent of Holmes's mind was different. Like Bowditch, he was delighted with the possibilities Paris presented. But where the one deplored the absence of such institutions in his own country, the other observed that the French people appreciated their privileges.

You look in vain for the traces of that wanton spirit of mischief which with us defaces everything that can by any possibility be soiled or mutilated.

He had earlier observed that "every Frenchman behaves to his neighbor like a gentleman," his attention characteristically focused upon manners and good breeding.

"The soldiers, to be sure, stand at the gates of many of the public institutions," wrote Holmes describing his explorations to his family. But except as one of these guardians of order affected him, the young man did not immediately see that there might be some connection between the presence of the soldiers and a Frenchman's appreciation of his privileges. He took the wrong gate one day at the Tuileries and was brought up short before he had gone very far in the direction of the apartments of Louis-Phillipe. *"On ne passe pas,"* said the soldier and the American postponed his visit to the king of France who had given up pretending to be democratic ever since he had moved from the Palais-Royal to the Tuileries.[35]

Louis-Phillipe's daughters might look surprisingly like Ann Saltonstall, but his soldiers on review were something "of which a militia muster can give you no idea."

It is something I never expected to realize in my own sight . . . to see the long line of cuirasses glittering on the bosoms of tall broad stately Norsemen, and the lancers with their little tri-colored pennons floating from their unaimable weapons and those dense masses of infantry with their bayonets undulating and sparkling under your window and all this with the music of a hundred instruments ringing and rolling around you.[36]

It was, indeed, a new experience for a young man whose notions of a spectacle were founded on the annual procession of the Governor and his troop of lighthorse on their way to the Cambridge meeting-house for commencement day.

"One must pick up some notions on geography, for instance, and on politics." The left bank did not present to this nineteenth-century traveler the face of dissipation, but there were

89

revolutionaries even at Mme. Morel's dining-table. All through the *arrondissement* of Luxembourg there were students eager to fight. Over the Café Procope's coffee, excited republicans read their journals, made their jokes about the pear-shaped countenance of the king, and wrathfully discussed the government project for fortifying the city. The pretended defenses are "to be so placed that in the event of what kings call insurrection and people revolution, they may knock Paris to pieces with her own cannon." Luckily, the young man told his parents, his mind did not take a revolutionary turn or he might, like his fellow-boarder,

have had the pleasure . . . of being kept under lock and key through all the fine doings of July, and of having my room entered and finding myself and my friends in the guard-house under the name of a political association. . . .[37]

The "fine doings of July" began for the Americans in Paris with an Independence Day dinner when "that inextinguishable old gentleman M. Lafayette and his progeny stirred up our patriotism with their presence." The New Englanders were very much in evidence at the gathering, and a hot-headed Jacksonian naval officer suspected that these sons of Federalists had not drunk their toasts to the President Andrew Jackson with the proper enthusiasm. He demanded to know "if this is a meeting of the Hartford Convention or of Citizens of the United States." The Bostonians did not take the insult quietly. Holmes's friend James Russell was on his feet in an instant—"his mustaches curling like a sultan's—hissed in his very eyes & called on the company to cut off the buttons of his uniform and turn him out; and this to an officer, a dead shot, who had killed his man already." But there was no duel after all; the ill-mannered naval officer got himself entangled elsewhere. On the whole, the party was a dull affair in spite of the excitement, partridges stuffed with truffles, and fifty kinds of wine, "to say nothing of the scrape's costing seven dollars to each enthusiastic republican." [38]

It was nothing like the show the Frenchmen put on for their holidays, however unrepublican. It was not July 14 that was

celebrated in 1833, but July 27-29, a three-day fiesta for the
"revolution" of 1830. The 27th was a day of mourning with
much display of crape and amaranth and the sound of melancholy music, but on the 28th there was a day of rejoicing—
compulsory rejoicing assured by a number of preliminary
arrests and by the king's soldiers who were out in full force
to forestall any demonstrations against the government.

Everything went off very quietly. I gave a franc for the privilege of
standing on a table and saw the whole scrape. The queen and princesses
and a little whiteheaded prince in a coach as gingerbready as King
Pippin's . . . and Louis Philippe on horseback bowing ferociously—and
then soldiers for two or three hours pouring through the Rue Castiglione
a very wide and beautiful street as if they would flow forever like the
rivers.

In the evening, there was a tremendous concert, followed by
superb fireworks, general illumination—the dome of the
Panthéon looking "like a vast hemisphere of fire"—and a naval
display on the river. The third day was given over to every
kind of theatrical show.

The young man, recalling commencement and election
days, suddenly felt like a country boy. "I have a little better
notion now than I once had of the difference between a population of sixty and eight-hundred and ninety, thousand
people." There was that amusing sign "Hôtel de L'Univers
et des États Unis" which must have seemed doubly ironic to
him in his letter-less state; perhaps America was a mere ap-
pendage to the universe.[39]

But all through the summer there were visitors, and part of
the pleasure of being "naturalized" was showing them about.
Tom Appleton had turned up in June after a too expensive
stay in England; the "medicals" made his coming the occasion
of a party. They dined at Prevost's in the Palais-Royal and
watched the "gambols of the children" at the Théâtre des
enfants. With Appleton, Holmes made his first visit to the
Louvre; it was very near closing time, but foreigners were admitted every day and the two went again immediately to spend
three exciting hours. It was Titian who caught Holmes's ad-

miration when he got over being astounded at the mere number of things to be seen.[40]

To Appleton even then Paris was Paradise; he would make his famous phrase about "good Americans when they die" later; right now he was bent on pleasure of the fashionable kind and the "medicals" went with him. Holmes had already regretted that he had not gone to the theater more during his first month in Paris. His failure, he feared, "betrays a want of taste" and besides it was a good way to learn the language. He soon made up for the omission. The party in the Palais-Royal and the visits to the Louvre were followed by dinner at a fashionable restaurant, and an evening at the Théâtre français where he saw Mlle Mars who for all she showed her fifty-eight years had a voice "perfectly clear and pure," and her pronunciation was "perhaps the best model of classic French." [41]

These Bostonian dwellers on the left bank took all their pleasures with a certain solemnity. Holmes assiduously cultivating his "taste" bought a few engravings and a good many books from the familiar stalls on the Quai d'Orsay. He visited the galleries and detected in himself signs of improvement.[42]

He delighted to wander the streets of Paris and not all the pleasures of the *flâneur* could be ticketed as educational; one could not be constantly shopping for self-improvement. He told his parents that he was "old and tough." "The skim milk sentiment of my younger days [he was twenty-four] has hardened into the white oak cheese of maturity." [43] The very elaborateness of the conceit gave him away. He never forgot the old lady at the head of the Pont des Arts from whom he bought violets.

For the *flâneur* there were street vendors with odd and barbaric things to sell.

A fellow took a quantity of beetles, glued them into a little frame of paper so that he could make them stand upright—pulled off all their legs but two, glued a little straw on one of these—put a little cocked hat on their heads—and having equipped them in this manner placed them opposite each other in pairs. So you would see on his hat, where he exposed them for sale, a dozen pair of these little knights bowing their cocked hats and poking away at each other with a vivacity which authorized their manufacturer to demand two sous a pair for "les deux combatants." [44]

Holmes had not much money to spend and could not go in for the dandified dress of a Mason Warren, but he was "always famous for loving to look in shop windows." The windows of the Parisian shops were "very large, of fine plate glass, and crowded as if the clouds had rained jewelry upon them." There was infinite delight for an inveterate window shopper in the Palais-Royal, indescribably Parisian, but on the whole a Vanity Fair immensely satisfying only "if enjoyment is the object of life." [45]

He had, however, been plainly taught that the chief end of man was *not* enjoyment, and something of the puritan clung to him still. He went to plays with the thought of improving his accent; he shopped for books and medical instruments, and he stayed in Paris all through the summer, when most of the other medicals had gone off to Italy or England for holidays. With no letters from home and his friends away, he might have spent some lonely months if his classmate Isaac Morse and his friend George Crowninshield had not turned up.

At last, after five months, the mix-up about his mail was straightened out; a clerk had put the letters in a drawer where they had lain forgotten while the anxious young foreigner made his many inquiries. But now he had his letters. "You cannot have any idea of what a difference your letters made in my feelings." [46] His own letters promptly became more free and less repetitious than they had been when he was writing to a disturbing silence.

There were, however, one or two matters to be clarified. He was writing to anxious parents with strange American notions of the general wickedness of Paris. Even Dr. Warren, a father who had been to Paris as Abiel Holmes had not, had exhorted his son to attend church regularly, "most particularly in Paris" and warned him against companions "fond of theaters and dissipation." [47] What the minister said to his son is not hard

93

to imagine. Apparently the allusions to the theater had given alarm.

There is no need of cutting or tearing off this last page about the theaters; where society is far advanced they must exist and are a blessing; they are cherished and improved in proportion as it is enlightened, and the outcry of civilized Europe would explode their assailants, were they not, in Europe, confined to an inappreciable body of the community.

He went on, significantly, to call attention to the fact that his letters had not dwelt upon points of difference between his ideas and those of the people he loved; he was referring undoubtedly to religious ideas. He hoped his family would take his observations on the theater quietly and not waste a letter refuting them.[48]

There was so long an interval between a letter and its answer that some matters were hard to settle.

And once for all I say that you may trust me, and I beg you to remember that, in being in Europe for my good, I am here for yours. If I should think best to go to Italy—let me go. If I should choose to spend a few months in London—let me go. I have told you all this about money matters before hand,—as I was and am abundantly supplied without touching my letter [of credit] for several months to come. I will only mention as folks at home have odd notions sometimes, that I never risk a franc at any game in Europe and that none of us Boston boys take to that amusement. To conclude, a boy is worth his manure as much as a potato patch, and I have said all this because I find it costs rather more to do things than to talk about them.[49]

He had been a little extravagant at first; it took him a while to bring his mind "back to its center of equilibrium," [50] but, he assured his family, he had "no disposition to extravagance" and probably spent "less money on pure gratification than most students." He had talked with the others—"Jackson, Gerhard, Stewardson—all hard, very hard students who all exploded the idea of getting along for less [than] at least twelve hundred dollars a year."

He wrote with confidence and firmness and with no apologies. And, indeed, he had no need to make them. Abiel Holmes had much less cause to worry about his son than Stephen Longfellow had had to worry about his; or William Irving, to worry about his brother. "I tell you," Holmes wrote, "that it is not throwing away money, because nine-tenths of it goes straight into my head in the shape of knowledge." [51]

And so it did, for he had not let his troubles with the language, the flood of company from home, the excitement of strange sights and new experiences break the routine established the week after his arrival in Paris. He was something of a sight-seer, a convivial companion at the Trois Frères for the regular Sunday dinner with the "medicals," but he was first of all a student. Even before the regular fall session began, Monsieur Louis, seeing him take notes, had said, *"Vous travaillez, monsieur, c'est bien ça."* [52]

Scholar in Paris

Well I have a mind to see what is done in other
places of learning.

To BEGIN at once to follow Louis on his rounds at the
Pitié was probably not the wisest move Holmes could have
made, but the enthusiasm of the other medical students was
infectious. He had scarcely arrived in Paris when the earnest
Bowditch began singing the French pathologist's praises so
loudly that Holmes was incredulous. When Bowditch implied
that Louis was a better teacher than Dr. Jackson, Holmes was
quick to defend the man he so much admired. Bowditch, writing home, reported the encounter.

We had a fight (as he called it) for an hour, and the next day I heard
of his having said that either Louis was the greatest man that ever
lived in medicine, or that I was crazy.[1]

Holmes had quickly discovered that Bowditch was not so
crazy as he had seemed.

It was a love of sheer swank that made him report almost at
once to his family that he was "studying" with Louis, "one of
the first pathologists of the world." His French had not improved so much in two weeks that he could understand Louis's
close questioning of the many patients the doctor daily examined, and his résumé and discussion of each case. Probably
a good deal of his first instruction in medicine came at ten or
eleven over *sirop* and coffee when the students met for breakfast and talked over the morning's work. In the group were
several young men of promise. Jackson had done independent
work on the tuberculous patients he had studied with Louis;

Gerhard, a Philadelphian who was a formidable rival to the Bostonians and who already knew a good deal about typhus and typhoid, would publish in two years' time the book that would make plain once and for all the distinction between these two diseases. Bowditch was passionately interested in everything and zealous to reform American medicine and medical education. For all his tendency to be fashionable, Mason Warren was really trying to carry out his father's fifty-seven admonishments. He liked kid gloves, but the hands that wore them were those of an accomplished surgeon.

All these young men, with others less brilliant, like Stewardson and Copley Greene, had felt at once the contrast between the "languid scientific atmosphere" [2] of America and the concentrated one of Paris. "What should I have done had I not come to Europe," exclaimed Jackson. "My grand aim," wrote Bowditch, "shall be to . . . repay the immense debt of gratitude I owe to France." [3] More articulate than his friends, Holmes expressed what the others implied.

Merely to have breathed a concentrated scientific atmosphere like that of Paris must have an effect upon anyone who has lived where stupidity is tolerated, where mediocrity is applauded, and where excellence is deified.[4]

Paradoxically, the soldier-ridden capital of King Louis-Phillipe was in some ways more free than republican Boston. "Every possible avenue of science stands open like a barn door" wrote Holmes, mixing metaphors in his excitement.

The whole walls around the École de Médecine are covered with notices of lectures, the greater part of them gratuitous; the dissecting rooms, which accommodate six hundred students, are open; the lessons are ringing aloud through the great hospitals. The students from all lands are gathered together, and the great harvest of the years is open to all of us.

Not only did Paris open its institutions freely, but its student population was treated with more respect and given more importance than a similar group received at home. "More particularly in scientific matters," Holmes observed, "there is nothing at all resembling the patriarchal authority which so often has held, and has such a tendency to acquire, the place of sound reason." The meanest student was free to doubt and dispute if he questioned what he heard.[5]

And Holmes meant to make the most of what was offered him. He had never exclaimed aloud as Longfellow had done, "I *will* be eminent," but the ambition was there all the same. The young man who had given his friend Barnes practical observations on the dangers of marrying too early still calculated his chances. His letters to his parents suggest that his zeal was not wholly compounded of a disinterested love of science. Quite frankly he desired success and observed rather shrewdly the difference between a French and an American medical career. He worked and worked hard; he made the most of what came his way; and he responded to the sharp competition offered by men like Jackson and Gerhard.

The kind of practical advice he was likely to give himself is suggested by that he gave his young brother, whom he was inclined to patronize.

My dear child,

I advise you to give up your thin speculations and addict yourself unto facts. If you study law as I study medicine, you will find a disinterested love of knowledge grow up in a very short time. If I can study in Paris, I hope you can in Cambridge.[6]

The "dear child" might have reminded his smug brother of the way he had studied law in Cambridge; it must have taken great forbearance on the part of even the gentle John Holmes to let such exhortations pass without comment. A few months earlier, Wendell had written John:

When a body has got to your age he should give up all his idle fancies and notions and apply himself to some practical use, pleasantly if he can—odiously if he must. In about thirty years he will have money and character, and then he may go again to his cat's cradles and speculation. But just put off the age of action a little too long, and there is a great chance that you evaporate into "general knowledge," or dribble down into a half intellectual harlequin like Henry Channing.[7]

Had he not himself found a way to apply himself to some practical use, and that a pleasant one?

98

It is true enough that I am avaricious of my time, because I want to learn more than —— knows, and beat —— out and out in the nice scientific touches. I am, as usual, all medicine, getting up at seven and going to Hospitals—cutting up—hearing lectures, soaking, infiltrating in the springs of knowledge. There is a great deal more to be done than I was inclined to suppose, but the more the better when one gets into good working trim. I suppose you wonder, in looking over my meagre letters not to find them full of Parisian talk and gardens and statues and such—but to tell the plain truth, I see no more and hear no more of those things than you do. If you get discontented, send me word, and I will give up following the diseases of the skin at the hospital St. Louis, cut off a slice from my daily anatomy—drop Broussais's lectures—take a fashionable journal, a box at the Italian opera and become as amusing as possible. Well you may depend upon it that we never gain without losing—and I suppose if I should make verses nowadays (which heaven forbid!) my readers would think I had not grown much the better poet for crossing the water.[8]

His desire for a practical kind of success and the excitement stirred by the scientific atmosphere of Paris combined to make his interest in medicine even stronger than before he left home.

No small cause of his increased devotion was the stimulating teaching of Louis. With no trace of the theatrical in his nature, Louis was "tremulous and even timid in addressing a little circle of students." [9] Where other men with flashy manners and thundering rhetoric maliciously denounced or ran down their colleagues, Louis "was intently occupied with his patient, and seemed to be conscious of nothing but what related to him." [10] This judgment of John Collins Warren is echoed in Holmes: "He thinks of nothing but his facts and his 'laws.' " [11] Although the students whom he attracted—American, Swiss, English, and a few French—admired him to the point of idolatry, it was not the brilliance of his mind that attracted them. Even the worshipful Bowditch conceded that there, at least, others, Gabriel Andral, for example, surpassed him.[12] Holmes declared Louis's capacities "limited"; what kept his students around him was "his truthfulness, diligence, and *modesty in the presence of nature.*" [13]

His most immediate effect upon the young men who followed him through the wards, St. Charles and St. Paul, was to arouse in them a sense of great responsibility. With nothing like the feeling of his duty to society which Bowditch had, Holmes could yet observe in a letter of August 13, after two months' exposure to Louis:

We [Americans] are too far from the scientific centers of Europe, and the impulse given thirty years ago, by the French pathologists to the severe study of medicine, accumulating up to the present moment, falls more fully upon us than on our fathers. . . .[14]

And by November he declared himself "more and more determined to give my own country one citizen among others who has profited somewhat by the advantages offered him in Europe." [15] Bowditch, from his more altruistic perspective, had a similar determination to excite those younger than himself "to study science, for itself, and afford them every facility for doing so." [16]

"Science for itself"—"the severe study of medicine"—this was precisely what Louis taught.

There is something more rare than a capacity for judgement; that is the passion for truth, that state of the soul which does not allow us to stop in our scientific labors at that which is only apparently true, but which obliges us to continue our research until we arrive at the fact.[17]

Not even illness should oblige the investigator to stop short of the truth. Louis was kind and friendly to his students and called upon them when they were ill, but his passion for facts was sometimes at war with his sympathy. Bowditch, down with rheumatic fever, had kept at his teacher's bidding careful notes of the progress of the disease until finally he could no longer hold a pen. "But, my dear," said Louis, "you should dictate." [18]

After a few months' exposure to Louis, Holmes reported the core of his teaching:

I have learned at least three principles since I have been in Paris; not to take authority when I can have facts; not to guess when I can know; not to think a man must take physic because he is sick.[19]

His daily attendance upon Louis was curtailed when the winter lectures began, but even then he spent at least four mornings a week in the wards of the Pitié, going sometimes on Sunday. Like James Jackson, he probably appreciated the advantages of Louis's small classes. A clinical teacher like Chomel, who had two or three hundred students attending him, could not give his lectures at the bedside as Louis did. In so large a group there was no chance for the student to make examinations on his own and to check his observations against those of the teacher. In fact, the students who attended Chomel at the Hôtel Dieu could scarcely see the patients at all, for his classes began a half-hour before daylight, when the wards were dimly lighted by candles. In Louis's classes both teacher and student examined the patients with the stethoscope; the students heard the doctor's questions and the patient's answers; the full record of each case could be studied from Louis's careful tables in which all the facts were collected and from which his figures—his famous *chiffres*—were drawn. For the Americans Louis's thorough study of pathology was a new experience. As Jackson wrote his father:

On one branch he necessarily surpasses you, *viz.* morbid anatomy; for in our country it is impossible to follow this subject with such freedom, owing to the prejudices existing among us; and at our hospitals, our cases are necessarily imperfect, as we do not retain our chronic cases, as they do here, till death.[20]

Holmes became so devoted a disciple of Louis that he later wondered if perhaps he had not made a mistake in giving himself up so thoroughly to Louis and those of his colleagues who were scientists rather than practitioners. He did, in fact, give a disproportionate amount of attention to the pathologists, Louis, Chomel, and Andral; and to the surgeons, Marjolin, Roux, and Velpeau. He found himself scrambling at the end of his stay in Europe to fill in some obvious gaps in his knowledge.

In his first letter after the winter lectures began, he reported attending a lecture by Richerand, the physiologist, "a celebrated old gentleman in his day, now somewhat used up." [21] The "old gentleman" was only fifty-five at the time, and he taught a subject the young student might have given more

101

attention to than he did. Holmes never went again to hear
Richerand and later sampled only one lecture by the leading
French physiologist, Magendie; he seems never to have attended the classes of Longet or Flourens. Holmes could not,
of course, have known one of the greatest of the French physiologists, Magendie's student, Claude Bernard, who had not
yet begun to study medicine but was at that time suffering his
own attack of author's lead-poisoning and writing plays.
Holmes had reason later to regret his neglect of physiology;
halfway through his career as a professor of anatomy and
physiology in the Harvard Medical School he was obliged to
yield the physiological half of his subject to younger men, for
he could not keep up with a rapidly advancing branch of science in which he was ill prepared to begin with. In part his
choice of subjects seems to have been directed by his strong
sense of being in competition with a group of formidable
rivals; he followed Jackson and Bowditch into clinical medicine and Warren into surgery.[22]

The first lectures which he attended in the fall of 1833 gave
him a dramatic introduction to the war between the old and
new schools of French medicine. At the École de Médecine, in
the big lecture hall seating a thousand students, he listened
first to the Professor of Internal Pathology, sixty-two-year-old
François Broussais, and then to the thirty-six-year-old Gabriel
Andral, who would shortly succeed Broussais in office, as he
had already undermined him in authority.

By 1833, François Broussais's hold upon French medical
thought had slipped beyond recovery. His famous system of
physiological medicine, which assumed that the basis of all
pathology was gastro-enteritis, was now the object not only
of criticism but even of ridicule; but he was still fighting ob-
stinately, punctuating his sharp sentences with a flourish of
his spectacles. In scarlet-trimmed cap and flowing, black gown
he lectured violently to a half-empty hall, which, as the hour
came to its close, began to fill with students coming early to
get seats for the popular young doctor who followed him on

the lecture platform. "The doors creaked open and banged oftener and oftener, until at last the sound grew almost continuous."[23] Frantically angry, Broussais raised his voice and strove to drown out the sounds that symbolized his own defeat and the coming end of the antiphlogistic treatment he practiced. Broussais could do nothing by halves; a special feature of his practice was a lavish use of leeches, and the French breeders of the creatures did a brisk business in the days when Broussais was a power in French medical practice.[24]

Holmes did not bother to preserve whatever notes he may have taken on the irascible old man's lectures. Attending them, he was sure of a good seat for the next lecturer, Andral, notes of whose lectures on "Internal Pathology" were worth saving. Ten years younger than Louis, Gabriel Andral belonged also to the new "scientific" generation. The disciples of Louis were delighted to hear in Andral's lectures the principles of their master expressed with a style and eloquence Louis himself did not possess. James Jackson, Jr., had burst into rhapsodic praise when he first heard the young teacher.

The glory of the week has been Andral's introductory lecture on diseases of the brain. It was the most eloquent I ever heard, one speech of Mr. Webster's and a sermon or two of Mr. Channing's excepted. I could scarcely restrain myself it was so grand and beautiful. What powers of mind and vastness of comprehension has this man! What gave me peculiar pleasure, also, he declared boldly and freely for the numerical method, saying it was the only mode of advancing the science of pathology.[25]

This was high praise, indeed, from a citizen of a country that prided itself on its orators and from a young man not given to such outbursts.

The opening lectures, which Holmes heard on November 6 and 8, 1833, were certainly a contrast to the teaching of Broussais. Where the older man was convinced that he had discovered a theory that explained the etiology of all disease, the younger, after emphasizing the need for a knowledge of physics, chemistry, anatomy, and physiology, went on to speak of the "imperfection" of present modes of examination and of contemporary knowledge, frankly admitting that the medical profession worked in ignorance.[26] The admission of ignorance and the expression of skepticism about the current therapeutic practices were characteristic of this group of French clinicians and earned for them the name of therapeutic nihilists. To a great extent their teaching was negative, but at the same time it tended to correct old errors and to destroy misleading and false "systems" like that of Broussais. It was in vain that Broussais tried to indoctrinate his students with his theory; the eloquent Andral was busy reporting the results of his microscopic examination of the blood, relating his observations of disease to his studies of pathology, and refuting his colleague's doctrine with factual evidence. He examined critically, also, the theories of other system-makers: Brown, Hahnemann, and Tommasini; although his point of view precluded his taking such theories seriously, the questions of his students prompted his analysis of these systems.[27]

In dealing with the doctrines of Hahnemann, Andral applied the methods of Louis and reported his test of the homeopathic treatment on some four hundred of his patients. "It would not be philosophical," he told his students, "to say that the homeopathic treatment was of any use in any one of them, although some of them recovered." In fact, the only appreciable effect of this method of treatment was upon Andral himself, who had "trembling in the fingers" after constant handling of aconite. Nine years later, Holmes would use his notes from these lectures of Andral in his fight against quackery.[28] When Holmes later, rather grudgingly credited the homeopathists with helping to do away with heroic, or overdosing, methods of treatment, he was echoing Andral.

Jackson and Bigelow had already taught Holmes to doubt the efficacy of some of the established modes of therapy and to believe that every practitioner must fall back upon his own experience; the teaching of Louis and Andral, besides reinforcing this skeptical attitude toward drugging and bleeding, tended further to demonstrate that the uncontrolled, haphazard experience of the general practitioner was no safe guide to treatment.[29] When, in 1860, Holmes shocked the physicians of America by suggesting that the whole materia medica with a few exceptions might be tossed to the fishes with no harm done, except possibly to the fishes, he was following out the lessons he learned in Paris in 1833-34.

The sources of other medical writings of Holmes also appear to lie in these somewhat sketchy notes taken from the first series of lectures he attended. In 1877, when he addressed the Microscopical Society, he did not remember how often Andral reported the results of his use of the microscope, but his manuscript is evidence of the fact that, if no Frenchman taught the use of the instrument, one of them made its probable value plain—plain enough so that Holmes invested some of his not too plentiful cash in one of Raspail's microscopes to take home with him.

Other observations made by Andral can hardly be regarded as immediate sources for Holmes's later medical writing, but they may have lingered in the back of his mind to combine with other ideas gathered at a later date. Andral speculated, for instance, on the possibility of hereditary characteristics and weaknesses; he perceived a relationship between sex and hysteria, and between neuroses and certain diseases—notions that appear later in Holmes's "medicated" novels. Andral, also, in his references to contagion, had introduced the subject of puerperal fever, rather vaguely suggesting that "peritonitis in puerperal women in public establishments" [30] might be contagious; this idea Holmes would develop precisely and confidently in the most important of his medical essays.

Of much less germinal value for Holmes were the lectures of the Professor of Surgery, Marjolin, whose name lingered in Holmes's mind chiefly because of the professor's snuffbox. "It lies upon the table by him as he lectures, plain but of vast dimensions, and resounds like a subterranean cavern as at the close of an emphatic sentence, the ponderous professor calls upon it for vigor to begin another sonorous paragraph." [31] The poet was not altogether lost in the medical student; Holmes's impressions of the literary style of his professors sometimes stayed with him longer than their teaching. In one of his notes of a Marjolin lecture, he added beside his English entry the poetic French phrase which the professor had used to describe a patient's eyes—"*on voit des chandelles.*" [32] In the judgment of young Warren, Marjolin gave lectures which were "without exception the most thorough and most practical" of any he had heard.[33] So far as they can be taken as an accurate record of Marjolin's teaching, Holmes's notes show that he peppered his discussions of surgery with frequent references not only to his own cases but to those of others, noting particularly the errors of his colleagues, whom he did not hesitate to call by name, even when the erring surgeon referred to was a giant like Dupuytren.[34]

Besides faithfully attending Louis, Broussais, Andral, and Marjolin, Holmes sampled the work of other men during his first year; there are English notes for both the clinical lectures of Chomel and the surgical lectures of Roux, but he early abandoned attendance upon these men, postponing them until his second year. At St. Louis, Holmes followed the clinical lectures of Laurent Biett, director of this hospital for skin diseases. A man "not very fond of talking or lecturing," [35] Biett was devoted to his clinic, attending in the course of a year as many as 6,000 patients. Holmes seems to have had considerable respect for Biett; in a letter to his parents he quoted the dermatologist as "the highest authority in these matters" and offered them a diagnosis of a skin disease they had described to him. The ailment was psoriasis, considered by Biett as "formidable" only for its "obstinacy." The interesting fact for the modern reader is that Biett's advice, severe regimen, and his medication, arsenic, indicate that the modern dermatologist, so far as this ailment is concerned, is not very much ahead of his predecessors of more than a century ago.[36]

Besides attending clinical lectures at three hospitals and the regular lectures at the school of medicine, Holmes worked at his daily anatomy, a simple matter in Paris where every noon at an establishment about a mile from his rooms, the student for fifty sous could purchase a whole cadaver. In "a spacious courtyard with several neat white stalls, and a garden and a fountain in the middle," the American medical students in Paris might freely practice dissection and recall with irritation the "little infernal suffocating holes in which the unhappy native of our uncivilized land is often obliged to pursue his labors." [37]

It is not surprising that he had no time to write letters. "My weeks have now very little interest about them except such as is connected with my studies." [38] Even in the midst of the Christmas holidays, he was "obliged to go straight to l'École de Médecine," and could observe of the holiday season only that "the display of bon-bons—that is to say sugar things is *tout à fait magnifique*." [39] It was indeed "no trifle to be a medical student in Paris." [40]

Quite naturally the busy medical students kept pretty much to themselves, rather resenting any obligatory social engagements. When the banker Welles invited the young men across the river to dinner, they went dutifully, but came away in a rebellious mood.

We came to the conclusion that the dinner was detestable—but it was a business dinner you know and bankers should set a good example of economy.—Remarks as we were going home from the dinner.—Bob: Fellows I am hungry, will you go to the Trois Frères and get something to eat? Second voice. I am dry, shall we step in and take some beer.— I remarked that there was only one superfluity—the toothpicks.[41]

Nor were the visitors from America so welcome as they had been in the letterless and lonely summer; "hideous stranger Americans [were] animals generally to be avoided," and Holmes did not bother to attend the American Ball, an expensive affair. The French Mardi Gras, with its parades and carnival spirit, was more to Holmes's taste. He still went to the Louvre occasionally and to the theater to see Mlle Mars again.

But all this is nothing to medicine . . . bad correspondent as I am, you must contrive to prevent any of my dear friends and relations from getting outrageous, by the customary phrases 'much engaged in his profession,' 'time entirely occupied' and the rest.[42]

107

Back in Cambridge, however, the minister and his wife had read alarming tales of the state of affairs in France: there was some hint of trouble between France and the United States, but especially terrifying was the news of rebellion and civil war, of fighting in the streets between the French workmen and the soldiers of Louis-Phillipe. On April 13 Holmes tried to soothe his anxious parents with a calm account of the political situation. "French political matters are nothing to us American students, nor we to them . . . we should go to our hospitals just as quietly if there were forty revolutions." Even as he wrote, the strains of martial music came to him from the street, and from his window he saw a body of troops of the line. There was for Holmes, lover of spectacles, a certain fascination in the colorful soldiery of the king, but his sympathies were still republican. He knew now that the soldiers represent the "principle of intimidation."

One thing you must remember. A new generation has arisen since the French Revolution. The declarations for and against its principles and actors belong to the past—the appreciation of them belongs to the present. If then a single principle first advocated, or best advocated by Robespierre, or St. Just, or Danton, or Marat, is found to be true, let it be advocated again—and in common justice and truth in the name of that man whoever he was that [planted] it against the torrent of centuries.

Young Holmes was, however, completely the scientist. He commented on the news of the uprising in Lyons, remarked that Paris was sober but quiet, and continued, "There is no appearance of any row at present, which is to be regretted as I cannot otherwise see any gunshot wounds at the hospitals." [43] Before morning, barricades went up in the streets of Paris; revolutionaries fired upon the Dukes of Orléans and Nemours. In the rue St. Martin, the King's Guard stormed the house of a zealous republican. At six a.m., the soldiers attacked the barricades. At the Hôtel Dieu, the American medical students had their scientific curiosity satisfied; there were sufficient gun-shot wounds for study.[44]

His letter on French politics was one of the few he had found time to write during the busy season of the regular lectures; by April 30, he was ready for a vacation; the next day he was on his way to Strasbourg, expecting to be in England by the end of the month. With 4,000 of his original 11,000 francs left, he was rather nervous about money. As he explained to his parents, "London is very expensive . . . so if you wish to be in good season you had better see Mr. Welles and get some credit for the profligate or tell him to come home and set down education as a bad bargain." [45]

The next evening, Holmes, Bob Hooper, and Mason Warren set out in style in one of M. Lafitte's diligences, which they had all to themselves.[46] A three-day journey, through dull country and in rainy weather, was relieved by a comforting amount of the *"vin du pays,"* the country being the department of Champagne. The wine, reported Holmes, was "dog cheap—only some thirty sous or cents a bottle—very good, but not so explosive or vinous as you may drink at a soirée in Boston and oh! far below the Sillery frappé of the café de Paris." [47]

Near Strasbourg, the traveler felt himself in a different country; the houses and people were very "unFrench" and showed "that the centripetal force of one nation was expiring at its circumference." [48] In the city on May 4 they visited the cathedral, climbing to within forty feet of the top "by galleries and escaliers which seemed as if they would crack on lesser weight than our own." [49] At the Protestant church, they paid their respects to Marshall Saxe, but Holmes, who had no reason to love the Protestants of any sect, was irritated. "As a traveler I cordially hate the Protestants. Their churches are generally shabby enough, but when they have anything interesting in them it costs you an hour's trouble to get admittance. It was an evil day when men made the Lord's temple the den of the sexton." [50]

The next day they were in Germany in the domain of the Grand Duke of Baden, spending the night at the famous watering place not then in season. The tourists moved too fast to take much more than a Baedeker view of the country, spending only five or six hours even in Heidelberg "the most beautiful place I have yet seen." They did the conventional thing in

visiting the castle, which Holmes conscientiously described
for his parents, remarking upon the view with an allusion suitable for the puritan preacher, calling it "such a one as Satan
offered in his capacity of tempter." They were less conventional in visiting a small anatomical museum at the university
where Holmes rejoiced in "some very fine preparations of the
lymphatics by Tiedemann." "But this is nothing to you," he
added and, in all his accounts of his trip, he ignored the fact
that the three students made a point of inspecting hospitals
and medical museums wherever they were to be found.

In Frankfurt, they admired a Dürer painting, studied
human nature in a beer garden, enjoying the sight of "amiable-
looking folks, young and old junketing joyously together." [51]
The hospital was impressively clean; and there were exciting
rarities in the anatomical and natural history museums. After
attending a performance of *Fra Diavolo* which, being German
and different from the operas they had seen in Paris, was interesting but only passably well done in their judgment, they
traveled all night to Metz and there boarded a boat to take
them down the Rhine to Rotterdam. [52]

The first part of the boat trip was so full of "the romantic
and the wonderful that it seems as one looks back on it more
like a dream than a reality." He did not try a description: it
would be too "long, and tedious and tiring, for I never do such
a thing without labouring hard to be true and exact." His
parents could go to Byron for "any explosion of sentiment"
they may have expected. In fact, all he had to give them was a
discourse on Rhine wines, with special reference to the
"princely" Johannisberger, the same wine that became Longfellow's favorite. [53]

When romantic crags and castles and vineyards gave way to
less exciting scenery, the young men turned to their fellow-
passengers for entertainment. The eleventh day after their
departure from Paris found them in Rotterdam. For his family, Holmes made a proper accounting of the windmills, canal-
boats, tulip beds, and well-scrubbed streets they observed
during their week in Holland; [54] but in Rotterdam their first

concern was again an anatomical museum. At Leyden, where they spent the night, the young men pressed into service as an interpreter their landlady's twelve-year-old son. The boy was apparently impatient with his strange customers, who spent a whole day looking at anatomical preparations and specimens. He did them a good service, however, at the university museum. At Mason Warren's suggestion, he told the curator that the visitors were Americans, and on his own hook added that the fashionable Warren was the son of the emperor of the United States, a piece of misinformation that won them deferential treatment.[55]

The university, made famous in medical history by Boerhaave, had in Warren's judgment the finest museum they had yet seen. All three of them would remember that this was the university of their own Dr. Benjamin Waterhouse, who had introduced vaccination to America and had been a member of the first medical faculty at Harvard. Holmes asked his father to tell the old man, who was a neighbor in Cambridge, of their visit.[56]

In between museums they managed to get in a few picture galleries, a circus, an opera, and an organ recital, visiting The Hague, Haarlem, and Amsterdam before they returned to Rotterdam to take ship for England. On a dreary Sunday morning they arrived in London, trusted their luggage to a porter and "trudged to find St. Paul's coffeehouse, where we were advised to go by an erratic Dutchman we twice fell in with on our travels."

Of course after the gaiety of a Parisian Sunday, there was somewhat of the austere, not to say repulsive in the bald streets, and set faces which form such a contrast with the exhalation of happiness that hovers around the sister capital when the seventh day dawns—rather jocundly, but welcomed in their fashion by a great people who have as much right to their opinions as this nation of sulky suicides.[57]

Perhaps the London Sunday reminded him too much of the puritan Sabbath at home. The feeling of depression was not relieved by the discovery that 800 of his 4,000 francs were gone.[58]

111

A few days at St. Paul's Coffee House brought on a "paroxysm of the economical," and they moved to a lodging-house kept by a Mrs. Peters "where for two pounds ten a week, we have our sty. But we must fill our own trough—or to speak less irreverently, we pay besides for the abominable breakfast we insult ourselves with, and we dine at some hotel or chophouse. For a fortnight I believe we did nothing but grumble." [59]

No small source of their melancholy was the news which had come to them just before they left Holland. Their admired and brilliant friend, James Jackson, Jr., who had gone home several months before, had fallen ill not long after his home-coming. The news of his death was a shock to the travelers, for whom young Jackson had been a much respected fellow-student and beloved friend. The solemn, nineteenth-century rhetoric in which Holmes expressed his feelings to his parents and later to his old teacher Dr. Jackson does not go well in modern ears, but Holmes was sincere in his expression of admiration for Jackson's professional accomplishments and his affectionate nature. [60]

The group in London now included the Philadelphian, Stewardson. Among them they had enough letters of introduction to get admission to the hospitals and museums they wished to see. Holmes's brother-in-law, Usher Parsons, had given him a letter to Mr. Clift, curator of the Hunterian Museum. No better person could have shown them the famous collection of the great eighteenth-century physician; William Clift's fidelity to the idolized John Hunter was a matter of common knowledge; it was Clift who had accused Hunter's brother-in-law, Everard Home, of plagiarizing Hunter's work and of destroying the manuscripts to conceal his act. [61] Although at the time of Holmes's visit, the museum, which Clift tended with admirable devotion, was closed for repairs, the curator took Holmes and his friends through it. He showed them other kindnesses, inviting them to tea and taking them to a meeting of the Royal Society. Friendly, too, was the English surgeon, Edward Stanley, to whom Warren had a letter from his father. Stanley took the young men to dinner and allowed them access to his wards and the amphitheater at St. Bartholomew's.[62]

From May 20 until July 12, Holmes and his fellow-students devoted their days to the hospitals; they were not, however, impressed by what they saw of "the different manifestations of the English spirit of quackery." [63] In the 1830's the student who had once been subjected to the discipline of French science was likely to observe British practice with a critical eye. Holmes and his friends may have been prejudiced in advance by Bowditch's account of his inspection of the English schools and hospitals. Coming to Europe originally with the intention of dividing his education between England and France, Bowditch had taken one look at England and, without waiting for parental approval, had fled back to Paris, to the wards of the Pitié and the teaching of Louis. In his estimation there was no comparison between the two; the Englishmen were too far behind the times.[64]

Holmes had meanwhile acquired "a wonderful apathy to sights" and, further, a dislike of England and all things English, which touched off his "disposition to tartness and levity." His thinning pocketbook made him more irritated than ever with the expensiveness of England: still he paid out two dollars to stand in the crowded pit of the Royal Opera House and observe the "largest uncivilized spot in England"—the countenance of King William IV. Some of his money went for clothes, of which he laid in a good stock, but some of it went, too, for an orgy of theater-going which he neglected to mention to his parents, giving them instead a few caustic comments on the sermons he had heard.[65]

Nor did he mention going to Epsom Downs on Derby Day. The young man, who had run away from school to see a race, could not pass up the greatest race of them all. During his lifetime Holmes saw two Derbies, one in 1834 and the other in 1886. Recalling the first on the occasion of the second, he wrote:

The Derby Day of 1834 was exceedingly windy and dusty. Our party, riding on the outside of the coach, was half smothered with the dust, and arrived in a very deteriorated condition, but recompensed for it by the extraordinary sights we witnessed . . . the whole road between London and Epsom was choked with vehicles of all kinds, from four-in-hands to donkey-carts and wheelbarrows. . . .

It was no common race that I went to see in 1834. "It is asserted in the columns of a contemporary that Plenipotentiary was absolutely the best horse of the century." This was the winner of the race I saw so long ago. Herring's colored portrait, which I have always kept, shows him as a great, powerful chestnut horse, well deserving the name of "bullock" which one of the jockeys applied to him.[66]

For Holmes, the Derby was probably the pleasantest part of this holiday in England. Although he did not really like the English and became easily weary of sight-seeing, nevertheless, in the middle of July, he and Stewardson set out on a quick trip through England and Scotland, seeing a suitable number of castles and places of literary interest, and checking their experiences with those of their countryman, Washington Irving. At Stratford-on-Avon, they stayed at the Red Horse Inn where the landlady, "a mummy moved by machinery," showed them the poker Irving had clasped in his dream of dominion.[67] At Blenheim, they caught a glimpse of the "rascally Duke," [68] walking in his gardens, and admired his collection of paintings. "I have grown passionately fond of paintings," wrote Holmes, "and am astonished to find how my taste has improved with regard to them." Titian and Rubens were his favorites still. At Warwick, they ran into a village wake, called "the opening of the meadows"; but castles and village life, the buildings of Oxford, "old as the ark"; Scott's Abbotsford and Wordsworth's Lake Country did not tempt them to rest in their race through the country.[69] They stopped, however, for a fortnight in Edinburgh and two days in Glasgow to see hospitals and museums, and to call on medical men. They dined with the anatomist, Dr. Robert Knox, better known for his connection with the Burke-Hare scandal, that memorable case of grave-robbing and body-snatching, than for his book on the *Races of Man*.

Back in the Midlands at Manchester, Holmes, impatient for letters and now living on borrowed money, thought of going straight on to London; but the "idea of the railway was so tempting" that he gobbled his dinner and boarded a steam carriage bound for Liverpool. He was properly impressed by the speed of the new invention which traveled at "considerably more than twenty miles an hour."[70]

Writing from Liverpool on August 15, he was sick of being a tourist. "I shall hate the sight of a traveling guide for six months"; he was eager to get back to work.[71]

In London he was "delighted beyond measure to find two letters," and, feeling less desolate, he set out for Paris via the Dover-Calais road. The coach to Dover passed through Canterbury, where Holmes defied the coachman in order to take a quick look at the Cathedral. The Channel crossing was rough as usual, but Holmes was pleased to find himself a good sailor, although most of the passengers "said their breakfast backward."

At Calais he became a sentimental traveler and had his luggage carried to the Hotel Dessin. He had read Sterne's *Sentimental Journey,* and in a mood the eighteenth-century traveler would have approved, asked for the *remise,* climbed upon a coach-box, and read Sterne's "Preface in the *désobligeante.*"

Back in Paris, he wrote somewhat giddily on September 3, "*Me voila revenu!* Once more in the gay, the glorious city, where I have past [sic] so many happy days." Even the necessity of borrowing money again did not dampen his spirits.[72] He loved France and Frenchmen too well. In England he had witnessed an ugly scene, which left a bad taste in his mouth; he had seen a crowd of young Englishmen hunt down and stone an insane foreigner, a Frenchman. When he came later to give a lecture on national prejudices, his own admiration of the French came out clearly; and when he heard Emerson use his beloved Louis to illustrate an unattractive French trait, Holmes was moved to correct the speaker.[73] Personal

115

feelings and experiences could move him as abstract ideas never could.

A few weeks after his return to Paris, Holmes felt obliged to render his family a strict account of his precarious financial state. Apparently his father had suggested that he abridge his stay in Paris; a notion he had already refused to consider. He knew that the 5,000 francs spent in four months was against him. But on the trip, his expenses matched, dollar for dollar, those of his friends, all young men of good character. Their expenses had been those "necessary for young gentlemen." He intended to make the 3,000 francs he had just received go as far as possible—2,250 really, for he had to pay his debt to Stewardson.

I can dine for 18 sous. But I will not do any such thing. I pay five francs every day for my dinner and that is cheaper than I used to dine when Hooper and Warren dined with me. You shall know exactly how I have dined for the last fortnight.—Here is a specimen:

Bread	5 sous
Half a bottle of Beaume wine	20 "
Soup	12 "
A mutton cutlet	12 "
A quarter of a fricasseed chicken	115 "
Some sort of fruit	20 "

5 francs, 4 sous — and
5 sous for the *garçon*

—and that is the way that dinners cost a hundred and fifty francs a month—provided that you think it necessary to have clean waiters, good honest cooking, and not to have stale articles given you to eat.—My room and breakfast make very nearly but not quite a hundred more a month.

He had to pay also for private instruction, and shoes and boots, which "I trot to pieces at a terrible rate on these streets without sidewalks." He had been buying books for professional uses. Some money had to be spent on amusement. Would they then do the sums and judge if he be "very-very extravagant" if he spent the 2,250 in six months?

He hoped they saw how his money went and he appreciated their generosity. "It goes against my heart to scatter money so fast," especially knowing that other young men might have spent less, but "I have kept good company and have improved my mind and enjoyed myself." He did not mention that he had returned to Paris and his work more than a month before his friends, but he ended his September letters with significant announcements. Louis had given him free access to his wards, "a favor which he has granted only to a few, James Jackson was one of them." And he had been unanimously elected a member of the Société médicale d'observation.[74]

Medical Disciple

1834–1835

*He laid the foundation of future eminence by
application to his studies.*

As early as December 7, 1833, Holmes had attended
as a visitor a meeting of the Société médicale d'observation,
then in its second year of existence. Founded by three Swiss
students, the organization drew its charter members from the
followers of Louis, among them James Jackson, Jr. Strictly
limited to a "select corps" of Louis's students, the group might
well have had the character of a "Mutual Admiration Society"
as Holmes later described it.[2] It is noticeable, also, that the
number of French students in the group was relatively small.
Swiss, English, and especially Americans predominated. The
Americans besides Holmes and Jackson, were Gerhard, Stewardson, and Norris.[3] The preponderance of foreigners in the
society is probably explained by Louis's practice of showing
them special consideration. Bowditch reported the teacher as
observing *"Écoutez,* you are a stranger here and are to reside
here only a short time, and therefore, I will grant you what I
could not to a Frenchman." [4]

Even the international quality of the society hardly justified
Jackson's description of its ambitious intention "to make exact
observations all over the world"; [5] but the purposes were serious and scholarly enough to warrant Louis's insistence that
the group was formed for *"le travail, et non la vanité."* Its
founders had been "struck by the uncertainty of medical
knowledge." They were convinced that "this uncertainty
arises both from an imperfect observation of particular facts

118

and from the manner not less imperfect in which they are studied." To their way of thinking, observation was not easy; it called for a "long apprenticeship." Their society, then, "would have as its object to make the problems clear to those who took part in it, to teach them to conquer the difficulties, to made observation really useful by making it exact and precise, and finally to show how one can safely proceed from particular facts to sound generalizations." [6]

The "long apprenticeship" Louis himself had served in 1815-29, when, as clinical clerk under Chomel at the Charité, he had labored to confine himself to making exact observations in spite of the ridicule of many of his colleagues. And now by granting to his students the special privilege of observing cases in his wards—an honor which had fallen successively to the three Boston students, Jackson, Bowditch, and Holmes —and by directing, as its president, the work of the society, Louis was ensuring for his students thorough training in his methods of observation. The standards of the group were sufficiently high to warrant the attendance of Marshall Hall, the English physiologist who had shown the difference between voluntary action and unconscious reflexes. Chomel and Andral were also members.

The society, in accordance with the strict principles of its president and the zeal of its members, gave its candidates for admission a stiff competitive examination. In competition with two others, a candidate had to present a lecture on at least three observations on the same disease, followed by an analytical résumé of these cases which were then to be correlated with those recorded in the literature of the disease. Holmes satisfied this requirement on September 6, 1834, and on the 16th he received the secretary's formal notice of his unanimous election to the society. His position, however, was not secure until he had for six months assiduously attended the weekly meetings of the society and "participated in its labors." Any member absent three times in succession or ten times in a year was subject to investigation and dismissal if a majority of the members refused his explanation.[7]

Holmes was faithful in his attendance, foregoing the theaters and balls which attracted his friend Hooper, and missing altogether only three Saturday evenings during the rest of his stay in Paris. He had been a member less than a month and a half when he informed his friend John O. Sargent that the society had called on him "to the extent of thirty thickset pages—all French, and almost all facts hewn out one by one from the quarry." [8] Unfortunately, the thirty thickset pages, along with all the other records of the society, excepting the rollbook, were destroyed in the siege of Paris in 1871. Like Jackson and Bowditch, who had found a "new spur to study" [9] in the practice of its members of cross-examining those who presented papers, Holmes found that it put him "under obligation to be exact, methodical, and rigorous." He had now sufficient control over the French language to "take a case from a patient, write it off, read it uncorrected, and defend it against criticism." [10]

Apparently his command of the language led Louis, "his English acquirements not being considerable," to ask from Holmes a report on a work by Marshall Hall. Louis hoped to use the material in a book of his own. "But the methods of the Englishman, who put himself into everything, and the Frenchman . . . who kept himself out of everything, proved very hard to incorporate." [11] If the labor served no purpose in the end, it did bring Holmes the pleasure of dinner tête-à-tête with the Englishman, then visiting Paris, and it helped further to establish credit with his family.

The letter in which Holmes reported these honors contained also a plea for credit of a tangible kind. Warren, whose personal talents and professional ancestry make him a formidable rival, was to spend a third year in Europe. For the reputation at which he was "not ashamed to aim," Holmes asked for at least a second year. He needed money for private instruction particularly, for it was "of infinite professional advantage." [12]

In spite of his financial worries, the stimulus of the society and the freedom of Louis's wards helped Holmes to settle down for a second year of even harder labor than the one he had already put in. When Hooper and Warren joined him again before the fall lectures began, he left to them the job of showing the sights of Paris to two new members of their group. With Jackson and Bowditch gone, Holmes was left with Warren to uphold Boston's reputation against its rival, Philadelphia. "Philadelphia may dispute us the palm," he wrote his family, "I for one will try to make her work for it." [13] He was sufficiently absorbed to neglect his usually faithful letter-writing; he may, too, have been a little piqued at not hearing oftener than he did from home; in his busy winter of 1834, he let almost two months go by without writing.

The freedom of Louis's wards allowed him to continue his study under the favorite of the American students. Louis's "numerical system," with improvements, is now so automatically applied to the study of disease that today we do not think of the method as being in any way special as it most certainly was in the 1830's. The method called first of all for the careful noting of *all* the facts of a patient's history and the history of the specific ailment. Anyone who has been quizzed by an interne or nurse in a modern hospital knows that such information is now gathered as a matter of course. His system further called for the notation of all observation of the patient and all medicines administered during the course of the disease. These data Louis set up in tables for comparative study. He made these tables for the largest possible number of patients suffering from the same disease. He knew very well that one great source of error was the habit of jumping to conclusions on the basis of insufficient evidence; it was necessary to compare large numbers of cases before drawing conclusions. A sagacious general practitioner might avoid error after many years of experience, but he was still merely guessing. Louis, correlating a great number of observations and adding post mortem investigations to his studies of the living patient, could avoid guesswork.

His method was the means of correcting erroneous notions of treatment and it made possible accurate and early diagnosis.

Louis's studies of tuberculous patients, for example, made it possible to recognize the disease in its early stages. The work, begun by Laënnec, discoverer of the stethoscope, was carried on by his pupil, Louis. One of Louis's students, the American Gerhard, by employing the numerical system was able to establish once and for all the difference between typhus and typhoid fever. On the negative side, the application of Louis's system demonstrated the uselessness and the dangers of the practice of bleeding in the treatment of some diseases.

Yet the effect of Louis's teaching was in the end more negative than positive. None of his American students could return home and actually carry out Louis's practice and follow his example, devoting years of their time to clinical study. The teacher had sent two of his students home with instructions to spend ample time in observation and research before entering into actual practice. He had written directly to Jackson's father in an attempt to persuade him to allow that young man to carry out such a plan, but the American physician rejected the advice. When he came to write a memoir of his son after his premature death, he ruefully admitted that he may have been wrong in yielding to the pressure of American opinion which frowned upon a life of apparent inactivity.

But why could he not adopt the plan fully? Because in this country his course would have been so singular, as in a measure to separate him from other men. We are a business doing people. . . . he who will not be doing must be set down as a drone.[14]

Young Holmes had already observed for himself that difference between his own country and France.

This generation of American students would not carry back with them a zealous interest in pure science as a later generation was to do, but they did carry with them a skepticism which would have a salutary effect on American medical practice. It was this healthy skepticism; this mistrust of all armchair theories, of single-answer systems; and this sensible and useful attitude toward drugging that Holmes carried back with him. If he never became a searcher after truth in the laboratory, he did become a useful critic of medical practices and exposer of charlatanism, the more so because he was not inarticulate.

In the clinical lectures of Auguste François Chomel, which he began again to attend in 1834-35, Holmes found the methods of Louis approved. The genial head of the Hôtel Dieu had long been Louis's friend if not, in the American's judgment, his equal as a clinical teacher. A more eloquent and, ordinarily, more popular teacher than Louis, Chomel had an enormous following for his early morning rounds of the wards St. Lazare and Ste. Madeleine and his lecture later in the hospital amphi-theater. The sketchy notes which Holmes preserved and the amphorisms, which he later bound with those collected from the teachings of Louis,[15] give only a dim record of what he gained here beyond a reinforcement of what he was acquiring more directly from his labors at the Pitié.

Some of this second year was given over to the study of surgery, when it was too late to do more than sample the lectures of the surgical giant of the day, Baron Dupuytren, "a square, solid man, with a high and full-domed head, oracular in his utterances, indifferent to those around him, sometimes, it was said, very rough with them." Before the lecture season of 1834-35 had fairly begun, Dupuytren succumbed to the third stroke of apoplexy. Holmes had, however, a wide choice among a galaxy of distinguished surgeons, from Napoleon's favorite, Baron Larrey, at the Hôtel des Invalides to that "great drawer of blood and hewer of members," Lisfranc at the Pitié.[16] Holmes chose Velpeau, Amussat, and Lisfranc, whom he later abandoned for Dupuytren's successor, Roux.

Velpeau, the ex-peasant, had made his way through the rough competition of the Parisian medical world by dogged hard work and thoroughness. His students found his lectures sometimes too scholastic, full of divisions and subdivisions and rich with allusions to authorities all the way from Hip-pocrates to Dupuytren. But there was "a vast deal of sprightli-ness and good nature in the countenance and voice of Vel-peau." [17] Moreover, his sympathies were with the "new" school of French medicine, not with the blood-letters. When Jean Baptiste Bouillaud (along with Broussais and Dupuytren, one of the giants of the old school), made insulting allusions to Louis and his colleagues for their criticisms of the excessive use of the lancet, Velpeau, who was not given to quarreling with his contemporaries, spoke out vigorously in defense of Louis. Holmes made a note of the surgeon's remarks:

on the conduct of certain persons which apply marvelously to Bouillaud and in which he made severe comments on those who accuse their colleagues of killing their patients. For the rest the ideas of M. V. on the value of bleeding . . . agree very well with those of M. Louis.[18]

At the same time Holmes knew that in his own field of diseases of the heart, Bouillaud had made valuable contributions; he did not leave Paris without purchasing the Frenchman's latest volume on his speciality.

It was probably Velpeau's ponderous thoroughness that made some of his students consider him impractical; he was capable of spending an entire hour examining one small problem of treatment; even in introducing his own method of handling a fracture of the clavicle (still taught to medical students today), Velpeau scrupulously described two other methods of handling the fracture.[19] Young Warren, who had not on the whole been impressed with French surgeons or their work, found Velpeau "replete with the most true scientific and surgical spirit that I have yet met with abroad among the surgical world." [20] Holmes, some ten years later, labeled him "the first of the French surgeons." [21]

His opinion of Lisfranc was less generous. To Holmes, Lisfranc appeared as "a very large, coarse but not ill-looking man with a swaggering air and bullying voice," who attracted as his followers "a slovenly mob . . . of fellows with caps stuck on one side of their heads, unsavory with tobacco and unconscious of soap, who go leering and winking about the women's wards, and lounge with their hands in their pockets upon the gritty benches of operating theatres." [22] By the time he made this judgment, he had probably forgotten that his indictment included his thoroughly respectable, not to mention dandified, friend Mason Warren, who had chosen originally to follow Lisfranc instead of Velpeau because the former seemed to him the more practical and original surgeon.[23]

Quite possibly Holmes was prejudiced at the start, for in his first lecture Lisfranc made scathing allusions to doctors "who base their results on tables"—referring obviously to Louis—and boasted of his own long experience as a general practitioner. The listening student could not forbear a parenthetical observation of his own in his notebook: "such stupidity seeming to me inconceivable—but there it is."[24] Lisfranc was in the habit of denouncing his colleagues, calling even Dupuytren a "brigand." [25]

Holmes attended twenty-one of Lisfranc's lectures before he departed in disgust. He had seen both Lisfranc and Velpeau make bad mistakes in the course of an operation, but only the former tried to account for his patient's death "with a piece of juggling logic." Trained furthermore by both Jackson and Louis to employ the lancet and leeches sparingly, he distrusted Lisfranc's phlebotomizing. "I saw him on one of his morning visits order fifteen or twenty patients to be bled for no special reason except that he was in the depleting humor, and on the following morning after addressing a single question to each of them, I heard him gravely expatiate upon the benefit these patients had received." [26]

In retrospect, Holmes could credit Lisfranc for not making a mystery of the art of surgery and for setting down exact rules for his students. Yet he felt that he had heard Lisfranc say only one or two good things altogether. "One was in the form of a little spurt of eloquence upon the bodily degeneracy of the inhabitants of cities and the necessity of the pouring in of fresh country blood, all which rattling out from his broad chest and capacious larynx with half a dozen *sacrés* and a double tattoo upon all the *r*s was what a Frenchman calls *tout à fait magnifique*." This theme with variations is a common one in Holmes's writings when his breakfast-table chatter takes the form of lectures on health.

Holmes could admire an effectively turned figure of speech,

however uncongenial the subject-matter or the speaker might be; he alluded more than once in reminiscent passages to Lisfranc's "Homeric comparison between the thighs of the soldiers of the imperial army and the bodies of men such as they are at present." [27]

But he added, "I got along about as far as that with him, when I ceased to be a follower of M. Lisfranc." [28] And by January 1835, he had gone over to Pierre Roux, "essentially an operating surgeon, carnivorous, anthropophagous by nature." Roux, although he seemed "to place his whole pride in his manual dexterity," was apparently a less conceited man than Lisfranc. Holmes once saw him "check with great spirit and temper a burst of applause with which the amphitheatre resounded as he finished an operation of lithotomy; the only time I remember such an outrage upon propriety in the noisy operating rooms of Paris."

As a lecturer, however, Roux was "totally incomprehensible"; [29] and Holmes, who now claimed to think in French, found himself helplessly scribbling inadequate notes in a mixture of French and English. Fairly detailed descriptions of observed operations are mingled with such entries as this: " 'Suddenly, (and when I say suddenly, &c. &c.—) ((follows a parenthesis enormous and complicated.—)) Suddenly the skin becomes bluish &c. &c.' " [30] Holmes's notes were sprinkled with despairing "&c.'s" as he gave up trying to follow the rapid and intricate parentheses of M. Roux.

His notes on the lectures of Jean Amussat, whom he "attended for a good while," are similarly sketchy. "A gross egotist," Amussat gave up "half his course" to his own hobbies "as if the rest of surgery was incidental to these particular processes." Holmes was willing to credit Amussat with skill in his own department of "hydraulic derangements," but he preferred the broad and thorough teaching of Velpeau. The latter's good nature too was more pleasing than Amussat's jealousy. Holmes was ready to agree with the Brazilian student who remarked, "Do you observe that man?" pointing out the teacher. "He looks as if a cancer was eating out his heartstrings." Moreover, Holmes, who later had a reputation for an excessive tenderness of heart not compatible with the surgeon's work in the days before the use of anesthetics, was likely to be put off by any hint of cruelty in a surgeon's make-up. Amussat's experiments with animals, one of which he observed, seemed to him excessively cruel in proportion to their scientific value.[31]

On the whole, he seems to have got the best part of his surgical training in the company of his Swiss friend, Bizot. In the spring of 1835, the two young men bought instruments and practiced what they had learned on easily purchased cadavers.

It is an odd thing for anybody but a medical student to think of, that human flesh should be sold like beef, or mutton. But at twelve o'clock every day, the hour of distribution of subjects, you might have seen M. Bizot and myself—like the old gentlemen one sometimes sees at a market—choosing our day's provisions with the same epicurean nicety. We paid fifty sous apiece for our subject, and before evening we had cut him into inch pieces . . . here one who knows how to use his hands, and who gives his attention exclusively to the subject for a time, may, as I have said I have done, become an expert operator in a few weeks.[32]

Still neglecting such training in physiology as he might have had, and giving the greater part of his attention to clinical medicine and surgery, Holmes did attempt to fill in some gaps in his knowledge. He managed to get to St. Louis, where he had formerly attended Biett, to hear some of the lectures of Baron Alibert, a "talkative old gentleman with a good deal of learning and experience and a reputation of ancient date threadbare at home but still looking very well at a distance."

On fine days, Alibert's students waited for him under the trees in the hospital courtyard, where he gave his lectures. "At last a coach rattled up to the gate and a short stocky gentleman of sixty or more with a broad brimmed hat, cocked on one side of his head waddled into the presence of the assembled students and taking his place began somewhat in the manner of one of our celebrated auctioneers: *'Enfants de la Méthode Naturelle, êtes-vous tous ici?'* 'Children of the Natural Method, are you all here?'" Alibert's "Natural Method" of classifying skin diseases was, however, already being supplanted by that of his former pupil Biett, as Holmes recognized in his comparison of the two, shortly after their deaths. One left "his empty title behind him, the other a name more honored than any patent of nobility." [33]

Holmes managed, too, to work into his crowded days the lectures of the "Voltaire of pelvic literature," [34] the American-born Phillipe Ricord, specialist in venereal diseases, "a sceptic as to the morality of the race in general, who would have submitted Diana to treatment with his mineral specifics, and ordered a course of blue pills for the vestal virgins." [35] Since few men knew their subjects so well as Ricord knew his, Holmes justly advised:

> When the inexperienced youth who visits Paris for the first time, having yielded to the call of temptation, awakes some fine morning and finds himself suffering as Pope has it
> "Of wrongs from Duchesses or Lady Mary's"—he can hardly do better than take a cabriolet and drive to the residence of M. Phillipe Ricord:
> —No man will handle his feelings or his person more tenderly,—no man will send him away in a state of such philosophical acquiescence with a condition which according to Ricord is or ought to be the prevailing lot of mankind.

With a "treacherous" smile and a manner of speaking "full of levity, satire, and scandal," Ricord might appear to Holmes to be a "medical Mephistopheles"; but as Holmes knew, the syphilologist's instruction was invaluable. It was Ricord who first made definite the distinction between gonorrhea and syphilis, correcting the error of John Hunter. He also established and described the three stages of the latter disease. Even in 1835 English physicians were apparently still clinging to Hunter's error. Holmes reported quizzing Ricord on the subject.

> His answer was "*Je m'en fous* Carmichael was here for some weeks and could not find any real syphilis in our hospital. The English keep talking about their 'genuine pox'—who cares about their genuine 'pox' —*Je m'en fous*—" [36]

Holmes has left no record of his excursions into other branches of medicine, but from allusions in his letters home and in his medical notes to "l'Hôpital des enfants," one as-sumes that he gave a little time to the study of children's dis-eases. He also gave some attention to obstetrics, which he studied under a woman, Mme. Lachappelle. This training he was obliged to put to practical use. The only note of the event in his own records is a parenthetical entry after the date March 26 in the midst of his notes on Roux's lectures. The note reads "(*Jour de l'accouch publique*)." His friend Hooper, however, is communicative. His diary entry for that day reads:

One of my friends (Holmes) on going to Hôtel Dieu this morning fell in with two women leading another who was making most terrible cries occasionally, at last she made one more painful than the rest. When he went up to her to know what was the matter, they had just seated her on the sidewalk when she was accouched of a living child. My friend cut the apron string of one of the women for a ligature and cut the cord with his knife, took the child to a "Marchand de vins" and washed it, then sent it after the mother to Hôtel Dieu.[37]

Crowding into his two years what many of his friends ac-quired more leisurely in three, Holmes had summoned the necessary concentration for his heavy schedule. Never again in his life would he show such whole-hearted devotion to a single pursuit as he was showing now in his study of medicine. When Holmes wrote his family that not one among his fellow-students had "sought knowledge so ardently and courted pleas-ure so little," [38] he was taking a high tone, but he was not exaggerating. Hooper's diary records dinners, and balls, and theaters, but except for the party which celebrated the return from England of Warren and Hooper in October, and the farewell parties in the spring when the same two young men departed for home, Holmes stuck to his work, eschewing even a trip down the Seine and a visit to the races, a real depri-vation. The traditional weekly dinner with the other Bos-tonians at the Trois Frères he could not forego even when his money troubles became desperate.

To some extent the arduous work saved him from melan-choly, from worry over the debts he had to pile up in the spring, and from growing homesickness. It helped, too, to keep him nearly impervious to his family's continued pleas that he come home. In spite of his request that his family refrain from appealing to his feelings, his parents apparently made a point of their old age, of brother John's illness, and of their worry over the strained relations between America and France.[39] Holmes assured them of his affection, told them there would be no war, but firmly indicated his intention to finish his business.[40]

The financial situation early became serious. He had hoped to make his last allotment hold until March, but before December he began campaigning for more, and by January he was in debt. Amusements and even some necessary books he could give up, but not decent quarters and private instruction. His personal dislike for banker Welles made the painful business of borrowing doubly unpleasant. "I say once more that I do not want money to abuse, but to use and I want it, to quote our medical aphorism—'*tuto, cito, jacunde*'—that is to say *at once,* and without one word to impress more heavily upon me the sacrifices which I have called for so largely and so often." [41]

In February he was willing to make a few concessions, but he would not come home. It was not until March that he had the promise of more money, and it was very slow in coming. On April 13, he acknowledged the receipt of 3,000 francs, which had been sent out on February 24. But the letter enclosing the money still urged him to come home.

With many rhetorical flourishes but still with courtesy and dignity, he answered. His family had stopped short of ordering him home; if such an order should be forthcoming he would obey it; in the meantime he would go on working. He offered them three propositions: should he come at once on receiving their reply (it would take two months for a reply to reach him); should he wait until July and come with Hooper; should he spend two months in Italy and come home in the fall? "My original intention," he added significantly, "is the last." Then boldly, he listed his needs—passage money, money for books, instruments, and other medical supplies.

I beseech you as you value my peace rather to trust me with too much liberty—which I solemnly promise not to abuse—than to leave me in the situation of a dependent and perhaps a suspected foreigner,— My dear parents, you have done everything for me, but I too in lavishing my youth on my studies have been labouring for your honour and happiness.—

You are worried with the idea of war,—the chambers show every disposition to pay our debt and the idea of immediate hostilities is out of the question. . . . Do not then be distressed with imaginary evils—put on a little of the Roman spirit and above all if any pecuniary considerations disturb your quiet, remember that Dr. Channing is said to have been years in debt for his European residence and that I who am worth a hundred of him may pay my debts from my professorship. . . .

Now when you write be neither too despondent nor too tender, and reflect on the importance of every month which I pass here completing my education. Were I a parent and did a young man like myself call upon me for his counsel and his aid, I should consider no sacrifice too great that could advance his education—and I should hesitate long before I would say to him, pale and fatigued with study—leave Europe forever, the only one among your companions who has not been beneath the dome of St. Peter's.—A single word, suggested by over anxious economy or tenderness may plant a regret that will never be effaced and that has not been deserved.

It is not likely that the boyish countenance of young Holmes showed any "marks of long labour"; the labor was real enough, but he was healthy and had not stinted himself on food or lodging. From this lofty and effective rhetoric he descended to practical matters. For him to stand beneath the dome of St. Peters would cost them 4,000 francs.[42]

Whether persuaded by his son's eloquence or by the testimony of Mason Warren, whom Holmes made the bearer of another letter and cited as a witness to his zeal as a student, or whether too generous to deny his son, Abiel Holmes at any rate came through with the needed funds and sanctioned the trip to Italy.[43] At last relieved of debt and looking forward to the holiday in Italy, Holmes hurried about to complete his purchases and pack his gear to be sent home. The tone of his letters became promptly less rhetorical, as he excitedly catalogued the contents of the box. Besides two skeletons, a showy one for his brother-in-law and a little one for himself, he was

131

sending for Parsons some "new-fangled instruments," a set of botanical plates, and two new books, Malgaigne's operative surgery and Bouillaud's latest on diseases of the heart. For himself, he had bought a library of medical classics.

> You must not be astonished at finding so many old books among my collection—they have all been bought slowly, one by one, deliberately chosen on account of their intrinsic value, and I venture to think are one of the most valuable little collections which a young man has sent home to America. . . . If you choose to send for them you can have them carried out to Cambridge and John can amuse himself in over hauling them—as a young doctor's purchases require to be sifted before they are submitted to profane eyes.

> I put in a favorite engraving of my own which I have always had hung up in my room and which may be stuck up where your fancy may choose to place it. There are a few Alduses to regale the anti-quarian eyes of father—a portfolio of engravings of all sorts—a microscope &c.

The money came just in time for him to send off this box; there was not time to put in presents for them. "However, steal the pictures—maraud among the Alduses—empoign the microscope and wait for further importations." The joyous letter is dated July 4 and concludes with a P.S. "Independence day—Vive l'Amérique," a betrayal of a growing nostalgia which is toned down with the mundane addition "there are some things for Mason Warren in the box." [44]

On July 18, 1835, he attended a meeting of the Society of Medical Observation and on the 20th in the company of two friends, he was on his way to Switzerland. As might be expected from his plan "to see as much as fast and as cheap" as he could, Holmes's journey through the Alps and down through the Italian cities and back to Paris through Marseilles and Lyons produced hurried and perfunctory letters. Nature in Switzerland and Art in Italy were accepted ingredients in a young American's European education, and part of Holmes's arguments for making the trip had been based on the plea that "all the other fellows did." He confessed that seeing sights was "the most tedious of occupations," but he dutifully saw them, coming away from Switzerland with his recollections "all set . . . in a gigantic frame of snowy summits and arrowy peaks" and hurrying through the Italian cities to find "the eye—fatigued and the susceptibility worn out with over exercise." [45]

Milan, Venice, Bologna, and apparently Florence were nothing at all to the week's experience of Rome. He reported his taste and notions as "essentially different after seeing the best works of the old masters," but the objects he chose to mention were those conventionally singled out by nineteenth-century taste. It was the magnificence of the ancient Romans that gave him the greatest shock. "It surpassed all the ideas I had entertained so far that I can hardly yet believe my own eyes." For the art of the Middle Ages or the Renaissance he had felt himself somewhat prepared; even the engravings in his father's volumes of Rees's *Encyclopedia* had given him something to go on.

The immense numbers of pillars of precious marbles, of polished granite and porphyry—the gorgeous vases and gigantic baths sculptured often from a single mass of jasper or granite or porphyry—the innumerable statues and busts—the tremendous ruins of the Colosseum—of the baths of Caracalla—the triumphal pillars and arches, astonish altogether one who has formed his ideas of antiquity from a few old copper coins and a collection of broken earthenware.

Quantity and mass and richness were all he had time to register before embarking for Marseilles.[46]

Held up in quarantine in the French port, he turned to his jackknife and an old medical volume for consolation. In a shop in Venice he had bought a vellum-bound copy of Nicholas Tulpe, subject of Rembrandt's portrait of the doctor. The Dutch author's 228 cases whiled away the time Holmes did not spend laboriously cutting a chain of wood like the prisoner he was.

His letters home tell nothing of his visits to bookshops, where he added to his medical library and indulged the antiquarian interests aroused probably by his father and Dr. Winslow Lewis, his first teacher of anatomy. Almost half a century later the recollections of his dash through Italy and

133

Southern France were dim in his mind, but the memory of a
rainy day in Lyons was clear enough. In a dingy bookshop in
the French city, he found a copy of the work of the sixth-cen-
tury physician Aëtius. But his most exciting find was a volume
"marked *rare,* and [which] was really *très rare,*" for it was the
first edition in Greek (1532) of the Aphorisms of Hippocrates,
edited and prefaced by a doctor more famous for his wit than
for his medicine—François Rabelais. When Holmes finally
presented his medical collection to the Boston Medical Library, he said that the "accession of a book . . . was an event
almost like the birth of an infant." He had with reason boasted
to his parents of the library he was sending home.[47]

Now, in the summer of 1835, his thoughts, as he told his
family, were tending more and more toward home. Back in
Paris in early October, he prepared to leave. On the 17th, he
attended once again a meeting of the Société médicale d'observation. The 1st of November saw him in Havre where
he boarded the packet ship *Utica,* bound for New York.
Among the passengers was "Williams the Oculist," who made
the mistake of handing over to the young medical student two
copies of a pamphlet about himself and his particular brand
of quackery, unwittingly providing Holmes with ammunition
for the warfare he was later to undertake against all kinds of
medical charlatanism.[48]

He was home in time for Christmas; in January, in three
days, he dashed off from his notes and from the books in his
own library, his essay *Acute Pericarditis.*[49] He had not taken
his medical degree before he went to Paris; this hastily written
essay was his way of fulfilling the thesis requirement. In February he appeared before the faculty of the Harvard Medical
School to pass successfully his final examinations. He was voted
the degree on February 11 [50] and on May 22 [51] became a member of the Massachusetts Medical Society.

Doctor

1836–1839

He was, therefore, willing to resume the office
of schoolmaster, so as to have a sure, though
moderate income for life.

WHATEVER HIS REPUTATION as a zealous student in
Paris, he could not have forgotten that among his friends at
home he was a poet and a wit. In November 1834, a year before he returned to America, John O. Sargent had written to
ask him for some verses. With more fancy language than was
altogether necessary, Holmes had refused his old friend. "The
blossoms" of his "flaunting youth" had fallen. He was unwilling to desert "one who had so often borne" him "company
—shoulder to shoulder—quill to quill—paragraph to paragraph—in more than one aspiring periodical," but the day of
a serious medical student in Paris had left no room for verse-
writing.

The electricity for that day is pretty thoroughly drawn off—and in fact
if I who somewhat labour in literary paturition—were to attempt that
which invariably exhausts my powers, I should wrong myself for too
small a matter.

No John, a heavier burden from my own science if you will, but
not another hair from the locks of Poesy or it will be indeed an ass's
back that is broken.[1]

Although he had refused to write, his literary friends did
not forget him in his absence. In the *New England Magazine*
for October 1835, Park Benjamin, reviewing a literary annual, *The Boston Book,* lamented the lack of verses from
Holmes, and launched into a eulogy of his friend.

The productions of O. W. Holmes, though circulating all over the
Union and in England, in the newspapers and literary journals, have

not won for their author that meed of fame which he deserves; simply because they were published under different signatures and at different times—and without the slightest care for their preservation. Deeply engaged in the study of an arduous profession, their author placed but little value on his genius for poetry; his verses were written as the amusement of leisure hours, and we will venture to assert that, so indifferent is he with regard to their destiny, he is utterly unconscious at this moment whether they are still afloat or have vanished like other gilded bubbles on the surface of popular regard.

Benjamin went on to remark that Holmes's pieces had been appropriated by other versifiers and palmed off as originals; he thought it not improbable that they had made "a reputation for many a starveling bard." [2]

The poet was not utterly unconscious, however; he had been home scarcely a month before he tried his hand again at verse-writing. Probably he had seen Benjamin's puffing paragraphs and was then the more willing to contribute to the new periodical, the *American Monthly Magazine,* edited by Benjamin and Charles Fenno Hoffman.

His first contribution, "An Evening Thought," expressed in its opening stanza a feeling that was echoed in most of the poems he attempted in this first year after his long silence:

> . . . something colder in the blood,
> And calmer in the brain
> Have whispered that my youth's bright flood
> Ebbs, not to flow again.[3]

In "The Last Reader," he represented himself as poring with a melancholy pleasure over the poems he had written in his "youth"—he was then twenty-six. He professed not to be distressed at the notion that his lines may be forgotten.

> What care I though the dust is spread
> Around these yellow leaves,
> Or o'er them his sarcastic thread
> Oblivion's insect weaves? [4]

In the heat of their composition, he had been rather proud of these last two lines; they had occasioned a "paroxysm . . . a burst of the most insane enthusiasm and self-gratulation." The editor of the *American Monthly Magazine* on his own initiative had altered "sarcastic" to "corroding"; the wrathful poet promptly refused to write any more "until he would promise to keep hands off."

Holmes, always sensitive to praise or censure, was particularly so as he tried out his talents in 1836. His college friend, James Freeman Clarke, spotted the unsigned poem "La Grisette" in the April number of Benjamin's magazine and recognized Holmes's style. The gratified author was moved to confess his feelings.

I had not written a stanza while abroad, and I felt on first sitting down as if the power of writing had passed away . . . and left me high and dry upon the sand, my sails and pennons all flapping in the wind—my keel wedged into the solid shore of fact—and with no hope of ever bounding again over the billows of poetry. So it was, however, that after writing one or two of these pieces, particularly "Our Yankee Girls" and "The Last Reader," I thought them remarkably good—at least for me, and was in hopes other people would think so. But several of my friends seemed to think I had fallen off,—and one in particular, who always professed a great liking for my verses, stopped me one day to tell me that the "Grisette" was poor stuff,—namby-pamby. . . .

This troubled me somewhat—I supposed I was running to seed—and when I found one of my offspring altered and mutilated in the magazine, where it was published, it settled the matter, and I determined not to write any more at present. Some time since I was appointed ΦBK poet for the coming anniversary, and, as I accepted, this occupation will be enough to keep me quiet.

But he was not thinking about poetry he assured Clarke, rather unconvincingly, after several pages when he had talked of nothing else; he was thinking of medicine. He had published his poems anonymously that no one might suppose him "ambitious of being considered a regular scribbler." What he desired was a "regular occupation, one which can support me and give me a hold on the community in which I live, and which my love of observation and the habits which I have formed for the last few years have rendered to me the most delightful of employments." He concluded his letter with thanks to Clarke for soothing his "perturbed spirit." [5]

For a young man who did not want to be regarded as a poet,

Holmes's behavior seems odd. Making public appearances and publishing a book are strange ways to seek anonymity. When he accepted the invitation to be the Phi Beta Kappa poet at Harvard and repeated the poem for another commencement—Brown University, he was receiving recognized literary distinction. Obligingly, too, he prepared some verses for the Harvard centennial and even went so far as to sing them himself. Publishing the Phi Beta Kappa poem was a customary procedure, but Holmes made the most of the occasion and gathered together the stray poems that had been circulating anonymously for five years, fixing once and for all the authorship of a number of extremely popular verses. By publishing the volume of poems, he could capitalize on his literary fame and at the same time bow himself off the stage. Holmes was not insincere when he wrote the final paragraphs of the introduction to the volume *Poems* which came from the press in November 1836.

I have come before the public like an actor who returns to fold his robes and make his bow to the audience. Already engaged in other duties, it has been with some effort that I have found time to adjust my own mantle; and I now willingly retire to more quiet labors, which, if less exciting, are more certain to be acknowledged as useful and received with gratitude; thankful that, not having staked all my hopes upon a single throw, I can sleep quietly after closing the last leaf of my little volume.[6]

In the Phi Beta Kappa poem itself, Holmes entertained the audience with topical allusions that ranged from the facetious to the melancholy; he satisfied their desire to be amused and their wish to be moved to lofty sentiment, but he began with references to "my boyhood's time," which could be suggestively mated with "neglected rhyme," and he ended with a pointed reference to his present ambitions in the realm of science. Although its theme was poets and poetry, the poem, called "A Metrical Essay," concluded with some elegiac lines for young Dr. James Jackson and references to all they—Jackson and he—had hoped to be.[7] To couple his own name with Jackson's and refer to their common ambition was to make a

138

very plain statement. All Boston knew of the brilliant son of Professor Jackson.

The result of these intended farewell appearances can be imagined. Editors wrote asking for verses; Emerson recommended Holmes as a possible lecturer on the lyceum platform.[8] Reviewers objected to his "literary suicide"; no less solid a periodical than the *North American Review* protested:

There is no profession so engrossing as to leave no time for poetry; and the mind must be of a very unmanageable sort, which any intellectual pursuit would unfit for the practical business of life.[9]

Many years later Holmes came to the conclusion that his mind was unmanageable; at the moment, he was finding that the study of medicine seemed "to take away both the pleasure and faculty of poetical composition. So far has this been carried that a little illustration of a picture which I had promised long ago to one of my friends has cost me more pain to elaborate than two or three *formidable* essays on professional subjects written in the meantime." [10] He could not stop writing altogether, but he did not want to keep his reputation going "in a series of periodical gaspings"; [11] he therefore consistently refused all editors of giftbooks and magazines unless they were old friends and he happened to have something on hand. In one week in 1838, three requests came in. One of them was from Clarke, then editing the *Western Literary Messenger*. Holmes wrote:

I have come to the conclusion to repel two of my petitioners, one by a churlish silence, and the other by an unctuous or rather saponaceous refusal, and to dispose of the third, that is yourself—by sending such a specimen of fancy work as shall prevent you from too rashly repeating the request.[12]

Although sometimes willing to play master of the revels for his Harvard friends, he could not always play that role. His classmates had to be content with a letter in 1839.

I feel much obliged to the Committee of the class for remembering me and my old tricks, which I should be too happy to play over again for my class mates if I could be amongst them at their dicennial meeting. . . . If I could send you a song as my representative I should be very well contented . . . but I do not dare to promise even this. Songs are the trout of Helicon, and after one has caught a certain number they are shy of biting. I will throw out my best summer fly the next rainy day and if anything is caught you shall receive it by the mail.[13]

Telling himself that his inclination to write poetry was a failing and a disease, Holmes had begun at once to establish a reputation as a doctor. Even before giving his "Metrical Essay," he had obliged the Harvard faculty to recognize talents quite different from those he displayed on the platform. The Harvard audience knew that the poet of the day was also the winner of the Boylston Medical Prize for a dissertation on "Direct Exploration." The question proposed by the prize committee had been announced long before Holmes returned from Europe. It seems likely that he did not tackle the subject until after his return, producing in a short time a clear and thorough answer to the question: "How far are the external means of exploring the condition of the internal organs, to be considered useful and important in medical practice?"

The essay is not an original piece in the sense that it contributed anything startlingly new to the subject. Its value would be wholly for the occasion. Very shrewdly he decided not to waste any time on means of examination long known and generally accepted; he disposed of those means dependent on vision and touch at the start, and concentrated upon what was new—technique dependent upon hearing.

The physician's problem was, after all, to determine what was going on inside a patient; insofar as his ailment showed itself in outward signs visible to the eye or palpable to the touch, the doctor had some objective signs to go by and was not dependent upon the unreliable and vague testimony of the patient. In the days before anesthetics, the surgeon could not go about opening up patients to find out what was wrong inside them. Before the invention of a galvanometer, he could not record the invisible, impalpable, and inaudible changes in the muscles of the heart by means of an electrocardiograph. In 1836 the newest means of getting at the inaccessible interiors of patients were those employing not electrical machines, for there were no machines, but the physician's ears, aided by the stethoscope.

And these new means, after paying due respect to the ancients for their use of percussion, Holmes considered. As he pointed out, the technique of percussion described by Auenbrugger (1761) and revived by Corvisart (1808), and the technique of auscultation discovered by Laënnec (1815) had not completely reached the English-speaking world until 1821, when the first translation of Laënnec's work was published in England, an American edition following in 1823. The standard *Dictionary of Medicine* had only recently changed its article on auscultation from its original unfavorable notice to a favorable one. Holmes in 1836 was quite right in assuming that these new means either were not known at all or were regarded skeptically even by reputable and well-known physicians. Holmes's own teachers, Jackson and others, had taught the methods of Laënnec, and in Paris, where Laënnec's disciples were perfecting his work, the use of the stethoscope was a matter-of-course; but in general there was still sufficient doubt among American physicians to warrant Holmes's essay and to give it, at the moment, a value beyond its personal value to the ambitious contestant for a prize.

Written with a clarity and precision of style that would have pleased his Harvard teacher of rhetoric, Edward Tyrell Channing, and garnished with effective allusions to the ancient medical authors, which would delight Winslow Lewis, the essay could be read with pleasure and understood even by the general reader. There is a little decoration, just enough to give it a literary flavor and not enough to constitute overdressing. Abiel Holmes's sermons show the same neat use of the decorative classical quotation. The committee liked it, at any rate, in spite of the apologetic Latin tag by which it was identified (the author's name being unknown until the decision was made). "Among toils and tedium," Holmes had signed his paper.

"A liberal friend of medical science," Dr. George Cheyne Shattuck, was willing to pay the expenses of publication of the prize-winning essay and the two runners-up. The Boylston Prize Committee had therefore recommended that the Massachusetts Medical Society see to the publication of a volume to "be gratuitously distributed to each fellow of that Society, and to every other respectable physician in Massachusetts," and to be volume VII in a series called the *Library of Practical Medicine*. This book with Holmes's name on its title page appeared a few weeks before his *Poems*.[14]

He had meanwhile hung out his shingle at 2 Central Court, his old boarding-house, but it is doubtful that he ever seriously intended making a name for himself as a general practitioner. It was the security of a professorship that he had dangled before his parents' eyes when he wrote to ask for money to continue his study in Europe. His campaign for winning distinction in his field seems to have been planned with that object in mind. Going out for prizes as a medical essayist was more likely to earn him an academic post than to get him patients. He did not rest with the honors he had won in his first year home. If there was anyone in New England in December 1836 who had not heard of Dr. Oliver Wendell Holmes, poet and physician, he was to hear of him before another year went by.

He had won the approval of his former teachers early. In September 1836, Drs. John Collins Warren and Jacob Bigelow were recommending him for a job at the Boston Dispensary. Bigelow referred to his "zealous devotion"; Warren remarked upon his amiable disposition and concluded: "Dr. Holmes has so well established his reputation for medical acquirement that it would be unnecessary for me to say anything on this topic." [15] The post of a visiting physician in this charity organization would allow Holmes, as he well knew, more opportunity to continue making observations after the manner he had been taught by Louis than he could make as a young and new doctor in private practice.

Somewhat inefficiently organized, the Boston Dispensary operated on a system which required each patient to present a ticket given him by a patron of the organization. This arrangement was not very satisfactory, for it left the patient dependent upon individual subscribers. Dr. Holmes found himself begging tickets from his friends so that his patients could get the treatment they needed. He was required to attend only those "regularly recommended," [16] but some of the poor people of the Broad Street slums could not wait upon such recommendations.

Observing the conditions under which these people lived, Holmes was forced to conclude that many of them got well in spite of, rather than because of, medical treatment. When in 1860, in a controversial address before the state medical society, Holmes spoke out against the abuse of medicines and false assumptions of their usefulness, he was moved to recall his experiences in Broad Street.

> Medication without insuring favorable hygienic condition is like amputation without ligatures. I had a chance to learn this well of old, when physician to the Broad Street district of the Boston Dispensary. There, there was no help for the utter want of wholesome conditions, and if anybody got well under my care, it must have been in virtue of the rough-and-tumble constitution which emerges from the struggle for life in the street gutters, rather than by the aid of my prescriptions.[17]

A similar observation he recorded in 1837 in a critical letter to the managers of the Dispensary, declaring that the goods of the apothecary were not enough; what many of these patients needed were proper diet and warm clothes.

There were other weaknesses in the set-up of the charity which called forth Holmes's criticisms. The lack of any proper consulting room was a disadvantage for the patients and the doctors. Moreover, such a consulting room, if provided, would be useful for medical students who could there observe cases. Louis's precepts were obviously in his mind here.

One other criticism made by Holmes at the end of his year of service suggests that he was not aware of the power held by a small group of doctors associated with the Harvard Medical School. He recommended that physicians be appointed not on the personal say-so of doctors, who were likely to show favoritism, but by competitive examination.[18] The young doctor had taken his instructions seriously; the managers had asked their physicians to make criticisms and they got them. It did not occur to Holmes to do more than record his observations; the instincts of the agitator were not in him.

About the time he began his work at the Boston Dispensary, he started to collect material for another Boylston essay on the subject of the history of intermittent fever (malaria) in New England, a project which obliged him to open a large correspondence with New England physicians.

When Holmes undertook to answer the Boylston Prize Question "To what extent, and in what places has Intermittent Fever been indigenous in New England?" he was tackling a problem abandoned by the Massachusetts Medical Society, which in 1834 had appointed a committee to take on the same task. The committee's circulation of a questionnaire had evoked only two responses, and the project had been given up for lack of information.[19] Holmes, aware of the medical society's failure, went at the chore of gathering information by soliciting his intimate friends and besieging fellow-physicians with batteries of personal letters. What the medical society's printed circular failed to accomplish, Holmes's private letters achieved.

But the job was tedious and discouraging. The information came in slowly, when it came at all, and some of it seemed too slight to warrant the effort. Tempted at times to give up, he still persisted in the task of wading through the arid pages of town histories and the curious but rarely rewarding—for his immediate purposes—works of the colonial historians and puritan divines. Mistrusting indexes, he went through his sources page by page, "with the exception of some few ecclesiastical papers, sermons, and similar treatises of Cotton Mather, which being more likely to cause a fever than to mention one, I left to some future investigator." [20] His wit could not be held in abeyance even in so dreary a job as searching for a needle in the haystack of puritan theology.

Meanwhile friends like the devoted Phinehas Barnes, agreeably quizzed the doctors in their neighborhoods, drawing out

144

of them recollected facts not procurable in any other way; brother-in-law Dr. Usher Parsons performed a similar service. Dr. Jackson was helpful; former fellow-students generously interviewed the experienced doctors in their regions. Some doctors, personally unknown to Holmes, co-operated none the less and kindly answered his questions.

Gradually he built up a collection of material which he thought might make a useful if humble contribution to the medical history of New England. He had no false notions about the value of the finished essay. "I am fully aware that this dissertation contains much that is arid and wearisome; that its pretentions are of the humblest nature, as presenting little more than the details of facts, and that very often in the language of others." [21] But he expressed, too, some satisfaction in "having explored some neglected sources of knowledge, and of having rescued a few perishing traditions from forgetfulness." [22] And to the finished essay, he attached the appropriate motto "Perserverando." There is some amusement in observing that to suggest the arduous labors of historical research he used a quotation from *Paradise Lost* as his father before him had done for the same purpose.[23]

Much less perseverance was required for the second manuscript upon which he worked in the early months of 1837. The material for his essay on neuralgia and the best modes of treating the ailment was easily accessible; organizing and writing the paper presented no problem to a young man as facile with the pen as Holmes. He had nothing original or spectacular to offer, but what he had to say he could say well. He offered his own evaluations of contemporary ideas on the subject without expecting that others would agree with him but hoping that they were made upon the "plain dictates of reason." He left it to "the reader's sagacity to discover" the few instances in which prejudice determined his judgments. It requires no sagacity, however, to spot the sarcastic paragraph rejecting the doctrines of Broussais, one of the passages which does, indeed, "add vivacity to a dull discussion." [24]

Shortly after the manuscripts of the two essays were submitted to the prize committee, the *Boston Medical and Surgical Journal* printed a prophetic notice. "It is strongly suspected that a very peculiar manifestation of talent will be exhibited in the writings of the competitors this present year." [25] In August the results of the competition were announced; Holmes had won both prizes. The medical journal was moved to observe: "It is almost useless to contend with him in an enterprise of this kind." [26]

Winning three prizes of this kind was a quick path to professional distinction; gathering the three essays into a volume was a sensible if opportunistic gesture. Holmes knew very well the measure of the three essays; he gave the one on intermittent fever the first position in his book, and it was the only one he ever thought later of reprinting. Holmes knew that no paper hastily gotten up to meet a deadline could be free from error. He knew, too, that usable observations on two of the subjects—those on direct exploration, and neuralgia—could not be made except after long and controlled study of the problems implied. The brief introduction which he supplied for the printed volume (published January 1838) anticipated, as he intended it should, the judgment of one critical reviewer. If the *Boston Medical and Surgical Journal* in a burst of provincial pride was ready to shower him with praise,[27] his ex-fellow-student, W. W. Gerhard of Philadelphia, was more discriminating. Reviewing the book in the *American Journal of the Medical Sciences,* Gerhard banished "Direct Exploration" as neither useful nor necessary, labeled the neuralgia essay as uninteresting, and gave the essay on intermittent fever all his praise.[28] As recently as 1944, a modern authority, Dr. Erwin H. Ackerknecht, called Holmes's paper "still the best regional history of malaria thus far written." [29]

In the midst of these triumphs, Holmes's father died. The Reverend Abiel Holmes had preached his last sermon in January 1837 on the appropriate text, "The vanity of life a reason for seeking a position in heaven." [30] The quarrel in his church had long since ceased to be a subject of gossip in the town of Cambridge; he had lived to see the building of a new church,

designed by Washington Allston, and had preached the fitting
sermon for its dedication. But Dr. Waterhouse, the minister's
friend and neighbor, had not forgotten the church quarrel
and its aftermath. Recording the death of his friend in his
journal, he wrote:

> His new society gave him a colleague, and they apparently labored
> harmoniously, but after all it was not a garment without a seam. . . .
> Dr. Holmes received worse treatment from his Orthodox brethren than
> from the Unitarians who took the first steps to remove him. He had
> reason to pray—"Save me from my friends." When he preached in their
> new meeting-house, he was undermined by his false brethren. Deacon
> Wm. Hilliard, his putative friend, was the first person who spoke his
> discontent, and the necessity of giving him a colleague. I thought it ad-
> visable, and a help his years and feeble health required; but I was
> averse to a high-toned Calvinist or a high-flown Unitarian. Holmes
> aimed at being a liberal but conscientious man, which he was. But he
> is dead, and has left behind a very respectable character. Abiel Holmes
> was really a righteous man. . . .[31]

Nor had the son forgotten the fiery trial of 1827-29. Expressing his and his family's objections to the Rev. William
Jenks's desire to write a biography of Abiel Holmes, the son
released long pent up emotions, making it clear that the feelings he expressed were his own.

Nor is there much in his theological career upon which I can dwell
with pleasure. For many years quietly established at Cambridge, he was
respectably but not conspicuously stationed as a minister.—There was
hitherto little in his long career to attract notice to his pulpit. He maintained a kind of middle station between two opposing parties, as yet
unmolested.

The time having come when he stood in the way of the theological
tacticians then managing the church militant, he was sacrificed.—His
course as a clergyman, peculiarly delicate and difficult amidst the conflicting opinion which raged around him, showed all the amiability and
some of the weaknesses of his character.—But his last years were tran-
quil, and we may try to forget those scenes in which, alas, he suffered
for himself while he acted for others. . . .

His religious life, in any considerable detail cannot be wanted by
the more liberal members of our vicinity and our city, for his principles of faith were of the old orthodox standard—nor by the present
orthodox party—for it was by their agency that he was torn in his old

age from his people, and finally rejected and supplanted in his authority . . . the two great parties which divided our community crowded against him each from his own side—one pressing upon his Calvinist faith, the other upon his liberal principles of intercourse and orderly habits of public ministration, with much care and policy for their own interests, and too little anxiety with regard to him.

The life of such a clergyman and of such a time may perhaps deserve to be written. But God forbid that at this period the machinery of modern Jesuitism should be unfolded as it was brought to bear upon my father's happiness. The history of some of his last, but not the very last of his years, would reveal a series of Machiavellian contrivances to delude and beat down a simple hearted man and his opposition, worthy of a better nest of conspirators than a deacon's fireside. . . .[32]

That this outburst was not enough to release all the young man's inward feelings became apparent later when the professional life he was now trying to make for himself was pushed into the background and he took to writing again. Deacons would be ridiculed, high-toned Calvinists exposed, and kind-hearted clergymen honored when he came to write his novels. But such means of release must wait another twenty years.

Although his daughters had married and his older son taken to living in Boston, the minister had refused to sell the Cambridge house to the Harvard Corporation. He left to his widow, his sons, and his surviving daughter no very great estate, but there was sufficient property to enable Sarah Wendell Holmes and brother John to live comfortably on in the Cambridge house until the mother's death twenty-five years later. Less aggressive and less ambitious than his brother, John Holmes was content to live quietly in Cambridge and to assume the responsibility of caring for his mother while Wendell went on to make his successive bids for distinction. The older son was not unaware of the fact that he had "always been liberally treated" by his parents and that at John's expense. "I have," he admitted to his father's friend, "been a little inclined to usurp Benjamin's portion." [33]

In the following year Holmes realized in part his ambitions for a professorship. He got his first teaching experience in 1838 when he allied himself with Jacob Bigelow, Edward

148

Reynolds, and David Humphreys Storer to form the Tremont Medical School. In time the Tremont School was incorporated, and eventually it merged with the Harvard Medical School, but at its inception in 1838 it was modeled after the informal school which Holmes himself had first attended as a means of filling the three-year apprenticeship requirement for the degree.

From the apothecary Metcalf, the doctors rented an upstairs chamber at 35 Tremont Row which they turned into a dissecting room. Lectures and examinations were given at regularly scheduled times. The school became famous in its day for the opportunities for clinical study it offered. Small clinical classes were rare in the established medical schools of the time; but the Tremont School offered daily attendance at the Massachusetts General Hospital, the Eye and Ear Infirmary, and the Lying-In Hospital. Holmes taught physiology and pathology, and heard recitations in anatomy. He also gave a short course in surgical anatomy, and taught the use of the stethoscope and the principles of auscultation. David Storer taught obstetrics and chemistry; Reynolds, surgery and anatomy. Jacob Bigelow gave the clinical instruction, taught his own specialty, materia medica, and gave the lectures in theory and practice. As time went on, the school added special subjects to its offerings, the first being a course in the use of the microscope. This was Holmes's offering; he was one of the first teachers of medicine in America to introduce his students to the instrument, which is now a common part of any grade school laboratory, but which was then unknown.

The school adjusted its program to fit the regular Harvard schedule so that the student who enrolled in the Tremont School and at Harvard received a full year's organized work. It is not surprising that a large number of students who pursued this program came eventually to make a superior showing in their profession; they had the advantage over young men who got their training by the old-fashioned apprentice system.[34]

Holmes's association with the medical men of Boston had

149

begun early; in 1836 he had become a member of the Boston
Society for Medical Improvement. This small group of doctors
met twice a month on Monday evenings to discuss cases and
to hear papers. A paper, in fact, was required of every member
on penalty of a fine and, eventually, disqualification; failure
to attend and to take part in the discussions with reasonable
frequency was also grounds for dismissal. These rigorous
standards, ultimately abandoned, were in force during the
period when Holmes, as an active practitioner, was a member.
The reports of the meetings indicate that he could be depended upon for contributions of various kinds, but particularly for his knowledge of medical literature and history. He
helped to build up the society's library; and, as an anatomist,
he contributed to its museum.[35]

His first papers naturally rested upon his European experience. In December 1836, he gave an "interesting" defense of
Louis's numerical system;[36] a year later his "admirable" sketch
of Parisian lecturers evoked a request for more of the same.[37]
When the club debated the question of the difference between typhus and typhoid fever, Holmes was vigorous in his
support of the discoveries of his fellow-student Gerhard.[38]

It is no surprise to find him also acting the part of poet for
the society's annual anniversary party. For the first anniversary he attended, his verses, which for obvious reasons do not
survive, were "a very ingenious and highly wrought description of the two scourges of the human race, malaria and
syphilis." [39] The combination seems a little odd; but the first
obviously grew out of his current investigations of intermittent fever, and for the second, he had a distinguished precedent in Fracastoro's sixteenth-century poem, which gave the
disease its name.

Of Holmes's verses for the anniversary of 1838, there is only
a bare mention; the secretary's uncommunicativeness is
natural, for Holmes himself was keeping the society's records for this year. As a secretary, he had not so far grown out
of his Hasty Pudding days that flashes of cleverness did not
now and then get into the otherwise sober records of the Club.

When two of their number were called away from the party of 1838, the secretary noted: "The hilarity of the Company was temporarily diminished, and the Census of the city permanently increased during their absence." [40]

It was for this group that Holmes would produce the most famous of his medical works, a story to be told in its proper place.

Altogether Dr. Holmes was probably too busy for any very active social life, but he enjoyed enough of it to call down on his head a warning from his friend Barnes, suggesting that he cut down his engagements.[41] Barnes had also resumed his old role of advocate for marriage. He had been watching the announcements for some such news of Holmes; and being himself on the edge of matrimony he was eager to persuade Holmes to follow him,[42] a suggestion to which the young doctor was not indifferent. One of the first poems Holmes had written on his return to Europe was a eulogy of "Our Yankee Girls," and "A Metrical Essay," in its oral version, had contained an allusion to some special "Mary" waiting in the audience for the poet.[43] In February 1838, he received the news of Barnes's marriage a little enviously. "And so you are married. I wish I were, too. I have flirted and written poetry long enough, and I feel that I am growing domestic and tabby-ish. I have several very nice young women in my eye, and it is by no means impossible that another summer or so may see my name among the hymeneal victims." He did not intend to dally any longer; in two years he would be, he thought, too old.[44]

One of the young women in his eye was Amelia Lee Jackson, daughter of Judge Charles Jackson and niece of Dr. James Jackson. Holmes must have had ample opportunity to meet her, but he had certainly not committed himself in 1838; at least the following letter from Amelia to her cousin, Henry Lee, Jr. (one of Holmes's patients) does not sound like the letter of a young woman with prospects of marriage in mind.

We shall soon be in town and then for parties and dissipation. For my part I almost dread this winter. I think a girl's life at my age isn't the most pleasantest by any means; she is in the most unsettled state: a young man can occupy himself with his business and look forward to his life and prospects, but all we have to do is to pass our time agreeably to ourselves. Not that we have not enough to occupy ourselves in carrying on our education, but I think everyone likes to feel the *necessity* of doing something, and I confess I have sometimes wished I could be poor to have the pleasure of exerting myself. . . .

She considered attending a history course during the winter, but feared that no exertions would ever make her a scholar, an achievement she would leave to her brother and her younger sister.[45] Probably the anticipated dissipation of the Boston winter season of 1838-39 included some attention from the verse-writing doctor.

By September 1838, when Amelia Jackson was contemplating her winter without enthusiasm, Dr. Holmes was comfortable in the knowledge of a new professorship, one that would not interefere with his work in the Tremont School.

On July 24, 1838, at their annual meeting, the Trustees of Dartmouth College had voted "to go into the choice of a Professor of Anatomy" and had chosen Oliver Wendell Holmes. On July 12 the young doctor had written a dignified letter indicating his willingness to accept the position if it were offered him, and on August 7 he received official notice of his Dartmouth appointment.[46] In September the annual catalogue of the college included in its list of officers the name of the Boston physician, who would begin his duties the following August. And, confidently, the catalogue announced:

Although the Trustees have deeply to regret the resignation of Professors Mussey and Oliver, by whose labors chiefly the medical branch of the College has been for so many years sustained, yet from the known character of the gentlemen recently elected to fill the places thus vacated, they do not apprehend that the advantages afforded to Medical Students will in any of the departments be materially abridged. . . .[47]

The "very agreeable appointment" at Dartmouth meant only fourteen weeks away from Boston and assured him of some $400; not much, but certainty counted for something to a young man whose eye was wandering in the direction of a wife. He had a year in which to get ready for his new job. The

preparation meant something more than planning lectures.
When Dr. Mussey left Dartmouth, he took with him from the
museums of special and morbid anatomy his valuable private
collection, a void which the 1838 college catalogue promised
to fill "with all possible despatch." The same catalogue announced:

Arrangements are already in progress for supplying, previous to the
next lecture term, by means of collections and purchases at home, and
importations from abroad, whatever may be essential for illustrating
the several branches of the course.

The arranger was the appointee to the professorship of anatomy and physiology, and the catalogues of 1839 and 1840, as
well as his bill to the college, bear witness to his energy in
fulfilling this part of his obligations. Even today, apart from
unlabeled osteological specimens which seem to date from
Holmes's two years at Dartmouth, there is in the Dartmouth
Medical School Museum a labeled dissection showing the
nervous system of a child's head—Holmes's work. Besides re-
plenishing the college museum and supplying specimens and
preparations necessary for his teaching, Holmes had also to
prepare the medical school's annual circular.[48]

Meanwhile, during this busy spring of 1839, Dr. Nathaniel
Potter, of the University of Maryand, was pursuing him with
the offer of a chair of surgery in the university's Medical
School. The young doctor was to consider the possibility of
being a surgeon in Baltimore and an anatomist in Hanover,
a notion which was apparently at once discouraged by both
parties to this plan. His old teacher, Dr. Jackson wrote: "You
are unwilling to desert your country, and I should be sorry to
see you desert what I regard as your calling." [49] The authoritative voice of a prospective Dartmouth colleague spoke candidly and firmly. The gist of Dr. Dixi Crosby's letter of advice
was an emphatic "no" to the Baltimore position. The doctor
tempered his sternness with:

Now my dear Sir however you may feel and act, believe me all I have
said has come from a heart filled to overflowing with the kindest feelings and sincere attachment. From the first I liked you (a homely phrase

says you) and if you decide to go you will carry with you my warmest friendship. . . . Ask some of your wise heads and see if they talk as I do. . . .

Wise heads prevailed. Holmes refused the Baltimore offer.[50]

A few months before the term at Dartmouth was to begin, the New Hampshire Alpha chapter of Phi Beta Kappa remembered that the new member of the medical faculty was also a poet and promptly asked him for a poem for commencement; Longfellow had been their poet in 1837; Emerson, their orator in 1838. The new Dartmouth professor could not very well refuse, although his poem had to be "written in great haste amid numerous pressing engagements." [51] Once in Hanover and lodged in the Dartmouth Hotel, to be his home for three months in 1839 and 1840, Holmes might from the balcony look down upon the common in gala dress for commencement. Two years earlier, Longfellow had stood on the same balcony and described the scene in his journal.

Under the great maple trees near the hotel, was drawn up during the day a line of pedlar's carts; from which the said pedlars sold their wares at auction, with loud outcry and such wit as they were masters of. The crowd of clowns bought cheap or bought not at all: and up and down walked those, who had made great bargains, wearing new hats from which the yellow paper had not been removed, or holding in hand a tin pail or a tin tunnel.[52]

More dignified entertainment was provided by the orators of the day; in 1839 they were Edwards Park of Andover Theological Seminary; Alexander Everett, brother of Edward Everett; and the Reverend Calvin E. Stowe, husband of Harriet Beecher Stowe. These respectable gentlemen had given long and learned speeches on solemn subjects. Stowe, it is true, had caused a smile accidentally when he drew analogies between Queen Victoria, "a young maiden of eighteen," and Martin Van Buren, a "red-whiskered widower of sixty," but on the whole the orations were dreary.[53] The audience was probably grateful for the rounds of laughter the last speaker of the day provided in his jingling rhymes. In a lengthy notice of the festivities of the day, the reporter for the *Boston Daily*

Atlas saved his warmest adjectives for Dr. Holmes, showering upon him flattery the doctor was to receive too often for his own good. With most of its superlatives deleted, the *Atlas* account goes as follows:

> It was in truth a splendid performance. It consisted of a series of pictures of human life, whose colors varied "from grave to gay, from lively to severe." Among them were—The Forest at Summer Noon—The Forest in Winter—The Ball Room in Winter—The Rustic and the Cit (who attempted to use the flail, and whether he hit the grain or his *head,* was sure to make the *chaff* fly)—The Tenants of the Hospital—The Betrayed Maiden and her Lover—The News of the Town, as reflected in the press by scribblers, who are obliged to mix white and blue lies, like soda powders in white and blue papers, before they can make them sparkle! . . . I have ever regarded Holmes as one of the very first poets in the country, and I know the performance of which I am speaking, will raise him higher in public estimation.[54]

The author of the poem was less enthusiastic about his "slip-shod lay"; [55] neither the eulogies of the *Atlas* reporter nor the requests of Professor Hubbard moved him to publish it; [56] the whole poem was not rescued from limbo until one hundred years later, although Holmes did give away a few excerpts from it to persistent editors.

Ironically, the newly appointed Professor had made his first appearance in his old role of Poet.

Medical Reformer

*He in this year gave at once a proof of his
benevolence, quickness of apprehension, and
admirable art of composition.*

A FEW DAYS LATER the new Professor of Anatomy and
Physiology gave his introductory lecture. He defined his subjects by analogy: "One shows us the wheels and levers of the
machine which we are to study; the other sets them all in operation." Dr. Holmes proposed to present the two subjects together.

Precisely in the same manner as the young machinist does not confine himself to studying the pumps and pistons and cylinders of a
steam engine for one quarter and then busy himself during the next
in reading how they move when in operation, but in the examination
of each part, enquires what is its utility? why is it here—how does it
act—just so should the young anatomist constantly associate in his mind
the function of a part with its structure, so far as nature allows him
to perceive such a connection.

Interweaving history and fact, Holmes gave his lecture a
major theme of an exhortatory kind. The scientific atmosphere of Paris had not faded from his memory. "Wherever
sound observation silences . . . scholastic babbling, even if
it cannot substitute any positive fact in the place of the idle
speculations it overturns, it removes a mountain from the path
of the student." He would not be sorry to see one of his students "crucifying himself in the first ardor of his industry,
upon the thorny processes of the spheroid, or diving beneath
the fourth layer of the muscles of the back to drag up drowned
science by the locks from the fathomless channels of the verte-

brae." The principles of Dr. Louis are not improved by being thus represented in the imagery of Shakespeare, but the speaker's intentions were good. The lecture concluded with critical allusions to "sneering practical men" and an exhortation to pursue knowledge for its own sake. Holmes here held to a lofty ideal and did not see any separation between the practitioner and investigator; later he was to put himself in line with the "practical" men whom here he criticized.

The poet's imagination colored parts of his lecture. He told his students of the ancient physician Galen's journey to Alexandria to see a skeleton. "Yet we have only to order such a preparation and it comes just as certainly as the box of claret from Bordeaux and the bale of silk from Lyons, that lie by its side in the Havre packet." [1] The illustrative material he had been commissioned to order from Paris had arrived just in time for his lectures.

Holmes had only three months in which to acquaint his students with the complexities of his double subject; but possibly his flair for making the minutiae of anatomy both clear and interesting could help him make so short a period of study valuable. Steering clear of arid technical jargon, Holmes was in the habit of fixing in his students' minds the details of descriptive anatomy by means of concrete analogies. He also had to include in his short course surgical anatomy, and some chemistry; for in 1839 the Dartmouth Medical School offered no chemistry, a deficiency repaired the following year. It is with reason that Holmes described the "chair" of Anatomy and Physiology as a "settee." If he thought the burden too great, he had only to recall that Nathan Smith, the founder of the Dartmouth Medical School, himself the entire faculty, had taught the whole medical curriculum of four major courses.

Accepting the Dartmouth position had one drawback. He had to leave to his collaborator, Dr. Jacob Bigelow, the work of seeing through the press the American edition of Marshall Hall's *Principles and Practice of Medicine*. When the volume came out in October 1840, it had many defects, for which

Holmes was obliged to apologize to critical correspondents. A few years later he was inclined to apologize for doing the work at all. It was precisely the kind of job he soon criticized severely (recognizing his own defection) both in reviews of books and in his report as chairman of the American Medical Association's committee on medical literature.

A review, published in 1843, gives his own description of this means of getting professional notice:

A new fashion is growing up among our publishers, upon which we will bestow a parting word. . . . . A work is published in England, embodying the labors of some man of talents. . . . The giant of our all-devouring press snuffs it in the wind—

Fee, faw, fo fum,

I smell the book of an Englishman.

Before the work, however, can be trusted to the American public, it must find some responsible citizen to alter, improve, amend and answer for it, some young physician, whose notebook might show that he has occasionally prescribed an "Anderson" for his grandmother, or practiced on himself with Rochelle powders before breakfast; or some surgeon, who has cut a few corns and strapped a broken head or two— is selected as the sponsor. The favored youth opens the book in the natural intervals which characterize uncut volumes, skims the content of those leaves which are free from adhesions, pours a calm whiff of cigar smoke into such as are merely united at the top, and occasionally pokes the first joint of a finger into those which . . . have only one entrance. In half an hour he manufactures a dozen superfluous impertinences which he calls "Notes". . . . And this is the way the works of the London practitioners . . . are ushered into the American market, under the patronizing shadow of some minute fungus, no more competent to criticize, still less to amend, his original, than a turnspit to carry the paddle wheels of the Great Western. . . . Our scientific reputations are becoming to a frightful extent parasitical, built up on mere typographical association of names. . . .

Holmes and Bigelow did much more than blow tobacco smoke down the uncut leaves of the English edition; their revisions were minute and careful, using both Bigelow's wide knowledge of American botany and his researches into self-limiting diseases, and Holmes's knowledge of modern French medicine. Their work was not of the superficial kind burlesqued by Holmes. If Holmes himself fitted his own caustic description of the young practitioner, Dr. Bigelow was hardly in the same category. Nevertheless, Holmes was moved to remark in the review quoted: "We would not be too sweeping in a censure which might reach ourselves. But we have actually become ashamed of this jackdaw style of making a reputation." [2]

Meanwhile, although achieving that reputation was not proving too difficult, it was harder to put his reputation of being a poet in its proper place. Even the correspondents whom he had quizzed in his investigations of intermittent fever had reminded him of his verses, addressing him as "Dear Laureate Dr.," requesting the volume of poems, or calling him a "queer genius." "What the deuce can a man of your imagination," asked Dr. C. P. Coffin of Lowell, "find of interest in hunting up dry facts?" [3]

The begging editors were treated to refusals, but the second invitation of the Harvard Phi Beta Kappa Society in 1837 —this time asking for a song for the dinner—Holmes had accepted. This was, of course, the year that Emerson was the Phi Beta Kappa orator. Holmes must have heard the address he later called America's literary Declaration of Independence, "The American Scholar." There is no record of what he thought of it at the time. But he had no taste for metaphysics, as he had long ago indicated to his rival poet in his college class, James Freeman Clarke. Like Emerson the son of a liberal minister, and like Emerson, too, starting his career as a preacher, Clarke found no barriers in the way of becoming a follower, if not an imitator, of Emerson. Young Dr. Holmes, however, brought up in orthodoxy and then exposed to the rationalism of science, was not likely to be moved by the speaker. In 1836, Holmes had included in "A Metrical Essay," a brief elegy for Emerson's younger brother, Charles Chauncy Emerson. The elder Emerson had called at his rooms in Paris in 1833, but this casual acquaintanceship was not enough to bring Holmes within the orbit of his influence. The doctor's life, after all, brought him into closer relations with men like Jacob Bigelow, and Dr. Walter Channing, who said of Emerson's lectures that they made his head ache.[4] All that in the 1830's and '40's could connect Holmes with Emerson was the tenuous thread of the doctor's repressed interest in poetry, an interest Holmes indulged, as on this occasion, only to please his friends at their social gatherings.

It was Emerson, however, who had suggested Holmes as a possible lyceum lecturer; and in 1837 Holmes made his debut on the lyceum platform. From then on he assumed the role of lecturer irregularly until the 1850's, when he became a constant performer. His earliest lectures were not reported in contemporary newspapers, which tell nothing of his first appearance beyond the date—December 7—and the place—the Boston Lyceum. He has left his own record, however, of some of his early titles. The title "Cities" suggests that Holmes probably drew upon his European experiences for subject matter, no doubt extolling his beloved Paris at the expense of the—to him—gloomy city of London and the too hastily visited city of Rome. But this is only conjecture, for the lecture survives in only two tantalizing fragments in one of the doctor's notebooks.[5]

The first lecture he ever gave was probably "English Versification." This was his offering for the Warren Street Chapel series on December 19, 1837.[6] Since it is unlikely that he prepared more than one lecture for his first season, it may be assumed that he had given this one on December 7. It is not hard to imagine its content; Holmes was likely to lavish his praise upon the eighteenth-century poets, upon Goldsmith and Pope. Irritated by false rhymes or rough and unfamiliar rhythms, and admiring lucidity, Holmes reveals in his own verses the qualities he was likely to recommend to a lyceum audience. Some sixteen years later, Holmes confessed to having spoken slightingly of Tennyson in an early lecture—undoubtedly this one.[7]

Whatever prompted him to undertake lecturing, he could not have found these early ventures particularly lucrative; at the most, he could receive ten or fifteen dollars for a performance; possibly the extra dollars were of some use to a young man whose medical practice was not then extensive. At any rate, his teaching and practice were by 1840 sufficiently lucrative to allow him to think seriously of marriage. Holmes had sometime in 1839 taken up new quarters at 35 Tremont Row, over the shop of the town's most noted apothecary, Thomas Metcalf. The establishment was directly opposite that of the King's Chapel sexton, old Martin Smith, who in the event of the failure of doctor and druggist "would do all that circumstances permitted for our late patient." [8]

Since 35 Tremont Row was also the address of the Tremont Medical School, housing its library and dissecting room, it might be supposed that Holmes was carrying professional devotion to an extreme. He was not to live there long, however. Two months before he was due to return to Dartmouth for his second term, Holmes went over to King's Chapel, where across the top of an official blank he wrote the injunction: "Please marry me by the name of *Wendell.*" [9]

On June 15, 1840, the ceremony was performed and presumably the minister obeyed the groom's order. Holmes had finally fulfilled his long-restrained desire for domesticity and settled his romantic eye upon one young woman, Amelia Jackson. The father of the bride, Judge Charles Jackson, was not a wealthy man but he was well-off and able to present the couple with a house at 8 Montgomery Place, not far from the church which Holmes thereafter attended, and the Tremont School. [10]

The marriage was the occasion for some speculation among the friends of the bride. The Jackson girls had apparently a reputation for being over-devoted, both as daughters and wives. "Amelia is a singularly energetic and effective woman and too devoted as a wife,"—this was Waldo Higginson's judgment. He thought it possible that marriage had changed her. "I think though Wendell has vastly improved her intellect, so that she makes a much better appearance in society than I ever expected—her soul is more that of a woman of the world—She realizes less frequently that the world is not all." [11] He was not entirely sure of his judgment; the doctor was making his wife too worldly perhaps. [12] A feminine gossip's picture of the marriage is rather different. "Dr. Holmes & Amelia were here the other evening & the little doctor was in his brightest & most entertaining mood, talking about the different quackeries, although his wife had read him a lecture just before leaving home on the impropriety of talking about his profession. . . . Amelia . . . is as happy as ever." [13]

We may suppose that Holmes was also as happy as ever. On March 9, 1841, he wrote his sister Ann a significant letter.

Last evening between 8 and 9 there appeared at No. 8 Montgomery Place a little individual who may be hereafter addressed as
—Holmes, Esq.
or
The Hon.—Holmes, M. C.
or
His Excellency—Holmes, President,
etc. etc. but who for the present is content with scratching his face and sucking his right forefinger. Amelia had a favorable time of it and is now remarkably comfortable.[14]

The then nameless baby acquired his father's name and ultimately fulfilled the spirit if not the letter of his father's prophecy. The father kept a record of his son's progress. At the age of twenty months, the future Justice of the Supreme Court of the United States had advanced to the stage where he identified himself as someone named "Auber" supposed to be "Oliver" or " 'Enny" supposed to be "Wendy." Six months later, the parent was probably overdoing it a little when he noted that the boy could "say almost anything now," unless, of course, the baby was already showing that he had inherited his father's garrulity.[15]

There is nothing to tell whether the doctor delivered his son or not, but the record of the birth of his second child is in his own medical casebooks under the date October 20, 1843 and the mother's initials, "A. L. H." The clinical entry concludes "Child a female—weighed with clothes and white handkerchief 7¼ lb." [16] A week or so later Mrs. Henry Lee, Sr. wrote to her son: "I must not forget now to announce a youthful Amelia, whose grandmother thinks is the *'Spec'* to use her own term, of the family, & there are *many* rivals I assure you—

Wendell & his wife are both much pleased that it is a daughter." [17] In 1846, a son, Edward Jackson, completed the doctor's family.

The doctor supported his ménage by teaching and practice and by occasional lecturing. His relinquishing of the Dartmouth position after two terms and his refusal to accept an offer from the Berkshire Medical School suggest that his practice had increased sufficiently to make such excursions from home unnecessary. His practice—so far as the casebooks can be taken as evidence—was just what one might expect of a young general practitioner. The families who sought him out went through the usual round of births, measles, mumps, and influenza. Because of his Paris training and probably his essay "Direct Exploration," he was called in by other doctors chiefly to examine tuberculous patients, of whom he had a number himself. Occasionally a distraught young stranger, suffering from a venereal disease or the aftereffects of an abortion, would come to the doctor's office to be given a moral lecture as well as medical advice. But the doctor's entries indicate that his chief object of indignation was the charlatan whose advertisements, freely allowed in all newspapers, had duped his patients. He was, apparently, sparing with drugs and lavish with advice about hygienic practices.

One entry sketches him in a dual role—that of doctor and of a young man in Boston society. He sandwiched a wedding and reception in between attendance on a confinement case, getting back from the reception just in time. Another shows the worried doctor looking for a vanished patient—a young Irish girl who had come to the house one day and sent her sister the next, but who had left no address. Another shows him spending twenty-four harassed hours at the bedside of a woman dying miserably of cholera morbus. There are several entries describing the shy, consumptive girls—the New England type—reluctant to submit to examination, the type of girl whom Holmes constantly uses as an example of the New England woman.

The notes were apparently not meant as an office record, but rather as a repository for observations which in one way or another the doctor thought interesting; there are detailed notes of autopsies, of cases examined with other doctors, of follow-up reports. One entry reports his own microscopical examination of a cancerous tumor of the breast. He had probably begun to make use of the microscope and possibly even to teach its use to his students at the Tremont Medical School before December 1842; but the casebook entry of the date is the first record of his use of it.

His own health gave him some trouble and the casebooks include clinical notes on the progress of his own bronchial troubles and toothaches, for which he dosed himself with restraint, employing hot wine or gin and water for the one and laudanum for the other.[18]

During these first years of practice, the doctor worked all through the summer and made his rounds on foot. In a few years more he was able to afford a long summer vacation and to keep his own horse, a possession not without its dangers, for the doctor's delight in speed made him something of a public menace.

He was meanwhile turning his medical knowledge to account in a direction other than that of private practice. If his wife felt that there was some impropriety in talking about his profession at social gatherings, she could not very well object to his using his ideas on the lyceum platform. He had begun his role as a lecturer with a subject suited to a poet (English versification); for his appearances in the thirties, he had prepared lectures based upon his travels: "Cities," and "National Prejudices," 1839. In the last of these, his love of France and all things French came out in jests made at the expense of the English. It was, in fact, a personal prejudice that made the center of his lecture; and the "eloquent tribute" to England with which he concluded must have been somewhat vitiated by the body of the lecture.[19]

But in 1840, he began to use the lyceum platform as a means to expose the flourishing quackeries of the day. On that subject he could not be silenced. Neither a brother nor a fellow-poet was spared his contempt when either succumbed to the blandishments of hydropaths or homeopaths. John Holmes, whose wit his Cambridge friends considered the equal of Wendell's, turned his brother's feverish concern with the evils of homeopathy into a family joke and went calmly off to Brattleboro to take the water-cure in spite of his brother's scorn. Boston hostesses came to feel that it was wise to keep Longfellow out of Dr. Holmes's way lest the doctor read his fellow-poet a lecture on the medical errors by which he was deluded. There is no record of Holmes's ever scolding William Cullen Bryant on the subject, but it is not likely that he showed unwonted forbearance when he came face to face with him, for Bryant was president of the homeopathic society. Much as he respected their poetic talents, he thought his fellow-poets ignoramuses in scientific matters.

The views to which his patients, his family, and his friends had perforce to listen were presented to the public in four lectures in 1840 and 1842. The lecture for 1840 was "The Natural Diet of Man," and there the followers of Sylvester Graham and William Alcott were the targets for the doctor's wit and indignation. Translating the technical language of the chemist and comparative anatomist into images comprehensible to the layman and illustrating his points with witty if sometimes far-fetched analogies, the doctor demolished the arguments of the two popular vegetarians and exposed them to ridicule.[20]

For the most fashionable and learned of the Boston lyceum audiences of the day, Holmes prepared the most serious of his lectures against charlatanism. The Society for the Diffusion of Useful Knowledge was an organization as dignified—possibly as pompous—as its name; its secretaries were normally chosen from among those who had made reputations as men of learning and of standing in their professions. Among those who served in that position were John Gorham Palfrey, Daniel Webster, and Holmes himself. In fact, Holmes was the secretary for the season of 1841-2; his newspaper announcement of the series for the year schedules, for February 2, 19, and 26, a group of three lectures by him, entitled "Scientific Mysticism." The three lectures dealt separately with the subjects "Astrology and Alchemy," "Medical Delusions of the Past," and "Homeopathy." The first survives in manuscript and the second and third were combined to make the published essay *Homeopathy and Its Kindred Delusions*.[21]

For these three lectures, Holmes took an approach less popular and a tone less frivolous than he had used for his others. His wit was less flashy and his analogies more fitting and more serviceable than usual. In "The Natural Diet of Man" his exposures of false reasoning had been casual, made simply by the way; in these three lectures he is at great pains to reveal and to emphasize the false reasoning, the abuse of evidence, and the misrepresentations which marked the thinking of the advocates of homeopathy and of its founder, Samuel Hahnemann.

He had organized these lectures with some care in order to bring out the essential similarities between the quackeries of the past and those of the present. He drew effective parallels between the charlatans of different periods and the follies of their unthinking advocates. And all that he had to say in 1842 had a direct bearing on the contemporary form of quackery, which he exposed in a manner so temperate and just that one newspaper was prompted to regret that the doctor had held both his wit and his temper in check when he dealt with the homeopathists.[22]

If for the modern reader the subject-matter of the published version of the lectures has only an antiquarian value, Holmes's revelation of the way in which the lay mind has for generations operated when exposed to the fallacious "arguments" of medical charlatans has still a usable value. Much of what Holmes had to say is applicable to the way many people today respond to "medical" articles of the kind that appear in popular magazines, or to the gossip of people whose ailments form their chief topics of conversation, or to the modern advertising of patent medicines.

In his lecture on "Medical Delusions," Holmes treated at some length the history of the once-famous "Metallic Tractors." These instruments, the invention of a Connecticut Yankee, Dr. Elisha Perkins, were "simply two pieces of metal, one apparently iron and the other brass, about three inches long, blunt at one end and pointed at the other." Dr. Perkins claimed that by drawing his tractor "over the affected part very lightly for about twenty minutes" he could effect remarkable cures of any kind of complaint, all the way from rheumatism to a tumor.[23] Perkins made a good thing of his invention, for he sold the tractors, "the intrinsic value of which might perhaps, amount to ninepence" for five guineas a pair. Naturally the purchasers of this expensive item were its most ardent advocates. "A man who has paid twenty-five dollars for his whistle," observed Holmes, "is likely to blow it louder and longer than other people." [24]

He scored another direct hit upon gullible laymen when he observed: "There is a class of minds which is more ready to believe that which is at first sight incredible, and because it is incredible, than what is generally thought reasonable." As an example he offered the line of thought pursued by the devotees of astrology who argue that because there is still some mystery in the motions of the planets, there is every possibility that the planets have some hand in the personal affairs of men.[25]

That "the statements of the unprofessional public" have much to do with the spread of any form of quackery, Holmes recognized; but:

those who know nothing of the natural progress of a malady, of its ordinary duration, of its various modes of terminating, of its liability to accidental complications, of the signs which mark its insignificance or severity, of what is to be expected of it when left to itself, or how much or how little is to be anticipated from remedies, those who know nothing or next to nothing of all these things, and who are in a great state of excitement from benevolence, sympathy, or zeal for a new medical discovery, can hardly be expected to be sound judges of facts which have misled so many sagacious men who have spent their lives in the daily study and observation of them. . . . Medical accuracy is not to be looked for in the florid reports of benevolent associations, the assertions of illustrious patrons, the lax effusions of daily journals, or the effervesent gossip of the tea-table.[26]

Such incompetent judges would be easily impressed by a homeopathist's exulting claim to having "cured" a case of jaundice in twenty-nine days, but, said the doctor, "I happened to have a case in my own household, a few weeks since, which lasted about ten days, and this was longer than I have repeatedly seen it in hospital practice, so that it was nothing to boast of." [27]

The public response to the lectures varied from the *Boston Post's* wish that the doctor had been less mild in his attack on the homeopathists, to the violent and florid pamphlet of a follower of Hahnemann, Robert Wesselhoeft, who seemed to think that to call Holmes an example of French materialism was to answer his arguments.[28] A literary paper, the *Quarto Boston Notion,* reporting on the second of three lectures, expressed the wish that "Dr. Holmes would publish a collection of his prose writings, including the lectures he has delivered within three or four years. They were inimitable of their kind. His style is quite remarkable for its terseness and point, and overflows with verbal wit and beautiful imagery." The writer of the article enthusiastically recalled Holmes's contributions to *New England Magazine*—the two papers "under the general title of the Breakfast-Table"—from which he had extracted some sentences which pleased him.[29] Holmes's literary reputation clung to him even in the observations of his professional colleagues; the writer of the notice in the *Boston Medical and Surgical Journal* described him as "alike celebrated for ready wit, a good song, and candid investigation." [30]

It was a candid investigation that he would produce in the year 1843. Settled now permanently in Boston, Dr. Holmes resumed his faithful attendance at the meetings of the Society for Medical Improvement. He still provided verses in "his usual witty manner," [31] and saw to it that the society's library was enlarged. It was in this period of the early forties that he made a large number of contributions to the society's museum.

Holmes's birthplace—the gambrel-roofed house

Dr. Holmes, seated second from left, with members of
the Boston Society for Medical Improvement—c. 1843

One of his papers for 1841 was on "Medical Characters in Paris," [32] about whom the group had earlier expressed a wish to hear again. For another meeting he prepared a paper on giants and managed to produce a real one for illustration. Mr. Freeman, advertised as the "Giant from the West," obligingly (for five dollars, that is) came around to the society's rooms to exhibit himself.[33] The doctor's interest in such abnormalities was excessive, but he was not alone in his curiosity. One of his wife's numerous cousins described a visit made to a dwarf with Dr. James Jackson and Dr. Holmes. "Uncle James and Dr. Holmes were both perfectly crazy about him, went to see him very often & Uncle J. went around the family urging them to go see him." [34]

More important, however, in June 1842, another of Holmes's former instructors, Dr. Walter Channing, was bringing to his attention a subject of vital significance. At a meeting of the Boston Society for Medical Improvement on June 28, the obstetrician reported upon thirteen "fatal cases of puerperal fever." [35] Five months later, on November 28, Channing gave an account of a second series of cases,[36] a report which, in the minds of his audience, would necessarily be colored by facts which they had learned at a meeting in October. For that meeting on October 11, 1842, at which Holmes presided, Dr. John Fisher gave an account of two cases, the one of a physician, the other of a medical student, who had suffered dissection wounds incurred while performing an autopsy. The wounds of both became infected, and both became seriously ill; the doctor, after a long siege, recovered, but the medical student died. The autopsy had been upon the body of a woman who had died from puerperal—childbed—fever, that disease which alone accounted for the terrifyingly high mortality rate among women in confinement.[37] Meanwhile, in Philadelphia a whole series of puerperal fever cases occurring in the practice of local physicians had prompted Dr. Francis Condie to address the Philadelphia College of Physicians on the disease. In the course of his speech he suggested the possibility that the disease might be contagious.[38] It was no new suggestion; English physicians had for the past fifty years made the same observation from time to time, but the leading obstetricians and the standard texts on their subject either did not mention the possibility of contagion, or if they did mention it, did so only to reject the idea. The Philadelphia *Medical Examiner* for January 21, 1843, for instance, printed a letter, about the cases upon which Dr. Condie had reported, in which the author—a leading American obstetrician, teacher of the subject, and author of the standard text—dismissed the idea of contagion as nonsense, accounting for the extraordinary number of cases in the one physician's practice by the fact that his practice was very large.[39]

Dr. Holmes, a careful reader of medical journals, began in December to look up information about the disease.[40] On January 9 the subject of puerperal fever again came up for discussion before the Boston society. The meeting made so sharp an impression on Dr. Holmes that he entered a note of it in his casebook.[41] Not only did Dr. Channing report further cases of puerperal fever, but also Dr. John B. S. Jackson gave an account of another death from a dissection wound; like the medical student in Fisher's report, Dr. Barker of Lynn had died after performing an autopsy on a puerperal patient.[42]

Ill himself during most of January, Holmes nevertheless turned up for the meeting of January 23. The subject of the last meeting was resumed; "Dr. John Jackson asked the opinion of the Society as to the contagion of Puerperal Fever, and the probability of physicians communicating it from one patient to another. An animated discussion followed and on motion of Dr. Jackson it was voted that it be continued at the next meeting." [43]

Dr. Holmes's borrowings from the Athenaeum Library suddenly jumped in number.[44] As his researches led him on, he began to badger his friends whose experience in practice was larger than his. It did not take long for the mounting array of factual evidence to arouse the doctor. His study had convinced him not only that puerperal fever was highly contagious but that obstetricians, nurses, and midwives were active agents of infection, carrying the dreaded disease from the bedside of one mother to that of the next. And it was this last terrible fact that moved him to action. In "a great heat and with passionate indignation," [45] Holmes wrote the argument for the prosecution.

Twenty-one days after Dr. John Jackson asked his question, Dr. Holmes presented to the group the answer. The secretary's entry reads: "Dr. Holmes read a paper upon the Contagion of Puerperal Fever. On a motion made by Dr. Storer, seconded by Dr. Jackson, it was voted that Dr. Holmes be requested to publish the paper." [46]

He was so convinced that he began his essay with a scornful refusal to treat the matter of contagiousness as in any way debatable. "I would not consent to make a *question* of a momentous fact which is no longer to be considered as a subject for trivial discussion, but to be acted upon with silent promptitude." [47] It was the ex-law student who spoke, rather than the doctor, playing the roles of prosecuting attorney and judge, marshaling the ordered array of evidence, delivering the charges, and passing the sentence. The etiology, the morphology of the disease interested him not at all. It was the one fact— that the obstetrician is himself culpable—that he sought to demonstrate; doctor after doctor, from among the dead and the living, were called upon to give their testimony. And no jury could fail to render a verdict of guilty.

There is no tone deep enough for regret, and no voice loud enough for warning. . . . God forbid that any member of the profession to which [a woman] trusts her life, doubly precious at that eventful period, should hazard it negligently, unadvisedly, or selfishly.[48]

He ends his essay with eight rules for the obstetrician, concluding:

Whatever indulgence may be granted to those who have heretofore been the ignorant causes of so much misery, the time has come when the existence of a *private pestilence* in the sphere of a single physician should be looked upon, not as a misfortune, but a crime; and in the knowledge of such occurrences the duties of the practitioner should give way to his paramount obligations to society.[49]

No one before Holmes had attempted to gather together the records of individual physicians; no one had surveyed the literature of the disease. Holmes found that as early as 1773 Charles White of Manchester had concluded that puerperal fever is contagious and advised precautions. From time to time after that date, other doctors had speculated upon the possibilities, with different degrees of conviction. In 1795 Dr. Alexander Gordon, of Aberdeen, had been certain of the fact, on the basis of his personal experience. Thomas Denman in 1801 and Robert Collins in 1835 had expressed a similar conviction, the latter appreciably reducing the mortality rate in a Dublin hospital by using disinfectants.[50] Holmes called upon all these helpful witnesses as he marshaled his evidence in a manner more clear and incontrovertible than that of his predecessors. He collected their suggestions for precautionary measures and added a few of his own, emphasizing the physician's moral and social responsibility. What perhaps was most important, no one before Holmes had clothed the damning facts in persuasive eloquence, informed by passionate indignation and unshakable conviction.

But the Boston Society for Medical Improvement was a small private club of local physicians; however valuable its activities were to individual members, its doings were not likely to attract much attention outside Boston. In 1843, however, the society had undertaken to publish a magazine, *The New England Quarterly Journal of Medicine and Surgery,* and in the fourth number, the issue for April 1843, of the only volume of the magazine ever published, appeared at pages 503-530, Holmes's essay on "The Contagiousness of Puerperal Fever." This periodical, which had only a small circulation, and a few offprints from it, which Holmes had struck off for himself— in too small a quantity as he later realized—were the only means by which his arguments and evidence were disseminated in their entirety.

An abstract of the essay appeared in the July issue of the *American Journal of the Medical Sciences,*[51] a periodical with a much wider circulation than the abortive magazine of the

Boston Society for Medical Improvement. The two-page abstract was a much less persuasive argument than the original, for Holmes's own essay was powerful in the sheer weight of the number of cases cited by him and in the moving quality of his rhetoric. It was not, however, the essay itself, but this brief abstract which attracted attention. The *American Journal* was flooded with communications on the subject not for months, but for years afterwards, the most lengthy and important being the account of Dr. Samuel Kneeland in the issue for January, 1846.[52]

It was the abstract which William Farr, pioneer medical statistician and Registrar-General of Great Britain, commented upon for ten pages in his Fifth Annual Report; he did not see the original essay. Holmes, who reviewed the Registrar-General's reports for the Society for Medical Improvement, was pleased to find his ideas there noted, although regretful that the abstract had led Mr. Farr to say that he had not gone far enough. But on this subject, Holmes showed no trace of conceit. His indignation over what he did not hesitate to call the criminal negligence of the members of his own profession was sincere, passionate, and impersonal. "But any concern I may take personally in the matter is trifling," he said in this review, "compared to the great interests involved—the lives of hundreds and thousands of women who are liable to be poisoned in their beds by a pestilence that walks at noonday into their chamber—and charges it may be a guinea a visit for dispersing the deadliest of diseases to a young and innocent mother." [53] In 1852 Copland's *Medical Dictionary,* in the article on the disease, took up the argument *for* contagion, giving full credit and praise to Holmes's essay of 1843, and printing his conclusions in full.

But for a period of about a dozen years, the question of whether or not puerperal fever was carried from patient to patient by negligent doctors remained a matter of debate. The files of the *Boston Medical and Surgical Journal* show that the subject became a matter of frequent comment immediately after Holmes's 1843 essay was published. Anxious country doctors guiltily and honestly reported their experiences and their conviction that the disease was contagious.

But the prevailing opinion seemed to be that the question was unsettled. A little over a year after Holmes read his paper, Dr. Channing (who had not been present on February 13, 1843), read a paper of his own *against* the contagiousness of the disease. "From his own experience he would never hesitate to visit other patients and to take charge of women in labor, when attending puerperal cases as a consulting physician." [54] American textbooks of obstetrics still did not recognize, did in fact deny, the contagiousness of the disease. Even in New England, where physicians had had more chance than they had elsewhere to become familiar with Holmes's whole argument, the subject was still open enough to warrant the Massachusetts Medical Society's appointing in 1849 a committee of obstetricians to investigate it. The wording of the committee's instructions indicates that there was still some question about Dr. Holmes's views, but that it was necessary to act upon them. The committee was, therefore, to investigate precautionary measures. [55] The general concern with the subject seems to have fluctuated considerably until 1852 when Dr. Hugh L. Hodge, Professor of Obstetrics in the University of Pennsylvania, published a volume *On the Non-Contagiousness of Puerperal Fever*. In 1854, a second Philadelphia physician, Dr. Charles D. Meigs, Professor of Midwifery and the Diseases of Women and Children, at Jefferson Medical College, saw fit to include in his book *Childbed Fevers,* a long attack upon the concept of contagion. He himself preferred to attribute the many deaths from this disease "to accident, or Providence." [56] Both Hodge and Meigs, who, as obstetricians, supposed authorities in their field, and professors, could not brook any idea which called their authority in question, were abusive and violent in their allusions to Holmes. Meigs, for example, tried to dismiss Holmes's essay as among "the jejeune and fizzenless dreamings of sophomore writers." [57] In Europe, Semmelweis was being greeted similarly with abuse and insult for his insistence upon the contagiousness of the disease and the necessity of taking precautions. Coming to that conclusion in 1846, he had instituted hygienic practices in his hospital wards and had published his findings in 1847, only to encounter opposition much more vindictive than that accorded Holmes, who was fortunate in having his ideas accepted by his immediate colleagues so that he never suffered the Hungarian's personal martyrdom. It is significant that Semmelweis's authoritative support came from men who were *not* obstetricians, men like Skoda and Hebra.

The impulse to answer Meigs and Hodge may have come first from Holmes's old Dartmouth friend, Elisha Bartlett, who asked for a copy of the essay that he might have ammunition against the Philadelphians. "How the hungry heads of that Hydra keep shouting out!" he wrote.[58] But it was Meigs's book which finally evoked response. In January 1855, Holmes republished his essay under the more meaningful, if cacophonous, title *Puerperal Fever as a Private Pestilence*. To it he added an introduction, addressed particularly to medical students. "I had rather," he wrote, not without sarcastic intention, "rescue one mother from being poisoned by her attendant, than claim to have saved forty out of fifty patients to whom I had carried the disease. Thus I am willing to avail myself of any hint coming from without to offer this paper once more to the press. The occasion has presented itself, as will be seen, in a convenient if not flattering form." [59] At the art of polite insult, Holmes was considerably more adept than his opponents.

To Holmes the fact that the doctrine he had advanced in 1843 was still treated as a *question* was sufficient reason for reprinting the original essay. Moreover, he knew that Professors Meigs and Hodge were "sure to be listened to, not only by their immediate pupils, but by the profession at large." [60] Their power was that of men assumed to be authorities on the subject.

These two reflections unleashed all Holmes's powers of eloquence; and for once, at least, his eloquence was not out of proportion to the significance of the subject. At the close of the introductory material added in the 1855 essay, Holmes wrote:

I am too much in earnest for either humility or vanity, but I do entreat those who hold the keys of life and death to listen to me also for this once. I ask no personal favor; but I beg to be heard on behalf of the women whose lives are at stake, until some stronger voice shall plead for them. . . . let it be remembered that this is no subject to be smoothed over by nicely adjusted phrases of half-assent and half-censure divided between the parties. The balance must be struck boldly and the result declared plainly. . . . Let it be remembered that *persons* are nothing in this matter; better that twenty pamphleteers should be silenced, or as many professors unseated, than that one mother's life should be taken. . . .

Indifference will not do here; our Journals and Committees have no right to take up their pages with minute anatomy and tediously detailed cases, while it is a question whether or not the 'black death' of child-bed is to be scattered broadcast by the agency of the mother's friend and adviser. Let the men who mould opinions look to it; if there is any voluntary blindness, any interested oversight, any culpable negligence, even in such a matter, and the facts shall reach the public ear; the pestilence-carrier of the lying-in chamber must look to God for pardon, for man will never forgive him.[61]

After such an appeal, any reader would find it hard to ignore the evidence set forth in abundance. *The American Journal of the Medical Sciences,* which had recognized the 1843 paper with a two-page abstract without comment, acknowledged the 1855 paper with an enthusiastic review.[62] Dr. Walter Channing changed his mind and wrote an article confirming Holmes's views. A year later, in a communication to the *Boston Medical and Surgical Journal,* an obstetrician remarked that the contagiousness of puerperal fever was now generally admitted. "There are those in other sections of the country who deny its contagion—but they have been nearly silenced by the masterly essay of Dr. Holmes." [63] In the same year the committee on medical literature of the American Medical Association added the 1855 essay to its list of recommended titles.[64] A reviewer of the 1857 edition of Meigs's *Obstetrics* corrected him for the error to which he still clung, and cited as the final authority Dr. Oliver Wendell Holmes.[65]

Occasional Poet

He ... exerted his talents in occasional composi-
tion.

A MONTH AFTER his puerperal fever essay was first printed, Holmes received a plea for some verses. Across the bottom of the letter from Harvard's Phi Beta Kappa Society, he noted that he had already given them a poem in 1836.[1] Still he obligingly served as a vice-president for the annual dinner and produced some couplets for "An After-Dinner Poem." The poet's mood was satiric, but his time was limited and he observed quite justly that:

> in strains like these
> The native juice, the really honest squeeze—
> Strains that, diluted to the twentieth power,
> In yon grave temple might have filled an hour.[2]

The allusion to the homeopathic doctor's method of diluting his drugs is characteristic of the whole poem, which darts from one topical allusion to another: the Dickens dinner of the year before, the current fashions in dress, in verse, in medicine, in philosophy—leaving in each a barb of wit. The transcendentalists fare badly. Holmes had obviously been reading the *Dial.*

> Here babbling "Insight" shouts in Nature's ears
> His last conundrum on the orbs and spheres;
> There self-inspection sucks its little thumb,
> With "Whence am I?" and "Wherefore did I come?"
> Deluded infants! will they ever know
> Some doubts must darken o'er the world below
> Though all the Platos of the nursery trail
> Their "clouds of glory" at the go-cart's tail?

> Oh might these couplets their attention claim
> That gain their author the Philistine's name! [3]

Three years later Holmes wrote a letter in which he revealed a change in his attitude toward Emerson's poetry, as well as an awareness of his own limitations. Acknowledging a volume of Emerson's poems, he admitted that he had read them at first, as they appeared in the *Dial,* more for their faults than their virtues, feeling irritated by false rhymes and awkward rhythms and baffled by the obscurity of some passages.

It is by the way very strange to me that you who recognize the constancy of the rhythmical element in nature should sometimes undervalue it as you do as a means of expression—and as if to disprove your own profession on this point I have noticed that almost every passage which has struck me most by the beauty or strength of the thought has made the language that conveyed it melodious in spite of your carelessness.

The best poems and passages in this volume of yours may be perhaps those that to me are vague and mystical. I have nothing to do with thoughts that roll beyond a certain width or orbit—I know them only by the perturbations their influence occasions in my own narrower range—but my sight is not strong enough to make out their substance. We must be modest in these matters I know—much that to you returns a clear and simple image seems to me to refract and distort the divine idea it professes to transmit—my organs are very likely to be in fault, but this is one of the last things that the dull eyed and limited can discover.

He found himself coming back to many of the poems ("Monadnoc," for one), liking the "wild strawberry flavor" of some, and admiring—with a reservation—the "unquestionable genuineness . . . with which your descriptions of common scenes and feelings are wrought." His feeling was finally that, in spite of what were to him defects, Emerson was "one who loves, reads, and interprets nature." He wrote his letter not to offer the poet praise, which he supposed Emerson neither cared about nor needed, but to let him know that "one mind so different in tendencies and habits from many of those whose intercourse with your own has been closest, has been able to enter with delight into the recesses of your robust but infinitely subtle intelligence." [4]

For his satiric allusions to Emerson in his "After-Dinner Poem," Holmes expected—with reason—to catch it from Emerson's admirers, but as an occasional piece the poem was too momentary to warrant more than civil praise for its felicity. Not a "professional" poet, the doctor was primarily an after-dinner versifier, who could be counted on to help honor a visiting celebrity like Dickens, to produce appropriately patriotic lines for a celebration of the landing of the Pilgrims, or to lighten the solemnities of the inauguration of a college president with lines that make fun of his own role. In his poem for Edward Everett's inauguration, "A Modest Request," the poet imagines himself peacefully enjoying a pleasant morning in his own back parlor, but unfortunately:

> No iron gate, no spiked and panelled door,
> Can keep out death, the postman, or the bore.

"The door-bell jingles" and the poet takes a letter from the box.

Dear sir,—
> In writing on a former day,
> One little matter I forgot to say;
> I now inform you in a single line,
> On Thursday next our purpose is to *dine.*
> The act of feeding, as you understand,
> Is but a fraction of the work in hand;
> Its nobler half is that ethereal meat
> The papers call "the intellectual treat". . . .
>
> And since success your varied gifts attends,
> We—that is, I and all your numerous friends—
> Expect from you—your single self a host—
> A speech, a song, excuse me, *and* a toast;
> Nay, not to haggle on so small a claim,
> A few of each or several of the same. . . .

The poet naturally becomes a little hysterical at the demands made upon him, while his wife tries to soothe him and offers him a strong drink. The rest of the poem is the speech, song, and toast, as requested, for the dinner on the occasion of Edward Everett's inauguration as President of Harvard College.[5]

Holmes's appearances as an occasional poet were becoming numerous, and the occasions themselves were more public than before. He had from the first been in the habit of amusing his fellow-physicians with verses, and he had twice appeared in the role of Phi Beta Kappa poet. In 1842 at a city affair, the Dickens dinner, the English consul in Boston, T. Colley Grattan, had been moved to remark that the "chairman's four *vices* were as good as the four cardinal virtues of any other man." [6] Of the four vice-presidents for this occasion, Holmes was the one to be called on again and again to fulfil a similar function.

In these poems of the forties, his themes are contemporary manners and customs, follies upon which he made his own critical comment. The most ambitious of them, a long poem "Urania," was first delivered before the Boston Mercantile Library Association on October 14, 1845. Opening with allusions to his profession as a doctor, he described himself as still loyal to the Muses, specifically to Urania, a "truant, not recreant" to the claims of poetry. What he was not willing to admit to begging editors, he confessed to his audience.

He knew that his audience was on the alert for jokes; "remembering some expansive line let loose among the nuts and wine," they were all impatience till the opening pun. Recalling "The Height of the Ridiculous," Holmes observed:

> I know a tailor, once a friend of mine,
> Expects great doings in the button line.

The unfortunate poet was in the position of all persons who have got themselves too good a reputation as jesters, and he tried here to put his audience in a frame of mind suitable to the seriousness he felt himself. He did not want to play the "stage buffoon." [7] What happens in the poem is what so often happens when a wit deliberately forsakes his natural role; Holmes becomes sentimental. In proportion as he tries to be more serious, he becomes less natural.

His subject matter ranges from the "duty of religious charity" to advice on such minutiae as correct pronunciation and suitable neckwear. His expression varies accordingly from over-strained rhetoric to good colloquial phrases. The reader does not suffer when the insidious demands of the poet's rhyme lead him to over-expansion of the thought, so long as the thought is satiric; but no allowances, that can be made because the poem was meant for oral delivery, can excuse some of the turgid passages where the poet labors to give weight to commonplace solemnities. As he drops from the lofty to the trivial, he changes his language from that of conventional poetic diction to that of plain talk, much to the reader's relief. Holmes, who never pretended that boredom was not sometimes a condition of life, gets off the following realistic situation.

> I tell in verse,— 't were better done in prose,—
> One curious trick that everybody knows;
> Once form this habit, and it's very strange
> How long it sticks, how hard it is to change.
> Two friendly people, both disposed to smile,
> Who meet, like others, every little while,
> Instead of passing with a pleasant bow,
> And "How d' ye do?" or "How's your uncle now?"
> Impelled by feelings in their nature kind,
> But slightly weak, and somewhat undefined,
> Rush at each other, make a sudden stand,
> Begin to talk, expatiate, and expand;
> Each looks quite radiant, seems extremely struck,
> Their meeting so was such a piece of luck;
> Each thinks the other thinks he's greatly pleased
> To screw the vice in which they both are squeezed;
> So there they talk, in dust, or mud, or snow,
> Both bored to death, and both afraid to go! [8]

In the concluding portion of the poem, he turns arbitrarily to the subject of a national poet, commenting upon the romantic desire for a "native bard" which had so often been expressed by American writers. Although he was no less critical of America's cultural dependence upon England than Emerson, and although he believed that any writer needed to draw his material from his own environment, he had no faith in:

> . . . . the odd notion that the poet's dreams
> Grow in the ratio of his hills and streams,

and he mocks the idea that the aforesaid "bard":

> Pink of the future, fancy's pattern-card,
> The babe of nature in the "giant West,"
> Must be of course her biggest and her best.[9]

In another way, "Urania" shows Holmes leaning to the right in matters of moment in the period. Although the poem begins with mildly radical views on religion, it ends with some middle-of-the-road political reflections. What he foresees from the antislavery struggle is disunion. The vagueness of his political allusions, the use of ambiguous images, and the windy rhetoric would be likely to prevent any listener from getting the full import of his lines. But one private reader of the poem, James Russell Lowell, missed none of its implications and was prompted to write the author a long letter of criticism.

In 1846, Lowell and his young wife were living at Elmwood in Cambridge; Lowell had just finished his stint as editor of the *Pennsylvania Freeman* and was not at the moment the editor of any of the antislavery journals, but he was a contributor to them; his sentiments on the matter of the Mexican War were of course being made very plain through the mouth of the irrepressible Hosea Biglow. It was that period in Lowell's life when he was most actively the advocate of causes which would then be considered radical; he had, moreover, grown out of the unsympathetic attitude toward Emerson and the Emersonians which he had expressed satirically in his schoolboy poem for his graduation from Harvard College. In 1846 he was at all points very far to the left, as Holmes very obviously was not. He seems, moreover, to have been so far fired with reformer's zeal that he was ready to undertake the reformation of a fellow-poet, his senior by a decade. His letter, which unfortunately does not survive, was written shortly after he read the poem; Holmes's reply is dated November 29:

I have read your letter, as I believe, in the same spirit as that in which it was written. There is nothing in its frankness which offends me—on the contrary, that is the very quality in it which makes it valuable and acceptable. . . .[10]

Lowell had accused him of lining up against the "Causes" of the day: peace, temperance, claims of the poor, reform in general, and antislavery. Although he saw no justification for the Mexican War in which the country was then engaged, Holmes could—in lines echoed years later by his son—observe:

> I cannot shut my eyes to the beauty of heroism and self-devotion which the battle-field has witnessed. I think our fathers were right in taking up arms to defend their liberties, and I have even now a mitigated and *quasi* kind of satisfaction in hearing of the courage and constancy of our countrymen in so poor a quarrel as we are engaged in.[11]

As for temperance, he was not a teetotaler; he admits to having written verses "in which the pleasures of convivial excitement were, perhaps, too warmly drawn." But these lines he had never printed. That he was "not wholly insensible to the significance of this particular reform" was borne out, he wrote, by the fact that he refused to rent a store to a grocer, "knowing that rum would be retailed from it." The gesture meant a substantial loss.

For the poor, he was "ready to lend . . . cordial support to such practical measures as furnishing them with better dwellings and similar movements." He was not an out-and-out conservative, as Lowell seemed to think, being a firm republican in politics. "The idea of my belonging to the party that resists all change is an entire misconception." Among physicians he was at the extreme left.

> I may be lazy, or indifferent, or timid, but I am by no means one of those . . . who are wedded for better or worse to the *status quo*, with an iron ring that reason cannot get away unless it takes the finger with it.

As for slavery, he considered "disunion the most vital matter at present," but he was "glad there are always eloquent men to keep the moral sense of the world alive on the subject." In what is plainly an allusion to Longfellow's recently published *Poems on Slavery*, Holmes observed justly that "nothing is so flat and unprofitable as weakly flavored verses relating to it. Did you ever see a volume of lines—not by you or me—that illustrated this fact?"[12] On these issues Holmes would not change his mind for another decade.

In spite of his avowed fidelity to literature, Holmes did not regard himself as a professional poet, although he allowed a small edition of his poems, reprinting those in the 1836 volume and adding a few written since that date, to be published in England. His appearance as an "occasional" poet, his publication in England, and his production of a poem like "Urania" for the lyceum platform, however, kept his literary reputation alive while he gave most of his time and energies to the profession of medicine. He still refused to consider himself as "one of the regular army of litterateurs," [13] as he told the persistent editor of *Godey's,* Sarah J. Hale. To another editor, John Keese, he admitted that writing for print had charms. "If I once open the door to these requests not only will less worthy editors swoop upon me like so many kites, but I shall be like the wolf that has tasted blood and get the itch of writing into my finger-ends again." If Mr. Keese should be ill, however, the doctor was ready " *'saigner, piquer, et clystériser,'* in the words of Molière's comedy, until you cry enough." [14]

As his casebooks show, his practice had grown more extensive. Among his patients were John Lothrop Motley and his family; Charles Sumner's brother George; John T. Morse, whose son, now three years old, would eventually write the doctor's biography. Morse, whose recollections of his subject as a doctor included memories of unpleasant doses, has not much to say about Holmes as a practitioner. Toward the end of his life, Motley, however, writing Holmes from England, where he was in the hands of the royal physician, wished himself in America and Holmes back in practice that he might be treated by his favorite doctor. [15]

The desire Holmes had expressed to his classmate, Clarke, in 1836 was now being realized. He had secured the position in the community that he so much wanted. Harvard had called him back to serve on examination committees; the Massachusetts Medical Society asked him not only for verses to brighten their annual dinners but also for work on the committee to improve the state's system of compiling vital statistics, on the committee to correct the records on insanity

184

among Negroes, on the committee on publications. He was now acting as secretary for the Boylston Prize committee. He was a member of the American Academy of Arts and Sciences, ultimately its recording secretary, and an active contributor to its proceedings, usually offering some small anatomical discovery or some new improvement in his microscopes.

"Fifteen years," he had told the members of the Boylston Medical Society in 1844, "are required to obtain a good city practice . . . where no accidental aid, or peculiar good fortune conspires with the requisite industry and ability." [16] The speaker's accidental aid had come in the shape of his connections with Dr. James Jackson; Holmes's own experience lay behind the address, delivered to an audience of medical students, on the subject of their "positions and prospects." The content of the speech was not entirely worldly and personal. He had told them, too, of the new discoveries to be hoped for from the use of the microscope, the development of chemistry, and the wholesale wiping out of the errors of the eighteenth-century empirical systems. Not without justifiable vanity, he could not suppress an allusion to his own essay on puerperal fever.

He had prepared his listeners to encounter the kind of misunderstanding and suspicion that George Eliot was to dramatize in *Middlemarch* with her doctor-hero, Lydgate, who like Holmes had been exposed to French science, specifically to P. C. A. Louis. Quoting from a medical poem he had offered his colleagues the year before, the poet-doctor had expressed with fervor the respect for science he had learned in Paris, for a kind of science that can survive misrepresentation and charlatanism:

> The feeble sea-birds, blinded in the storms,
> On some tall lighthouse dash their little forms,
> And the rude granite scatters for their pains
> Those small deposits that were meant for brains.[17]

Editors still pursued him only to receive the inevitable "no"; by 1846 he had a new reason to offer for his refusal—the patients at the Massachusetts General Hospital. Two new

185

wings added to the hospital made it necessary to enlarge the staff of visiting physicians and surgeons. Holmes, Henry I. Bowditch, and John Dix Fisher were appointed as physicians; Jonathan Mason Warren, Samuel Parkman, and Henry Jacob Bigelow, as surgeons. The *Boston Evening Transcript* reported the appointments with vague disapproval and with a reference to "inexperienced" men.[18] With one exception, the men appointed had been in active practice for at least a decade; the exception was the twenty-eight-year-old Henry J. Bigelow, who might be described as "inexperienced"; it was Bigelow, however, who would very soon play a major part in a dramatic event of the year.

On Monday evening, November 2, 1846, young Bigelow in a state of great excitement came to call at 8 Montgomery Place.[19] He wanted to read a paper to Dr. Holmes—a paper so important in subject that its writer was certain that what he had to say would be heard around the world. It was natural for Bigelow to seek his former teacher's opinion of the literary quality of his paper; he probably counted also on Holmes's appreciation of the events his paper described—events which Holmes had not witnessed. The paper was primarily an account of two operations performed at the Massachusetts General Hospital on October 16 and 17; on those dates Holmes was well occupied at home, for his third child, Edward Jackson, was born on the 17th.

At ten o'clock on the morning of October 16, a group of surgeons and medical students had gathered in the amphitheater of the hospital. The surgeon, seventy-three-year-old John Collins Warren, was ready and waiting; the patient, who was to be the subject of an experiment, may presumably have been a little nervous, all the more so because of the delay. The instigator of the experiment, W. T. G. Morton, was fifteen minutes late for his appointment. If the Hollywood version of the adventures of the dentist Morton improved on the story to the extent of making the patient a touchingly pale maiden with no unsightly blemish for the camera's eye, instead of an unromantic youth with a congenital tumor on his neck, it was entirely faithful to the fact in representing the hero's last-minute entrance. The real Morton had actually spent a sleepless night trying to get together an effective inhaler, an instrument he needed for his part in the performance which was to make such an impression on the youngest of the hospital surgeons.

A few moments after his arrival, Morton could tell the surgeon that his patient was ready; the operation itself was a simple one of a kind Warren had often performed in his long career; but this operation differed from the others in one respect. The patient felt almost no pain. The dentist Morton had rendered him insensible with sulphuric ether. On the following day, Morton again administered ether to a patient upon whom Dr. George Hayward performed a somewhat more complicated operation than the one of the day before. This time the patient felt no pain at all.

Henry J. Bigelow knew that he had witnessed the first successful step in the conquest of pain. For the surgeon, the discovery removed the greatest obstacle in the way of his further progress. For the patient, it brought immediate relief from the horror of the operating room. The doubts of the value of the discovery and the fears of its possible dangers which disturbed other surgeons did not affect Bigelow. He tried out the ether on himself; he observed the effects of it upon Morton's dental patients and listened to the dentist's accounts of his experiments. By November 2, he was ready with his paper, reading it aloud to a listener who recognized the importance of the discovery. On November 18, the paper, with additions, was printed simultaneously in the *Boston Daily Advertiser* and the *Boston Medical and Surgical Journal*. On the 21st, Dr. Holmes addressed the following letter (italics mine) to the dentist Morton.

Everybody wants to have a hand in a great discovery. All I will do is to give a hint or two as to names—or the name—to be applied to the state produced and the agent.

The state should I think be called *"Anaesthesia."* This signifies insensibility. . . .

The adjective will be *"Anaesthetic."* Thus we might say the state of Anaesthesia or the Anaesthetic state.

I should have a name pretty soon, and consult some accomplished scholar . . . before fixing *the terms, which will be repeated by the tongues of every civilized race of mankind.*[20]

In the long years of bickering about who discovered ether anesthesia, Holmes followed the lead of his colleagues on the hospital staff and gave his support to Morton against the rival claimants: the Boston chemist Charles Jackson, the dentist Horace Wells of Hartford, and Dr. Crawford Long of Georgia. The principle behind this allegiance to Morton was that the credit belonged to him who made the discovery known; it had been Morton who persuaded a distinguished surgeon to make an official trial of ether. Holmes was willing to write a personal letter to his former classmate, Isaac Morse, Congressman from Louisiana, when Morton pressed his claim before Congress.[21] He was not, however, willing to make himself Morton's active champion. In 1857 when the irate dentist asked his help against Charles T. Jackson, Holmes refused. As he explained to Dana:

Although it is clear as day that J jumped up behind, he is a good natured fellow enough, and one does not care to tug at his little red ribbons and other "crachats" as the Frenchmen coarsely call those decorations—But if the question is publicly agitated once more, my testimony and opinion will be where they always have been with Mr. Morton—the winter of whose discontent I hope yet to change into "etherial mildness" (Thomson).[22]

Holmes could not forbear a pun under any circumstances. When Boston debated the question of erecting a statue to the discoverer, Jackson or Morton, Holmes could not resist the opening and suggested that the monument be dedicated to "ether."

Holmes's role in the drama of 1846 was a small one, but it was one more link in the friendship between him and Henry J. Bigelow, an association which was to have its effects upon the course of medical education. Both men were then on the staff of the Tremont School, and both were soon to join the faculty of Harvard.

When John Collins Warren performed the memorable operation on October 16, he was about to begin his last year of service at the Harvard Medical School, where he had taught anatomy and surgery for thirty-one years. In February, Warren sent in his resignation; on April 7, the *Boston Medical and Surgical Journal* prematurely announced the appointment of Oliver Wendell Holmes as Parkman Professor of Anatomy and Physiology, describing the new professor as "a talented and eloquent lecturer, and an accomplished scholar and man of science." [23] The appointment had not yet been confirmed by the board of overseers, and Holmes himself did not receive the notice of his still tentative appointment until two days after the *Journal's* premature announcement.[24] By the end of April the matter was definitely settled, and Holmes was writing President Everett to resign from the college examination committee upon which he was supposed to serve, giving his work at the hospital and his position as a member of the faculty as his reasons.[25]

Dean of the Medical School

1847–1850

*He was generally seen with a circle of young
students around him whom he was entertaining
with his wit.*

THE CHAIR to which Holmes had been appointed did
not carry with it any salary; named in honor of George Parkman, it was the college's recognition of Dr. Parkman's gift of
land on North Grove Street upon which the medical school had
just erected a new building. As a new member of the medical
faculty, Holmes inherited with the other professors a burden
of debt; the much-needed new building cost more than the
faculty had bargained for, and the debt had to be paid off from
the faculty's earnings, out of which came, also, all the expenses
incurred for their courses. A professor's compensation was derived wholly from the fees paid by the students who elected to
attend his lectures. As Professor of Anatomy, Holmes was in a
slightly better position than his colleagues, for he had always
the largest number of students. But his income, like that of his
colleagues, would at best be uncertain and had to be aug-
mented by labors outside the school—by private practice,
teaching, and, in Holmes's case, by lyceum lecturing. For one
member of the Harvard medical faculty, this financial insecurity led to a tragedy. For all of them, it was a powerful
factor in their subsequent stand on the subject of medical
education.

In 1847, however, the move into a new building and Warren's resignation were the signals for a few improvements in
the college program. The Hersey Professorship of Anatomy

Bowdoin Square, Boston;
Boston-Cambridge horse-car in the foreground—1853

Massachusetts General Hospital (left) and Harvard Medical School—1853

and Surgery which Warren had held required its incumbent to give lectures on anatomy to undergraduates. Receiving the notice of Warren's retirement, the Harvard Corporation voted to appoint, as the new Hersey Professor of Anatomy, Jeffries Wyman who would lecture only to undergraduates; the Parkman Professorship being created especially for the Medical School. The teaching of operative surgery was separated from anatomy and allocated to the Professor of Clinical Surgery, George Hayward. Two new "subjects" were recognized: physiology in the Parkman Professorship, and pathology in the new post assigned to John Barnard Swett Jackson. These changes brought the faculty and the subjects taught up to seven so that when the new term began in November 1847, the Harvard Medical School was in that respect in line with the resolutions passed in May by the newly founded American Medical Association. The Medical Faculty now included, besides the new appointees, John Webster (chemistry), Walter Channing (obstetrics), John Ware (theory and practice), Jacob Bigelow (materia medica), and George Hayward (surgery).[1]

Channing relinquished the post of Dean of the Medical Faculty to Dr. Holmes, who held the post for six years, 1847-53. As Dean, Holmes had a number of tedious clerical duties to fulfil. Besides making out the school's circulars and its reports to the college, Holmes acted as intermediary between the faculty and the college. Curiously, although the school functioned almost completely apart from the college, the overseers now and then interfered in bothersome ways. Over so small a matter as the format of the diplomas, for instance, there was trouble. The college had ordered a very expensive one for which the medical faculty had to pay; their protest was greeted with the announcement that a faculty had no legitimate existence and no authority as a body.[2] The ambiguous political relations between the college and the medical school, like the uncertain financial arrangements, affected the attitude of the older members of the faculty when the question of reform came up.

The perennial question of the admission of women went

through various stages of indecision, counter-decision, and general confusion. Holmes as Dean encountered the problem at once. He was himself not opposed to teaching women, and his recommendation to the overseers that Harriot K. Hunt be admitted was unequivocal.[3] The overseers remained consistently opposed to admitting women; the medical faculty fluctuated from time to time, but usually Holmes was the solitary advocate for women. He was not prepared, however, to fight for their rights.

His literary talents probably had something to do, also, with his being called upon to give the school's opening address. On November 3, the Harvard Medical School was officially opened with a public introductory lecture by Professor Holmes. Such lectures, the traditional way of opening the college term, Holmes described as advertisements; in 1879, looking over his collection of them, he felt as if he were handling "Barnum's posters." [4] In 1847, Holmes may not have thought of his maiden speech at Harvard as a circus poster, but for its purpose it was as successful as anything Barnum could think up. The newspapers as well as the loyal *Boston Medical and Surgical Journal* were moved to comment on its brilliance; and three of Holmes's non-professional friends promptly asked if they might enroll in his course. Theodore Parker, William E. [?] Channing, and Thomas Dwight were promised tickets, and Theodore Parker, to whom the tickets were sent, was told that the professor would be glad to have them all in his class, but warned that they might be tired out with details. Holmes assured Parker that his feelings would not be hurt if they all gave up after the first dozen.[5]

The "best discourse ever given," as the local medical journal described it, was less factual and less witty than Holmes's usual public utterances. It was essentially the expression of its author's respect for his profession.[6] He thought the founding of the American Medical Association, to which he had gone as a delegate, was the most important evidence of the contemporary spirit of the profession. The national association was founded, Holmes told his audience, for the purpose of improving medical education and medical practice; the profession ought to welcome, not to fear, its criticisms, to look upon it as a source of benefit, not of danger.

The critical purposes of the association Holmes himself carried out. In 1848, as chairman of the Association's committee on medical literature, he turned in a report that caused not altogether favorable comment. He spoke out vigorously against the poverty of mind revealed in the country's medical writing; he deplored the profession's servility to England and the "habit of indolence generated by the easy acquisition of a foreign literature which seems to answer every necessary purpose." The country's numerous medical journals were even more parasitical than the authors of books. "The ring of editors sit in each other's laps, with a perfect propriety, and great convenience, it is true, but with a wonderful saving in the article of furniture." [7]

Meawhile at Harvard he was proving his reputation for eloquence. As a teacher at the Tremont School, he had become known for being able to make the subjects he taught interesting and exciting, even amusing, and for being able to make the dusty subject of anatomy lose some of its dryness. None of his students supposed him to be a brilliant scientist or a discoverer, although from time to time he added some small piece of information to anatomical knowledge; he was, however, thorough and conscientious.

The room where the doctor lectured was too small and crowded from the first—airless and uncomfortable. The hordes of students plunged down the steep tiers with a thunderous energy that threatened to break through the floor. The hour was one o'clock. Already overstuffed with words— their whole morning had been given to hearing lectures— weary and hungry, the young men challenged all the talents of the lecturer to keep them alert and attentive. Many of them were half-educated country boys; fewer than twenty-five per cent of them were college graduates. To this ill-prepared and weary crew, Holmes had to teach the essentials of his double subject in the space of less than four months.

His motto for the year, he had said in his introductory lecture, would be "illustration." And to fulfil this end he labored during the spring and summer. A connoisseur of anatomical iconography, Dr. Holmes could become excited and enthusiastic over any good example of it. It seems likely that his son's interest in fine engraving and particularly in Dürer may have been aroused by the handsome plates in the old books the doctor was so fond of. If it had been possible, Holmes would have liked to use nothing but the most beautiful plates; as it was he hired an artist to prepare copies. "I have spared no man's library," and he named Winslow Lewis and Agassiz as being especially helpful. He felt it important "to render visible everything which the eye can take cognizance of, and so to turn abstractions and catalogues of names into substantial and objective realities." [8] He got together charts, diagrams, models—all that would serve this end—all paid for out of his own pocket. The college anatomical museum, gift of his predecessor, John Collins Warren, provided other illustrative material; Holmes himself contributed to the museum a number of items, some preparations of his own making.[9]

He fixed up for himself an apology for an office in a "spacious but obscure and irregular crypt" [10] under the steep tiers of benches in the amphitheater where he met his class. Here Holmes went over his illustrative material, making certain that it was complete and good. The essential item was, of course, the dissection for the day. Holmes chose his demonstrators for their skill, and about this part of the work he was exacting. He gave these young men full credit, saying on one occasion that he thought a good demonstrator was more important than a good lecturer,[11] and showing always a lively admiration for a well-prepared specimen.

Part of his success as a lecturer was owing to this capacity for enthusiasm, an unrecapturable quality, the existence of which we take on faith although some of it is hinted at in such verses as "The Living Temple" originally called "The Anatomist's Hymn." The brain he describes as follows:

Then mark the cloven sphere that holds
All thought in its mysterious folds.
That feels sensations faintest thrill,
And flashes forth the sovereign will;
Think on the stormy world that dwells
Locked in its dim and clustering cells!
The lightning gleams of power it sheds
Along its hollow glassy threads! [12]

It is not a good poem throughout because of its unintentional surrealistic effects, but it suggests the poet-doctor's feelings. There is, too, a letter to his own teacher of anatomy, Winslow Lewis, in which he described an elaborate dissection used to illustrate the mechanics of respiration. The figure had been laid open at a different depth for each of the lobes of the lung and had been fitted out with a gadget to make the lungs function. The cadaver, as he described it, seems macabre to the lay reader, but Dr. Holmes obviously thought it beautiful.[13]

What might not be fixed in memory by these means, he impressed upon his audience by using his flair for analogies, pinning down terms with picturesque similes. The fimbriated end of the Fallopian tube was like the fringe of a poor woman's shawl; the mesentery, like old-fashioned shirt ruffles; the minute coiled tube of the sweat gland, like a fairy's intestine; the double-lobed brain, like a walnut.[14] Where possible he avoided overtechnical language, having a personal distaste for the jargon which spoke of "ligating" instead of "tying." Where necessary, he suggested mnemonic devices, using rhyme or ribaldry as fixatives. Where no radical change of nomenclature has come about, rhymes, credited to Holmes, are still the common property of medical students.

It goes without saying that the wit which charmed a dinner-table was not in abeyance in the amphitheater, but it was there of a somewhat different quality. Some of his jests, those that survive, are not printable; their ribaldry is innocuous, but they are not funny in type, being the kind of thing that goes over only when heard. He may have produced an effect, but he was hardly being brilliant when he opened his lecture on the female genitalia with "My subject this afternoon is one with which I trust you young gentlemen are not familiar." It is not to be supposed that he missed up on any chance for a pun, but none survive. His reference to the bile ducts provoked from a student "I prefer mine broiled," a *sotto voce* remark the doctor did not miss, commenting "Young man, aren't you usurping my prerogative?" [15] The same student thought Dr. Holmes and the surgeon Bigelow the best lecturers in the college and recorded in his diary the students' pleasure when Dr. Holmes took over the dissecting room for a term. "Every muscle, bone, or organ suggests some witty story." [16]

He was so successful at the job of managing his large classes at that worst of all hours, the last in a long morning of lectures, that for the rest of his thirty-five years as a teacher, no matter what changes were made in the schedule, that hour was always given to Dr. Holmes.

His wit and vivacity made him, also, the center of groups of admiring students at the monthly medical school parties.[17] A few of his colleagues perhaps suspected that the Parkman Professor's obvious liking for attention was inconsistent with proper modesty, but what could they expect when the doctor produced for their amusement lines like the following, in which the students call up the professors for examination? The poet made himself the first victim, calling up the Professor of Anatomy in the conventional way:

> Call Number One—Professor Bones.
> Take down his age and name.
> Now ask your question, brother Jones.
> Professor, hear the same.
> There, take your place, look in my face,
> Stand up upon your legs
> And tell me why it's all a lie
> That men are hatched from eggs?
> Oh Professor
> Professor, can't you tell?
> I rather guess that you'll confess
> The ovum is a *sell*.

What do you say? You all vote *Nay*.
Professor Bones may go.

His friend Henry J. Bigelow was called out with a personal allusion. The surgeon's fondness for splendor and elegance of dress was well known.

> Professor Bougie you'll proceed
> To tell us what you know.
> Explain this fact. When you extract
> A polyp or a wen,
> Why are you dresst in all your best,
> Among these plain young men?
> O Professor!
> Professor, can't you tell?
> Why, when you take a tumor out
> You needs must *cut a swell!*
>
> Professor Bougie stand aside.
> We cannot let you in!

The poet was personal, too, in his allusion to the Professor of Pathology, the curator who was "always found a grubbing round" in the anatomical museum. J. B. S. Jackson's intense devotion to the Warren Museum was a matter of record. His approach was not a little like that of the virtuoso; and, although in his day a much respected pathologist, he could commit surprising absurdities. He once reported in the *Boston Medical and Surgical Journal* an autopsy on a woman who long ago had been impaled on a pitchfork to the permanent derangement of her internal organs. Dr. Jackson described the whole very carefully, giving a full history of the case, and then concluded proudly that the museum possessed not the pathological specimen one expects, but the genuine original pitchfork! In Holmes's poem, the curator is made to commit a pathological pun.

So is the Dean, then, (c.1859) David Humphreys Storer, Professor of Obstetrics. In fact, the poet was so far gone in his punning-spree that he produced three obstetrical jokes, of which one is surely enough.

> You know full well as people tell
> The branch that you profess:

> Why is the gravid matrix like
> To Adams his express?
> O Professor
> The reason I will state:
> Because they both *contract* to make
> *Delivery of freight.*

Needless to say, the faculty flunks its examination, but the kind-hearted and politic students are made to drive a bargain; the professors will be passed if they agree to repay the kindness.[18]

Holmes did not intend his comic poem as a satire on the way he and his colleagues conducted their final examinations; but the perfunctoriness of his mock examination may have seemed ironic to some of the more intelligent members of the class for whose pleasure it was written. To a number of the students who were graduated from Harvard before the reform of 1870, the school appeared too "easy," and too large to make it possible for the students to receive the best training. The best of them were also students at the smaller private Tremont School where they concentrated on getting the clinical instruction and special subjects not to be had at Harvard, and where, too, they found their fellow-students fewer in number and less "rough" in character.[19]

At the Tremont School, not only were the students sure of decently small clinical classes in three of the city's hospitals and at the Boston Dispensary, but also they were able to get an unusual amount of instruction in special subjects. Holmes offered courses in microscopic anatomy and in auscultation and percussion; Jeffries Wyman gave a course in comparative anatomy; Agassiz taught embryology; and Dr. George Gordon, and later Silas Durkee, dermatology. Its two terms —March through July, and September through October— made a strong supplement to the four-month session at Harvard; its classes in the regular subjects of the medical course were based on the Harvard lectures and were conducted in the form of recitations and examinations rather than in the form of lectures. The close connection between the two

198

schools was excellent for the students who attended both schools. About one-third of the men who received their medical degrees from Harvard enjoyed the advantages of the Tremont School.

The appointments of Holmes and J. B. S. Jackson and, in 1849, of Henry J. Bigelow, drew the Tremont School even closer to Harvard than it had been before; the fact that Louis Agassiz and Jeffries Wyman of Harvard were now also giving special courses at the Tremont School tightened the bond in another direction. From 1847-1853, Holmes as Dean of one school and Secretary of the other was responsible for the advertisements and catalogues of both; he went so far in pointing up the connection between the two schools that Professor Ware was moved to urge him to go slow.[20] The connection, however, was real enough to warrant Holmes's representation of it by sometimes running a single advertisement for both schools.

For the eighty or ninety students who attended only the two terms of lectures at Harvard required for the degree, the connection between the two institutions was no benefit. Nor were their opportunities improved when, in 1858, their faculties identical, the Tremont School merged with Harvard and became the summer session of the latter. Even with the merger, the Harvard medical faculty did not alter the length of its winter session—four months—and attendance at two winter sessions alone was required for the degree.

It is not surprising that Holmes and others of the Harvard faculty stood out in the meetings of the American Medical Association in opposition to the many proposals for lengthening the lecture terms of the regular medical schools.[21] They had a vested interest certainly in a private institution like the Tremont School; and their perspective, stiffened by ten years' experience, did not change when the private school became a summer session; the delegates from Massachusetts continued to oppose or ignore the resolutions of the national association. Proud—and justly so—of the quality of the instruction they offered and of the curriculum in the combined schools, they were blind to the fact that these virtues bene-fited only a fraction of their own students.

No small cause of their blindness was the financial ar-rangement under which they worked—as even an under-graduate like James Clarke White could see. Each professor, dependent upon the number of individual tickets sold for his course, was bound to prefer a program which kept the basic medical expenses of an individual student low and yet allowed a good number of others to buy as much as they could afford. Twenty years of such a system made Henry J. Bigelow, for example, Charles William Eliot's bitterest op-ponent when the latter came to reform the whole university; the wavering Holmes here followed Bigelow's lead, and the basis of their opposition was the conviction that the school would lose students and money.

Men like Holmes with outside sources of income and Bigelow with his large surgical practice were not, of course, wholly dependent upon ticket-selling for their livelihood. Only one member of the faculty at the time of Holmes's ap-pointment was in that precarious position. The fact that John Webster, Erving Professor of Chemistry for twenty years, received a pittance for lecturing at the college in Cambridge did not ease his financial insecurity. He was a poor man and heavily in debt. On the afternoon of November 23, 1849, he busied himself picking up after his lecture at the North Grove Street building, as he waited harassed and desperate, for a caller—a creditor who knew that the tickets for the 1849-50 term of medical lectures had just been turned in and that his debtor would have some cash. Dr. George Parkman entered the building erected on the property he had given the Medical School, about a quarter of two to collect his debt; he came in response to a note sent him by Webster. The Professor could not pay; he hoped to stall off Parkman's demands and dissuade him from carrying out the threat to have him turned out of his job.

A week later all classes at the Harvard Medical School were

called off; through the building on North Grove Street tramped a coroner's jury holding an inquest on the body of Dr. George Parkman, whose dismembered remains had been gradually gathered from various parts of the building.

When the notice of Parkman's disappearance had been printed in the *Boston Evening Transcript* on November 24, Littlefield, the janitor at the medical school, had remembered that he had seen Parkman there; he had been suspicious, too, of the odd behavior of Professor Webster who was spending more than a normal amount of time behind the locked doors of his laboratory. Reporting his suspicions to two members of the faculty, he had been ordered to continue his investigations but on no account to report them to the Dean. The reason for this injunction is not clear unless it is accounted for by Holmes's reputation for more squeamishness than is customary in a man in his profession. On November 30, Littlefield had broken through the rear wall of the privy connected with Webster's laboratory and found a pelvis, a right thigh, and a left leg.

Further search of the school revealed a thorax and a left thigh packed in a tea chest filled with tan and covered with minerals in the corner of the same laboratory. In the furnace of the laboratory was a large mass of human bones, fused slag and cinders. Here, too, were found the block of mineral teeth and the gold filling which proved the connecting link in identifying the remains as those of Parkman.[22]

On December 8, the medical school classes were resumed. Regarding their colleague as innocent until proved guilty, the medical faculty met with formality to appoint a committee "to consult Professor Webster about filling the vacancy occasioned by his absence." Dr. Ware and Dr. Holmes, the committee appointed, politely called upon Webster in prison, where he was awaiting trial for the murder of Parkman; and on the 12th, the medical faculty voted to accept Professor Webster's suggestion that Professor Horsford of the Lawrence Scientific School take his place.[23]

In the trial of Webster, Holmes appeared as a character witness for the defense (his classmate Ned Sohier was one of

Webster's lawyers) and a medical witness for the prosecution; as the latter he was called upon to back up the expert testimony of his fellow anatomist Jeffries Wyman. Naturally, the murder and the professor's trial created a long-lasting sensation. The medical school was obliged to open its doors to a curious public as well as the jury. Several years later, Charles Dickens, paying his second visit to America, wanted to visit the scene of the crime. Holmes took him around and answered his questions while the creator of Bradley Headstone, Mr. Crook, Fagin, and a choice selection of other villains chalked up his impressions.[24] As the medical school's official historian observes, "This was a period of grievous mortification and distress for all Harvard men." [25] It continued to be so until the memory of the affair faded away, and the case became significant only in legal history, in which it is cited as an important instance of a conviction for murder on circumstantial evidence. While the stigma of the crime lasted, however, its effects were sometimes ironically apparent. More than twenty years later a Williams professor's wife indignantly refused to entertain in her house a Harvard professor; her son, a Harvard professor himself, tells the story with some amusement, for the rejected guest was James Russell Lowell.[26]

Lyceum Lecturer

1848–1853

*But his lively mind could not be satisfied with-
out more diversity of employment.*

WITHIN A YEAR of his appointment to Harvard, Dr.
Holmes became wholly the teacher—teaching medical students anatomy and lyceum audiences a little of everything.
In January 1849, he notified his patients that he was giving
up private practice; [1] in April he announced his resignation
from the hospital staff.[2] But these changes did not mean more
undisturbed hours at home with his family, for by 1851
Holmes had become a member of what he called the "fifth
estate"; [3] he was a full-time public lecturer.

For five years, 1851-56, Holmes made daily appearances
throughout the lecture season in countless small towns and
cities in New England and New York State, eventually traveling as far as Cincinnati and Louisville. At noon five times
a week he lectured on cells and tissues and bones to his
medical students; evenings found him in Salem, or Charlestown, or Roxbury, lecturing to the townspeople on "Love of
Nature," "Byron," or "Literary Tribunals." His family could
not have seen much of him during the lecture seasons which
normally lasted from October through March. To keep a
lecture date at any distance from Boston, he had to hurry
from the medical school to the station; to be sure of meeting
his class the next day, he had to travel back late at night. If
the lecturing schedule meant leaving town for more than
a day or two during the school year, he doubled up on his
medical lectures, making up the work ahead of time; usually,

however, he arranged his tours so that his lectures in distant towns came in October or March.[4]

Traveling constantly by slow trains or in cold carriages through snow-covered New England was not the most comfortable way to spend the winter evenings. Once he had to spend a whole night in an icy coach on a drift-bound train. Often the secretaries of nearby lyceums left it to the lecturer to provide his own transportation; [5] a Boston liveryman long remembered the impatient little doctor dancing up and down in the stable doorway and demanding a carriage and horse in a hurry. A journey to any distance meant spending the nights in strange beds in cold country inns; "family men get dreadfully homesick. In the remote and bleak village the heart returns to the red blaze of the logs in one's fireplace at home" and to his children "if he has any youthful savages." [6]

Holmes had entered slowly this "trying and dangerous business of lecture-peddling." For twelve years (1838-50) he had given occasional performances before Boston and out-of-town lyceums; but his experiences were not of a kind to encourage him to do more. "No one had heard of me, and few people knew what a lecture was. There was no literary public; we had to create the taste, and uphill work it was I can tell you." There was no particular attraction in lyceum lecturing in the days when "the managers of forlorn institutions tried to beat him down to a few dollars, when he had to walk miles over plowed fields to reach some remote town, and then, send his agent out into the highways and hedges to beat up an audience." [7]

Yet Holmes had kept his eye on the lecture-room, noting in a memorandum book agents' names and fees offered even when he did not accept the invitations; he had rarely let a year go by without making at least two or three appearances; he had published two of his lectures as separate books: *Homeopathy and its Kindred Delusions,* and *Urania.* The publication of a volume of poems in 1848 had served to remind prospective lecture audiences and lyceum secretaries that Oliver Wendell Holmes was the author of "The Last

Leaf" and "The Height of the Ridiculous." In August 1850, he had published *Astrea,* a Phi Beta Kappa poem for Yale University; in both 1849 and 1850 he had made public appearances in Pittsfield, Massachusetts—appearances duly and flatteringly noticed in the widely circulated *Springfield Republican.*

Dr. Holmes had gradually become a literary lion and, as he himself observed, the lecture-room of the period was a fine lion-trap. "It is but a question of dollars and cents," he continued, "and without any infringement of dignity, the greatest lion in the land will not only come and sit down before the audience, but roar and shake his mane, and lift his paws by the hour." [8] That lecture audiences came as much to get a look at a celebrity as to hear what he had to say is obvious from the newspaper reports; Holmes's face and figure were inevitably a "disappointment," although few reporters went as far as "P.P." of Lawrence who candidly observed that the doctor's face was "as ugly" as his own.[9]

For lions and their roarings the wealthy city lyceums were willing to pay at more than double the rates they had offered in the forties. Until the depression of 1857, the lyceum platform was something of an Eldorado for those lecturers popular enough to get regular invitations. The rates for a single lecture in a city of any size were from fifty to seventy-five dollars; New York City lyceums offered as high as $100, and would go as far as twice that for an imported celebrity like Thackeray.

Lecturing had in fact become a business. As Holmes observed, it had "its market, with its rise and fall of stock"; the lecturer was a "merchantable commodity." By 1850, everyone from Maine to Missouri knew what a lecture was. "In little damp vestries, and in stately halls, in country and in city, popular lectures are thronged." [10] In larger cities the halls were specially built for the purpose; the opening of Smith and Nixon's establishment in Cincinnati in 1855 was a fashionable affair. The first evenings were "expected to be a series of the most brilliant festivals, as all of Cincinnati's literary circles, as well as her beauty and fashion, will be generally represented." The celebrity for the opening night, James Murdock, Shakespearean reader, fell ill, but:

Fortunately, Mr. [*sic*] Oliver Wendell Holmes . . . had arrived in town a short time previously, and as he himself stated, in his traveling dress, and with his address necessarily in traveling condition, he nevertheless delivered a lecture replete with wit, humor, and brilliant reminiscences of the great poet of the nineteenth century, Lord Byron.[11]

The lecture-room had not become exactly what Emerson had hoped for it when in 1841 he described his expectations to Carlyle.

I am always haunted with brave dreams of what might be accomplished in the lecture-room, so free and so unpretending a platform,—a Delos not yet made fast. I imagine an eloquence of infinite variety, rich as conversation can be with anecdote, joke, tragedy, epics, and pindarics, arguments and confession.[12]

Most of the lecturers were men like Holmes, not men like Emerson; of the difference between them, Holmes was well aware as he showed when he begged Emerson *not* to come to one of his lectures. "I am forced to study effects. You and others may be able to combine popular effect with the exhibition of truths. I cannot." [13]

The variety Emerson had hoped for was realized only in a superficial way, especially as audiences came to look more and more for the excitement of staring at celebrities, the prestige of attending a fashionable affair, and the relaxation of enjoying a minimum of instruction with a maximum of amusement. A good deal of Holmes's popularity, for instance, seemed to rest upon his ability to give his audiences the comforting illusion that they had received instruction in the midst of their laughter. That the popular taste, however, had swung away from the type of lecture that was primarily instructive or informational is plain from Holmes's own experiences. In his almanacs, in which he recorded his lecture engagements, he noted the lecture or the type of lecture asked for. To eight requests for "History of Medicine," there were forty-one for "Love of Nature," [14] in which occurred a fanciful passage so hilarious that no reporter could ever get it down.[15]

The two lectures named suggest the changing tastes. "History of Medicine," which Holmes offered in 1851, was a revised version of a lecture he had given first in 1842 and then twenty-four times in 1848.[16] Like all his lectures in the forties it was "educational," based on professional knowledge, and prepared after some digging in library sources, as his withdrawals from the Boston Athenaeum show. The early lyceum audiences really wanted to be instructed, and they wanted particularly scientific information: but when in 1853 Holmes was invited by the Lowell Institute of Boston (an organization known for its erudite lectures) to give the series for the following year and expected that a scientific discourse was desired, he was told that "the public . . . was tired of all this; audiences could no longer be entertained by sulphurated hydrogen, nor a megatherium from the flood. . . . "[17]

"Love of Nature," on the other hand, although it drew upon its author's specialized knowledge, was a spontaneous, fanciful piece in which Holmes indulged all his fondness for hyperbole, for daring analogies, for pointed satiric sketches of human types—the entomologist "who gives insects long names and short lives, a place in science and a pin through the body," the virtuoso who "if a thing is naturally large . . . must have it of the smallest; if small, then he must have it of the largest; if striped, he must have one spotted; if spotted, then it must be striped"; the virtuous rural citizen, "temperate in material things, and in things intellectual, totally abstinent." Light, entertaining, inconsequential, the lecture seems to hover on the edge of some serious thought almost Emersonian, but it hovers only.[18]

Probably even more significant of contemporary tastes are "Lectures and Lecturing" and its companion piece "The Audience"; Holmes was not the only one who chose these subjects in 1852 when lyceum audiences had become too sophisticated to take most lecturers any more seriously than they would take jugglers. And as a word-juggler Holmes left little to be desired. His audiences were generally so pleased that he could make fun of them with impunity.[19]

Why Holmes, at this time, chose to become what he described as "the slave-merchant of his own children" [20] must be a matter of conjecture; but certainly the financial rewards were of some importance; his earnings for his first big season, 1851-2, were about $1200,[21] a relatively large amount for those days, equal in fact to the whole salary of the Smith Professor of Modern Languages at Harvard, Henry Wadsworth Longfellow. The wares Holmes offered for this price were three lectures: "History of Medicine," "Love of Nature," and "Lectures and Lecturing." As essays in a magazine, even supposing there had been a really good one at the time, they would not have brought a fraction of that sum.

Nor would they, in a magazine, have brought him the same kind or amount of fame, if the attention he received from Boston to Buffalo, and Augusta to New York can be called fame. The newspapers were not always flattering; their response, particularly outside Boston, was uncertain, and Holmes was at first wary of exposing himself. Writing in the summer of 1851 to James T. Fields about a possible engagement before the New York Mercantile Library Association, he remarked that he had asked $100 for his performance, and added "one thing is certain, that I am not going to expose myself to the lifted leg of New York Puppyism and Puffer Hopkinism for nothing." [22]

Holmes soon discovered that he did not have too much to fear. Until an unfortunate address in December 1855, the publicity he received was flattering, even fulsome. The citizens of Portland were disappointed in his appearance but found his lecture "irresistibly attractive"; the lecture audiences in Albany were delighted with his sentimental allusions to their city as the hometown of his Dutch ancestors and flattered by his offering them a special poem, an "extra" in the lecture.[23] As a student of effects, Holmes knew well the value of such personal allusions.

When finally in September 1855, Holmes was able to accept an invitation to lecture in Louisville, he was all but snatched off the train to attend a civic banquet for a former governor of Kentucky; the reporter for the *Louisville Daily Courier* watched every mouthful the doctor ate and observed with gratification that the eastern celebrity tasted all "our western fluids." [24] Kentucky fluids being what they were and are, one hopes that the doctor was able to follow his usual practice of chasing his drinks with large quantities of black tea. If attention, popularity, a kind of fame was what Holmes desired, the lecture-room provided it in generous measure.

Other motives may have pushed him onto the platform. The lecture after all was a form of talk, and Holmes's loquaciousness was a matter of common gossip, of concern to his wife, of mingled feelings to his friends who, much as they enjoyed his chatter, sometimes regretted that he talked too much. For some members of his audience, Holmes's obvious enjoyment of his own wit was one source of his charm; he was clearly having a good time talking; to other critics, his manner smacked of conceit.

Being a form of talk, a kind of extended conversation, the lecture allowed Holmes freedom for his pin-wheel mind. The discursiveness that is a defect in some of his long poems was probably pleasing to the half-attentive lyceum audiences of the 1850's. Holmes's mind spun from notion to notion with more speed than the restraining form of the couplet properly suggests; the prose lecture allowed his fancy to run naturally. Sometimes he found himself talking in verse, especially as he got toward the end of his lectures when his sentences fell not only into rhythm but even occasionally into rhyme.[25] He got into the habit of decorating the close of his lectures with verses if they came easily enough. And throughout his lectures, even critics who did not like his opinions and who had no respect for his intellect found what they described as a "poetical quality," and noted the brilliance and wit of his images.

The flat newspaper reports of Holmes's lectures do not wholly reveal the quality the reporters vainly try to indicate with words like "sparkling" and "effervescent," but they do suggest the doctor's whirling firecracker style. As a matter of fact, Holmes often used the fireworks image to describe his own things, recognizing that printed talk of his kind had too much the character of fireworks the morning after. Yet it is plain from the reports that his pyrotechnics were the same which he would use to such advantage later in the Breakfast-Table books. His method in his lectures differs from that of the books only in being less controlled and more flighty. His nervous and exuberant fancy does hit, now and then, on a point that sticks even in the form of cold newspaper type: "The first material production of America is not a church, or children, or a jackknife, but a stump. And the first intellectual product is a man to get upon it and make a speech." [26] And—"As the head is all the better for an occasional shampooing, so the mind needs to be rubbed down with the generalities of humor." Over-zealous reformers are victims of "inflammation of the conscience." [27] The lecture-room gave Holmes a chance to talk, and to talk in the fashion most natural and satisfying to him. He did not particularly mind giving the same lecture forty-one times in a season; [28] besides he added special introductions, touched them up and made changes from time to time, tossing out an old anecdote for a new one—something fresh that had happened just the other day. He apparently had more than one version of each lecture, choosing from the lot the ones most suited to the audiences, for obviously what went for a back-country town would not do for New York.[29] The traveling was arduous, but preparing and giving the lectures was no hardship.

Another less conscious motive may have drawn him into the lecture business. Sometime during the forties the not too busy general practitioner had scribbled some notes in the back of one of his casebooks—six pages of phrases, lines of

verse, aphorisms, fragmentary thoughts, images—a salma-
gundi suggestive of the writer's state of mind. A good many
of these fragments are "medical" in the sense that they de-
rive from his professional experience; but is it a general practitioner only who observes "Sick people fix on *trifling* affections to call attention to. Make themselves the pivot and
spin like beetles"? Other entries are detached images—"Fleet
of butterflies"; some are ambiguous, suggestive but not trans-
latable: "Couch it gently—convey it in vague hints and quilted
words"—"Attempting to write poetry like Herbert's or
Donne's." Such fragments as the following seem to give the
lie to Holmes's pose as the amateur rhymester.

> Union of melody and thought in the poet—
> Crystallization of thought in poetry—
> The poets dream. The birds high in the air
>   The pendulum. The Cathedral—
> *The one Thought.*—
> He is not worthy of the name of poet who does
> not find the materials of art inexhaustible and
> is not always able to recreate himself as it
> were. . . .[30]

If no one of these fragments is complete enough to warrant
speculation, the six pages together suggest that the doctor's
mind was not wholly on his profession, that, in spite of his
consistent and careful resistance to the pleas of editors, he
had not cured himself of what he pretended to regard as a
disease. In the lecture-room, the incurable fever had a chance
to break out.

Holmes probably was not sorry to find that in the fifties
the popular demand had shifted from scientific subjects; the
choice of "The English Poets" for the twelve lectures asked
for by the Lowell Institute was his own, and it led him into
reading more widely in literature than he had been in the
habit of doing.[31]

He had always kept up with his contemporary Americans,
some of whom, of course, sent him their books as they came
out. His letter of appreciation for Hawthorne's gift of *The
House of the Seven Gables* shows him exercising his critical

faculty more boldly than he did anywhere in the Lowell
Lectures.

> I think we have no romancer but yourself, nor have had any for
> this long time. The imagination of our lean countrymen has always
> seemed to me as emaciated as their faces. I had been so morbidly set in
> this belief that but for your last two stories I should have given up
> hoping and believed that all we were to look for in the way of such
> spontaneous growth were such languid, lifeless, sexless creations as in
> the view of certain people constitute the chief triumphs of a sister art
> as manifested among us.
> But there is rich red blood in Hester, and flavor of the sweet fern
> and the bayberry are not truer to the soil [than] the native sweetness
> of our little Phebe! The Yankee mind has for the most part budded
> and flowered in pots of English earth—but you have fairly raised yours
> as a seedling in the natural soil.—My criticism has to stop here—the
> moment a fresh mind takes in the elements of common life about us
> and transfigures them I am contented to enjoy and admire and let
> others analyze. . . . Only one word then—this,—that the solid reality and
> homely truthfulness of the actual and present part of the story are
> blended with its weird and ghostly shadows with consummate skill and
> effect—this was perhaps the special difficulty of the story.[32]

He began the preparation of the Lowell lectures in Pittsfield in the summer of 1852, writing Folsom at the Boston
Athenaeum to send him the books he needed. Confessing that
his poetical and critical library was not very rich, he wrote
for the works of Shelley and Coleridge, for Wordsworth's
Prelude, for critical works by the Schlegels and Hazlitt, and
for Leigh Hunt's *Imagination and Fancy.* On his return to
Boston in the fall, he raided the Athenaeum for magazines,
following particularly the criticism of Jeffrey through the
files of the *Edinburgh Review.* He seems to have looked
especially for what the poets he had chosen had to say of
each other; and although using biographical sources, he kept
his attention focused upon the poets' work rather than their
lives.

When he had worked his materials into their final shape,
cutting out a superfluous general introduction and trimming
two lectures on Wordsworth down to one, the series he offered
was as follows:

On Tuesday evening, March 22, 1853, Holmes gave his first lecture. Behind him, accentuating his small figure, was spread a huge screen upon which former lecturers, as Holmes reminded his audience, had displayed their materials—"bones of fishes, bodies of ditto, Egyptian hieroglyphics, geological strata"—and to which like schoolmasters they pointed with a twenty foot rod "to stir up the entire menagerie of dry bones." [33] And then with characteristic candor the doctor spoke of his expectation that little of what he had to say would be new and much might be objected to. He would simply tell them what he thought of the poets he had chosen. Holmes had studied effects to good purpose; the audience was sufficiently enchanted not to mind when the doctor mocked the verses of the extremely popular Samuel Rogers and made fun of Campbell's "Gertrude of Wyoming."

The lecture was so completely successful that, according to one reporter, "Dr. Holmes may claim to have revived the early popularity of the Lowell Institute Lectures." [34] Another newspaper observed: "No opening lecture promises such a course." [35] But both these observations come from conservative papers, the second from the *Boston Evening Transcript* that so doted on Dr. Holmes that its reporters frequently became incoherent with ecstasy. The *Commonwealth,* which loved neither Boston nor Holmes, may have been close to the truth when it observed: "the brilliant little doctor is a great favorite with Boston—she considers him, so to speak, one of her crown jewels . . . the Holmes diamond, then, had no sooner appeared upon the crimson velvet of the Lowell pulpitum, than a jocular feeling took possession of the audience. His peculiar magnetism makes itself felt before his voice is heard." The *Commonwealth* could not deny that the doctor's "electric battery has full command of the risible muscles which he can convulse to any extent," but "to the other muscles he is less formidable." [36] But whether the *Commonwealth* made fun or the *Transcript* exhausted its superlatives, the doctor drew the crowds in such numbers that he was obliged to give each lecture twice; both evening and afternoon performances were jammed; season-ticket holders were turned away from the door as the doorkeeper helplessly let the mob in. "Even leaning against the wall [was] a luxury difficult of attainment." One disgruntled reporter observed:

> The *Courier* of today speaks of the *solid men* of Boston. Let him attend an afternoon lecture, and he will receive an impression (a painful one, perhaps,) of the *solid women* of our city.[37]

Parts of the series repeated in Cambridge, New York, and Louisville were equally successful; and the lecture on Byron and Moore became part of Holmes's regular repertoire.

Holmes had no illusions about their value;[38] he knew that he had designed them with his appraising eye more steadfastly fixed upon his audience than upon his subjects. His severest critics accused him of making up to his audience, of dishonestly courting their favor. Such a judgment implying insincerity on Holmes's part seems harsh. He made fun of Carlyle's criticism of Scott, laughed at over-earnest reformers, exposed Wordsworth's worst infelicities; but that he did so in order to make a bid for popularity is unacceptable. Holmes thought of the function of the lecturer as that of a teacher, but a teacher outside the classroom; it was not the lecturer's place to take sides, to be a positive reformer of evil, but rather to be a corrector of excesses, a restorer of balance. He seems to have thought the lecture-room the ideal place for non-partisan comment, the place where irritations might be soothed, where

214

earnestness might be lightened with a jest. He did not, however, feel that a lecturer had to lean over backwards not to
offend anyone or that he had to compromise his own opinions
to please a particular group.

In the Lowell lectures Holmes did not attempt to impose
on his audience a theory of poetry, although in his final lecture
he offers a vague and elastic definition. "Poetry is the expression or creation of beauty in language that harmonizes with
the beautiful." [39] That he valued poetry highly is suggested in
his lecture on Keats. Referring to the poet's medical studies,
he observed:

> It is a good thing to save a few lives, but it is better to infuse a new
> life into our language. At twenty-two when he should have been putting
> up the sign "John Keats, Surgeon, the slightest favors or fevers grate-
> fully received," he did better; he published Endymion.[40]

Nothing is so apparent in these lectures as Holmes's rejection of a narrowly moralistic approach to poetry. He nowhere
states such a rejection, but collating all the newspaper reports
and criticisms of his lectures gives this impression. He appeared to regard the moralist, whether of the domestic, social,
or transcendental variety, as one maiming his own capacity to
appreciate a poem. There was, however, a noticeable difference in his manner of handling these moralists; the domestic
type was treated with an almost paternal tenderness; the
transcendentalists and social reformers were satirized. He led
his audience gently around the blockade of Shelley's atheism;
but he slashed into Carlyle's essay on Scott, using his wit lav-
ishly to mock Carlyle for belittling Scott. Holmes would always find Carlyle an irritating mystery, however hard he tried
to understand the man he called a dyspeptic dogmatist.[41]

Possibly he supposed that the reformers could take care of
themselves; they were certainly not inarticulate. The critics
for the *Boston Daily Commonwealth*, for example, inclined
to regard the doctor with tolerant amusement at first, became
sarcastic and acid after the third lecture—the one in which
Holmes attacked the idolized Carlyle.[42] From that moment
on, the *Commonwealth* was out to get the doctor; his lecture

on Wordsworth provided ample material for its scorn. Even the doting and faithful reporter for the *Boston Evening Transcript,* which had welcomed the attack on Carlyle with indecent delight, was somewhat set back by Holmes's treatment of Wordsworth.[43] William Cullen Bryant's paper, the *New York Evening Post,* normally forbore any critical comment, but could not help adding to its report of Holmes's lecture on religious poetry that the subject seemed "more within the compass of the lecturer's powers than the one on Wordsworth."[44] Holmes tried hard to be just to a poet for whom he felt more awe than liking; there is no injustice in his adverse criticism except as the flippancy he tries to check breaks out now and then in the wrong places. It is after all very easy to laugh at Wordsworth. It seems likely that the criticism of this lecture set Holmes to exploring Wordsworth further; he came to like him in the end.

Holmes's method of handling his subjects is unanalytical; he describes, or throws out undeveloped observations, illustrating his remarks with quotations. The quotations are usually omitted from the news accounts, obscuring Holmes's meaning; moreover, the reader has no confidence that the rendering of his words is exact; it, therefore, seems dangerous to draw conclusions about his capacities as critic from single passages, even one that is so provocative and that looks so good as the following:

> Wordsworth's power never passed beyond his own personality, and he merely described men and things as he found them. He cannot be illustrated, because he only adds quality to pre-existent objects, and creates nothing.[45]

One other isolated passage echoes a thought Holmes had expressed before in writing both Emerson and Hawthorne of what pleased him in their work; in the lecture on Southey, Holmes observed: "But it was certain that no poet who wrote of foreign scenes mainly, could have such an influence and name as he who takes the pith and marrow of his works from the soil on which he treads."[46]

Taking the series as a whole, and allowing for Holmes's conception of the lecturer-audience relationship, the modern reader can find little in his dicta—as far as they go—to quarrel with. Holmes does not force his poets into any narrow theory of poetry; he never makes the mistake of criticizing a poet for not doing what he never intended to do; and he does not deal in odious comparisons. Beyond leaning rather heavily on Leigh Hunt's distinction between imagination and fancy, he does not rely on any critical jargon, but uses instead images and quotations to express his ideas. He here lays himself open to his critics, however, by sometimes choosing unfortunate images or anecdotes to illustrate a point—illustrations which his critics perversely take literally although Holmes no more meant them to be taken literally than Swift did his *Modest Proposal*. His failure is usually not an error in judgment, but an error in taste. He is too quick to sacrifice his subject and his point to his wit.

His personal preferences are plain; he likes Campbell, Coleridge, Shelley, and Browning; Mrs. Browning he respects. About Byron, a poet "of passion," he is enthusiastic. To Holmes, Wordsworth is all intellect; and lack of passion is in Holmes's eyes a major defect. Of Tennyson, the doctor's opinion has changed since the days when he made fun of his verses (1838), and he now likes him almost as much as he does Byron. But the "most truly poetic poet of the century" is Keats; "his philosophy is that of the artist." [47]

Brought up on Augustans, exposed early to the eighteenth-century men of "sensibility," Holmes took his starting points there—Popeian resonance determined his taste in melody and made him slow to hear another kind of music; eighteenth-century "poetic diction" made him only too ready to spot the fallacy in Wordsworth's theory and the English poet's worst offenses there. Holmes knew very well that his affection for Moore was in part sentimental, bound to memories of his Cambridge childhood. What Holmes called passion in another poet ran too close to sentimentality in his own verses; only his humor, and that not always, saved him from error. Another "man of sensibility" and wit, William Makepeace Thackeray, who heard these Lowell Lectures and was himself making a splashy success in the American lecture-room, went home to England to declare that the best thing he had seen in America was Oliver Wendell Holmes.[48]

Summer Resident

His introducing his ... opinions and even preju-
dices ... cannot be fully defended.

Aᴄᴛᴇʀ ᴛʜᴇ ʙᴜsʏ and trying winter with its constant
lecturing, Holmes was probably happy to escape to Canoe
Meadow in the Berkshires. The family income had allowed
him to buy the property adjoining the Wendell lots; nearly
300 acres lying on either side of the Housatonic River just
south of Pittsfield gave him a farm and woodlot where, for
seven summers, he escaped the heat of Boston and rested from
the grind of continual traveling. Holmes, who went about
with a tape in his pocket to measure the biggest trees wherever
he found them, planted orchard and forest trees. The farming
he must have left mostly to his caretaker; but he reported with
ingenuous pleasure on the state of his strawberries and potatoes so that a medical colleague was moved to hope that the
doctor was as successful in delivering potatoes as he was in delivering lectures.[1]

Here, too, he had a chance to spend some leisurely hours
with his family. The family was growing up—Wendell, 13,
would soon be taller than his father. Getting his southern
classmate up-to-date on the news of his children, Holmes described them:

The oldest . . . shoots, fishes, swims, draws in summer and is one of
Mr. Dixwell's . . . favorite scholars. Amelia, my next, is ten years old, is
a nice little body, can swim across the Housatonic, and is a clever little
scholar without being a wonder. Ned, aet. 7, is something of what we
used to call a "buster"—great at practical jokes, red in the face, up-
roarious, aggressive, indomitable, loud in voice. . . .[2]

and, he might have added, generally known as the young pugilist.

This was the period when Pittsfield, Lenox, and Stockbridge drew as their summer visitors literary men from the rival cities of Boston and New York. There were also lion-hunters ready to rope in such distinguished company as Melville, Hawthorne, and Holmes. On August 5, 1850, one such gentleman, Mr. Dudley Field, corralled his literary neighbors for a day of pleasure at his place in Stockbridge. Herman Melville and his guests Evart Duyckinck and Cornelius Matthews came down by the cars from Pittsfield; [3] they found Holmes, "a slight apparition . . . with a glazed India Rubber Bag, in hand," at the station. It was as "Mr. Town Wit, whose clever verses and *jeux d' esprit* are on every tongue," that Cornelius Matthews described Holmes in his account of his visit to the Berkshires for Duyckinck's paper, *The Literary World*. They were soon joined by Nathaniel Hawthorne, with whom came a bridal pair, Mr. James T. Fields, the publisher, and his wife Annie, "the violet of the season."

Their host had planned a morning of mountain climbing, a pleasure for which the plump Fields in his patent leathers and his wife in her new blue silk were not too well prepared; but the whole party somehow got safely to the rocky top of Monument Mountain, "rambling, scrambling, climbing, rhyming—puns flying off in every direction, like sparks among the bushes." At the summit, where the romantics in the crowd were ready to contemplate nature, "somebody attempts a pun —we believe it's the rogue, Town Wit." [4]

A gathering storm sent the party to improvised shelter; Fields protected his curled whiskers and his wife's new dress in the shadow of a convenient rock. The inventive Holmes got out his jackknife and made himself an umbrella of branches. He was ready to turn the Byronic setting into a city drawing-room and tended to the business of opening and serving the champagne [5] while Matthews read the romantic "Story of an Indian Girl," William Cullen Bryant's poem on the inevitable legend of the mountain where the company was gathered.[6]

Edward Jackson Holmes

The Holmes children:
Edward Jackson, Amelia, and Oliver Wendell, Jr.–c.
1855

Dr. Oliver Wendell Holmes—c. 1857

When the storm cleared, the party scattered over the cliffs, "Melville to seat himself, the boldest of all, astride a projecting stick of rock," like Ishmael at the masthead of the *Pequot* in the novel he was then writing. The nervous little doctor, on the other hand, peered curiously but uneasily about the cliffs; they affected him, he said, like ipecac.[7]

He was in a happier element at the dinner-table later, "sitting erect in his chair, bristling with eyes, collar, and ears alert." As usual it was he who set the talk of sea-serpents, of the condition of poetry.[8] "He said some of his best things and drew the whole company out by laying down propositions of the superiority of Englishmen." Or so Duyckinck reported, but since Holmes was too passionate a provincial himself to have offered such contentions unqualified, it seems more likely that the theme he set was his notion of the effect of climate on constitution, a subject he reports having argued about with Melville. On this occasion "Melville attacked him vigorously," and the battle was on, while Hawthorne, the observer, sat in his customary silence, and James T. Fields "smiled with internal satisfaction underneath his curled whiskers at the good tokens of a brilliant poem from Holmes in a few days at the Yale celebration." How Duyckinck knew what Fields was thinking is a mystery.[9]

After dinner the party went exploring again in Icy Glen, "a dark and slippery region, with oozing rocks for stairways, and rotten logs for bridges." For mountain tops and towering cliffs Holmes had no taste, but the icy grotto was on his scale. While Hawthorne and Holmes engaged "in the neck-endangering progress through the treacherous gully," their publisher lamented his girth. It was probably Holmes who suggested that if he really wanted to get thin, he had only to pay his authors bigger royalties. Matthews, in his report, like Duyckinck in the letter quoted, shows a curious clairvoyance about the workings of his Boston rival's mind. "Such a face of melancholy we never in our mortal life witnessed as did our Boston Bibliophile put on when he saw his two prize producers—now under way with a volume each—the Essayist and the Town Wit," undertake the perilous passage of Icy Glen.[10]

Such a sharp sense of rivalry accounts probably for the review of Holmes's Yale Poem, *Astrea,* Matthews came to write a few months later. No doubt malice lent an edge to Holmes's excellent satire on the pseudo-critic, and sharpened his wit when he turned from the Boston to the Manhattan variety, but Matthews was too quick to feel the sting. Poem and review are equally provincial, but Holmes knew that he was being so, while Matthews denied the charge, betrayed himself by boasting, and made observations more foolish and unjust than he needed to. The only good word he had to say for the poem was about the passage on the moral bully which satirizes the fanatical reformer. As satiric couplets, the passage on pseudo-critics is quite as good as the one Matthews chose to admire, but the reviewer was thrown so far out of line that he saw no resemblance and was led to find fault where no fault existed. He protested, for instance, the doctor's use of medical images, listing the professional terms separated from their context.[11]

Writing Duyckinck in November, Holmes explained patiently that his satire was not personal and that it applied only to those who merit it. He objected, with reason, to the reviewer's injustice:

> It is a small matter, but the *animus* which allows such license might lead a critic to great acts of injustice. In quoting the word "posteriors" as in my poem—I fear it was a fling, not a slip—you lead your readers to think that I am indecent as well as dull. It is an old story, but let your critic remember the hint when he sits down over his next author.[12]

Pittsfield was not all vacation; the poem which provoked the above exchange had to be prepared for the press; the citizens knew that they had a poet and doctor in their midst, fellow-physicians called him on consultations and the ladies asked for poems. And since the publication of his *Poems,* he had been the victim of correspondents who sent him manuscripts and asked advice. A fellow-sufferer, Hawthorne, asked him, in 1851, to help on a committee to judge manuscripts (apparently for some contest in Albany): Holmes answered with his most showy fireworks.

> I don't want to refuse anything you ask me to do. I shall come up, I trust, about the first of June. I would look over the Mss. in question, as a duty, with as much pleasure as many other duties afford. To say the truth I have as great a dread of the *Homo Caudatus, Linn. Anglice* (,) the Being with a Tale, male or female, as any can have.
>
> "If foes they write, if friends they read me dead," said poor Hepzibah's old exploded poet.—Still, if it must be I will stipulate to read a quantity not exceeding fifty six lb avoirdupois by weight or 18 reams by measure or "tale",—provided there is no locomotion in the case—the idea of visiting Albany does not enter into my programme of intentions. I do not know who would serve as a third or a second member of the Committee—Miss Sedgwick if the Salic law does not prevail in Berkshire, is the most natural person to look to. But the real truth is the little Albaneses want to see the Author of the Scarlet Letter and don't care a sixpence who else is on the Committee. That is what they are up to. So if you want two dummies, on the classical condition *not to leave the country except in case of invasion,* absentees, voters by proxy, potential but not personally present bottle-holders, I will add my name to that of Latimer, Ridley & Co. as a Martyr in the cause of Human Progress.[13]

Obviously to stay in one place for a few months was a luxury he would not willingly relinquish; he may have resigned (1853) as dean of the medical school to be relieved of the burden of tending to the school's clerical affairs in person or by correspondence. It did not occur to him to give up his professorship; medical lectures were "a very expensive luxury" but permanent, as he wrote to Whipple who had tried to persuade him to take on an extended lecture tour in 1853.[14]

As it was, he continued to lecture nearly every night in the week, borrowing "Byron and Moore" from the Lowell series for the 1853-4 season, and adding two new lectures, "The Americanized European," and "Literary Tribunals" for 1854-5. The first of the new lectures grew out of that notion he had argued about with Melville—climate and constitution.[15] Of the second no full report has yet been found; his text a quotation from Pope's "Essay on Criticism," Holmes "launched forth into an extensive and spirited review of the attributes of authors, critics, lecturers, and editors. Between lecturers and editors, he drew a comparison which elevated the former to the highest sphere of influence, while the latter (poor fellow!) he placed in rather reduced circumstances." [16] This observation from the *Boston Journal* falls midway between the adulation of the *Transcript* and the damnation of the New York papers.

1855 was Holmes's year to call down upon his own head a variety of condemnations. It was then that he reprinted his puerperal fever essay to stir up a small tempest that this time would make his idea stick. At the same time he was causing a furor of a very different kind and one that attracted an enormous amount of attention. The indignation of a Hodge or Meigs was as nothing compared to the wrath Holmes brought down upon his head in December 1855, when he addressed the New England Society in New York City and expressed a criticism of the extreme abolitionists and the Maine Law for prohibition.

Horace Greeley's *Tribune* let fly the first blast; and throughout the North, abolitionists, free-soilers, and temperance men followed suit; even personal friends like Theodore Parker and relatives like Wendell Phillips publicly expressed their disapproval; Emerson privately voiced his regrets to his brother-in-law, Dr. Charles T. Jackson, who relayed them to Holmes, and Charles Sumner sent him a pamphlet to educate him to happier views. In the confusion, the Boston newspapers mourned over him like a fallen angel, even when they actually agreed with Holmes and shared with him the compromise point of view of Daniel Webster.

The Websterian point of view is obvious in Holmes's address and it is not unexpected. In 1850 Holmes had been one of the many signers of the long letter of congratulation sent by Massachusetts men to Webster after his Seventh of March Speech; he was probably led to do so by his friend, R. C. Winthrop, conservative Massachusetts politician whose advice Holmes followed on more than one occasion. However much consideration of political expediency may have directed the opinions of a Winthrop or a Webster, I doubt that Holmes, in his innocence, was anything but sincere. His ethical position appears wholly honest. In his notes for the unfortunate address he expressed his point firmly. "If we have made a compact with moral barbarians, keep it or undo it," [17] a thought he softened in language for the actual speech. In his address, Holmes did not depart from the position he had hinted at in *Urania*, described in his letter to Lowell in 1846, and made more plain in the verses called "The Moral Bully," part of the Yale Phi Beta Kappa poem *Astrea*. What prompted him to introduce into this particular speech his somewhat ingenuous and offside thoughts on the slavery problem is less clear; he could not help knowing that he would offend some of his listeners. It seems possible that his correspondence with Isaac Morse, the Louisiana congressman, may have had something to do with it. Morse had been writing Holmes frequently for the past few years, expressing himself with more and more vehemence. In July of this same year, he had bitterly refused to come near his old classmates—"I'll see them all *damned* before I will go see people who won't stand by the Constitution." [18] It was in the fall of 1855, too, that Holmes had been so royally and flatteringly welcomed in Louisville. He had been introduced by the toastmaster with allusions to his being a Yankee, but "whatever may be his politics, his heart's all right."

His heart *was* in the right place; but his head, when it came to politics, was incredibly innocent. He liked the role of peacemaker and thought it a suitable one for the poet and lecturer; but when he set out to correct the reformers for their raucous voices and bad manners and attempted to soothe their tempers —not denying their grounds for indignation—he was patting a tiger and should not have been so naïvely hurt when it turned and bit him. In Louisville he could arouse good-natured laughter with a pun: "Will you hear me who to-day, for the first time, have drenched or washed myself in the waters of Kentucky. What can I say? Need it be anything here that I will regret when I go home. Let me tell you that I am for Union,

225

and have at home three pledges to attest my devotion, one of them over-topping myself," [19] a jest that led him easily into verses expressing what the *New York Tribune* called his "Union-saving" sentiments.

In New York the effect of such sentiments was very different. A few mild paragraphs in the middle of an innocuous, rather windy and provincial after-dinner speech were misrepresented and distorted in paper after paper until Holmes was reported in the *New York Herald* as having expressed this monstrous thought: "there was not a pickaninny in America that if it could get food enough would not grow to wind its caul around the neck of the Union." Of course, he said no such thing, nor anything remotely like it. It is almost impossible to find a phrase or sentence in the printed speech that could lend itself to such gross distortion. Holmes did say with simple—simpleminded, if you like—honesty that in a pinch, his sympathies were with white men, although as he tried to explain to Parker, "an African or an Indian in the right, is better to me than an Anglo-Saxon in the wrong." Holmes had some reason to be indignant with the newspaper tirades against him, but he kept his direct expressions of indignation for private correspondence. To Parker he wrote:

To have every honest word one utters lied or blundered over by a drunken reporter, and then commented on by a partisan editor who has lived for years on personalities and keeps a paper for his passions as a bully keeps a brothel for his harlots; this is the lot of him who ventures to say any honest thing not dictated by a caucus or an association.[20]

Publicly, he kept his temper and wrote no contradictions, with one minor exception,[21] for he knew the wisdom of an observation made in his lecture on "Critics and Criticism": "A speaker is not in the slightest degree responsible for anything any single reporter makes him say. He is not bound to contradict any misstatement, if he does, it may be inferred that he sanctions all he does not contradict." [22]

One feels that Holmes is in the right when he answers Parker's accusation of pro-slavery sentiments:

I find various passages in my poems in which I attack what I have called in one place "moral bullies." I recognize the existence of such a class among us. I received a most disgusting letter from one (a vegetable-feeder) once, after delivering a lecture in defense of a mixed diet.—I enclose an article illustrating the same kind of character as it shows itself in behalf of the Temperance movement. I recognize the same thing as manifested at times in the Anti-slavery cause. Wherever it is found, it is to me a fair subject of remark in prose or verse. I don't want to be *bullied* into Heaven by the pulpit—neither do I wish to be called hard names to make me better and more humane. But surely my attacks on this spirit, as shown in moral warfare, do not prove that I am a glutton, or a drunkard, or a defender of slavery.[23]

To Sumner he wrote: "I would have done by a black man, I hope and believe, as Jonathan Jackson, my great uncle did. I would fight for liberty in Kansas." [24] And to Emerson (italics Holmes's):

If the law of conscience *carried out fully only by the ultra-abolitionists,* had been proclaimed in strict accordance with the law of love, I believe the question would be far more nearly solved than it is at present. But they have used every form of language calculated to inflame the evil passions and the consequence is that growing sectional hostility, the nature of which is the disruption of the government which Mr. Parker thinks is near at hand.[25]

In his address Holmes had expressed his respect for the ultra-abolitionists; to Parker he speaks of talking over with Wendell Phillips their inflammatory methods.

Up to a point it is not hard to follow and in part accept Holmes's views, allowing for his political ignorance; but it is impossible to understand his seeing, as he tells Parker, "nothing blamable" in his thought that "the white race at the south must always have the upper hand"—an observation that throws into ironic relief his remark, à propos the journalistic abuse of himself, that it is painful "to be spoken of as a brute when one is a man." Ironic, too, is his remark to Emerson "you know very well that everything much praised or abused has some underlying principle and therefore *my case* has a certain interest."

Holmes justly thought of himself as being very much like other people—a notion he often expressed—and in accepting the doctrine of racial inferiority and adding to it the conception that he was a "Trustee of Providence for all races as for all individuals weaker and dependent on"[26] him, he was probably representative of many an abolitionist as well as slave-owner. Within the limits of his ideas, he was more honest than either. He was not, as he told Emerson, "undergoing any process of moral disintegration. . . . I may be wrong, but I wish to be right more than ever. How easy it would be to join a party and be popular! . . . Please not to mourn over me then, as one that is lost to truth. I love honesty in you too well to be wholly wanting in it myself." [27]

These letters were written in March; by May even Holmes could read the bloody evidence of Kansas; looking back upon the course of his feelings during the antislavery conflict, Holmes later (1864) wrote that it was "the Kansas iniquities which first opened my eyes to the base designs of the mighty slave dynasty." [28] Following hard upon the burning of Lawrence, Kansas, came Senator Brooks's attack on Sumner. Of Holmes's political views from that point on we have no sign until the war itself, but we can read his silence as evidence of either a change of heart or possibly a conviction of his own incompetence.

The barrage of criticism, some of it reasonable and polite, did not immediately frighten Holmes from the lecture-room, although from the moment of the New England Society address, the press, hitherto on the whole friendly and extremely flattering, was likely to treat Holmes with mockery, some of it malicious. His new lecture for the 1856-7 season, "Critics and Criticism," a revision of his earlier "Literary Tribunals," was not calculated to endear him even to editors not horrified by his political views. In it, he apparently used his wit like a scalpel, and his subject for dissection was the newspapers; naturally the press retaliated by not reporting his lecture at all.

Less obnoxious to journalists was "The Lyrical Passion." Like many of his lectures and the few medical reviews he published about this time, this piece is exuberant in its fancies.

Nothing delighted Holmes so much as the multiplication of figures of speech. Where one analogy would do, he lavished all his imagination could bring forth, taking an obvious pleasure in spinning out an image, working it for all it was worth and more than good taste should allow. At best this lecture is a flashy and superficial "history" of poetic feeling that reads like a rehash of his 1836 poem, "A Metrical Essay," couched in too many clichés and overdressed in sentimental imagery. Holmes was not the only lecturer who had run out of suitable material and fallen into a stereotyped pattern. After six boom years, the lecture business was falling off; its popularity had begun to wane even before the lyceums began to feel the effects of the depression and become aware that their lecture series were operating at a serious loss.

But into this lecture, Holmes introduced a few poems of his own; and one of them, "At the Pantomime," is timely enough in its theme for quotation here. Holmes could, after all, recognize a prejudice when he saw one.

> The house was crammed from roof to floor
> Heads piled on heads at every door;
> Half dead with August's seething heat
> I crowded on and found my seat,
> My patience slightly out of joint,
> My temper short of boiling-point
> Amidst the throng the pageant crew
> Were gathered Hebrews not a few,
> Black-bearded, swarthy,—at their side
> Dark, jewelled women, orient-eyed. . . .
>
> Next on my left a breathing form
> Wedged up against me, close and warm. . . .
>
> Then woke the evil brood of rage
> That slumber, tongueless, in their cage. . . .
> Up came their murderous deeds of old,
> The grisly story Chaucer told,
> And many an ugly tale beside
> Of children caught and crucified. . . .
>
> The show went on, but, ill at ease,
> My sullen eye it could not please,

In vain my conscience whispered, "Shame! . . ."
I thought of Judas and his bride,
And steeled my soul against their tribe:
My neighbors stirred; I looked again
Full on the younger of the twain.
A fresh young cheek whose olive hue
The mantling blood shows faintly through;
Locks dark as midnight that divide
And shade the neck on either side;—
So looked that other child of Shem;
The Maiden's Boy of Bethlehem!

—And thou couldst scorn the peerless blood
That flows unmingled from the Flood,—
Thy scutcheon spotted with the stains
Of Norman thieves and pirate Danes!
The New World's foundling, in thy pride
Scowl at the Hebrew at thy side,
And lo! the very semblance there
The Lord of Glory deigned to wear.[29]

The two lines that express with such effective concentration the whole ugly nature of prejudice are a second try, a revision made in 1874. A comparison of the first version with the final one shows, better than elaborate discussion, in what direction Holmes's mind was to develop. The first does not show the psychological insight of the second. The quotation which follows is from the 1856 manuscript.

Then rose the $\begin{cases} \text{sinful} \\ \text{nameless} \end{cases}$ words that slip
From darkening soul to whitening lip [30]

—these lines do not go beyond a description of a present emotion; even the second reading "sinful" implies merely a superficial moral judgment. But the 1874 version accomplishes all that the first does and much more, evoking the images of Spenser's monster in the Den of Error and the hideous offspring of Milton's Sin and Death, and communicating the complete psychological state:

Then woke the evil brood of rage
That slumber, tongueless, in their cage.

230

Holmes was nearly fifty when he wrote the first version of "at the Pantomime"; but he was on the verge of a change which Emerson in 1862 described with some accuracy. "Holmes came out late in life, with a strong sustained growth . . . like old pear trees which have done nothing for ten years, and at last begin and grow great." [31] The change began in the lecture-room and might have been cut short there had not a combination of circumstances made Holmes abandon lecturing as a regular practice.

The physical ordeal of lecturing had begun to tell on his health; the asthma that had troubled him from time to time was aggravated by constant exposure, by anxiety, and by the emotional strain of being away from home. Probably, too, the knowledge that lectures were becoming a less popular commodity and that he himself was a somewhat tarnished favorite helped to bring him to the point of drastically curtailing his lecture engagements. A third circumstance may have crystalized the decision for him. In 1856, a Dr. William Treadwell bequeathed to Harvard University $50,000 to establish a chair of anatomy and physiology, but he tied the bequest down to a condition that was plainly a criticism of Holmes, for he stipulated that the holder of the professorship was on no account to be allowed "to lecture before the Lowell Institute, Lyceums, or other establishments for amusing the public." [32] The Harvard Corporation, which had no reason at all to be dissatisfied with its Parkman Professor, who was known for his conscientiousness and excellence as a teacher, refused the legacy, but Holmes on his own account may have taken the criticism to heart. He began to cancel some of his engagements and to refuse others. Although his diminishing income obliged him to sell the Pittsfield property—he was advertising it in the spring of '56—he adopted the policy of refusing invitations that took him away from home.

The experience of lecturing had given Holmes an outlet and an audience, but its effects were not of the best. His friend Motley may have overestimated Holmes's potentialities, but he was right when he wrote in 1857: "But you can't do what

231

I wish you to do, except upon two conditions—one, devotion of your faculties and your time to the one great object—the other, cotton wooling your ears absolutely to all hand clappings and greasy mob applause of mercantile lecture rooms."[33] He was hitting here at Holmes's greatest weaknesses. Never overestimating his own work, nor taking the praise lavished on him as being anything more than journalistic stereotypes, Holmes still could not keep from responding to the flattery. He even knew that his plays for effect, however well they went down with an audience, were bad for him. He confesses to having learned "to take out the really good things which don't tell on the audience, and put in the cheaper things that do." He admitted that "all this degrades him, of course."[34]

It might as well be said right here that Holmes never did follow Motley's first injunction. "Devotion . . . to the one great object" Holmes had shown only as a medical student, and imperfectly as a doctor, gradually allowing requests to provide verses for special occasions and invitations to lecture to encroach upon his professional life. "See here, my son, what industry can do" his father had told him long ago, pointing out the moral of the bookworm, but the moral was lost on Holmes. Until he was nearly seventy-five years old, when it was a little late for the kind of devotion Motley had in mind, Holmes divided his talents; he taught medicine, he wrote for the *Atlantic Monthly*, and he entertained his fellow-citizens at dinner-tables and public functions.

It was too late, in 1857, for the versatile doctor to change his habits, but it was not too late for him to stretch his mind a little more and make a better showing before the public than he had in the lecture-halls. He had begun to think of publishing, not the lectures—he had no illusions about those—but some of the poems he had used as ornaments. Characteristically hesitant and uncertain, he did not send them to *Putnam's Monthly* as he thought of doing.[35] But opportunely for Holmes as for other New England writers, a new magazine, paying high prices and ably edited, was in the offing.

Autocrat of the Breakfast-Table

1857–1858

*Many of these excellent essays were written as
hastily as an ordinary letter.*

AT THREE O'CLOCK on the afternoon of Tuesday, May
5, 1857, eight men were gathered at the dinner table in the
Parker House. The host for the occasion, Mr. Moses Dresser
Phillips, head of the publishing firm of Phillips, Sampson &
Company, was a practical businessman who ordinarily took
no more than thirty minutes for his dinner; but this time he
did not leave his table until eight o'clock after the "richest
day intellectually" he had ever had. At his right sat Ralph
Waldo Emerson and at his left Henry Wadsworth Longfellow. Next to Emerson was Oliver Wendell Holmes, and on
the doctor's right sat James Russell Lowell. Opposite Holmes
was John Lothrop Motley, the historian. The gentleman opposite Lowell was J. Elliot Cabot.

The eighth guest at the foot of the table was a person of
small importance in the host's eyes—"my literary man," Phillips called him; but to Francis Henry Underwood the dinner
was not, as it was to his employer, the beginning of a venture,
but the culmination of a scheme he had long had in mind—
the founding of a magazine.

Through William Lee, the junior partner in the publishing house, Underwood had finally aroused the interest of the
skeptical Phillips, who now on May 5 sat proudly at the head
of his table of distinguished guests—"that brilliant constella-
tion of philosophical, poetic, and historical talent." On the
following evening the group met again—this time the authors

played host to the publisher—and Underwood's magazine was a settled project, with Professor Lowell as editor and Dr. Holmes as godfather, for Holmes gave it its name—*The Atlantic Monthly*.[1]

Undiscouraged by his own failure in 1853 or the recent folding of the promising New York magazine, *Putnam's Monthly,* and undeterred by the inauspicious financial conditions of 1857, Underwood had been working all during the spring to get the local writers and his employer Phillips to put the project into effect. He had turned first of all to Lowell, of whose interest he could be sure, for Lowell had tried such a scheme himself with the *Pioneer* in 1843 and had been ready to contribute to Underwood's abortive periodical in 1853.

There was no dearth of possible contributors; Boston, Cambridge, and Concord were, if anything, overflowing with varied talent. And as Lowell knew, if Underwood perhaps did not, a magazine to be permanently successful needed not the popularity that comes from catering solely to the tastes of the mob but rather the less spectacular popularity that comes from "as much variety as possible." "It is not merely necessary that the matter should be good," he had told Briggs, the editor of *Putnam's,* "but that it should be individual." [2]

Some such idea as that must have been in Lowell's mind when he made his acceptance of the editorship of Underwood's magazine dependent upon being able to secure the contributions of writers like Holmes. It was in 1884—nearly thirty years later—that Lowell wrote Holmes: "When I accepted the editorship of the *Atlantic,* I made it a condition precedent that you were the first contributor to be engaged." [3] It seems likely that the often-quoted passage is a piece of kindly exaggeration, for Lowell knew well enough that Holmes would be pleased to think that the magazine to which he had so long contributed had never been able to get along without him.

A more reasonable assumption is that Lowell, who knew the value of variety, urged Holmes and other conservative thinkers and writers upon Underwood to offset the latter's choice of contributors who were radical—specifically antislavery—in their views. Underwood's first attempt to found a periodical had been a literary and anti-slavery magazine with the star contributor Harriet Beecher Stowe, whose best-seller, *Uncle Tom's Cabin,* he had seen through the press in 1852. It seems probable that the desire for balancing the weighty and radical with the light and conservative determined the choice of Edwin Percy Whipple, an agreeable and fashionable critic, who like Holmes had won an enormous following as a lyceum lecturer. Whittier and Mrs. Stowe, on the other side of the political fence, were appealed to for non-political contributions, and Emerson was asked to get something from Thoreau. Lowell's wish was to make the magazine "free without being fanatical . . . to unite in it all available talent of all shades of opinion." [4]

After some delays, the new periodical made its first appearance with the issue for November. On page 47 appeared the two most provocative of its nineteen unsigned contributions—the one, four quatrains entitled "Brahma," and the other a prose piece called "The Autocrat of the Breakfast-Table." In spite of the magazine's policy of keeping its articles anonymous, there could be no secret about the authorship here. The Autocrat might claim in his paper that he talked "like a Transcendentalist" and pretend that his friend "the Professor" had written one of the verses he offered, but few readers were deceived. It was obviously Dr. Holmes who rattled on about mathematics, mutual admiration societies, puns, the naturalness of conceit, and self-made men, and who wound up his paper as he had wound up his lectures, with a poem or two. As for "Brahma," only a real transcendentalist like Emerson could have written the baffling sixteen lines beginning "If the red slayer think he slays."

Emerson's poem was parodied and talked about everywhere, some readers covering their bewilderment with mockery and others trying to understand it. "If I'd called it "Jehovah," Emerson later remarked dryly to his daughter, "everyone would have known what I meant." *The Autocrat* caused no such discomfort but evoked fulsome praise; some of it is so thick with exaggerations that by comparison a modern radio commercial is a model of restraint. Even a southern paper the *Charlestown Courant,* which could scarcely find one good word to say of the *Atlantic,* with all the "ugly African features that marked its birth," grudgingly admitted that *The Autocrat* was "clever" and that it saved the magazine from dullness. Whatever form it took, the furor over page 47 of the first number of the *Atlantic* was useful advertising; Underwood could report to his editor that "the orders for the second number are doubling those on the first." [5]

Part of the success of the first number was owing to the Jeremiahs who had anticipated its failure. It was so good that the prophets were confounded. The pre-publication talk was in its way good publicity. Proud Bostonians were quick to point out its virtues to the birds of ill omen and to continue to beam upon the baby long after its delivery. Born of two ugly parents—the antislavery controversy and the financial depression—the child was beautiful, and Boston never got over praising it and spoiling it in consequence. The magazine, highly approved in England, became a touchstone of "culture," a fact amusingly illustrated in an observation made by Thomas Wentworth Higginson. Visiting a rural town in the—to a Bostonian—hinterlands of Pennsylvania, he observed of the natives that they were not only literate, but cultured—nearly all took the *Atlantic.*

The fortunes of *The Autocrat* and the *Atlantic Monthly* were closely bound to each other; nearly every flattering notice of an issue of the magazine had its special praise for the Breakfast-Table papers and its reminder of Dr. Holmes's popular verses. Writing from England, Motley reported to Holmes that the *Atlantic* was a favorite of the critical members of the Athenaeum Club. English readers were already familiar with Longfellow and Emerson; of Holmes they had known only the little that one volume of verses could tell them; the *Atlantic* gave him an English audience. At a dinner party, reported by Motley, it was Thackeray who introduced the subject of *The Autocrat,* asking his neighbor on the other side of the table, " 'Have you read the Autocrat of the Break-fast-Table by Holmes in the new *Atlantic* magazine?' He then went on to observe that *no man in England* could now write with the charming mixture of wit, pathos and imagination—that your papers were better by far than anything in their magazines." [6]

News of this kind provided the Autocrat with the answer to the indirect question with which he had ended his first number. Rarely offering his literary wares on his own account, Holmes was in the habit of waiting to be coaxed. When he ended his first paper with the remark that he has said a good many things which he might print "some time or other, if urged . . . to do it by judicious friends," [7] he was asking if his audience wanted more. And before three issues of the magazine appeared,[8] there was no doubt that the public was clamoring for the Autocrat's breakfast-table chatter; the writer's own breakfast-table became swamped with fan-mail, his correspondents, English and American, telling him what to write, offering him stories, protesting his statements, and asking his opinions. By the fourth issue, he announced that he was so well pleased with his boarding house that he intended to remain there perhaps for years.

The papers which he produced for successive issues of the *Atlantic* owe very little to the two original numbers of the *Autocrat of the Breakfast-Table* which had appeared in the *New England Magazine* twenty-five years earlier.[9] Only the fiction that the Autocrat rules a boarding-house breakfast table is preserved. The young Autocrat had been a cocky youth, arrogant in manner, and affected in style, standoffish in his attitude toward his fellow-boarders, protecting himself behind a façade of pseudo-sophistication. He had strung together isolated aphorisms, carefully made-up epigrams. The new Autocrat is an easier, more natural, more candid man than the other.

So personal is the Autocrat's talk that the biographer has the sense of standing at the doctor's elbow as he wrote each paper; again and again the stimulus for a piece of conversation was some event of the doctor's life, something which had happened just now. In September Holmes visited "Governor" Swain of Naushon Island;[10] the Autocrat's second paper, written on his return, gave a discreet account of the island and its host, famous for his hunting parties at which the literary guests were expected to provide verses. Holmes went to a class reunion in January; in the fifth number of *The Autocrat,* the Professor's intoxication of pride in the "Boys of '29" was described. The doctor let his *alter ego* be more sentimental than he dared to be in his own person of the Autocrat. In June the Holmes family moved into a new house at 21 Charles Street; the thoughts evoked by the change went into the August paper he was then writing. The new house overlooked the Charles River, giving the doctor a convenient place to moor his little boats, kayak-like affairs, in which he sculled out towards the harbor nearly every morning before breakfast. The boarders were promptly treated to a lecture on the healthful pleasures of rowing. He was called in at the last minute to pinch-hit for Rufus Choate, a formidable orator, at Dartmouth's commencement; his reminiscences of Hanover appeared in the September number. He was, in fact, in danger of being too personal. Motley recognized an allusion to himself as one of the wise men of Boston; Holmes had quoted in the sixth number Motley's famous saying—recently attributed to Frank Lloyd Wright—"give me the luxuries of life, and I'll dispense with the necessities." The historian wrote the Autocrat: "If you ever so much as hint at my existence again, I'll never forgive you."[11]

At the beginning of the first essay were five paragraphs on the general theme of mutual admiration societies. The Autocrat blushed to report that he did not belong to such a group. But in May and again in August 1857, he had been a special guest at the Saturday Club—a "stranger" according to Emerson's journal—first for a birthday dinner for Louis

Agassiz and second for a farewell party for John Lothrop Motley, both original members of this "Mutual Admiration Society" upon which the Autocrat in his first paper cast an admittedly envious eye.

Weaving a conversation-piece out of reminiscence, literary allusion, provincial pride, and distaste for the vulgarities of the American press, the Autocrat introduces a clever arrangement of what he euphemistically calls the "false premises" of the literary snob who has not been asked to join such a society. The passage works itself neatly down to the revealing truth. The false premises are:

First, that men of talent necessarily hate each other. Secondly that . . . habitual association destroys our admiration of persons we esteem highly at a distance. Thirdly, that a circle of clever fellows, who meet together to dine and have a good time, have signed a contract to glorify themselves and to put down him and the fraction of the human race not belonging to their number. Fourthly, that it is an outrage that he is not asked to join them.[12]

Although Holmes nowhere in the passage calls the Saturday Club by name, its members could not miss the fact that the Autocrat had them in mind. Near the close, he heaps up allusions to similar gatherings in literary history; the groups who met with Jonson and Shakespeare at the Mermaid Tavern, Addison and Steele, or Johnson and Reynolds in their London coffee-houses were flattering analogies to those who on the last Saturday of every month sat at the Parker House dining-table with Agassiz and Longfellow.

In September, about the time Holmes's first paper went to press, Motley wrote him from Europe asking to be remembered to "all the members of our Club which I hope you have regularly joined by this time." [13] And on the afternoon of October 31, almost simultaneously with the publication of the first number of the magazine, Agassiz and Benjamin Peirce stopped at 8 Montgomery Place on their way to the Parker House. They came as official escorts for Dr. Holmes, the new member of the Saturday Club.[14]

It was only in such a gesture that the group was in any

way formal in its proceedings; there were no by-laws and no officers, although Agassiz sat at the head of the table "by native right of his huge good fellowship and intense enjoyment of the scene." [15] The ordering of the wines and the seven-course dinner was usually left to the lawyer and gourmet, Horatio Woodman, one of the original founders of the club, whose taste for the society of the great men of his community won him the label of "genius broker." [16] No secretary, had there been one, could have recorded the nuances, the wit, the complexities of the conversation that passed back and forth across the dinner table for some six hours.

The Club was "strung like a harp with about a dozen ringing intelligences, each answering to some chord of the macrocosm," wrote the Autocrat for his third paper; and he went on to describe the kind of dinner-table talk such a gathering produced: "that carnival-shower of questions and replies and comments, large axioms bowled over the mahogany like bomb-shells from professional mortars, and explosive wit dropping its trains of many-colored fire, and the mischief making rain of bon-bons pelting everybody that shows himself." [17] At the Parker House, Holmes could not play the Autocrat, for his companions were not meek school-mistresses, or uncertain divinity students, but scientists, Peirce and Agassiz; poets, Lowell and Longfellow; lawyers, Rockwood Hoar and R. H. Dana; a musician, Thomas Dwight; a historian, Motley; a philosopher, Emerson. Even men-about-town like Sam Ward and Tom Appleton, whose main business in life was with dinner parties, could keep their end up fairly well in talk with men of larger intellects than their own.

If few records of the talk survive, there is some suggestion of the kind of subjects tackled. For the meeting of January 30, 1858, Emerson brought as a guest Bronson Alcott. Obviously the latter did not think the conversation quite up to his own lofty level, but he thought the talk "spirited." It turned chiefly "upon Personal Identities, the distinctions, physical, and metaphysical, between man and beast. *I* would have discriminated more fully and finely between the three-fold forces of *brute, human, and divine,* in whose mixture and interplay life itself consists; but the company were unused to such analysis, and talked to the senses the more becomingly, as naturalists, and observers can." [18] The last observation suggests that Agassiz and Holmes carried the burden of this particular conversation.

Another observer's account of some Saturday Club table-talk suggests what happened when the three most garrulous members of the group fell into debate. Motley set off the fireworks with a proposition with which Holmes immediately disagreed; then Lowell broke in, differing with both of them. In the three-cornered battle that ensued, the disputants all talked at once, "with an occasional ringing sentence thrown in by Judge Hoar for the benevolent purpose of increasing a complication already sufficient to tax the resources and wit of the combatants." Whipple, reporting the affair, went on to observe:

Still, in the incessant din of voices, every point made by one was replied to by another or ridiculed by a third, and was instantly followed by new statements, counter-statements, arguments and counter-arguments, hits and retorts, all germane to the matter, and all directed to a definite end. The curiosity of the contest was that none of the combatants repeated anything which had once been thrown out as irrelevant, and that . . . the course of the discussion was as clear to the mind as though there had been a minute's pause between statement and reply. . . . The other members of the Club looked on in mute wonder while witnessing these feats of intellectual and vocal gymnastics. If any other man than Judge Hoar had ventured in, his voice and thought would have been half a minute behind the point which the discussion had reached . . . judging by the ear, I came to the conclusion that in swiftness of utterance Motley was two-sixteenths of a second ahead of Holmes and nine-sixteenths of a second ahead of Lowell.[19]

Perhaps Lowell and Motley knew only too well that the best way to keep Dr. Holmes from monopolizing the subject was to talk at the same time. One wonders if Lowell's obvious relish in reporting in his letters occasions upon which any member or visitor managed to bring the doctor up short is not touched with a little malice; he was a brilliant talker himself and much less likely to ride hobbies than the doctor, but apparently not quite so quick. Delight in seeing Wendell Holmes the object of another's wit as well as a special affection for John Holmes and appreciation for the good jest may have prompted him to record the following:

The Autocrat giving an account of his having learned the fiddle, his brother John who sat opposite, exclaimed, "I can testify to it; he has often fiddled me out of the house as Orpheus did Eurydice out of the infernal regions." [20]

At his imaginary breakfast-table, Dr. Holmes could say what he liked and let the Autocrat win every round. If it were necessary to provide him with an opponent, Holmes had only to call in one of his counterparts to Sairy Gamp's Mrs. 'Arris—the Professor or the Poet—and stage a debate with himself. Yet he does include among his boarders the young fellow called John who in his role as deflater, if in no other respect, resembles his creator's brother.

The intensely personal quality of the Autocrat's papers does not lie, however, in such chance resemblances between the boarders and people Holmes knew; it comes from the real spontaneity of the papers. With no over-all design in his mind, Holmes wrote each one to meet a monthly deadline. So casually are the papers written that he does not even bother to adapt his allusions for the actual publication date. Nor is there any attempt to give the papers an artificial unity. The slight romance—the Autocrat's wooing of the Schoolmistress—was an afterthought; it is not until the ninth number of the twelve that Holmes makes his breakfast-table dictator regard the young girl among the boarders as anything more than a barometer to register the pressure of his wit. Quite likely his correspondents had badgered him to put into his papers that essential of magazine prose, a romance. The type of correspondent who browbeat Louisa May Alcott into digging up a husband for Jo March in *Little Women* undoubtedly went after Holmes on behalf of the Schoolmistress.

Many other elements in the papers were plainly evoked by

the fan-mail he began to receive after the first numbers and by press notices of the magazine. Almost the whole of the third paper grew out of the Autocrat's sensitivity to criticism; he hated to be called "droll" and his personal feeling here led him to an impersonal and effective contrast between wit and wisdom:

There is a perfect consciousness in every form of wit,—using that term in its general sense,—that its essence consists in a partial view . . . whatever it touches. It throws a single ray, separated from the rest,—red, yellow, or blue, or any intermediate shade,—upon an object; never white light; that is the province of wisdom. We get beautiful effects from wit,—all the prismatic colors,—but never the object as it is in fair daylight. A pun, which is a kind of wit, is a different and much shallower trick in mental optics; throwing the *shadows* of two objects so that one overlies the other.[21]

When a correspondent asked where he got his analogies, the Autocrat was moved to a lyrical outburst, with a slight transcendental flavor about it. He exclaimed, "Nothing is clearer than that all things are in all things, and that just according to the intensity and extension of our mental being we shall see the many in the one and the one in the many." [22] The universe is swimming in an "ocean of similitudes and analogies"; out of it he plucked "The Chambered Nautilus."

Starting out his fifth paper, the Autocrat recalled the heady experience of writing the poem and opened with an extravagant and excited description of his feelings in such moments of creative action. The poem justifies his excitement; he had never before and would never again hit the same level in a wholly serious lyric.

Not all the poems in *The Autocrat* were written at the moment; some were verses dragged up out of old lectures. That the lectures provided him with raw material he admits when he allows the deflater John to call him on a passage. In fact, it is possible to trace a good many passages to their parallels in the lectures. And, asks a boarder, doesn't he "read up various matters to talk about?" The Autocrat says not, although for the next paper, the Professor's essay on old age, Dr. Holmes borrowed Cicero from the Athenaeum, and later Michaux on North American trees for his tenth paper. Such recourse to books was apparently rare; even here his object seems to have been only to check with sources he already knew. For the most part the Autocrat, obeying his own rule: "Talk about those subjects you have long had in your mind," rides his hobbies hard. Pseudo-science, moral bullying, the art of conversation, vulgarisms of speech and behavior—all these themes which he had been for many years exploiting in verse and in lectures—recur again and again in the Breakfast-Table papers; the variety of his images and illustrations saves his reiteration of these themes from becoming monotonous. Although he comes back to some of them with the persistence of an Uncle Toby, he can still surprise his reader with some fresh expression of his thought.

For example, the Autocrat's insistence that logic of itself is of slight value appears in many guises—in a mildly derisive description of the mathematical mind (a passage colored by its author's own failings as a mathematician), in a number of neat illustrations of the absurdity rigid logic can lead to, in references to the futility of logic in a debate between two people who have no basic assumptions in common. This scorn of logic *per se* finds its final and best expression in "The Deacon's Masterpiece"; the One-Hoss Shay:

> That was built in such a logical way
> It ran a hundred years to a day,
> And then, of a sudden, it . . . went to pieces all at once,
> All at once, and nothing first,—
> Just as bubbles do when they burst.
>
> End of the wonderful one-hoss-shay.
> Logic is logic. That's all I say.

In it, Holmes satirizes effectively any logical system (not necessarily Calvinism) supposed by its authors to be perfect, uncorrectable, and therefore, everlasting. A thought at which he had nibbled in talk, in verse, and in his private correspondence is here given complete expression.[23]

Unpremeditated and "dipped from the running stream"[24] of the author's thoughts, *The Autocrat of the Breakfast-Table*

justified the subtitle given it when it appeared in book form—
"Everyman his own Boswell." For the November number of
the *Atlantic,* which appeared shortly before the book, he
prepared an imaginary interview with the Autocrat's landlady who is made to remark, "Folks will be curious about
them that has wrote in the papers," and obligingly the landlady furnishes a realistic verbal description of Dr. Holmes.

This gentleman warn't no great of a gentleman to look at. Being of a
very moderate dimension,—five foot five *he* said, but five foot four more
likely, and I've heard him say he didn't weigh much over a hundred and
twenty pound. He was light-complected rather than darksome, and was
one of them smooth-faced people that keep their baird and wiskers cut
close, jest as if they'd be very troublesome if they let 'em grow,—instead
of layin' out their face in grass, as my poor husband that's dead and gone
used to say. He was a well-behaved gentleman at table, only . . . had a
way of turnin' up his nose when he didn't like what folks said, that one
of my boarders, who is a very smart young man, said he couldn't stand no
how, and used to make faces and poke fun at him whenever he see him
do it . . . nothin' could hurry him when he was about his vittles. Many's
the time I've seen that gentleman keepin' two or three of 'em settin'
round the breakfast-table after the rest had swallered their meal and the
things was cleared off, . . . and there that little man would set with a
tumbler of sugar and water,—what he used to call O Sukray,—a-talkin'
and a-talkin'. . . .[25]

Well-advertised and indecently puffed in the *Boston Transcript,* the book sold 10,000 copies in its first three days, and
more than double the number in the next few weeks.[26] In
the heat of his success, Holmes was tempted to accept an offer
made him by a New York publisher, Bonner, who wanted
a weekly column for his paper, the *Ledger;* but Phillips,
who paid cash and paid well, raised his offers enough to
persuade Holmes to abandon the notion of going elsewhere.[27]
From that point on, Holmes remained so faithful to the
Atlantic Monthly and to Ticknor and Fields (the publishing
house which soon took over the magazine and most of its
authors) that only in one or two special instances did his
work appear over any other American imprint.

The year 1858 came to an end with Dr. Holmes as a literary hit of the season. American and English reviewers showered him with praise; the latter found him the first creditable claimant to the honors they had conferred on Washington Irving. Meanwhile, the Autocrat's "friend," the Professor, had got two papers ready for the next series.

Professor at the Breakfast-Table

1859–1861

The history of his mind as to religion is an important article.

A T FIRST GLANCE, the Professor, who in January 1859 took over the Autocrat's chair at the breakfast-table, would seem to be the same man. He rides the same hobbies; he borrows some of the Autocrat's favorite images; his monthly papers owe something to his immediate experiences. But as the Professor at the Breakfast-Table, Holmes makes fewer jokes than he does as the Autocrat; his talk is less jerky, less lively; he pays more attention to his fellow-boarders. That he makes a serious attempt at characterization of three figures, (Iris, Little Boston, and the Model of all the Virtues) that he tries to hint at mysteries of plot and character, and that he introduces into his papers—especially toward the end—a number of action-scenes—these facts suggest that Holmes wanted to write a novel, didn't dare try it right away, but thought he'd practice a little.

As the Autocrat he had declared that every man had at least one novel in him and that he might try his hand at one eventually.[1] It was the Autocrat, however, who had remarked that "good jockeying" was important to authors: "Judicious management; letting the public see your animal just enough and not too much; holding him up hard when the market is too full of him; letting him out at just the right buying intervals."[2] The tentative story-telling of the Professor's papers is partly the jockeying of a practical man, partly the hesitancy of a timid one, and partly the fumbling of a man who had not made up his mind as to what his novel—when he got around to writing it—would be about. Holmes found the answer to the last question in the process of writing the Professor's papers; he found it in his character Little Boston.[3]

The grotesque little figure, whom the Professor first sees as a threat to his inherited sovereignty at the breakfast-table, plays many roles before the papers end. He is at the beginning a figure of not ungenerous fun—very obviously the Professor's *alter ego.* Holmes is laughing at himself when he says "What shall I do with this little man?—There is only one thing to do,—and that is, to let him talk when he will. The day of the Autocrat's monologues is over." [4] From a humorous little provincial, bursting with local pride, Little Boston changes rather abruptly to a bitter satirist; then, temporarily deprived of a speaking part, he becomes a medium through which Holmes attempts to bring out his heroine, Iris. By the final paper, he is as far as possible from being a figure of fun; he is the symbol and spokesman for a double theme that Holmes had asserted in *The Autocrat* and expanded in *The Professor,* and that he would dramatize in *Elsie Venner,* the novel he was on the verge of writing.

The interpretation of Little Boston as "a device by which [Holmes] disclaimed personal responsibility when he was afraid of shocking his readers," [5] seems untenable. Holmes was not in the least afraid of shocking his readers; in fact, he rather liked to do so. As the Autocrat, he had deliberately shocked the Divinity Student who, of course, was conveniently docile and easily awed. The religious press and private correspondents were not so meek, nor were they so polite as the Divinity Student. Scenting blasphemy in the Autocrat, orthodox believers of every sect, save the Unitarians, found it on nearly every page of *The Professor,* for the more numerous and violent the attacks, the more aggressively Holmes developed his religious reflections.

Holmes's claim that he never read abusive and adverse criticism is not a statement of fact, but rather an expression of affected indifference. In a scrapbook, obviously put together by Holmes himself, appear a large number of clippings of articles by the indignant defenders of orthodox religious beliefs.[6] Even as the first number of *The Professor* appeared in the *Atlantic*, Holmes was getting into trouble with his current lyceum lecture on "The Chief End of Man." As far as one can judge from the inadequate newspaper accounts, the lecture is an innocuous development of its text, taken from the Westminster catechism. To his contemporaries, however, his unorthodox sermon was heresy and insult. His suggestion that man's chief end might vary with the individual and might be sought and found in the course of his earthly life seems scarcely to be an extreme expression of rugged individualism, for the whole is tempered with a classical plea for harmony and balance, for the development of the whole man.[7] Apparently what terrified his audiences was the fact that he dared to take liberties with the conventional interpretation of the text. As Holmes came to observe, orthodox Protestants were curiously timid about accepting the responsibilities of their Protestantism and were as ready to cling to the raft of authoritarian dogma as those whose faith was based upon acceptance of authority.

Holmes could please the Unitarians with his desire for free inquiry and open discussion—the lecture and the Professor's papers earned him the post of principal speaker at the Unitarian Festival in May 1859. But he outraged the orthodox. In December 1858 the *Congregationalist* printed a dramatic report of a direct encounter between Holmes and his critics. The story is probably apocryphal, but that it should be told at all is suggestive. The Winchester·Library Association is reported as having requested that Holmes *not* give "The Chief End of Man." Holmes is supposed to have answered that he would give "that or none." The Committee replied, "None, then." "This," said the *Congregationalist*, "is very creditable to the young men. No lyceum lecturer has the right to outrage the religious sensibilities of an audience and the man who would do so ought to be proscribed." Holmes clipped the tale from the paper and put it in the scrapbook among a collection of items, written in the same spirit, that accumulated as he turned again and again to theology in *The Professor at the Breakfast-Table.*

In the first person singular, Holmes maintained some kind of poise in the face of the violent attacks of the evangelical press; in the disguise of Little Boston, he could, conveniently, lose his temper and at the same time laugh at himself for doing so. It is Little Boston who breaks out into a passionate satiric sketch of the anonymous newspaper writer.[8] The "Levi" who took exception to the Professor's theology and expressed his wrath in the *Boston Courier* of March 4, 1859, —the clipping is in the scrapbook—is only one example of the critics who are objects of Little Boston's satire. It was in March, of course, that Holmes was writing the fifth paper of *The Professor* in which his *alter ego's* satiric sketch appears; thus closely are the papers related to the attacks of the religious press, which found Holmes a more dangerous contributor to the *Atlantic* than Emerson.

Holmes could not let the subject of religious beliefs alone; presumably the May paper was to settle the matter. The Professor had found "a fly in his teacup"; he had not known "Truth was such an invalid" that it could not bear the fresh air of inquiry.[9] But he provoked with this paper a deluge of criticism to which he could not keep from replying. The matter was so much on his mind that in July he was nervous about calling for Harriet Beecher Stowe, whom he was to escort to an *Atlantic* party; the lady was, after all, the daughter of Lyman Beecher, whose brimstone sermons preached in his own father's church Holmes could not forget. He wondered if she would disapprove of him *very* much.[10] Of course, the doctor meant the remark as a joke, but it was symptomatic; moreover, it was probably a letter from her to which he had referred in the fifth of the Professor's papers.[11] At the party itself, the subject still pursued him; he devoted most of his time demonstrating to Mrs. Stowe's husband, an orthodox minister, that all swearing originates in the pulpit.

It must be added that he was not the only member of the

party bent on trifling with conventional sensibilities; it was Lowell who started the to-do about champagne, knowing very well that the Stowes were teetotalers; it was Lowell, too, who worked hard to prove to the Victorian Mrs. Stowe that *Tom Jones* was the greatest novel ever written. The witness for the aggressive talk of Holmes and Lowell is T. W. Higginson. Another of the special guests, Harriet Prescott Spofford, recalled of Holmes only that he "talked incessantly" and that she was "diverted from any act of memory by observations of the gesture with which he tossed back his head for asparagus and the amazing celerity with which he ate his ice." [12]

Holmes knew the value of critics like the one who attacked him with an irrational barrage of theological clichés and wound up anticlimactically with the suggestion that he was no fit company for Harriet Beecher Stowe; [13] but he could not be wholly indifferent to the mass of such criticism, and he could not help being disturbed when men he knew and respected went after him. He knew what he was talking about when he wrote for the August number that the reformer's "greatest spiritual danger was the perpetual *flattery of abuse.*" In the poem which follows, he suggests there is danger in being:

> Too kind for bitter words to grieve,
> Too firm for clamor to dismay. . . .[14]

He himself was neither, and, in the ninth paper, in the person of Little Boston, burst out:

The time is at hand when religion must be AMERICANIZED! Now, sir, you see what Americanizing is in politics;—it means that a man shall have a vote because he is a man,—and shall vote for whom he pleases, without his neighbor's interference. If he chooses to vote for the Devil, that is his lookout;—perhaps he thinks the Devil is better than the other candidate; and I don't doubt he's often right, Sir! [15]

And abruptly, the heroine's devotion to the little cripple, hinted at mysteriously before, is explained in terms of his religious independence, giving Holmes a chance to recall his own struggles with the unpleasant dogmas of his father's church. It becomes very plain at just this point in the Professor's paper, that that conflict is not won. Holmes is no serene Emerson confidently offering the results of private reflections; he is a man on the defensive, thinking on his feet, in part to justify his rejection of his father's creed and in part to work out his own. One suspects that some of what appears to modern readers of Holmes as psychological insight, anticipating twentieth-century ideas, is the result of introspection and rationalization forced upon him in the midst of this battle. He was an old man when he wrote in his autobiographical notes: "No child can overcome these early impressions without doing violence to the whole mental and moral machinery of his being. He may conquer them in after years, but the wrenches and strains which his victory has cost him leave him a cripple as compared with a child trained in sound and reasonable beliefs." [16] What he here expressed with admitted reference to himself, he offered in *The Professor* and in the novels which follow as a general proposition. In his battle against all faiths which accept the doctrine of original sin, he protested with passion its dangerous effects on sensitive children.

Significant of his altered feelings in this running warfare with the religious press is the fact that, in the ninth number, Little Boston is made to fall ill; a dying man, he can no longer be laughed at. Moreover he is now referred to as "the Little Gentleman." In the subsequent papers, the religious theme seems to have been pushed temporarily in the background as Holmes busies himself somewhat vaguely with Iris, a Hawthornesque heroine in so far as her problem is that of a woman of genius. But beyond an intention of leading up to Little Boston's death, Holmes had no clear idea of where he was going in his story. The three papers which follow are melancholy and sluggish, befogged with mystery, and relieved only by a few flashes of the Autocrat's old vivacity and humor. The eleventh paper, recalling youthful superstitions, and dwelling upon deaths he has watched as a doctor, works around to the religious theme and closes with a hymn.

The reader has the feeling that the author is marking time, filling up space, until he reaches the end.

In the final paper, the Divinity Student is made to invade the room where Little Boston lies, and there made to feel the presumption of his act in the face of the little man's passionate independence and his physical deformity; he is made to do so not because Holmes had planned the scene from the very beginning, but because in the course of his religious conflict, he had reached the point where he needed to dramatize both his own faith and his belief that the human will is a "limited agency," a "drop of water imprisoned in a crystal." [17] One cannot help feeling that the whole passage, beginning with the Divinity Student's concern for the Little Gentleman's spiritual welfare and ending with the death scene, was written at the same time as the ninth paper in which he first falls ill. With more energy and life than he shows in the intervening papers and more lucidity, Holmes rushes through sharp satire to the climactic and passionate speech in which the dying cripple is made to reply to the Divinity Student, whom Holmes sacrifices twice, once upon his own rationalism and once upon his *alter ego's* passion.

That after the little man's outburst the scene drops off into gross sentimentality cannot be denied; but a biographer has somehow to forgive Holmes for literary sins, if a critic cannot, for it is impossible to doubt his honesty. Hoping for peace with his critics, he ended his series with the best known of his hymns, "Lord of all Being, throned afar."

Playing a minor accompaniment to the developing religious theme in Holmes's *Atlantic* papers is a medical motif. He began to see his old bugbear homeopathy as analogous to the contemporary vogue of spiritualism. The Professor, in a moment of pique, describes them both as retributory plagues: the one visited upon medicine for its slavish adherence to old forms of practice and disproved theories of disease; the other, upon theology for its old-fashioned approach to moral problems and its demonstrably untenable beliefs.[18]

The analogy pleased him; and in the following year, on

May 26, 1860, he gave it in altered form to his colleagues in the Massachusetts Medical Society.

The address, *Currents and Counter-Currents in Medical Science*, offers a reasonably accurate representation of the intellectual temper of the period of which it speaks. "Those new tables of the law, placed in the hand of the geologist . . . have remodelled the beliefs of half the civilized world"; [19] the consequence, of course, is the unsettling of traditional ideas and growing skepticism. It is, suggests Holmes, this last terrifying state of mind that sends men scuttling behind the protecting barricades of the oldest dogmas or those of the newest mystical fancy. With the newest fancies in medicine, he had dealt elsewhere; in this address he turned his batteries upon the dogmatists within the regular profession—the practitioners of the "heroic" method who still existed in sufficient numbers to justify the general statement that "the community is overdosed."

How could a people which has a revolution once in four years, which has contrived the Bowie knife and the revolver, which has chewed the juice out of all the superlatives in the language in Fourth of July Orations, . . . which insists on sending out yachts and horses and boys to out-sail, out-run, out-fight, and checkmate the rest of creation; how could such a people be content with any but the "heroic" practice? What wonder that the Stars and Stripes wave over doses of ninety grains of sulphate of quinine, and that the American eagle screams with delight to see three drachms of calomel given at a single mouthful.[20]

The administration in large doses of drugs of known danger and unproved value was to Holmes the major crime of the profession. To him the essential duties of a physician were to *prevent* disease, to ensure the best hygienic conditions for both the sick and the well, to make accurate diagnoses and prognoses, and to make the patient as comfortable as possible. The administration of drugs (chiefly to relieve symptoms) would then be incidental to this last. In Holmes's judgment, the dogmatic old-fashioned practitioner's faith in drugs was sheer superstition but once removed from a primitive belief in evil spirits. It was, furthermore, a pusillanimous yielding to the ignorance and folly of patients. The bulk of contemporary medical literature was directed too much to the eulogies of favorite nostrums, to irrational and untested claims of cures effected by them; meanwhile, Holmes pointed out, the patent-medicine manufacturers and homeopathists got rich.

"The causes of disease, in the meantime, have been less earnestly studied in the eagerness of the search for remedies." [21] The few careful observers who had given their energies to the study of causes were unappreciated if they were not abused. Holmes reminded his listeners that the few well-tested specifics in use were discovered by laymen, not by doctors. These few specifics, along with opium, and the "vapors which produce the miracle of anaesthesia" might be saved out, but for the rest, "if the whole materia medica, as now used, could be sunk to the bottom of the sea, it would be all the better for mankind,—and all the worse for the fishes." [22] In the process of accounting for the persistence of a practice repeatedly called in question by the discoveries of contemporary science, Holmes, in effect, implied that the majority of contemporary practitioners were ignorant, timid, unintelligent, lazy, and greedy.

Not unnaturally, some members of the profession were indignant. Even before the address appeared in print it was attacked; a small group of members of the society met on the following day to discuss and to pass by a narrow margin a censorious vote disclaiming agreement; the printed essay received the usual range of comment all the way from lavish praise to abuse; by now Holmes was sufficiently inured to vituperation almost to welcome it. "A loud outcry on a slight touch," he decided, "reveals the weak spot in a profession, as well as a patient"; [23] moreover, on medical matters, he was on solid ground, confident of his knowledge and sure of the support of the medical men he most respected.[24]

The *Atlantic Monthly*, in the meantime, was still flourishing; its subscribers now numbered 40,000, in spite of the financial failure of the publisher, Phillips, and the injunction laid by some preachers upon the members of their congregations not to read its subversive pages. Ticknor and Fields had bought the magazine and were continuing Phillips's liberal rates of pay. The magazine was clearly a success, and no small part of its popularity was due to Holmes.

The enthusiastic reception of his work in some quarters is accounted for by the reader's surprise; Lowell, who had been fairly confident at the start, was not the only one "astounded"; other critics confessed they had not supposed he had it in him. Now that he had begun to produce in his monthly papers something which was taking shape as a novel, there was fresh reason for surprise. *The Professor's Story,* published as *Elsie Venner,* fumbles somewhat at the start as the doctor presents his hero, Bernard Langdon, in one setting and then arbitrarily transfers him to another as if he had not entirely settled upon his plot. Once Bernard is installed as a teacher in Silas Peckman's boarding-school for girls in the village of Rockland, the professor's narrative is under way and moves as smoothly as Holmes's gadfly mind would permit.

For his setting, Holmes drew upon the villages he knew best: Pittsfield, Hanover, and the Cambridge of his youth. The "mansion houses" are those of Cambridge's Tory Row and the less pretentious "genteel houses" are almost identical to Holmes's birthplace; Pollard's Tavern is Porter's, remembered from college days even to its famous "flip." New Hampshire legend and Hawthorne supplied him with a convenient avalanche; and a number of New England towns suggested Rockland with its single overshadowing mountain. The school was suggested by The Young Ladies' Institute in Pittsfield, for one of whose public occasions Holmes had provided a poem.

In so far as Holmes presents the village types and its social hierarchy realistically, he anticipates the local colorists, but the rendering of the New England village is only incidental to his story, amusing filler in a narrative spun out to fill so many columns in a monthly magazine. Holmes never would write a carefully constructed novel, and he had too little power of invention to do more in the loose framework of a rambling tale than write essays and wittily turned character sketches. The Autocrat has in fact done no more than abandon his boarding-house fiction, cut down the amount of his discursive table-talk, and add a number of half-described and half-dramatized scenes rather loosely basted together by plot-threads. The whole is given a specious unity by periodically arousing curiosity about the strange and bewildering heroine of the story—Elsie Venner. The few segments of plot are finished off with the conventional devices of marriage, death, and banishment. It is all done in a pleasantly casual manner that makes each scene the stimulus for the Autocrat's reflections, expressed directly or through the medium of the village doctor.

The story does, however, have a central theme—the theme shadowed forth in Little Boston and plainly stated as early as *The Autocrat* in the following passage.

When I compared the human will to a drop in a crystal, and said I meant to *define* moral obligations, and not weaken them, this was what I intended to express: that the fluent, self-determining power of human beings is a very strictly limited agency in the universe. The chief planes of its enclosing solid are, of course, organization, education, condition. Organization may reduce the power of the will to nothing, as in some idiots; and from this zero the scale mounts upwards by slight gradations. Education is only second to nature. . . . Condition does less, but "Give me neither poverty nor riches" was the prayer of Agur, and with good reason. If there is any improvement in modern theology, it is in getting out of the region of pure abstractions and taking these every-day working forces into account.[25]

The illustration of this theme is the character Elsie Venner, a person in whom the will is reduced to a point where her behavior is abnormal; the "force" which effects this limitation is organization. At the risk of being implausible, unscientific, and inartistic, Holmes chose the most obvious means of making it plain that Elsie's behavior is due to no fault of her own, but is inherent in her physical make-up. Holmes used as his base a variation on the familiar old wives' tale of pre-natal influence, which had sufficient currency in his own day to be the subject of discussion at medical meetings and of bizarre stories solemnly reported in medical journals. He created an ophidian heroine and offered as the cause of her abnormal behavior the fact that her mother was bitten by a rattlesnake before the child's birth, the poisoning producing in the girl a dual personality, half-snake and half-woman. He then proceeded, in effect, to dare anyone to hold the unfortunate creature accountable for her acts. In dramatizing his theme of the limitations of the will, Holmes did indeed take "an extreme case to begin with,"— a case he knew might not be plausible from "an aesthetic or physiological point of view," [26] however obviously it illustrated his point.

He failed to see that to make Elsie an acceptable character and not merely an academic illustration of his text he had to take some thought for her plausibility from both those points of view. A Hawthorne might have managed to induce in his readers that "willing suspension of disbelief" necessary before a modern reader can go the whole way toward accepting the character, but Holmes could not. He was unable to achieve that fusion of the real and unreal he had so much admired in *The House of the Seven Gables*. His failure there shows up distressingly in his Gothic character, Dick Venner, and in the melodramatic scene on rattlesnake ledge where Elsie rescues the hero with a snake-charming act that no reader imbued with Dr. Holmes's rational spirit can accept. There can be no enchantment in the aura created by both the raconteur and the raisonneur of the story, the Professor and the country doctor, both rationalists and scientists. But if a reader can somehow ignore the inept Gothic touches and if he is willing to take the pre-natal poisoning for what it is worth to Holmes's thesis, there is no question but that Holmes makes his case.

That is not to say that he persuaded his opponents. The religious press was up in arms from the first number of the novel; the *Northwest Christian Advocate* of Chicago saw fit to run a series of articles warning its readers against the story as its plot was unfolded month by month. When it finally appeared in book form, the Chicago journal heaved a sigh of relief that the doctor was done "deriding the only principles capable of holding society to its moorings." Said the Chicago writer: "His diluted Emersonianism is at last bottled and corked and labeled." Meanwhile in the East, even in Boston, center of diluted Emersonianism, the doctor was being greeted as a Mohammedan. On the whole his critics, not without good reason, were as confused as they were shocked by the doctor's theology.

It cannot be said that other critics showed much more sense in their appraisals of the book than irate fundamentalists. Victorian modesty was outraged by the doctor's indelicacy and accused him of violating the secrets of the consulting-room. The self-appointed press agent of the *Boston Evening Transcript* strangled himself on his own adjectives; and Lowell's review is that of a man walking on eggs for fear of offending a personal friend. Poor in quality, the reviews seem significant only in their quantity, their number suggesting the extent of Holmes's contemporary fame. The "dearest inmate of our bosoms" (San Francisco), the "American Sterne" (London) was expected (by Philadelphia) to contribute to "the everlasting glory of his nation," provided he didn't become too infected with that "curious product . . . Bostonian philosophy"; he had produced "one of the best American novels, and the best story of New England life, that it was ever our fortune to read," (New York).

None of the contemporary critics of *Elsie Venner,* whether or not they could accept his theology, followed out the implications of his suggestion that Elsie was a case for the doctor. An indignant Wesleyan evangelist, who declared that what Elsie needed was prompt exposure to a Methodist revival meeting, illustrates the extreme of obtuseness, but the Methodist had rejected Holmes's major premise and could not be expected to look upon her as sick, not wicked. Other critics sentimentalized over poor Elsie or, in a burst of humanitarian feeling agreed to judge their fellow-men less harshly.[27]

And at that, they were closer to a reasonable response to the story than modern critics who hail Holmes as the great anticipator of Freud; such a judgment is extravagant both in implying that Holmes was alone in such anticipations and in estimating the extent of them.

Elsie's "case" presents analogies to those which might be found in a modern doctor's notes. Holmes, however, was offering in Elsie the results of observation only; he did not attempt to go beyond description into analysis of the psychological problem Elsie presented. Even when his own contemporaries wrote commenting on the similarity between Elsie and cases of "moral insanity" they had observed, Holmes was merely pleased to find his character more plausible than he thought she might be. By accident, her self-isolation, her behavior with her father, her recourse to violence, her orgiastic dancing—all look like a knowing selection of details; but these details are combined with others not drawn from a doctor's casebook. Elsie is, in fact, a haphazard mixture of whatever would contribute to her total effect, whatever would make her appear terrifying and half-human. Holmes gives her a long neck and diamond-shaped eyes; he uses allusions to myths of werewolves and magical transformations of men into creatures; he adds the "evil eye," throws in a little animal magnetism, and garnishes the whole with some accurate symptoms of hysteria.

Holmes's conception of Elsie's character depends upon a physiological not a psychological assumption. He rests his case on an actual poisoning of the human embryo, and presents Elsie as having the physical characteristics of a snake, even to literal cold-bloodedness. Her changes of mood, her shifts from torpor to activity are seasonal, dependent on climatic changes not motivated by emotional experiences. She is not shown as having the delusion that she is half-snake; she is actually made so. When Holmes makes Elsie's Negro attendant exclaim that Elsie is "not a woman," he is not—as a modern commentator has suggested [28]—implying that she is homosexual, but that she is not human, that is, a snake.

The doctors in the story—the medical student Bernard Langdon, the village doctor Kittredge, and the "professor" (Holmes), whom Bernard consults, are all bewildered by Elsie. Dr. Kittredge employs with Elsie the "expectant method" of treatment; he is Holmes's dramatization of the "leave-it-to-nature" faith which he admired in his old teachers James Jackson and Jacob Bigelow. Young Bernard is simply full of questions, questions which the Professor can answer only by urging a charitable attitude toward one's fellow-man, whose perversity may come from "drunken ancestors, abuse in childhood, bad company, from which you have happily been preserved, and for some of which you, as a member of society, may be fractionally responsible," [29] familiar notions in nineteenth-century humanitarianism. Helen Darley's slight hysteria even the medical student, Bernard, understands; and Dr. Kittredge is up to coping with the troubles of the vacillating minister Fairweather. For psychological problems of a more complicated kind Holmes had no explanations to offer. Dick Venner, born of a New England father and Spanish mother, has tendencies to violence like his cousin, but these Holmes explains away with the familiar stereotyped notions of southern blood.

He admits his mystification in the words of Helen Darley, who says, "Yet there are mysteries I do not know how to account for. . . . We had a girl that *stole* in the school and one who tried to set us on fire—children of good people. . . ." [30] The Professor, in fact, expresses his ignorance directly, and, at the same time, he indicates the line of thinking he is beginning to follow: "Until somebody shall study this [automatic action in the moral world] as Marshall Hall has studied reflex nervous action in the bodily system, I would not give much for men's judgments of other's character," [31]—in short, he says that there ought to be a science of psychology.

Both the story, with its poisoned embryo, and this observation, with its allusion to Marshall Hall, indicate that Holmes expected to find that there is a physiological, a mechanical, explanation of mental aberrations. The kind of psychology he was looking toward hardly seems to have much in common with that of Freud, as has been suggested. *Elsie Venner* is not a study in psychology, consciously undertaken as such. The major theme of the novel is one that has psychological as well as moral implications, but Holmes's focus is clearly on the latter; he touches the former only in so far as he recognizes that insanity is a sickness and that was no new idea in 1861.

But the doctor's clinical approach to human behavior and his eagerness to demonstrate the limitations of the human will, as a medical man sees them, would soon lead him around to the psychological side of his major theme, and by 1866 he would be ready to tackle a new patient, less difficult than Elsie. Moreover while Holmes in his own haphazard and intuitive way was beginning to realize the need for a science of psychology, other investigators were making organized attempts to establish such a science. Holmes appears not as an originator but as a sensitive index to the times.

But at the moment, in the early months of 1861, as the last chapters of his story appeared in the *Atlantic Monthly*, the minds of most men were on problems more immediate than speculations on free will, original sin, and aberrant human behavior. Dr. Jacob Bigelow was writing Holmes that the novel had helped him through the "protracted parturition of Abraham Lincoln." [32] Dr. Holmes suddenly saw his cousin Wendell Phillips and his friend Governor Banks in a new light; the war they had prophesied was now at hand.

Patriotic Orator

1861–1865

He was at all times indignant against . . . false patriotism.

Wʜᴇɴ Dʀ. Hᴏʟᴍᴇs joined his classmates for their annual reunion on January 3, 1861, the poem he brought them was not the usual lavish display of affection. The news of December 20—South Carolina's secession—and a letter from Isaac Morse "having a strong political and secessionist flavor" had provoked the fiery lines of "A Voice of the Loyal North." Silent on political matters since the error of the New England Society address, Holmes now broke out, his always strong patriotic sentiments at fever temperature. Of the south-erners he wrote:

> God help them if the tempest swing
> The pine against the palm.[2]

When the lines appeared in print, Holmes found himself again under fire from the press; the *Courier,* organ of the po-tential copperheads upon whom Holmes would pour his scorn throughout the war, turned the line about and exhorted the poet to be calm.[3] Calm he could not be and, if he had not by nature Whittier's capacity to turn out rousing political verse in quantity, he managed in the next four years to indulge his taste for flamboyant rhetoric on several occasions.

Dr. Holmes was not the only member of his household struck by what he himself diagnosed as "war fever." In April he received the second of two solemn letters from Cornelius Felton, President of Harvard. The men knew each other too well for formality, but President Felton assumed his gravest

263

tones, for he was writing to the father of an erring student whose misdemeanors were all the more surprising, coming as they did from a senior, "an excellent young man," [4] one of the best in the class. After three years and a half of exemplary behavior, the doctor's eldest seems to have gone berserk. The catalogue of his sins is long; as an editor of the *Harvard Magazine,* he was responsible for "rude and unbecoming allusions to members of the faculty";[5] he had received an admonition for "repeated and gross indecorum in the recitation room of Professor Bowen"; his latest offense was hurling a brick through a freshman's window.[6]

The young man very soon committed a fourth academic crime; answering President Lincoln's call to arms, he departed from Cambridge without waiting for President Felton's consent to his departure. It was Dr. Holmes who hurried to Cambridge to get Felton's approval, and by two o'clock the same day, young Wendell was in uniform and on his way to Fort Independence.[7] In June, President Felton was constrained to write again to the father; this time to have him remind the inaccessible son of his examinations.[8] Felton seems to have been the victim of an excessively conscientious devotion to his duties as a disciplinarian; in the midst of the war, he wrote to no less a father than Abraham Lincoln that his son had just been admonished for smoking in Harvard Square.

As for the erring son of Dr. Holmes, he apparently neglected his examinations, but he did turn up for his classday exercises, where he fulfilled his destiny and served as class poet. After all, "the tendencies of my family and myself have a strong natural bent to literature," as he wrote in the class book.[9] Although one of the top-ranking scholars in his class, he was not, as was the custom, given a part in the commencement day program, the traditional recognition of scholastic standing. He probably did not care; he was occupied with more important matters.

His proud father, however, was indignant and showed it plainly although he made no formal protest. Felton, who encountered the wounded father at every turn during the commencement week ceremonies, felt obliged to write a long letter of explanation.[10] In his answer, Dr. Holmes, showing a normal parental concern and employing his best literary style, set forth his reasons for thinking an injustice had been done. It is possible that, along with disappointment and parental pride, there went, also, some anxiety about his son's reputation, an anxiety stirred by the catalogue of sins so faithfully reported to him during the year. Dr. Holmes, whose own judgments were always intensely personal, may have felt that the Bowen episode had played a part here. His son's "indecorum" in the professor's classroom coincided with his own quarrel with the professor in meetings of the American Academy of Arts and Sciences.[11] Whatever lay behind his feelings, the letter was *not* a formal protest, but a candid explanation of his views upon which, obviously, he expected no action to be taken.

Meanwhile in July 1861, the object of fatherly concern was not yet a lieutenant, and the doctor was busy ensuring for him a commission. On the morning of July 10 Dr. Holmes and Motley (just returned from England) were waiting in the lobby of the Parker House to see Colonel William Greene. Dr. Holmes would see his son in Greene's regiment in case the lists for Colonel Lee's Twentieth were already full. The news of the death of Longfellow's beautiful wife postponed military affairs. Two days later Holmes with Motley went to Readville and there settled the matter of young Wendell's commission.[12] The doctor's letter of introduction from the Governor's Military Secretary indicated that the Governor would be pleased to see the commission granted. The commission came through a few days later.[13]

Before the fateful early weeks of April, Holmes had seen through the press *Elsie Venner* in book form, and a collection of his medical essays. Now he could not write, save to pour out, with more raw passion than power, his patriotic sentiments. His best poem, if one can somehow not shudder at its central thought, is "The Sweet Little Man, Dedicated to the Stay-at-Home Rangers" [14] which expresses effectively in corrosive lines the doctor's contempt for young men who had not, like his son, rushed instantly into the front lines. He could not put his heart into anything else, and in May, writing a prologue for a collection of his poems, *Songs in Many Keys,* scheduled for fall publication, he calls the verses "toys."

> It matters little if they pall or please,
> Dropping untimely, while the sudden gleams
> Glare from the mustering clouds whose blackness seems
> Too swollen to hold its lightning from the trees.[15]

For the September *Atlantic,* in an essay "Bread and the Newspapers," he expressed as well as described the general temper of the public in the first months of the war; his description is so accurate that it makes uncomfortable and ironic reading today. The essay has its personal confessions, too—of paternal pride, of exposed provincialism.[16]

While his literary labors seemed suddenly insignificant, his work at the medical school became increasingly important. For the new term to begin in November, Holmes acquired new microscopes and new preparations and borrowed from Agassiz specimens prepared by Hyrtl, the famous Viennese anatomist. The overseers' committee, making its annual inspection in January 1862, came away with an enthusiastic account of the Parkman Professor's department, in which it found "considerable addition to the facilities for instruction beyond the valuable and established means of past years." The writer of the report—presumably the chairman, Hitchcock—was so overcome with delight that he became extravagant.

Microscopic anatomy has now become an enjoined and systematic part of the practical course of instruction in this school. The means and materials for demonstrations in this branch have been liberally supplied by the Professor of Anatomy. . . . The dissecting knife and achromatic lens verify the vivid word painting and magical descriptions of the eloquent professor and if dead bodies in the lecture-room are not literally *moved* by his "Songs in Many Keys," they are made under the microscope to glow with scientific truth and wondrous beauty. If, with these facilities for instruction, students are not inspired with enthusiasm in the study of human anatomy, they ought charitably to be considered as victims of either *ramollissement* or mental petrifaction.[17]

Mr. Hitchcock had been inspired certainly; and so apparently had two of Holmes's former students (he had been giving informal instruction in the use of the microscope for a good many years) and to these young men, Waldo Burnett and John Dean, Holmes refers proudly in his Introductory Lecture, given November 6, 1861, *Border-Lines in Medical Knowledge.*

Its theme "Science is the topography of ignorance," the lecture strikes out along the edges of contemporary knowledge. In the midst of his discussion of the countless questions still unanswered by physiologists, he digresses to the subject of phrenology. In *The Professor* he had made fun of the phrenologist—having just visited one and amused himself by having his bumps read; here he says of phrenology:

It does not stand at the boundary of our ignorance, it seems to me, but is one of the will-o'-the-wisps of its undisputed central domain of bog and quicksand.[19]

Yet he thought that phrenology (he had been reading a good deal of Lewes),[20] stripped of its delusions, suggested the direction a new science—"call it *anthropology*"—might take. "Let it study man the individual in distinction from man the abstraction, the metaphysical or theological lay-figure. . . . The whole physiology of the nervous system, from the simplest manifestation of its power in an insect up to the supreme act of the human intelligence working through the brain, is full of the most difficult yet profoundly interesting questions." On the subjects of reflex action, instinct, intellect, will, "our knowledge is in its infancy." [21] Clearly by "anthropology" Holmes meant to imply what we could call "psychology," but he was still looking to the physiologist to supply the deficiency.

On Thursday, the day after delivering this lecture, Dr. Holmes was in the cars on his way to Philadelphia. On October 21, the day of the Battle of Ball's Bluff, his friend James Freeman Clarke had come to 21 Charles Street with the first and most frightening of the three telegrams the family would receive.[22] The lieutenant had been seriously wounded. Letters from him and from Dr. William Hunt of Philadelphia had soon allayed the first fears and offset the grim newspaper accounts.[23] And now, Dr. Holmes was going to meet his son and escort him home. The wounded hero did not want for medical attention; besides Dr. Hunt, Holmes's old friend of his Paris days, Norris, had attended the young man in Philadelphia. When the wounded lieutenant was safely home, Dr. Henry Jacob Bigelow opened the wound, with Dr. Hodges acting as anesthetist.[24] Within a month the lieutenant was up and about, going with his father to breakfast at James T. Fields's house, and entertaining a procession of admiring girls; by April he was caught up in a "round of gaieties and late nights." [25]

As for the doctor, "I am busy with my lectures at the college," he wrote to John Lothrop Motley, with whom he carried on, all through the war, an energetic correspondence. Motley, now American Minister to Austria, was eager for news, which Holmes conscientiously supplied him; and at the Saturday Club, Holmes was his friend's official representative. Motley had no objections to the letters being read aloud, but he did not want the newspapers to get hold of them. The American Minister had good reason to fear the latter; in their unexpurgated versions, the letters that went back and forth across the Atlantic make lively reading, for the two men could match each other passion for passion, Motley infecting Holmes with his own indignation at European southern sympathizers, and Holmes passing on to Motley his wrath at copperheads and Jeremiahs and those who complained about taxes. Holmes, with a cynicism unusual for him, wrote, "our people are worked up to the *paying* point, which, I take it, is to the fighting point as boiling heat (212) to blood heat (98)." [26]

Motley's letters encouraged Holmes. "You remain an idealist, as all generous natures do and must," wrote the doctor. "I sometimes think it is the only absolute line of division between men,—that which separates the men who hug the actual from those who stretch their arms to embrace the possible." The tone of wrath that informed such poems as "Never or Now" and "Choose You this Day Whom you will Serve" came out in the letters. "You know quite as well as I do that accursed undercurrent of mercantile materialism, which is trying all the time to poison the fountains of the national conscience. You know better than I do the contrivances of that detested horde of mercenary partisans who would in a moment accept Jeff Davis, the slave-trade, and a southern garrison in Boston." [27]

When he wrote on the evening of his fifty-third birthday, still fresh in his memory was a letter from an English friend, Frederick Locker, who had told him that northern men had said war with England was their intention; Locker obviously believed it. To Motley, Holmes wrote, "The revelations we have had from the Old World have shed a new light for us on feudal barbarism. We know now where we are not to look for sympathy." The letter wavered between depression and enforced faith—"the only thing that keeps a man up in times like these"; and he was filled with disgust at those persons who are in a "state of spiritual anemia."

Part of his depression came from a personal sorrow; ten days before, after a visit to her daughter in Salem, his mother Sarah Wendell Holmes had died. "Keeping her lively sensibilities and sweet intelligence to the last," [28] she had grown old gracefully, well-protected by the devoted John, who felt her death more sharply than his brother did. The doctor probably was not unprepared for the loss; he had dedicated his last volume of poems to her; he had referred to her in an *Atlantic* article. Sarah Holmes was, after all, ninety-three; her longevity she left to her sons and her soldier grandson, who would overrun her mark by two years.

At midnight on September 17, within a month of his mother's death, came the telegram announcing that his son, now a captain, had been wounded in the battle of Antietam. It sent Dr. Holmes off on his memorable hunt after the captain. There would have been no hunt, if the handsome captain had not been so susceptible to pretty girls—one of them learned, too, who could help him plot a letter in Latin to his father. In Hagerstown the wounded soldier had been given shelter and attention so agreeable that he lingered among his

269

new friends instead of going on to Philadelphia as his father expected. Meanwhile the doctor, already on his way, missed his son's letter saying that no escort home was needed. The father's nine-day search for his son made good copy; he was not so anxious that he could not talk to those he met on his circuitous journey. His eager curiosity about all he saw in the course of his circular wanderings between Philadelphia and the battlefield of Antietam was not necessarily, he thought, evidence of any lack of feeling.

Some might naturally think that anxiety and the weariness of a prolonged search after a near relative would have prevented my taking any interest in or paying any regard to the little matters around me. Perhaps it had just the contrary effect, and acted like a diffused stimulus upon the attention. When all the faculties are wide-awake in pursuit of a single object, they are sometimes clairvoyant in a marvelous degree with respect to many collateral things.[29]

Once the captain was found and safe at home, the doctor was perhaps a little too quick to get the tale of his search into print, but "My Hunt After the Captain" is decently restrained in its allusions to the object of the search. It is worth reading, and readers, then, may judge for themselves if in its seventy-seven pages the three that concern his son are not written with due respect for the soldier's dignity.

If the publicity of his father's article distressed him—and there is no direct evidence that it did—one wonders why he told another poet a story that soon got into verse—George Henry Boker's "The Crossing at Fredericksburg." The poem describes the affecting scene of the captain lying ill in his tent and insisting that the flaps be thrown back that he may watch the course of the battle. The poem was reprinted in a Boston newspaper with a note identifying the hero of the poem as a captain in the Massachusetts Twentieth—sufficient to name him to his friends.[30]

If there was any friction between father and son, one suspects that no house would be big enough for two vain men, both of whom liked to talk and both of whom liked an audience of pretty women. The son had the advantages of inches and looks, but the father had the advantages of experience and fame, advantages being now offset by a uniform and a hero's name. The father frankly admitted, "I envy my white Othello, with a semicircle of young Desdemonas about him listening to the often told story which they will have over again." [31]

It is not surprising that except for an agreeable piece of medical history for his friend Winthrop, Dr. Holmes wrote little in 1862. The doctor's friends, whom he had obliged so often with verses, knew him to be reluctant; in July, Judge Hoar, begging him to come to the Phi Beta Kappa dinner, had told him he was not expected to say a word or write a poem or do anything unless he wished.[32] After more than a quarter-century of almost automatically responding to Harvard toasts of one kind or another, Holmes could not come empty-handed; he gave them "An Old Graduate's Song." He had brought them also the vigorous appeal to arms, "Never or Now." But for the most part, he was engaged in the business of his generation—reading the newspapers:

> The newspaper is as imperious as a Russian Ukase; it will be had, and it will be read. To this all else must give place. If we must go out at unusual hours to get it, we shall go, in spite of after-dinner nap or evening somnolence.[33]

But in 1863, his son at home, his uncertainties worried out in letters to Motley, and his natural hopefulness encouraged by the news of northern victories, the doctor was ready to take the public stage again when the Boston City Authorities asked him to give the Fourth of July oration. It was a literary type of which he had often made fun; its sentimentalities, its bombasts, its adjectives, and its clichés were all too familiar. In 1863 the times demanded something out of the ordinary, yet the traditions of the occasion had to be respected. Holmes met the moment with the best of the very good rhetoric of which he was capable, when personal emotion and confidence in the justice of what he had to say were nicely balanced. He had not exposed his weather-vane sensitivity to the breezes of public feeling and opinion in the past three years for nothing.

Out of this exposure grew the "Inevitable Trial." Its

formal rhetoric makes it seem impersonal; but read against the letters to Motley, its closeness to Holmes's experience is obvious. Whether he knew it or not, he spoke with eloquence for the multitudes of kindly, reasonable, if ordinary, men of good will who could not endure the surgery of war without the anesthetic of idealism—the thin kind that readily spills over into sentimentality.

He had not so far changed from what he had been in 1855 that he could write in his own emancipation hymn a "Laus Deo" like Whittier, or find the aspects of the reformers anything but "unlovely and forbidding"; but now "whether they please us . . . or not is not the question. Like them or not, they must and will perform their office, and we cannot stop them. . . . If you strike at one of their heads with the bludgeon of the law, or of violence, it flies open like the seed-capsule of a snap-weed, and fills the whole region with seminal thought which will spring up in a crop just like the original martyr." [34]

One by one he picks up the complaints and criticism of the day and those his rational thought does not demolish are knifed with wit or drowned in such old-fashioned eloquence as the following:

There are many languid thinkers who lapse into a forlorn belief that if this or that man had never lived, or if this or that other man had ceased to live, the country might have gone on in peace and prosperity, until its felicity merged in the glories of the millennium. If Mr. Calhoun had never proclaimed his heresies; if Mr. Garrison had never published his paper; if Mr. Phillips, the Cassandra in masculine shape of our long prosperous Ilium, had never uttered his melodious prophecies; if the silver tones of Mr. Clay had still sounded in the senate-chamber to smooth the billows of contention; if the Olympian brow of Daniel Webster had been lifted from the dust to fix its awful frown on the darkening scowl of rebellion—we might have been spared this dread season of confusion. All this is but a simple Martha's faith, without the reason she could have given: "If Thou hadst been here, my brother had not died." [35]

And there is too much chatter about financial ruin. "For the multitudes who are unfortunate enough to be taxed for a million or more, of course we must feel deeply, at the same time suggesting that the more largely they report their incomes to the tax-gatherer, the more consolation they will find in the feeling that they have served their country." One observation, "If our property is taxed, it is only to teach us that liberty is worth paying for as well as fighting for," [36] has its analogy in a saying later credited to his son: "Taxes are the price we pay for civilization."

The oration drew him back to the lecture platform temporarily. After "The Inevitable Trial," Dr. Holmes's lyceum lectures for the 1863-64, 1864-65 seasons were anticlimactic. The theme of the first grew out of the Fourth of July oration, specifically out of those passages which repudiate the Old World. The germ of the lecture is in a letter from Motley who had exclaimed, "Well we are weaned at last!" [37] His subject being American intellectual independence, Holmes called the lecture "The Weaning of Young America." It was Holmes who later described Emerson's "American Scholar" as our Declaration of Intellectual Independence; he now saw some signs that such freedom has been realized. He had often rebuked his professional colleagues for their inertia and their submission to Europe, and his report on medical literature in 1848 had been eloquent on the subject. Now he tried to catalogue America's achievement in all fields, but exposing his uncertainty, he lapsed into exhortation, expressing his faith in the existence of hidden talents and genius in the American people.[38]

The Fourth of July oration provided also the seeds for the second lyceum lecture: "New England's Master-Key," [39] which is, as its title suggests, a piece of provincial boasting. His friend Motley was very much in his mind and, along with other New England historians, came in for somewhat lavish eulogy. At best the lecture is a cleverly, if ornately, expressed catalogue of the achievements of New England in various fields of knowledge; the pressure of the war had temporarily stretched Holmes's imagination, but he had now fallen back into his natural position. He knew his weakness here, describing himself as being as thoroughly provincial an American of the

Boston variety "as ever looked at his own reflection in the Frog Pond."

In literary work of any other kind he had not much interest during this period. In June 1864, Ticknor and Fields were after him for "An American Story." Their terms were tempting, but he had no need of money at the moment. In a private notebook kept about this time, Holmes had copied Dr. Johnson's observation that no one but a fool writes except for money, a notion with which Holmes seemed at times to agree. He told his publisher that he was willing "to wait until the stimulus is a little stronger. . . ." The proposition would give direction to his thoughts. Besides he wanted to be free to devote his time to his professorship which was "now very interesting" to him.[40]

His expanded courses in the use of the microscope and a series of special lectures on the subject in 1863 account for some of his feeling here. His enthusiasm for this subject was shared by a new member of the faculty, Dr. Calvin Ellis. Another addition to the staff in 1864 was Charles E. Brown-Séquard, the physiologist, whose investigations into the pathology of the nervous system were in the direction of Holmes's own speculations about human behavior. Dr. David Cheever, his demonstrator, to judge from his report of 1863, was an energetic young man bent on making many improvements, which Dr. Holmes approved. The dissecting-room had been refitted; Dr. Cheever reported it the best in the country and that on the authority of New York and Philadelphia teachers.[41]

The few of Holmes's writings not connected with the war grew out of his profession. It was to the average student that Holmes addressed his medical school lectures; such essays as "Sun Painting and Sun Sculpture" (1861),[42] "The Human Wheel, its Spokes and Felloes" (1863), and "Talk Concerning the Human Body and Its Management" (1869), were Holmes's successful attempts to bring some rudimentary scientific knowledge into the range of the average layman.

Novelist

1863–1867

I love to see my friends, to hear from them, to talk to them.

H OLMES, for all his love for his work, was too sociable to give it his whole attention; he liked a dinner party, a glass of champagne to make him forget he was a professor. Nor could the anxieties of the war affect the doctor's conviviality; Emerson thought the trait showed up in "My Hunt after the Captain" and, commenting on the essay in his journal, wrote:

> He is still at his Club . . . has the same delight in his perceptions, in his wit, in its effect, which he watches as a belle the effect of her beauty; would still hold each companion fast by his sprightly, sparkling, widely-allusive talk, as at the Club table . . . and yet the fountain is unfailing, the wit excellent, the *savoir faire* and *savoir parler* admirable.[1]

Emerson's judgment here was confirmed by experience a few weeks later when he met the doctor on the train; Holmes talked steadily for twenty miles.[2] The doctor could laugh at himself for his failing; of riding to New York with Julia Ward Howe, he wrote, "Mrs. Howe and I made a vow of absolute taciturnity at starting, and talked each of us the amount of an octavo volume of four hundred and fifty pages." [3] One supposes that the author of "The Battle Hymn of the Republic" could hold her own, the more so as Dr. Holmes described her elsewhere as "sharp, sometimes corrosive, irregular, not always safe."

Holmes liked the literary ladies of his day; there were rather too many of them in the field perhaps, and for some he felt a paternal pity even as he admired their courage. Mary A.

Dodge, he told G. W. Childs, then searching for contributions to a new magazine, was "a game fish, breaks your tackle." [4] They could be irritating, especially when they too persistently sought advice. There was that "foolish virgin" who clamored to have her manuscript back and neglected to provide her address. The doctor wrote frantically to Lowell:

> Do help me out of this scrape. How the deuce am I to know how to reach this insane female?
> > "Ann M. H.
> > > New York"!
> > —Needle Esq.
> > > Bundleofhayville
> > > > —shire.
>
> Please find her Mss. and anything that will tell her address, and Ann M. Hate her lifeless initials with an informing spirit. I shall insult my reason by sending a letter addressed to these senseless initials. [5]

Although he admired some of his feminine fellow-authors, Holmes could not help thinking that women who were not aggressively literary made the most charming companions. His neighbor Mrs. James T. Fields satisfied his tastes and furthermore provided the means for indulging his sociability. As the wife of the publisher and editor of the *Atlantic Monthly*, Annie Fields had always a flock of authors about her. Breakfast at Mrs. Fields's house and dinner at the Saturday Club were social gatherings where Holmes could satisfy his fondness for good company.

He cheerfully supposed others enjoyed such pleasures as much as he. Shortly after the publication of *Elsie Venner* and Hawthorne's *Marble Faun,* the two authors met at Mrs. Fields's. Her diary reports this conversation in which the persistent doctor badgered the reluctant novelist. Said the doctor:

> By the way I would write a new novel if you were not in the field, Mr. Hawthorne.
> I am not and I wish you would do it.
> I wish you would come to the Club oftener.
> I should like to but I can't drink.
> Neither can I.
> Well, but I can't eat.
> Nevertheless, we should like to see you.

But I can't talk either.
You can *listen,* though; and I wish you would.[6]

A dialogue of a different kind in which Dr. Holmes's vis-à-vis was not a reserved New Englander but an aggressive Englishman was reported by Lowell. The Englishman was a big red-faced man "of the bald-with-spectacles type. A good, roaring positive fellow. . . ." Anthony Trollope. Against this antagonist, Dr. Holmes "charged, paradox in rest—but it was pelting a rhinoceros with seed pearl." The Autocrat opened with:

You don't know what Madeira is in England.
I am not sure it's worth knowing.
Connoisseurship in it with us is a fine art. There are men who will tell you a dozen kinds as Dr. Waagen would know a Carlo Dolci from a Guido.
They might be better employed!
Whatever is worth doing is worth doing well.
Ay, but that's begging the whole question. I don't admit it's *worse* doing at all. If they earn their bread by it, it may be *worse* doing (roaring).
But you may be assured—
No, but I may n't be asshored. I *won't* be asshored. I don't intend to be asshored (roaring louder.)

"And so they went," wrote Lowell. "It was very funny. Trollope wouldn't give him any chance. Meanwhile Emerson and I, who sat between them, crouched down out of range and had some very good talk, the shot hurtling overhead." [7]

The Saturday Club did not give up its parties in spite of the war, although Longfellow, slowly recovering from the shock of his wife's death, and Hawthorne, beginning to show signs of his illness, came rarely. Motley, except for his flying visit in 1861, was there only in the letters Holmes read to them. Even Agassiz left them for a time, but no member of the club could have a birthday or go off on a trip without the club's taking notice of him. The club's blessing was a rich literary benediction—a speech by Emerson and a poem by Holmes being inevitably a part of it, with Longfellow and Lowell sometimes contributing. Holmes sent Agassiz off to the jungles of Brazil in 1865 with the following hopes:

From the Indians of the pampas,
Who would dine upon their grampas,
From every beast and vermin
That to think of sets us squirmin',
From every snake that tries on
The traveller his p'ison
From every pest of Natur'
Likewise the alligator. . . .
Heaven keep the great Professor.
May he find, with his apostles
That land is full of fossils,
That the waters swarm with fishes
Shaped according to his wishes,
That every pool is fertile
In fancy kinds of turtle. . . .

And he imagined the glorious welcome that will meet the scientist on his return, in which:

. . . the mighty megalosaurus
Leads the palaeozoic chorus.[8]

If prehistoric creatures were silent on Agassiz's return, the club members "joined hands, made a ring and danced around him like a lot of boys," except Emerson, "who stood apart, his face radiant." Agassiz, three times the doctor's size, "seized Holmes in his arms and took him quite off his feet." [9]

The club allowed its members to bring guests; the doctor brought his son and Jeffries Wyman, whose membership he proposed. They entertained celebrities like Grant, whose taciturnity Dr. Holmes found it hard to shake as with the zeal of the physiologist he probed the general about his capacity to sleep at any time and in any place.[10]

In 1864, the club celebrated Shakespeare's anniversary with an elaborate dinner that kept the committee—Emerson, Holmes, and Lowell—busy preparing it and gave them a few headaches afterwards as they tried to settle the bill. Wrote Holmes to Lowell: "Emerson says he can't cipher. My wife says I can't cipher. You say in your note $7.65 \times 2 = 29.30$ which is equally poetical arithmetic." [11]

Within a few months, the members of the club had reason

to worry about one of their number; they now all knew that Hawthorne's illness was serious. When Hawthorne returned to Boston after the trip on which his traveling companion, the publisher Ticknor, had died, he stopped temporarily at a hotel before going on to New Hampshire with his old friend, ex-president Pierce. There Dr. Holmes made the novelist a semi-professional call and observed that here was a case not to be tormented by superfluous examination. He asked a few questions, offered a little advice, and departed knowing that he could not make a favorable report to their literary acquaintances. Not long afterwards, the members of the club were gathered in Concord for the novelist's funeral. "All was so quiet and bright that pain and mourning was hardly suggested," wrote Emerson in his journal, adding, "Holmes said to me that it looked like a happy meeting." [12] It was Longfellow, not then writing a great deal, who produced the fitting poem about the occasion.

At the same time a younger generation of writers was showing itself; only a few would fulfil the promise some of their elders saw in them. "Mr. Howells—a young man of no small talent" [13] and a new contributor to the *Atlantic*—came as a guest to the Saturday Club. Lowell had already given a small dinner to introduce the newcomer to Fields and to the Autocrat, provoking from the doctor the familiar jest: "Well, James, this is something like the apostolic succession; this is the laying-on of hands."

Another future editor of the *Atlantic* had just moved to Boston in 1865. Thomas Bailey Aldrich had not yet written *The Story of a Bad Boy* and thought of himself chiefly as a poet. He sent his latest volume to Dr. Holmes who wrote:

Your danger is of course on the sensuous side of the *intellect*—you see what I mean—the semi-voluptuous sense of color and order, such as you remember in Keats' Endymion—is a very different thing from vulgar sensuousness.[14]

The war had scarcely ended before a southern poet, Paul Hamilton Hayne, was appealing to northern writers for the two necessities of a poet's life—books and a place to publish.

Holmes, like the others appealed to, was eager to help, sent the books asked for, and promised to consult Fields on Hayne's behalf. He knew the poems of Hayne and would use his "Across the Potomac" in his latest lyceum lecture, "Poetry of the War."

In this lecture, too, he would pay over-lavish compliments to two northern poets who, on the strength of their war poems, were taken for a time at least as writers of promise. Henry Howard Brownell, Hartford lawyer and Secretary of Admiral Farragut, had celebrated the naval battles of the war in his "Bay Fight" and "River Fight." There was some rivalry in the Holmes household about who knew the poet best. Lieutenant Colonel Holmes was "buttonholing all his friends like the Ancient Mariner," as he told them of his enthusiasm for Brownell; so Doctor Holmes wrote to the poet, enclosing, with his own letter, one from his son who declared: "I bullied and snubbed my daddy at tea the other day with my acquaintance with the great poets of the country." [15] While the lieutenant colonel buttonholed his friends, Dr. Holmes took Brownell to the Saturday Club and read his latest poem, the author apparently being too bashful to do so. As the "Battle Laureate" Brownell was presented to a large audience by the doctor's article in the *Atlantic Monthly*.[16]

Perhaps it was the younger Holmes who introduced his father to the extremely popular poem "The Old Sargeant"; both were enthusiastic about it and each preserved it in his Civil War scrapbook. The problem was to find the author, Forceythe Willson. Sometime in the early spring of 1865, John Hay, President Lincoln's secretary, came to dinner at 21 Charles Street. The talk turned to war poems, among them Willson's. Hay volunteered to search out the author and report back to the Holmeses. Much to their surprise, Hay, after inquiring over half the country—the poem had been first published in Louisville—found the poet in Cambridge, just across the street from Lowell's house. In May, Dr. Holmes sent Willson's address to Emerson, describing the poet as young and shy, "as strange as Hawthorne."

You would mean more to him than anybody else round him. . . . You might give him a hint and some day he will come up I think and spend an hour with you in Concord. Won't you drop him a line to encourage him? It is for his sake I ask it.[17]

Out of such talk and such experiences grew the lecture "Poetry of War." He had collected verses from the newspapers and periodicals and bought from street-vendors their best-selling broadsides; the material of his lecture ranges from the anonymous ballad "John Brown's Body," with its "ghostly imagery and anthem-like ascription," [18] to Emerson's "Boston Hymn" in which it is "the supreme voice that speaks." [19]

Deliberately eschewing negative criticism, Holmes managed to keep his praise temperate. As he had written Brownell in March, he supposed that negative criticism was necessary as surgery, but "thank God, it is not my business to practice either." [20] The result, of course, is a respectable lecture, but unexciting essay. Except for the omission of any allusion to Whitman, whose *Drum-Taps* had not been published when Holmes prepared his paper, the lecture gives an adequate indication of the kind and quality of the war verses.

As often in Holmes's writing, however, his by-the-way observations, thrown in as asides or used for transition, are better than his treatment of the main subject. Opening with a contrast between the northern ballad of John Brown and the southern song "Maryland, My Maryland," he observes the puritan quality of the first, seeing the second as a cavalier song, "appealing chiefly to local pride and passion." [21] The puritan-cavalier analogy comes in appropriately again when he comments upon the fascination the hard-fighting, hard-praying southerner Stonewall Jackson had for northern poets. "Possibly it may have been sympathy with his Puritan characteristics which drew us towards our vigorous enemy." [22]

Among the street ballads, he observes the preponderance of "mother songs," which, as their cloying numbers multiply, inevitably provoke healthy parody. "Dear Mother, I've come home to die" becomes "Dear Mother, I've come home to eat."

The way in which the excess is naturally corrected pleased him.[23]

Introducing Lowell's second series of Biglow Papers, Holmes observed, "I do not know whether it has been remarked how much American poetry and art tend to the feminine in their tone and subjects. . . . There is also a distinctly feminine character in much of our best authorship." Lowell seemed to him one of the few American writers in whom "the masculine element predominates." [24]

Holmes, naturally, paid his respects to Lowell's "Commemoration Ode," which he had heard on July 21, when Harvard honored its warriors and called upon its literary alumni to celebrate the occasion. The affair, initiated by Mrs. Holmes's cousin Henry Lee, was so elaborate that one guest, the wife of the sculptor William Wetmore Story, felt that there was too much "crowing." Borrowing the Autocrat's phrase, she observed that "all the world of mutual admiration was there, deciding, as it seemed to me, that the State of Massachusetts had fought all the battles and raised all the money and troops." At the opening exercises, a handsome stranger from Philadelphia distinguished himself with his short and moving prayer; the young man, Phillips Brooks, made such an impression that Boston had, of course, to take him in. At the after-dinner exercises, the introductions were given by Charles G. Loring; they were "awkwardly enough done," said Holmes. "It is a delicate thing to introduce a poet, he should be delivered to the table as a falconer delivers the falcon into the air, but Mr. Loring puts you down hard on the table—ca-chunk." [25]

Necessarily—for "what would a Harvard celebration be without Dr. Holmes?" [26]—the doctor was ready with his lines, called up to the tune of his classmate's song "America" and returned to his place with his own hymn "Union and Liberty." The newspapers spoke approvingly of Holmes and, of course, Emerson, but they had not a word to say of Lowell's ode, save blank allusion to graceful lines. Its length and form, its late place on a long program, and the physical difficulties of the occasion would have prevented most of the audience from knowing what they heard as Lowell read the lines, over which he had exhausted himself in frenzied composition and over which his friend John Holmes had wept. More than that, the news reporters had long been accustomed to hearing Emerson and Holmes on public platforms and had got into the habit of recognizing them with flattery of some kind.

A less questionable but more demanding form of flattery than that of journalists was that of correspondents—women so lavish in their expressions of affection that the doctor, as he had told the breakfast-table, was thankful for his unquestioned domestic respectability. Even the great were not above seeking gratuitous literary or medical advice; Henry Ward Beecher decided that his hay fever was related to malaria, spoke of having tried homeopathy, and asked the doctor to recommend to him some books on the subject. It is probably just as well not to try to imagine the effect of this letter upon the doctor. The ubiquitous Beecher family besieged him from all sides; Charles and Harriet wanted to write about religion. Holmes's theological notions drew any number of correspondents—a strange boy from Kansas who had struggled out of his old-fashioned faith with the help of the doctor's books; Henry James, Sr., a new neighbor to whose Swedenborgian limits Holmes could not go, but whose cheerfulness he shared; and at the other end Charlotte Dana who sent the doctor Catholic literature.

Elsie Venner was still in some readers' minds. An unsuccessful dramatization in 1865 served to remind Holmes's friends of his novel. One of them apparently had in his household a problem daughter and had asked his wife to give Holmes an account of her. Dr. Kellogg from the state asylum sent a letter a patient had written, as an example of another type of Elsie.[27] Early in January 1866 Dr. Horatio B. Storer, the gynecologist, wrote that he had been rereading Holmes's books; he became eloquent about *Elsie Venner*. Most books on education seemed to him poor, and he believed that "a book on education with a physiological basis" was needed.[28] Perhaps here was the impetus that set Holmes thinking about the novel he would soon begin to write—the American story Ticknor and Fields had asked for in 1864.

By September 12, the story, *The Guardian Angel,* was planned and partly written. James T. Fields came over to hear some of it read. The doctor was nervous, torn between reluctance and desire to read his book. His wife, apparently, was not happy that he thought of getting into print again and said so, fearful of the newspaper criticism. According to the scribe, Annie Fields, the conversation went on:

> Well, Amelia, I have written something now which the critics won't complain of. You see it's better than anything I have ever done.
>
> Oh, that's what you always say, Wendell, but I wish you'd let it alone!
>
> But don't you see, Amelia, I shall make money by it and that won't come amiss.

Mrs. Holmes was willing to concede that point, and the doctor turned to the publisher and got the necessary laugh: "If I should die before the story is finished, you wouldn't come down upon the widder for the money, would you now?" [29] He was generously enough paid for the times, $250 for each of the installments as it appeared in the *Atlantic* through 1867. [30] Moreover Fields gave it top billing, leading off every number for the year with the next installment of Dr. Holmes's novel. And to Fields, whom Emerson, reflecting the feelings of most New England authors, had called the "guardian and maintainer of us all," [31] Holmes dedicated the book.

The business of working on his book could not cut down his sociability; at the February meeting of the Saturday Club, "Dr. Holmes was in a great mood for talk." His rival Lowell, trying to get in a word, was rebuked by the excitable doctor, "Now, James, let me talk and don't interrupt me." A few days later, reading Lowell's poem for Longfellow's sixtieth birthday, the doctor put off the job of polishing up his May installment of *The Guardian Angel,* dashed off three tidy, if ordinary, quatrains for Longfellow, and insisted on going out to Cambridge with them although he was wheezing with asthma and his wife was reluctant to let him out. Fields, who called for him, promised to bring him home by twelve o'clock. And all the way, Holmes chattered about the dinner parties he had been to, his lectures, and the book.

In the course of his chatter he observed, "I was nothing but a roaring kangaroo when you took me in hand and I thought it was the right thing to stand up on my hind legs, but you combed me down and put me in proper shape. Now I want you to promise me one thing. We're all growing old, I'm near sixty myself, by and by the brain will begin to soften. Now you must tell me when the egg begins to look addled. People don't know of themselves." [32]

It was apparently Fields who encouraged the too easily swayed doctor to abandon his most suitable medium—the breakfast-table talk—for a form he had neither the craft nor patience to handle; being fiction, *The Guardian Angel* could not be the best thing he'd ever done, as he supposed. As in *Elsie Venner,* most of the dramatized situations of the story and all of the plot-turns have nothing to do with the main theme; a rescue from drowning, purloined legal papers, a mysterious land-suit, a question of paternity, the trials of a village poet, the romantic difficulties of a country girl—of all these only the first has the slightest organic connection with the problem of the central character. His notes themselves should have told him his error; for one note about a problem of structure, there are, conservatively speaking, twenty notes of notions and images waiting only the syntax of a sentence to transform them into breakfast-table talk.[33]

These notes are, in fact, just such "Thoughts on the Universe" as he assigns to Byles Gridley, one of the characters in his novel. Gridley, a retired professor, is the author of a stillborn book of aphorisms, epigrams, of *pensées* (Holmes had been reading Pascal [34]) on a wide range of subjects—the kind of thing Holmes could work up in the casual breakfast-table form or scatter through a provocative lecture, but could not get into a novel. They are, too, reflections which Holmes himself took seriously, but which his reading public took as only incidental to his fun. Possibly an unavowed realization of this fact, added to some wishful thinking, made him include in his story the episode in which Byles Gridley is suddenly wooed by a publisher, very eager to reprint in a large, new edition those "Thoughts on the Universe."

Another obvious personal fantasy appears in both *Elsie Venner* and *The Guardian Angel*. Both recall the schism in his father's church, not precisely as it happened, but with ironic twists, distortions which suggest very clearly how bitter an experience the church quarrel must have been. Uncommunicative at the time, he had burst out with his indignation after his father's death in the letter to Jenks already quoted. And now, more than thirty years after the event, he tells the story twice in versions less painful than the original.

The two orthodox ministers in the novels are not likenesses of his father, for they take their physical characteristics from David Osgood, the dignified old preacher whom he remembered from his youth; they resemble Abiel Holmes, however, in the contrast between their gloomy doctrines and their kindly natures, and both are provided with parishioners and deacons less generous than they are. In *Elsie Venner,* Deacon Shearer, leader of the church faction Holmes names for the "Vinegar Bible," becomes more and more dissatisfied with his minister's kindness, and at the end of the novel leads his followers to split off from the church. Significantly, the Rev. Dr. Honeywood does not, as Abiel Holmes did, follow his Deacon's lead, but remains behind to take over the liberal congregation of the town.

In *The Guardian Angel,* the Rev. Dr. Pemberton's deacon plays a minor role and is merely made the butt of a joke; Pemberton, however, has been provided, as Abiel Holmes had been, with an assistant, Bellamy Stoker, who is the villain of the piece, ultimately exposed and punished by his literary creator with a thoroughgoing kind of justice one would expect only of the puritan God of Wrath Holmes is trying to repudiate. Again, the good and kind old minister is left in his pulpit, this time in full control of his congregation, liberals and orthodox alike.

And Holmes knew in part what he was doing and, dimly, why. In November 1867, while *The Guardian Angel* was running its last installments, he wrote in a letter to Harriet Beecher Stowe:

> I have no doubt that I show the effects of a training often at variance with all my human instincts,—not so much from the lips of my dear parents, in both of whom nature never allowed "Grace" to lead them to any inhuman conclusions,—but from outside influences, against which my immature intelligence had to protest, with more or less injury to its balance, very probably, always after. I suppose all I write may show something of this, as the lamed child limps at every step, as the crooked back shows through every garment.[35]

Again his main intention in this novel was to demonstrate the limits of the human will; as he told the Massachusetts Medical Society in June 1867, *The Guardian Angel* is the "natural sequence" to *Elsie Venner* in showing "how in the normal order of things a series of inborn instincts and propensities" may act to inhibit the human will. "I describe the facts of inherited qualities as we who study families see them. I carry my subject through such exposures as our experience of life has shown us to be of too frequent occurrence." [36]

Born in India, orphaned early, Myrtle Hazard, the heroine, has been brought up in the gloomy New England home of a maiden aunt and bachelor uncle, the first a stern Puritan bent on breaking the child's will and forcing her into the Calvinist faith, the second a miser and eventual suicide. Another occasional member of this dreary household is a second self-absorbed and frustrated female poor relation.

When the story opens, the young heroine has, not surprisingly, run away from this ménage, disguising herself as a boy and escaping down the river. In the long night voyage, she has a "vision"—an experience Holmes borrowed from an account of a similar hallucination of the poet Forceythe Willson. In it she sees dimly the floating figures of her parents and her ancestors whom she imagines struggling for possession of her. Of this ancestry Holmes had already given a meticulous account, tracing his heroine's mixed strains through several generations including, among a number of imaginative but under-vitalized women, a religious martyr and a famous beauty. There was a touch of Indian there, as well as a military man, and a sea captain; the supposed primitive feelings of the first and the healthy bravado of the second and third manifest themselves later in Myrtle's behavior. The martyr, Ann Holyoake, and the beauty, Judith Pride, whose dim portraits fascinate their imaginative descendant, are the ones who contribute most to the heroine's character. She herself sees each in turn as her "guardian angel" until the supposed conflict between them is resolved; then, completely cured, Myrtle has no need of hallucinatory guardians and is quite ready to recognize that her protector has all along been the old tutor, Byles Gridley. The "cure," however, is not effected immediately.

The voyage of flight culminates in a near-drowning. Rescued and restored to her home, Myrtle lapses into hysteria, the second phase of her development.[37] In her hysterical state she is extremely suggestible and consequently vulnerable. Dr. Holmes's Victorian reticence does not conceal the fact that he regards his heroine's case as owing a great deal to her sexual development as well as to her inheritance. His contemporaries recognized and condemned his emphasis here. Successively, young Dr. Hurlburt, whose mesmeric power over the girl Holmes regards as dangerous, and the Rev. Bellamy Stoker, whose religion is the obvious mask of his sexuality, are banished from their association with the heroine by the fatherly guardian, the tutor Gridley. The first is dismissed by Gridley's appeal to the doctor's integrity; the second, by his forcing the heroine to face the fact that the preacher's interest in her has nothing to do with her spiritual welfare. Myrtle, made aware that the preacher's motives are far from "spiritual," is not pushed into a state of outraged virtue; "there was something in her own conscious-

ness which responded to the suspicions he had expressed."
Holmes here used the image of the undeveloped photograph
plate from which the picture emerges as the photographer
applies his wash. "In some such way the . . . warnings of
. . . Gridley had called up a fully shaped, but hitherto
unworded, train of thought in the consciousness of
Myrtle. . . ."[38] The shock of recognition brings on a
nightmare, not unlike the earlier hallucination in which
Myrtle had seen her ancestors struggling for possession of
her mind; in the dream, however, the dominant figures are
the two women, the martyr and the beauty.

It is the latter who wins, taking over the guardian role
from her predecessor as the heroine's struggles with herself
enter a third phase. Although the hysteric symptoms occasionally recur, she is represented as having recovered from
this part of her trouble; she is "cured," it must be noted,
by "nature," not by treatment. In her new phase, Myrtle
is aggressive and bold, behaving now, so the doctor implies,
under impulses inherited from ancestors healthier in body
and stronger in character than those who directed her toward
suicide, flight, and hysteria. At this point the guardian Gridley sends her to a fashionable city school, on the theory that
a change from the narrow village environment to one larger
and more demanding is necessary. Here again the motivating
inherited instincts lead Myrtle very nearly to excess; but a
final establishment of harmony among the conflicting impulses comes about naturally and automatically. In the child
and adolescent, the inherited traits are chaotic and conflicting; in the adult they are at rest and in balance.

Although Holmes was plainly again addressing himself to
laymen and theologians, he nevertheless in this novel developed his psychological theme, which in *Elsie Venner* is
only vaguely suggested. He would have the satisfaction of
finding his notions offered in a book published in the same
year as *The Guardian Angel,* a book which Holmes read.
Notes on Henry Maudsley's *Physiology and Pathology of the
Mind,* the first American edition of 1867, appear in Holmes's

black notebook. For his own library, he bought the same author's *Body and Mind*.

Two passages from Maudsley state Holmes's themes plainly: A human being's "father and mother, his grandfather and grandmother, are latent or declare themselves in him; and it is on the lines thus laid in his nature that his development will proceed. . . . The functional development [of the reproductive organs], taking place somewhat abruptly at puberty, works a complete revolution in the mental character." [39] And like Maudsley, Holmes expected the answers to questions suggested by such cases as that of Myrtle to come from the physiologist, studying, as Holmes put it in his preface, the "reflex function in its higher sphere." [40] All the materials for investigation which might have led him to fruitful ends he avoided, although he suggested a kind of suspended curiosity about them—about Myrtle's "Vision," her dream, her susceptibility to hypnosis; and about his own notions of "unconscious cerebration."

Meanwhile as his novel appeared in the magazine, his wife's prophecy of criticism was fulfilled from an unexpected and disturbing quarter; a new magazine, of a different type from the *Atlantic* but rivaling it in quality, carried in its pages monthly reviews of periodicals. The *Nation*, edited by Edwin L. Godkin, and financed in part by Charles Eliot Norton, could not be ignored. Holmes must have known that Norton was not personally responsible for the persistent sniping in the magazine column written by John R. Dennett, but he would have had to be utterly indifferent to criticism not to feel a temporary awkwardness. Norton was his friend—his cousin even in a distant way; Norton himself had been eager to claim the kinship when *The Autocrat* first appeared and had made a practice of inviting Holmes for an annual summer visit to Newport. But although there is ample evidence that Holmes was disturbed by the *Nation's* criticism, that it rankled long afterwards, there is no indication of a break with Norton, as has been rumored.

Holmes was wrong in supposing that the writer of the

Nation notices had some personal feeling against him.[41] Dennett obviously and justly felt that the doctor's popularity was greater than he deserved. Dennett's tone, however, in all his notices, is "smart." His criticism is the carping type likely, as Holmes told Brownell, "to unsteady the hand if one is not careful"; but he added a witticism that had no doubt a therapeutic effect: "After all if kings pay a fool to tell them their failings, authors need not complain if they get one for nothing." [42]

Dennett was obviously hard put to it to find something to say for each issue, but he felt obliged to deal with the *Atlantic Monthly* in detail every time; the result, of course, is that many of his observations are either trivial or vague. One of them, however, is as amusing as it is revealing. To a critic in the 1920's, when it was fashionable to berate the Victorians for their reticences, Holmes's handling of sex came in for a condemnation exactly the reverse of that he received from his contemporaries. In 1925 C. Hartley Grattan poured upon Holmes the scorn of the newly liberated; [43] in 1867 John Dennett lamented the "atmosphere of carnality" and went on to compare Holmes and Henry James, whose "Poor Richard" was running in the *Atlantic* at the same time. "We may remark here," wrote Dennett, "that in Mr. James's as in Dr. Holmes's treatment of women, the influence, the physical influence, of sex is very perceptible, but in Mr. James's stories it is not only refined but subtle—an aura, as it were, while the better known novelist deals with women as if he were a materialist." [44]

The *Nation* reviewer was, in the end, more offensive in his manner than his matter, for he said actually not much more than a personal friend could tell the author in a more tactful way. Judge Hoar, acknowledging a copy of *The Guardian Angel,* could let Holmes know that he thought *The Autocrat of the Breakfast-Table* the best thing he had done, by asking to be a subscriber to "Thoughts on the Universe."

The judge had had a chance, too, to observe a few hereditary influences first hand, for he had just heard the younger

Holmes present his first case, and thought the new lawyer very promising. Having the manner of his grandfather, Judge Charles Jackson, with the doctor's "expression every now and then coming out of it," young Holmes had not had the Jackson legal heritage crowded out of him by his father's poetry and anatomy.[45] A month later, Dr. Holmes was thinking of his son's heritage himself; to a correspondent he wrote à propos the general subject of heredity, " . . . luckily my wife is one of the smartest and most capable women going." [46]

Member of the Opposition

1867—1870 (1879)

The members of an university may, for a season,
be unmindful of their duty.

A<small>LTHOUGH</small>, when the steam was on, it was difficult "to carry the engine from one room to another," [1] Holmes managed to shift back and forth between his novel and his medical lectures. The latter, if they required from him little study in anatomy, called for constant alertness and agility in keeping up with the essentials of the latest discoveries in physiology, a tension which probably affected his judgment in the drama about to be enacted. The many discoveries in this branch of science, in chemistry, and in physics had determined the subject of his introductory lecture of 1861, *Border-Lines in Medical Science*. Now in 1867, when he came to write another introductory lecture, his acute awareness of the acceleration of scientific discovery and the contemporary agitation for reforms in education directed his thoughts as he prepared *Teaching from the Chair and at the Bedside*.

The lecture was written in something of a hurry, for the business of getting *The Guardian Angel* ready for book publication and the necessity of traveling to Montreal to secure the Canadian copyright had crowded the early fall months, and the trip had been made extremely uncomfortable by the recurrence of his now familiar trouble, asthma, which made it impossible for him to travel anywhere in comfort. The lecture obviously was written only a few days before it was given. As he told his audience, he expected to overrun his allotted hour, for "I can say with Pascal that I have not had the time to make my lecture shorter." [2]

The doctor's point of departure was the current clamor for an extension of the regular lecture course, already voted down by the Harvard faculty. Ignoring the other reforms suggested along with this one, he urged with eloquence and wit the superiority of clinical teaching to the lecture method and opposed lengthening the lecture term. His advocacy of clinical teaching cannot be quarreled with. Like many a defender of the *status quo*, Holmes had some sound observations and warnings to offer. "Just as certainly as we spin out and multiply our academic prelections we shall work in more and more stuffing, more and more rubbish, more and more irrelevant, useless detail which the student will get rid of just as soon as he leaves us." [3] With his own experience in mind, he suggested that the practice of medicine calls for wholehearted devotion and warned of the dangers of divided interests. Research in preventive medicine and in the causes and treatment of disease is a legitimate adjunct to the practice of medicine, but the student whose interest is in "pure science" ought never to hang up his shingle. Quoting Benjamin Rush who had said: "Medicine is my wife and Science is my mistress," Holmes observed: "I do not think that the breach of the seventh commandment can be shown to have been of advantage to the legitimate owner of his affections." [4] A specialist like Brown-Séquard was another matter, but, not seeing a time when specialization would be the rule rather than the exception, Holmes thought that a medical curriculum should be designed to meet the needs of the general practitioner.

To Holmes, the clinical training was the most practical part of the medical course; he did not wish to see the number of lecture subjects multiplied and disapproved the addition of courses in "pure science" on the grounds that such instruction was impractical. Sketching facetiously the possible results of such training, Holmes remarked that if doctors became too scientific and, in consequence, too impractical to tend to the immediate needs of their patients, the women of the world would indignantly express their dissatisfaction by taking over the medical profession themselves. He was here having some private fun with the young reformers of the Harvard medical faculty; for, in spite of their radical ideas, they were violently opposed to medical education for women. One of them had just recently written two successive editorials in the local medical journal—one advocating a reformed curriculum, the other opposing medical education for women.[5]

But for all the brilliance of the lecture in its parts, its whole is a blind defense of the *status quo*. One contributing cause of this blindness was his having focused his attention upon only one small part of the reforms being advocated—the lengthening of the lecture term—a point of view which necessarily narrowed his vision. More significant is his making the choice of focus in the first place. In choosing the subject of reform in education he was responding to the climate of public opinion which in his post-war period, as in our own, had become stormy on the subject of education in general. But in picking the one point, Holmes yielded to habit. Of all the proposals offered in 1867, this was the one which had been consistently offered from the very beginning. In fact from the founding of the American Medical Association in 1846 recommendations for lengthened terms had been repeatedly made and repeatedly voted down by delegates from the Harvard faculty. Holmes's lecture ironically illustrates his own notion of mental automatism; what was most familiar in the external stimulus had produced the habitual response.

Moreover, that response had been set in the days when the Tremont Medical School had been a separate institution, a profitable private business which would be threatened if its professors, nearly all of whom were also on the Harvard faculty, should be obliged to give more of their time to the "regular medical school." As long as the two institutions were separate, it was the Tremont School that had to be protected; and when they were combined, the protective habit transferred itself to the summer school. Holmes was forgetting that, although the Harvard program (with its combined winter and summer sessions and its recommendations about a graded program), was sound as a whole, the *only* part of it specifically required was just that part which he admitted was least valuable—the winter term of lectures.

Holmes was, of course, in the position of those members of an older generation who have made so many changes and adjustments in the course of their careers that they find it difficult to appreciate the changes being urged by the new generation coming up behind them. In the medical profession, this new generation, like Holmes's own, had been educated in Europe, in Vienna particularly, and in the 1860's the contrast between European and American medical schools was even greater than it had appeared to the young men who had flocked to Paris in the 1830's. Harvard's annual medical course was only four months long; in Vienna the course took ten months. Harvard required three haphazardly supervised years of study for the degree; Vienna, five, regulated by law. American examinations were oral, offered only at the end of the supposed three years of study and then in a perfunctory way. In Vienna, public examinations were given every six months.

It was by these European standards that younger men like James Clarke White and Calvin Ellis judged the school, which they had attended and where they now taught. It is possible that Holmes and Henry Jacob Bigelow, seeing these admirable products of their teaching, may have felt self-satisfied and failed to realize that these younger men might owe as much to their European experiences as to their Harvard training. Although frustrated in 1866 in attempts to bring about reforms, the younger men were so vigorous in their agitation that in 1868 the older members of the faculty, probably at Bigelow's instigation, put through a piece of legislation designed to hold back the reformers; they constituted the full professors as the "Executive Fac-

296

ulty," denying assistants, adjuncts, and instructors a voice in the government of the medical school.[6]

That the gesture was a futile one, Holmes knew. As he wrote to D. H. Storer on the occasion of the latter's retirement: "It cannot be long before the faculty is in charge of the younger men altogether."[7]

The time was even shorter than he had probably supposed; the professors enjoyed an interregnum of only one year. Early in 1870, the medical faculty graciously invited the new president of Harvard to attend its meetings. It was polite of them, but Charles William Eliot would have come anyway. And he kept on coming; in fact, "with an aplomb, a quiet, imperturbable, serious good-humor" that Holmes found it impossible not to admire, Eliot was "proposing in the calmest way to turn everything topsy-turvy." The old guard was astonished. Said one of them, "How is it, I should like to ask, that this Faculty has gone on for eighty years managing its own affairs and doing it well,—for the Medical School is the most flourishing department connected with the College,—how is it that we have been going on so well in the same orderly path for eighty years, and now, within *three or four months,* it is proposed to change all our modes of carrying on the school? It seems very extraordinary, and I should like to know how it happens."

"I can answer Dr. Bigelow's question very easily," said Eliot calmly, "there is a new President."

The reform of the medical school was only one of the objectives of Eliot; as Holmes observed, he turned up everywhere with an implacable determination that was overwhelming. Although Holmes thought the new president in danger of doing too much all at once, he nevertheless had "great hopes of his energy and devotion to his business, which he studies as no President ever did before."[8]

In the battle of the medical faculty that was only just beginning in 1869, the vigorous, strong-willed Bigelow led the conservatives, and the fiery, earnest James Clarke White led the reformers. There were political machinations behind the scene, as each party sought to win over the majority of the overseers, and long debates in the faculty meetings, scenes which Holmes found himself watching with modified amusement, for the comedy was a serious one and the principal actors brilliant. Between loyalty to Bigelow and admiration of Eliot, Holmes found himself playing the role of mediator, along with Calvin Ellis, who was as moderately in favor of reform as Holmes was moderately opposed to it.

The battle was not won when the medical school opened its winter term in 1870, but the man who gave the introductory lecture was James Clarke White. Calvin Ellis had begged him to go slow: "They will take your head off if you don't." But Eliot urged him on and promised to see to it that he had a large audience. "Well, White," remarked Bigelow as the younger man went forward to make his speech, "now we are about to catch it, I suppose."

And catch it they did, for White made no bones of the fact that he thought the practical spirit of American medical education was its "evil genius, its radical defect." Calvin Ellis's words of caution meant nothing and Eliot's encouragement much, as White took up Bigelow's challenge and declared the practical spirit "contemptible." He saw the throngs of American students in the medical schools of Berlin and Vienna as a reproach to America.

To those who may say that I am taking an unpatriotic view of the matter, that my estimate of medical education and our profession in America is too low and unfounded in fact, I will only reply: when I find the young men of Europe flocking to our shores and crowding our native students from their seats and from the bedside, when the fees of our best lecturers are mostly paid in foreign coin, and when thousands of wealthy invalids from across the sea fill the waiting-rooms of our physicians, then I will confess that I am wrong, and that of the two systems of education ours is the best. Until then I shall seek in the spirit and working of their schools the secret of their success, the cause of our failings.

In the audience, Emerson, an overseer of the university, was deeply moved; coming up to congratulate White, he declared that the lecture had "stirred him like a trumpet." [9]

And probably even that overseer, whoever he was, who called down Bigelow's scorn because he carried a horse-chestnut in his pocket to ward off rheumatism, would have sense enough to catch the drift of White's eloquence.

As for Drs. Holmes and Bigelow—they must have known that, in White's judgment, they were the two best lecturers in the school; they could not have missed the coupling of the allusion to "fees." In the end, it was Eliot's abolition of the fee system and incorporation of the medical school within the financial system of the university which actually made the reforms in the curriculum possible.[10]

For Holmes, the reform meant a regular salary which he rather liked, as well he might, considering that it was the highest in the medical faculty. He was further relieved of the necessity of scrambling for the physiology, for physiology became a separate department. The classes were smaller and the caliber of the students was better; it continued to improve as the entrance requirements were stiffened. Holmes could not say of these students as he said of others, that some of them belonged in kindergarten but for fear they would tread on the children.[11]

Describing the reforms to Motley, Holmes betrayed his old obsessive distrust of theologians when he observed the contrast between his own University and that of his father.

It is so curious to see a young man like Eliot, with an organizing brain, a firm will, a grave, calm, dignified presence, taking the ribbons of our classical coach-and-six, feeling the horses' mouths, putting a check on this one's capers and touching that one with a lash . . . and taking it all as naturally as if he had been born President. . . . In the meantime Yale has chosen a Connecticut country minister, aet. 60, as her president, and the experiment of a liberal culture with youth at the helm *versus* orthodox repression with a graybeard Palinurus is going on in a way that it is impossible to look at without interest in seeing how the experiment will turn out.[12]

By 1879 Holmes was completely caught up in the current of change. He was calmly telling his students that it was likely that a fourth year of study might have to be added to the medical course and proudly describing Harvard as "this institution which has to act as the tug-boat to drag other craft much bigger than itself out of their stagnant waters." [13] He rather enjoyed the spectacle of the Philadelphia schools of his old opponents in the puerperal fever debate following tamely in the rear of Harvard. He did not, however, so far delude himself as to claim, as Henry J. Bigelow did, that he was personally responsible for this new state of affairs.

Holmes had not occupied himself wholly with the battle of the curriculum during the interlude of 1867 to 1872. Although now out of the lecture game entirely, and deaf to his cousin Wendell Phillips's suggestions that he try the lyceum again, Holmes did consent in 1869 to give for the Lowell Institute a lecture, *The Medical Profession in Massachusetts*. The subject led him, unfortunately, back into the bad company—for him—of Cotton Mather and other Puritans. His exposures of their medical follies and, by implication, their theological ones occupy so much of his time that what promises to be a very good history of New England medicine comes out in a somewhat lopsided form. Nevertheless, drawing his materials from colonial manuscripts and literature, his father's annals, his brother-in-law's recently published history of witchcraft, he gave a sound as well as entertaining picture of colonial medicine.

In spite of his inclination to harp on the theology of his colonial doctors, Holmes showed in one respect an historical sense unusual for his time. In a period when town, county, and state histories, written from a narrowly provincial point of view, were common, Holmes at the outset of his speech declared it impossible to regard the events in the history of medicine as phenomena isolated geographically or intellectually. He represents his idea in figurative language:

A geographer who was asked to describe the tides of Massachusetts Bay, would have to recognize the circumstance that they are a limited manifestation of a great oceanic movement. To consider them apart from this, would be to localize a planetary phenomenon, and to provincialize a law of the universe.[14]

300

With this thought in mind, he constantly related what he has to say of colonial medicine to conditions and events in the old world.

He was, at the close of his lecture, hopeful for the future "in a community which holds every point of human belief, every institution in human hands, and every word written in human dialect, open to free discussion today, tomorrow and to the end of time." But this lyrical expression of the democratic faith was sobered by his fear that quackery and idolatry may be immortal.

We can find most of the old beliefs alive amongst us today, only having changed their dresses and the social spheres in which they thrive. . . . Names are only air, and blow away with a change of wind, but beliefs are rooted in human wants and weakness, and die hard. The oaks of Dodona are prostrate and the shrine of Delphi is desolate; but the Pythoness and the Sibyl may be consulted in Lowell Street for a very moderate compensation. . . . What shall we say of the plausible and well-dressed charlatans of our own time, who trade in false pretenses like Nicholas Knapp of old . . . or of the many follies and inanities, imposing on the credulous part of the community, each of them gaping with eager, open mouth for a gratuitous advertisement by the mention of its foolish name in any respectable connection? [15]

But during the sixties, the doctor's reading led him to exercise his wits less upon his old bugbears—puritan churchmen and medical charlatans—than upon his new mental hobbyhorse—psychology. Although the Athenaeum records of borrowings do not show which of the two O. W. Holmeses was taking out George Henry Lewes, James Mill, Herbert Spenser, David Hartley, and other writers who touched upon the subject, the doctor's entries in his black notebook and the references he would make in an address to be given in 1870 suggest that the psychological works that appear in the records from 1863 on were read by the doctor.[16] In his own library, he had, of course, such medical and physiological works as had a bearing on the general subject. Such notes as those on Maudsley's *Physiology and Pathology of the Mind* indicate that Holmes read, as one might expect, not so much for what might be new to him as for what

301

would echo his own thought. The Autocrat had talked of olfactory memories; he noted in Maudsley the same thought. The Autocrat had spoken of automatic thinking, and, in *The Guardian Angel,* of unconscious cerebration; from Maudsley, from Lecky's *History of Rationalism,* and finally from Leibnitz, he plucked out the now familiar idea.

Out of this haphazard reading grew his Phi Beta Kappa address for 1870, *Mechanism in Thought and Morals.* Making due allowance, as he asked, for occasional rhetorical flourishes and plays for effect in keeping with its function as an oration, the modern lay reader will find neither the manner nor the matter of his address too old-fashioned. Like most of Holmes's writing, the speech is a collection of unintegrated notions. In a mixture of fact, speculation, and humor, Holmes made effectively a number of points, to us commonplace, to his 1870 audience provocative and relatively new. He insisted upon the interdependence of mind and body, argued that mental disease is susceptible to cure, and attempted to establish the fact of unconscious thought.

Of inherited belief, he wrote that "obscure in their origins as the parentage of the cave-dwellers, [they] are stronger with many minds than the evidence of the senses and the simplest deductions of the intelligence." [17] Of prejudices, he said, "Old prejudices, that are ashamed to confess themselves, nudge our talking thought to utter their magesterial veto." [18]

Protesting the inefficacy of punishment—and incidentally defending contemporary scientists against the charge of materialism—he observed:

The next movement in moral materialism is to establish a kind of scale of equivalents between perverse moral choice and physical suffering. Pain often cures *ignorance,* as we know—as when a child learns not to handle fire by burning its fingers,—but it does not change the moral nature. Children may be whipped into obedience, but not into virtue; and it is not pretended that the penal colony of heaven has sent back a single reformed criminal. We hang men for our convenience and safety; sometimes shoot them for revenge. Thus we come to associate the infliction of punishment for offences as their satisfactory settlement,—a kind of neutralization of them, as of an acid with an alkali: so that we feel as if a jarring moral universe would be all right if only suffering enough were added to it. This scheme of chemical equivalents seems to me, I confess, a worse materialism than making protoplasm master of arts and doctor of divinity.[19]

Thinking of such problem characters as those he had attempted to turn into fiction, he quoted Shakespeare's lines:

> Pluck from the memory a rooted sorrow;
> Raze out the written troubles of the brain;

and hinted at the unsuccessfully handled theme of *A Mortal Antipathy,* to be written fourteen years later, when he spoke of the scars left by childhood experiences.

But as his title suggests, the doctor, in spite of his wanderings in that direction, was not approaching the problems of mind on the psychic level. Consistent with the methods of his time, he took the somatic approach. In his address, he described some psychological experiments of his own, made in 1867 and 1870; he was referring to his attempts to test the rate at which nerve impulses travel.[20]

As so often before, he had chosen his subject and his approach to it, with a sharp sense of the moment. In the early seventies psychology, studied on the somatic level, came into being as a recognized branch of medicine. The *American Journal of Psychological Medicine* was founded in 1870. In 1871, John E. Tyler, who had been a special lecturer on "Psychology and Medicine," would become a full professor at the Harvard Medical School, having his own department of neurology. In 1873-75, James Jackson Putnam would be added to the staff as special lecturer on mental diseases. It was Putnam who in 1909 would become, after a change of mind, "the chief prop of the psychoanalytic movement in his native land." So Freud described him.[21]

Poet at the Breakfast-Table

1870–1872

Besides, Sir, there must always be a struggle between father and son.

O N NOVEMBER 26, 1870, Dr. Holmes and his family moved into a new house at 296 Beacon Street. Holmes, whose Charles Street house had a river view, had embroiled himself at once in the public debate over the proposal to fill in the bay below Charles Street and enlisted the support of his brother-physicians who, having no property there, might be supposed to be unprejudiced.[1] Within a year the Back Bay district, reclaimed from salt flats and marshes, was a fact. The new neighborhood grew with all the rapidity peculiar to the expansive seventies. Before the end of the decade, Moses King, Cambridge printer of a *Handbook of Boston*, described the area as "the fashionable modern West End of Boston," and gave it a Victorian's highest praise in the phrase "refined elegance." [2] Dr. Holmes in making his move had led the exodus from Charles Street, now cut off from the river. He had chosen the property not so much for its fashionable atmosphere as for the view of the river and a place for his boats. A "brownstone front" with narrow front windows and a long flight of steps leading up to its front door, the new house seemed designed to turn its back on the street. The large, main rooms in the new house were at the back; the bay windows of the library on the second floor and the dining-room on the first overlooked the river.

The dinner table at 296 Beacon Street was a lively place, the talk quick and brilliant as each of the family in good-natured rivalry tried to score off the other.[3] Amelia could talk faster than her father; she was said to be the only person in Boston who could outtalk the popular minister Phillips Brooks. The doctor, "with a mind quick to perceive analogies," [4] moved by flashes of wit. The elder son liked to keep an argument open; Ned, the younger son, offered humor and intelligent observation to the talk.

All three of the young people in the family were on the verge of marriage; Ned, in fact, was already engaged to Henrietta Wigglesworth, "a very superior and charming girl," [5] as Dr. Holmes told his sister. In the following year Amelia's engagement to Turner Sargent was announced, and in 1872, Dr. Holmes was again writing his relatives to tell them of Wendell's engagement to Fanny Dixwell, "a most superior lady in every respect." [6]

Dr. Holmes became sharply aware of his age; along with the other "Boys of '29," he found it hard to keep up the annual fiction of youthfulness. "To be sure we are *young*—oh quite young. But somehow there seemed to be a general, though tacit, agreement that 11 o'clock was quite late enough for us to stay together," wrote Sam May, recording the class meeting of 1870.[7]

Holmes had scarcely settled in the house in which he was to die when he was obliged to sell the house in which he had been born. Since their mother's death John and Wendell Holmes had kept the Cambridge property in spite of Harvard's attempts to pry them loose from it; John, who never left Cambridge if he could help it, had lived on in the house, visited by Dr. Holmes and his wife, who came out during the spring and summer to tend the garden.[8] But the pressure of Harvard University under its new president brought about the long-resisted end.

As the brothers cleared the old house of papers and mementoes that took them back beyond their youth to the colonial days of their parents, they could not help but be aware of the changes going on so rapidly around them. John, describing the altering face of Cambridge, hit upon an image that effectively suggests the feverish activity of the times:

Cambridge is in the most furious stage of improvement heretofor known. They build, they remove buildings, they add and subtract parts, and at last have come to disemboweling large structures of recent erection with a fury like that of the Bacchanals, that they may have the luxury of re-placing the viscera.[9]

Wendell would keep his ghosts in his writing; he would shortly preserve the gambrel-roofed house as it had been in his childhood and turn the portrait of his ancestor Dorothy Quincy into verse; but John, who was the better philosopher of the two, quietly retired to the smallest street in Cambridge, the Appian Way. He could not, in his small lodgings, enter-tain his Whist Club and his countless friends in the same com-fort. He solved the problem of hospitality, however, by giving his friends oyster suppers in their own houses, carefully send-ing the oysters and crackers in ahead of time and finally ap-pearing himself with "a lank oil cloth bag, sagged by some bottles of wine. . . . He was forced to let us do the cooking and to supply the cold [sic] slaw, and perhaps he indemnified himself for putting us to these charges by the vast superfluity of oysters with which we were inundated for weeks." [10] In contrast to his friend Lowell, who periodically sought to re-form the world, and his brother Wendell, who felt obliged to talk with it on manners, religion, and medicine, John was "willing to let it go on experimenting until it gets wiser." [11]

While John was content to stand aside and observe the small world of Cambridge, the livelier Wendell, his energy un-diminished by his sixty years, needed the larger stage of Bos-ton. He might deny that he was "wedded to the pavement" [12] and claim that he loved the country passionately, but it is sig-nificant that he best enjoyed the company of men like his neighbor William Amory, a diner-out devoted to the city, "pre-ordained for Boston or the piazzas of . . . Nahant." [13] The latter seaside resort, next door to Boston, where Holmes spent several summers, was, in its season, simply the Saturday Club moved temporarily to a cooler spot. Tom Appleton was another of Holmes's favorites, to be welcomed as warmly now as he had been years ago when as young men they met in New York on the eve of sailing to Europe. Tom was the doctor's notion of a good talker, "witty, entertaining, audacious, ingenious, sometimes extravagant." Of one reunion with Appleton, Holmes wrote, as innocently as if he had never heard the sound of his own voice: "I never heard such a fusillade in my life." [14]

Motley was in Europe again, and Holmes resumed his role of keeping the historian up-to-date on the local gossip—the astonishing doings of President Eliot; personal news of his children's marriages; the Club, which was somehow less gay and exciting than it had been in the past. Lowell came less frequently; Longfellow seemed melancholy, finding life at home dull after a visit to Europe; and everyone was worried about Agassiz, gravely ill. But except for Eliot's machinations, there were few local sensations to record. In 1870, a visiting actor caused a mild furor; Charles Fechter's *Hamlet* only mildly interested the doctor, but he observed the excitement the player caused and remarked that Boston was "just the right size for aesthetic endemics, and they spare neither age nor sex." [15] The actor, at least, was one visitor for whom Holmes did not have to go through his rhyming paces.

He had, of course, been called out for the great Peace Jubilee in 1869. The ambitious projector of this occasion had something of P. T. Barnum's flair for the grandiose. In spite of the sardonic sniping of the New York papers and the skepticism of some Bostonians, Patrick S. Gilmore got his enormous chorus and orchestra trained, inveigled Liszt and Ole Bull into performing, and built a huge coliseum. When he came to touch Dr. Holmes for a poem, he found the doctor reluctant. Always entranced with any display of ingenuity, Holmes had been interested in watching the building of the city's first skyscraper (six stories); he had made himself some paper models of other architectural gargantuas and gone out occasionally to watch Gilmore's building in the process of erection. He was not, however, very eager to supply a hymn, to be sung by a chorus of school children, especially when the tune was set to begin with.[16] It was a bad poem, one of his worst, but it served its purpose as a minor item in the four-day program. No one, after all, could compete with the *pièce de résistance* of the affair—the rendition of the "Anvil Chorus" by a full orchestra accompanied by one hundred Boston firemen, in red jackets, performing on real anvils.

The Peace Jubilee was the first and last colossal affair staged by the city of Boston; the sarcasms of the rival Manhattan discouraged them from any more large-scale displays; but receptions for visiting celebrities and foreign ambassadors continued, statues and monuments were going up, and cornerstones being laid. For all of these Holmes was expected to perform.

In 1871, Boston, in an excessive display of unrepublican admiration for royalty, welcomed the Grand Duke Alexis of Russia. "The dinner the gentlemen gave was a handsome one," reported the doctor, "*thirty-five* dollars a plate ought to pay for what Californians call a 'square meal.'"[17] There were half a dozen speeches; Phillips Brooks distinguished himself. Holmes, as usual, hit the right tone in verses of welcome that no one would remember but everyone enjoyed at the moment. "Society" gave a Grand Ball for the visitor, whose youth and good looks enchanted the ladies. To the appraising eyes of the anatomist Holmes, he was a "superb specimen." Louisa May Alcott, a thoroughgoing democrat, observed with pleasure that the Grand Duke "would dance with all the pretty girls, and leave the Boston Dowagers and their diamonds in the lurch."[18] The Duke repaid this lavish hospitality with a small dinner at which Longfellow, Lowell, and Holmes represented the literary world.

Holmes was in good spirits in December 1871;[19] he had begun a new series of papers for the *Atlantic*. He could not be contented unless he was doing something besides lecturing at the college. In February 1870, he had told Fields that he did not want to write just then, but that he might want to later. Should he try a different audience if he could make a good thing of it? Meanwhile the editor, as Holmes reminded him, had "plenty of young blood" and did not need him.[20] By August, however, Holmes was suggesting that Fields come around and talk him "into a frenzy of ambition and composition." [21] But the frenzy was slow in coming; it was not until October 1871, that he wrote to William Dean Howells (since August, the *Atlantic's* new editor) and asked him to come to the house to talk things over. He thought it might be fun "to wake up his old congregation—their children and grandchildren." [22]

Returning to his boarding-house breakfast-table, abandoning all attempts at narrative (except for a little romantic seasoning and a device to bring the breakfast-table series to a close) Holmes still did not return completely to the manner of the Autocrat. Even had he wanted to effect such a return, he could not have done so.

The Autocrat of 1857 had been bold and eager, confident of his cleverness, delighting in paradox and surprise. The Professor had shown an unexpected earnestness, and a less unexpected vulnerability. Both had been answering stimuli in the immediate background: the Autocrat, those of his daily life; and the Professor, those offered by his readers and critics. Thrown off his balance by attack, Holmes had needed a safety valve and divided his breakfast-table authority between the Professor and Little Boston. The Poet of 1872 is, significantly, a very modest and retiring man, chastened if you like. He suspects that his audience is smaller than the Autocrat's and carefully addresses himself to the One Reader.

In *The Professor,* Holmes had brought one *alter ego* on stage; in *The Poet,* he brings three. His personality multiplying like an amoeba, Holmes now appears not only as the Poet, but also as the Young Astronomer and as the Master. The Astronomer is a melancholy young man, absorbed in his work in a lonely way—in too lonely a way the doctor implies. He owes something to the Astronomer in Johnson's *Rasselas;* but he also owes a great deal to the spectacle the doctor's older son was then presenting. It was at this time that the younger

Wendell Holmes was so engrossed in his work that he could not let his notes out of his sight and carried his brief case in to dinner with him. Nearly forty years earlier, the elder Holmes had been as devoted to medicine as his son was now to law; the similarity could hardly escape the doctor, preoccupied as he was with the question of heredity.

It is the Young Astronomer who writes the too liquid blank verse, "Wind-Clouds and Star-Drifts," that comprises most of the poetry of the book. One of his poems—they hardly deserve the name—develops the theme of the relations between youth and age, father and son. In "Master and Scholar" the "I" of the poem is supposed to be the Young Astronomer, but he is obviously the sixty-one-year-old poet, a fact which makes for ambiguity.[23]

The doctor had the subject very much on his mind. At Mrs. Fields's one evening, Charles Sumner indignantly objected to the criticism being heaped upon Agassiz by a younger generation of scientists. Holmes offered an explanation:

It means just this. Agassiz will not listen to the Darwinian theory; his whole effort is on the other side. Now Agassiz is no longer young, and I was reading the other day in a book on the Sandwich Islands of an old Feejee man who had been carried away among strangers but who prayed that he might be carried home that his brains might be beaten out in peace by his son according to the custom of those lands. It flashed over me then that our sons beat out our brains in the same way. They do not walk in our ruts of thought or begin exactly where we left off, but they have a new standpoint of their own.[24]

Holmes had committed "moral parricide" himself, or so the indignant orthodox press had told him, when he wrote *Elsie Venner* and in it protested the evil effects of a too rigidly orthodox training upon children. Even as he wrote *The Poet at the Breakfast-Table,* he picked up his father's copy of Calvin's *Institutes* with its notations in his father's hand. Not given to marking books, Holmes did enter in pencil on the rear end-paper a page reference for the passage in which Calvin upholds the doctrine of infant damnation. In ink he entered, initialed, and dated, March 31, 1872, a Latin note under one of his father's. Abiel Holmes's note reads: "See two pages in index at the end." The doctor added: "preserved in place by the son's care." [25]

In reading *The Poet,* one cannot help thinking that the doctor is feeling, as doubtless his own father had felt before him, the "bite of the serpent's tooth." In spite of its softening embellishments, one sentence in *The Poet* stands out. "As people grow older they come at length to live so much in memory that they often think with a kind of pleasure of losing their dearest blessings." [26]

Expressed obliquely, the father-son motif is one of the inner stories of *The Poet.* In the persons of the Poet and the Master, Holmes appears to tell another. Their dialogues offer his *apologia* for his life. As he knew and said in the book, his writing was a means to liberate his soul.[27]

In the fourth number of *The Poet,* he asks "suppose that your mind is in its nature discursive, erratic, subject to electric attractions and repulsions, *volage;* it may be impossible for you to compel your attention except by taking away all external disturbances. I think the poet has an advantage and a disadvantage as compared with the steadier going people. Life is so vivid to the poet, that he is too eager to seize and exhaust its multitudinous impressions." He is using the second person, but in the passage before, he had—more honestly—used the first person singular as he lamented an inability to give any subject his whole attention, and a tendency to be easily distracted.[28]

A year earlier he had answered the personal questions of S. Weir Mitchell, then beginning the neurological investigations that would lead to his theory of the nervous breakdown and the therapy of the rest cure. In his correspondence with the Philadelphia doctor, Holmes expressed emphatically what is so softly suggested in *The Poet.* Questioned by Mitchell about mental fatigue, Holmes answered that mental nausea took the place of fatigue with him:

I like nine-tenths of any matter I study but I do not like to lick the plate. If I did I suppose I should be more of a man of science. . . . I feel as if I were condemning my own intellect according to the judgment of many

311

persons. I have often regretted not having forcibly trained myself to the exhaustive treatment of some limited subject. . . .[29]

Looking at *The Poet,* the reader sees the figure of the Scarabee, who has done just that; toward the Scarabee, expert in a special branch of entomology, Holmes's attitude is ambivalent, respectful one moment and mocking the next. He summons Samuel Johnson to his aid to make fun of the Scarabee and his narrow specialism, but promptly turns to attack the eighteenth-century autocrat.

Continuing his confessions to Mitchell, he added: "But my nature is to snatch at all the fruits of knowledge—after that let in the pigs. A thoroughly detestable statement, but let it stand, for there is too much truth in it." [30] Holmes, describing the Master, his *alter ego,* expresses a similar thought about himself, but he turns the self-condemnation of the letter into self-defense in the book. The Master is:

a dogmatist who lays down the law, *ex cathedra,* from the chair of his own personality . . . who is not afraid of a half-truth . . . who says things preemptorily that he may inwardly debate with himself. . . . There are two ways of dealing with assertions of this kind. One may attack them on the false side and perhaps gain a conversational victory. But I like to take them up on the true side and see how much can be made of that aspect of the dogmatic assertion. It is the only comfortable way of dealing with persons like the Old Master.[31]

The letters to Mitchell show him aware of the significance of such passages as this and of such speculations as that on the discursive imagination of the poet. They suggest, too, a personal motive underlying his reiterated demonstration of the limitations of the human will.

Nobody but myself could tell it with all the reservations, qualifications, conditions of every kind, compensations, philosophical justifications, crack-puttying subterfuges and counterclaims to discursive intelligence which render life tolerable with such a vicious and kicking brain as I have described my will as bestriding.[32]

Taking these letters to Mitchell together with their parallel passages in the fourth paper of *The Poet* one can understand why his contemporaries continually observed that his actual talk was much better than his writing, why Emerson could list him among "My Men." It seems reasonable to assume that Holmes's talk had an edge to it, a sharpness he blunts with sentiment or evasion in his published writing.

Those notes which do not take the form of mere memoranda or are not so incomplete as to be ambiguous are evidence for such an assumption. The entry, in his notes for *The Poet*, which reads: "Afraid of my own personality (or another afraid of his)" [33] seems to express an insight that, in masquerade, comes out in the passage describing the Master. It is the Master who is supposed to be following the principle set down in the note, "I had rather say my say according to my own humor than follow the rules and produce 'a work of art.' . . ." [34] Unfortunately when Holmes himself got down to the actual business of writing for print, he did neither, except as he managed to do the first in an oblique manner, and as he accomplished the second in a poem or two.

Taken on its surface, *The Poet at the Breakfast-Table* is the book of a man who knew that age has put him on the sidelines. He was looking back down the century, all the time acutely aware of the present. His son in his state of feverish and rather lonely devotion to his work, the young men who had taken over the medical school, the young women who were clamoring for the vote, the specialists in medicine and science, and the "communists"—all these belonged to the present. Holmes knew that his view of these phenomena was conservative and prejudiced, but he thought that a man of solid prejudices, like the tree a cow scratches herself against, may serve a useful purpose. [35]

Possibly with the memory of his errors in the past, he handles the radicals of 1872 gingerly, appearing ineffectively as their defender, as a mediator between them and those who might be frightened by their threats of violence and revolution. He might have seemed less inept had he not implied that the radicals need not be taken seriously.

The radical ideas of the day, however, interested him less

than the scientific discoveries, and these he took calmly. He recognized that such discoveries have a way of unsettling old beliefs, but, he thought there was no need to go into hysterics about it.[36] And in his book, he discusses the effect of the Darwinian theory and the nebular hypothesis. Another subject of contemporary popular debate, the old notion of spontaneous generation, had been revived by the discoveries of the bacteriologists. Holmes gives a concise and lucid exposition of the experiment which tests the theory. Here too he appears as a mediator between the scientists and his readers, his object being to quiet the fears of the latter.

Especially interested in that field of science that is only beginning to emerge—psychology—he borrows from his *Mechanism in Thought and Morals* to reiterate his belief in the need for such study: ". . . the study of man has been so completely subject to our preconceived opinions, that we have got to begin all over again." [37] Looking back at *The Autocrat,* he found himself admiring that figure of speech in which he spoke of "depolarizing" words in order to divest them of the taboos and superstitions with which use had clothed them. In *The Poet,* he says: "The scientific study of man is the most difficult of all branches of knowledge. It requires, in the first place, a new terminology to get rid of the enormous load of prejudices with which every term applied to the malformations, the functional disturbances, and the organic diseases of the moral nature is at present burdened." [38]

Feeling handicapped himself by the lack of usable words, he borrowed from modern theories of evolution and physics to express his sense of the fact that what is called sin is a "vital process . . . a function, and not an entity." "We must study the lines of direction of all the forces which traverse our human nature." [39]

Francis Galton's studies in heredity pleased him; he was delighted to find in the modern investigator's *Hereditary Genius* that "there is a frequent correlation between an usually devout disposition and a weak constitution." The doctor had thought so all along and was excited to find his

notions of "pathological piety" confirmed. And he could
not help himself, but went on:

John Bunyan has got at the same fact . . . [he loathes Bunyan, remem-
ber]. He tells us, "The more healthy the lusty man is, the more prone he
is unto evil." If the converse is true, no wonder that good people, according to Bunyan, are always in trouble and terror, for he says,

"A Christian man is never long at ease;
When one fright's gone, another doth him seize."

If invalidism and the nervous timidity which is apt to go with it are
elements of spiritual superiority, it follows that pathology and toxicology
should form a most important part of a theological education, so that a
divine might know how to keep a parish in a state of chronic bad health
in order that it might be virtuous. . . .[40]

Although contemporary scientists could not distress
Holmes, who was prepared to accept their findings, other
signs of the times evoked irritation or laughter. Sentiment
acceptable in the early nineteenth century is now at a dis-
count. The doctor admits that sentiment "does not go a
great way in deciding questions of arithmetic or algebra, or
geometry. . . . But . . . it is a word not to be used too
lightly in passing judgment, as if it were an element to be
thrown out or treated with small consideration. Reason may
be the lever; but sentiment gives you the fulcrum and the
place to stand on if you want to move the world." In fact he
thinks that even "sentimentality," which is sentiment over-
done, is better than "that affectation of superiority to human
weakness which is only tolerable as one of the stage-properties
of full-blown dandyism, and is, at best, but half-blown cynicism." [41]

He is, however, in too good a humor to be everywhere
sarcastic. He has a good deal of fun with some burlesque
scenes: the modern young doctor, surrounded by formidable
instruments and full of learning, who hopefully examines an
ordinary bump on the head for signs of something esoteric—
Addison's disease, for instance.

He found another specialist of the times amusing—the
piano virtuoso. He described one he had seen. Her hands
jumped "at the piano as if they were a couple of tigers coming

down on a flock of black and white sheep, and the piano gave a great howl as if its tail had been trod on. Dead stop,—so still you could hear your hair growing. Then another jump, and another howl, as if the piano had two tails and you had trod on both of 'em at once, and then a grand clatter and scramble and string of jumps, up and down, back and forward, one hand over the other, like a stampede of rats and mice more than like anything I call music." [42]

Having protected himself with the fiction of his "one" reader, Holmes must have found his flattering correspondence comforting. Among his letters in May was one from Motley who thought the new breakfast-table papers were the "next best thing" to talking to Holmes. Motley, his recall from the Court of St. James's still rankling, was able, nevertheless, to think of his friend. Having heard of the doctor's poem for Grand Duke Alexis, Motley was moved to comment on the Russian-American friendship:

I do not know that I appreciate very highly that affection which is supposed to exist between Russia and America. At any rate, it is a very Platonic attachment. Being founded, however, on entire incompatibility of character, absence of sympathy, and a plentiful lack of any common interest, it may prove a very enduring passion.

As for Holmes's poem, Motley wrote: "Whenever there is a call for a national outpouring, off everybody goes, as a matter of course to tap you, and always you bubble fresher and fresher." He declared that Boston ought to vote Holmes a yearly butt of sack.[43]

The doctor, now in his sixties, was not so sure that his fountain could be counted on, and was actually saying "no" from time to time. Moreover, in 1871-72, the new medical school program made heavy demands on his time. Besides preparing new lectures for the lengthened course, he was ordering a collection of new illustrative material.[44] *The Poet,* family weddings, and the new lectures so fully occupied his time and so tired him that he even gave up the Harvard commencement functions and actually resisted a woman's pleas for a poem, telling her "No, my dear lady, I adore you, but I'll bet you can't coax me."

He was, in fact, a little weary of his "cornstalk fiddle"; [45] in September, refusing to take it up, he wrote the following eloquent letter to Thomas Wentworth Higginson:

> Your kind words are pleasant and your request is far from unreasonable, yet I must excuse myself from the very slight task—as it seems at least, to which you invite me.
>
> I am thoroughly tired of my own voice at all sorts of occasional gatherings. I have handled the epithets of eulogy until the mere touch of a warm adjective blisters my palm. I have tried not to do myself discredit by unseemly flattery, but I do really feel as if by force of repetition my welcomes were growing, if not unwelcome, at least outworn, and should in common propriety give place to something a little fresher. I have greeted representatives from all parts of the civilized and half-civilized world, and am expecting to be called on whenever the King of Dahomey or a minister from Ujiji makes his appearance.
>
> The most desperate attempts were made by men with argument, and women with entreaty, to get me to play Orpheus to the stones of the Pittsfield monument, but I resisted both successfully. These invitations keep coming to me all the time, and I mean to decline them all unless for some very special reason that happens to strike me full in the centre of volition.
>
> Here are Froude, and Edmund Yates, and George Macdonald, and nobody knows how many more—Tyndall and by and by perhaps Huxley and one must draw the line somewhere—suppose we say "Rhyming done here only for Crowned Heads or their representatives"? I have done England, France, Russia (twice), China, Japan, Germany (in the person of Ehrenberg), and so belabored my own countrymen of every degree with occasional verses that I must have coupled "name" and "fame" together scores of times, and made "story" and "glory" as intimate as if they had been born twins.
>
> I know you are on your knees by this time asking the Lord to forgive you for making a suggestion that I should try this last experiment on the patience of mankind. I cannot say whether He will forgive you or not, but you have my full pardon inasmuch as you have joined a very complimentary request with a word of praise, which, coming from so good a judge of what will bear praising, makes me willing to do almost anything except just what you ask me to.[46]

Septuagenarian

1872–1882

He that lives must grow old.

HOLMES WAS WEARY enough to want to do nothing but read story-books; dozens of correspondents, however, were persuaded that they were the "one reader" to whom the Poet addressed his remarks. The doctor faithfully answered them. His English audience had grown; the Breakfast-Table series circulated in cheap editions; yellow paper-covered affairs with his picture on them sold for one or two shillings, "to the detriment of your purse," wrote Motley, "but to the increase of your renown." The historian was delighted to see his old friend's familiar face staring at him from the bookstalls in every railway station.

Motley sent him a copy of the *Saturday Review* with its appreciative notice of *The Poet*. "It was not warm or enthusiastic enough but warmth and enthusiasm don't spout in the Saturday. Perhaps the dear 'Nation' may begin to discover your genius now that the model and object of its feeble imitation has sounded your praises." [1] The *Nation* was, in fact, more kind to *The Poet* than it had been to *The Guardian Angel*.

The literary world seems to have got in the habit of exchanging photographs; Tennyson sent his along with praise for the doctor's book. Holmes, under no illusions about his looks, did not pride himself on his pictures, but he looked "the camera in the face as good-naturedly as if it were going to make an Adonis" [2] of him. He sent his latest to those who asked.

Correspondence and medical lectures took up his time in the fall and spring of 1872-73. He fulfilled his desire to read story-books with *Middlemarch,* read a few scraps of science, and got caught up on the heavy journals. On Saturday, November 9, he was amusing himself puzzling out the tales in some Dutch children's books Motley had sent. The sound of fire-bells sent him to the north window, but there was no sign of smoke or flame in the towns across the river. Looking out of the windows on Beacon Street, he saw a great column of light above downtown Boston. "There was no getting very near the fire; but that night and the next morning I saw it dissolving the great high buildings, which seemed to melt away in it. My son Wendell made a remark which I found quite true, that great walls would tumble and yet one would hear no crash,—they came down as if they had fallen on a vast feather-bed." By Monday "all the world within reach was looking at a wilderness of ruins." An area of sixty-five acres below Washington Street was flat to the water's edge.

Holmes did not try to give Motley the whole story of the disaster. "Any reporter for a penny paper could tell you the story, I have no doubt, a great deal better than I can." Characteristically, he admitted his own momentary qualms as he watched the fire "eating its way straight toward my deposits." The doctor's candor sometimes shocked even his friends as they heard him cheerfully admit feelings they would themselves have been at pains to conceal. He could write, referring to an earlier Boston fire: "My mother used to tell me that her grandfather lost forty buildings in that fire, which made me feel grand, as being the descendent of one that hath had losses,—in fact makes me feel a little grand now in telling you of it." [3] But he did not think much of people who put on airs or assumed the grand manner on the strength of a distinguished ancestor, nor did he care much for those Boston dowagers whose "social knee-action" was so conspicuous. Charles Sumner's lack of humor did not distress Holmes so much as his tendency to think *"l'état c'est moi."* [4]

Holmes's vanity was very different from the senatorial grandeur of Sumner, for the doctor admitted to being constitutionally vain and turned the natural failing into a jest: "I have always been struck by the fact that a man bears superlatives about his own productions with wonderful fortitude." But he never allowed that vanity to lead him into overestimating his own talents. Emerson could account for his ability to produce the right lines for the right occasion as follows:

The security with which I read every new poem of Holmes is always justified by its wit, force, and perfect good taste. Dr. Holmes is the best example I have seen of a man of as much genius, who had entire control of his powers, so that he could always write or speak *to order:* partly from the abundance of the stream, which can fill indifferently any provided channel.[5]

The doctor himself described that talent as "a fatal facility" and his good-natured acquiescence as bad as "habitual drunkenness." [6] Lowell's praise of his poems evoked from the doctor the remark that he himself thought them often "too hopping." [7] He estimated his own writings justly, too, when he wrote to Paul Hamilton Hayne that there was "something of a real human life in them." [8]

He rarely undertook to write a piece of criticism because he knew that his kindness would be at war with his honesty and that his casual, personal way of reading might lead to injustice. Such critical pieces as he did undertake were tackled as favors for personal friends; his anxiety not to hurt the author's feelings gave such pieces a pussyfooting quality of which he was probably aware. He was likely to become prolix as he cushioned his blows with soft words. He could be sharp when the observation to be made was general. In an early review of a novel by a woman, he had counted himself grateful for a story "which does not rustle with crinoline, that most useful of inventions for ladies with limited outlines and literary milliners with scanty brains." [9]

In the few such notices written during the seventies, Holmes was at his best when he went off at a personal tangent. He reviewed Dr. E. H. Clarke's *Sex in Education* (1873) for the *Atlantic*. Through the fog of euphemisms necessary for a "family magazine" emerges the fact that Dr. Holmes did not question Clarke's physiology, but he doubted that the physiological differences between the sexes warrant completely different types of education. Holmes seems to have felt that the new psychologist, as well as the physiologist, needed to be called in consultation here: "the sweet poisons of adolescence are subtler than any Tofana ever mingled for his involuntary patients." [10]

He was incapable of saying no to every request for speeches or poems; he even came back to the lecture platform—to oblige some women. In a special Saturday afternoon series of free lectures on English literature, for women only, Dr. Holmes gave a lecture on versification,[11] concerning himself largely with technical matters; out of the lecture grew a short note for the *Boston Medical and Surgical Journal* on the "Physiology of Verse." It is an unfinished and suggestive investigation which offers the theory that poetic rhythms are related to pulse beats and respiration. He calls the tetrameter line the normal respiratory measure, guesses that connections may be found between a poet's favorite measure, and his deviations from physiological norms.[12] Sidney Lanier, then working on his book on English prosody, wrote eagerly to find out more about the doctor's reflections, but Holmes had carried them no further.[13]

For 1873 a review and a few poems were his chief literary productions. He turned down an invitation to attack the homeopathists again, thinking that neither his name nor style could be used to any good purpose.[14] He was enjoying his medical lectures, although the long flight of thirty-one steps to the lecture-room seemed to have doubled since 1848. The doctor had lost none of his pleasure in his subject, however. Medical-book salesmen, who caught him out in his crypt below the amphitheater, found him willing enough to talk but not to buy; he did not think much of their products. A connoisseur of the iconography of anatomy, the doctor described to them the beautiful engravings and woodcuts in his Vesalius and Sömmering.[15] Of his teaching, the ubiquitous President Eliot reported: "I never heard any other mortal exhibit such enthusiasm over an elegant dissection."[16] His enthusiastic praise was his demonstrator's reward for the careful labor necessary to satisfy Holmes's meticulous requirements. It was probably no accident that Holmes's demonstrators were always among the most promising of the medical school graduates.

Holmes's department now included Thomas Dwight, who would succeed him as Parkman Professor, and William James. Both James and Dwight have left accounts of their examination at Holmes's hands in the days before stiff, written finals were required. The doctor put Dwight through an ordeal of close questioning made comfortable only by the questioner's friendly manner and the informal surroundings of his house.[17] James, however, tells a different story. The doctor asked him to describe a small nerve in the head and getting an accurate answer, exclaimed, "If you know that, you know everything! Now tell me about your dear old father."[18] Professor Holmes was known to be similarly casual with students whom he supposed would end their days in a laborious, ill-paid, rural practice where common sense and knowledge of the patients might count for more than a knowledge of the minutiae of anatomy.[19] He seems to have adjusted his examination to the individual; his carelessness with James, then, may have been due to confidence in the young man's intelligence and a suspicion that he would never be a doctor anyway. That casual examinations had been the rule rather than the exception Holmes himself indicates in a chapter on the medical school which he contributed to the *Harvard Book* in 1875.[20]

Such unacademic behavior, however, had now undergone a radical change; to the labor of a hundred odd lectures a year was added that of reading two hundred examination papers. Introducing President Eliot at a commencement dinner, Holmes referred to the deluge of papers and described

Eliot as a man who "gets money out of his alumni and work out of his faculty." [21]

Eliot got enough work out of his Parkman Professor for the next nine years to keep the latter from yielding to the pleas of William Dean Howells, now editor of the *Atlantic*. Howells begged Holmes for a story. The doctor answered: "Am I not a little—too—ripe, let us say, for that kind of business which you and Henry James are carrying on so vigorously in your lusty manhood?" [22] He had thought about a story now and then, but he was too busy seven months of the year and preferred to lie fallow.

In spite of his professed boredom with the business of rhyming to order, he was ready to send a message to San Francisco, to open a New York theater, to commemorate The Boston Tea Party and the Battle of Bunker Hill; to inaugurate a Governor; to bury a doctor, a banker, philanthropist and a senator; to celebrate a housemaid's golden wedding, to save a church, to dedicate a Hall, to welcome the nations, to toast an English novelist, and to entertain the stockholders in a wharf. Fortunately not all these functions required his personal presence, nor were they the products of a single year. He was, in fact, quite modest during the interlude of 1873-76 when, after all, every city, village and institution was staging some kind of centenary.

His social life had "got up or come down," he was not sure which, to dinner parties. He had come to loathe the big public affairs—"those horrible cold dinners washed down with interminable spouting—and yet how often I have helped to make my fellow creatures miserable." The private ones were more to his taste; and if Holmes thought himself too ripe, his friends did not. He came apparently resolved not to do all the talking and departed ruefully aware of his broken resolution.[23] As American journalism began to make capital out of personalities, Holmes's reputation as a great talker became public property; Boston hostesses were obliged to trot him out for visitors. Such a reputation had its drawbacks: "It seems hard not to be able to ask for a piece of bread or a tumbler of water, without a sensation running round the table, as if one were an electric eel or a torpedo, and couldn't be touched without giving a shock." [24]

Boston society was meanwhile stiffening into the conventional mold to be satirized by the modern novelist, John P. Marquand. Two very different observers noticed the change; one a contemporary of Holmes, the other belonging to his son's generation. The doctor's old friend and rival as a wit, Tom Appleton, stayed away as much as possible, but when he did visit "stiff and chilly Boston," [25] he found Holmes a great comfort. To the sardonic and critical Henry Adams, teaching at Harvard and editing the *North American Review,* the complacency of that society was a dreary spectacle.

Dr. Holmes, who does the wit for the city of three hundred thousand people, is allowed to talk as he will—wild [mild?] atheism commonly— and no one objects. I am allowed to sit in my chair at Harvard College and rail at everything which the College respects, and no one cares.[26]

Holmes's "atheism" did not go wholly without reproof. Although for the Unitarian Festival, over which he had presided from time to time since 1857, he could describe orthodoxy as doing a strip act like a circus rider,[27] he was still occasionally receiving admonitions from orthodox correspondents. With many Biblical references, one earnest gentleman solemnly warned him to shun the horrible example of men like George Washington and John Adams. The doctor assured his correspondent that he owned a Bible and wished him a long life and final entrance into heaven, where "you will have the pleasure of meeting George Washington . . . and others you despair of." [28] Yet the correspondent's analogy was really acute, for Holmes's beliefs had come round to something like the deism of the eighteenth-century rationalists. Most of his correspondents, however, seemed to find his religious beliefs soothing, and Catholic readers were grateful for his understanding observations on their faith. The erstwhile heretic, blasphemer, and "moral parricide" now found himself an acceptable member of religious society; he was plainly much less dangerous than the skeptics and unbelievers springing up everywhere.

His good-natured wit was not reserved for dinner parties; as his generation became aging and ailing, the doctor took to calling unprofessionally on his friends. Old Dr. Jacob Bigelow, tied down by age and blindness, had at last got around to admitting his eighty-seven years. He used to try to disguise his age with an iron-gray wig, "the most admirably managed confession with extenuating circumstances that ever perruquier put together." [29] Dr. E. H. Clarke, Holmes's colleague and brother-in-law, was glad of the doctor's company. There were others in whose sickrooms Holmes was always a welcome guest. Motley, feeling the first signs of illness, wished himself home that he might talk with Holmes and hear him philosophize about it and "moralize it into a thousand similes. There would be some satisfaction in being shaky then. . . . " [30]

The peaceful complacency of Boston was somewhat shaken in 1874 by a local crime wave, by Coggia's comet (expected by some apprehensive souls to annihilate the world), and by the Beecher-Tilton case. "If it had been a settled fact that the comet was to hit the earth on the 22nd of July, late on the evening of the 21st people would have been talking of the great 'Beecher-Tilton scandal.' " [31] In 1869 Mrs. Stowe's article on Byron had caused considerable talk, but the charge of adultery brought against her popular brother Henry Ward Beecher was a sensation. It was the first of these excitements of 1874, however, that stimulated Holmes to a little writing. The psychologists of the seventies had turned their attention to criminals, and the humanitarians were discussing prison reform; the publications of the one group and the agitations of the other combined with the local situation to evoke from Holmes his essay "Crime and Automatism." The immediate stimulus was Prosper Despine's *Psychologie naturelle,* which had been sent him for review. Having met and talked with Frank Sanborn, Concord disciple of Emerson and prison reformer, Holmes consulted him for references on the subject. His essay is half a review of Despine and half a recapitulation of ideas expressed in *Mechanism in Thought and Morals*. Protesting the legal way of handling criminals, the doctor made observations on the law of a kind not likely to please his son; he called it "a coarse tool and not a mathematical instrument. . . . Of relative justice law may know something; of expediency it knows much; with absolute justice it does not concern itself." [32] But his remarks upon the opposition to psychological theories found an echo later in the writing of his son's contemporary, William James.

The essay offers nothing new for Holmes's thought, but it is curious to see him standing now squarely behind the humanitarian reformer. Sanborn as an abolitionist had had no support from Holmes; as a prison reformer, he had the doctor's help. Holmes showed no awareness of the social change that had gradually brought them together on the middle ground of a cautious liberalism, but he was aware of the altered focus of *thought*. It would be more accurate to say the altered focus of *conversation;* for just because Holmes's own thinking depended as much upon talk as upon books, his observations can be taken as an index of what everybody was talking about, that is, as an indication of when ideas, advanced much earlier, came to be common topics of social conversation. " . . . the issues of to-day really turn on points which within easy remembrance would hardly have been considered open to discussion except in proscribed circles." [33] The topics now were not the theories raised by theologians or the philosophy of Emerson. The points were those raised by statisticians, geologists, evolutionists, and—so far as Holmes was concerned —those investigators on the outer rim of the scientific coterie, the psychologists.

Holmes records the scientific temper of the times in another form. His verses "The Coming Era" suggest one characteristic of the late nineteenth century.

> Optics will claim the wandering eye of fancy,
>   Physics will grasp imagination's wings,
> Plain fact exorcise fiction's necromancy,
>   The workshop hammer where the minstrel sings.

No more with laughter at Thalia's frolics
  Our eyes shall twinkle till the tears run down,
But in her place the lecturer on hydraulics
  Spout forth his watery science to the town. . . .

The unearthed monad, long in buried rocks hid,
  Shall tell the secret whence our being came;
The chemist show us death is life's black oxide,
  Left when the breath no longer fans its flame.

Instead of cracked-brained poets in their attics
  Filling thin volumes with their flowery talk,
There shall be books of wholesome mathematics;
  The tutor with his blackboard and his chalk.

No longer bards with madrigal and sonnet
  Shall woo to moonlight walks the ribboned sex,
But side by side the beaver and the bonnet
  Stroll, calmly pondering on some problem's x.

The sober bliss of serious calculation
  Shall mock the trivial joys that fancy drew,
And, oh, the rapture of a solved equation,—
  One self-same answer on the lips of two!

So speak in solemn tones our youthful sages,
  Patient, severe, laborious, slow, exact,
As o'er creation's protoplasmic pages
  They browse and munch the thistle crops of fact. . . .[34]

About this same time John Fiske, preaching the gospel according to Herbert Spencer, was bringing down upon Harvard's head the old accusation in a new form. It was not heresy born of Unitarianism that was feared but atheism provoked by science. The sensitivity on this matter among the conservative graduates of Harvard was brought out unwittingly by Holmes in 1878. At the request of his old literary companion John O. Sargent, Holmes provided some verses for a meeting of the New York Harvard Club. It had pleased him in 1874 to see the original motto of the University—*Veritas*—inscribed on Memorial Hall, although since 1700, the college motto had been *Christo et Ecclesiae*. The theme of his poems is that the University "wants no narrower, no more exclusive motto than truth"; [35] and this he expresses in two sonnets. For all his repudiation of the puritan fathers, Holmes had at heart a flicker of admiration for them, which perhaps accounts for the fact that in the brace of sonnets the one on *Christo et Ecclesiae* has a trumpet note the other lacks.

He half-expected that some zealous outsider might object to a gesture that would support science against religion; to his surprise the protest came from within, and created a flurry of discussion about the college seal. The matter of the seal was a small affair and so Holmes thought it, caring only that it be understood that the spirit of the college was with *Veritas*, "which includes the other and everything else worth having." [36] A few years later Holmes would show himself upholding his own stand here and showing more courage in the face of public opinion than his younger colleagues.

Meanwhile Holmes was advancing toward his seventieth year, showing few signs of age and remaining mentally alert. His young voice, his lively manner, and erect carriage offset signs he himself saw. The successive deaths of his closest friends were reminders enough. His Andover schoolmate, Phinehas Barnes, whom he had seen rarely in the intervening years but with whom he had maintained a tenuous association, became seriously ill in 1870. Holmes tried to get the best medical aid for him Boston could offer, but his death in 1871 was the first in a long series.[37] In the seventies Holmes became almost a professional writer of elegies and memorials for his friends, his classmates, his literary associates, and his professional colleagues.

The death of Agassiz in 1874 meant for the older members of the Saturday Club a noticeable change; Longfellow did not like to come unless he could be sure of Emerson and Holmes, for he felt otherwise too much alone. Emerson's memory was already "hiding itself"; [38] he came less and less frequently.

For Holmes the greatest personal losses were the deaths of sister Ann, his son-in-law Turner Sargent, and John Lothrop

Motley. Motley's wife, that Mary Benjamin who so long ago had brightened Holmes's tedious ride to New York on his first trip to Europe, had died in 1874; the historian had shortly after come home to spend the summer in Nahant, and there he and the doctor had deepened an intimacy maintained before only in correspondence. In 1877 Motley died in England. It was in the order of things that Holmes should write a memorial biography of his friend and also that that biography should be personal and defensive. Holmes's wish is naturally to ensure his friend's good name, and he therefore unbalances his book by spending a great deal of time on the stories of Motley's recall from his two ambassadorial posts. As one of countless such memorial biographies produced for the then somewhat stuffy Massachusetts Historical Society, it is not distinguished save for its partisan warmth.

Like other Bostonians, Holmes saw in the deaths of Motley and Sumner reminders of the honorable political history of the past in contrast to the corruption and general villainy manifested in the Grant administration. The disorderly Tilden-Hayes campaign provoked from Holmes the lines of "How not to Settle It," in which he imagined the whole matter submitted to the arbitration of the class of '29, who promptly fight it out after the manner of the Gingham Dog and Calico Cat until nothing is left but fragments of coat tails, heaps of spectacles, a deaf man's trumpet, unpaid tax bills:

> And, saved from harm by some protecting charm,
> A printed page with Smith's immortal verses.[39]

In 1878, he was writing to Lowell—playing gossip for him as he had for Motley: "I don't want to write about politics; the subject is utterly odious. The ignoble aspect of the great republic (as it looks to me) at the present moment is enough to sicken any people of self-government—if there were anything better to be had. A real theocracy is the only government to be trusted, but I'm afraid that in the only one history tells about the priests had more concern in managing affairs than the Lord did."

In the same letter, the doctor exposed another familiar side of his nature; he remarked that Lowell's was the first letter from Spain he had ever had that did not mention a bullfight. "I wonder if you have been to one. I wonder if you have been to more than one. I wonder if Emerson would go to one. As for myself I confess to 'panem et circenses' from early boyhood. Gingerbread and a fight I could never resist in my early years. But I have grown more humane in the process of senile deliquescence and could not look on things now which used to give me those wicked heart-beats that made sin so attractive." [40]

He was still going to circuses, however; P. T. Barnum sent him complimentary tickets every year, and the tattooed man bore an endorsement to his authenticity by Dr. Oliver Wendell Holmes. The endorsement, Barnum assured him, was not in letters ten feet high, as Holmes had reason to expect.[41] There is very little difference between Barnum's posters and his private letters; he expected to come down upon Boston "like an avalanche. . . . My horses beat the world and I want you to share in the enjoyment they give to all lovers of that noble animal." [42]

It was difficult for Holmes to realize that he was already in his seventieth year. Putting the fact in writing, he felt "as if he were talking about somebody else, or reading in the obituary column of a newspaper, or scraping the moss from an old gravestone and spelling it out." [43] A year later on the actual birthday, he thought with a kind of "cheerful despair" that he would like to see Europe again, but he didn't expect to, except as a ghost. "I hope Heaven itself gives leave of absence now and then to spirits that have a weakness for their native planet." [44]

He would have fifteen more years to enjoy his native planet; he would go to Europe; he would write three more books; and he would live to see himself quite literally the "last leaf." So long as any of his literary contemporaries survived, Holmes could escape that fate to which American journalism now condemned the "great" of the land. He was not yet that freak of American publicity—a breathing monument. But with this birthday, the process of embalming him began. Harvard's Phi Beta Kappa made him president; the University gave him an LL.D. The New York Century Club enticed him out of Boston, and Mrs. Astor took care of him like a baby, personally tending to the business of waking him up in the morning.[45] The big affair, however, was the *Atlantic Monthly's* birthday breakfast given in December. Longfellow was ill, and Lowell was in Europe, but everyone else turned up—even the shy Whittier, bringing a poem, and Emerson, in spite of his hiding memory. Mark Twain, mindful of his sins at a similar birthday party for Whittier, spoke not without humor, but with respect. The women, Annie Fields, Julia Ward Howe, Julia Dorr, produced verses of more ingenuity than merit; and the men, half a dozen of them, recalled his kindness to youthful poets.

The guests were nearly all literary men, and it remained for President Eliot to testify to the doctor's professional life.[46] The *Boston Medical and Surgical Journal* noted Eliot's speech with approval, glad to claim professional honors and feeling obviously that doctors should have been better represented at the celebration. For Holmes, in the seventies, still made a professional showing outside his classroom.

He had been one of the six men who met on December 21, 1874, in Dr. Henry I. Bowditch's office to discuss the establishment of a Medical Library. The moving spirit was Dr. James E. Chadwick, who kept his somewhat aged friends awake nights discussing the problem. Four years later, they had a building and books. As President of the new Boston Medical Library Association, Holmes gave the dedicatory address and reaffirmed his faith in free discussion by declaring that the library should include not simply those works *approved* by the medical association, but those by authors whose theories or subjects might seem to conservative physicians to be beyond the pale; neither the old nor the eccentric and fantastic should be excluded, and he got in a plea for materials on anthropology and psychology although these subjects

331

might seem outside the domain of the practicing physician. Holmes felt that an enlightened and well-educated body of medical men is the best defense against ignorance and prejudice and that a good all-inclusive library is a tool for that defense.[47]

In 1876 he had appeared before a gathering of citizens meeting in Fanueil Hall to organize a movement for public parks. While most of the speakers offered aesthetic reasons for the desirability of such projects, or argued about finances or cited rival cities, Dr. Holmes confined himself to considerations of health—the health of children, particularly those children deprived of fresh air and sunlight. His short, concrete, single-minded argument is a sharp contrast to the windy harangues the other speakers offered.[48]

A similar wise simplicity shows in his address before the Boston Microscopical Society in 1877. He gives a brief and entertaining account of his own experiences, beginning with the magnifying glass his father brought from Salem. The two best American lens makers, Spencer and Tolles, whom Holmes had known from their earliest days, had paid him their respects a few days before in recognition of the doctor's interest in their instruments.[49] Characteristically, Holmes is extremely modest about his real accomplishment here; he was, after all, among the very first to introduce the microscope into a medical curriculum.

Although the practice of opening the medical school with an introductory lecture had been abandoned, Holmes seems to have given private introductory lectures for his anatomy classes. The lecture for 1879 survives in manuscript and suggests that seventy years had not noticeably dulled the doctor's wits. The question of admitting women had come up again; Holmes's observation explains in part his reluctance to agitate for what he would not deny to women.

I myself, all things considered, very much prefer a male practitioner, but a woman's eye, a woman's instinct, and a woman's divining power are special gifts which ought to be made useful. If there were only a well-organized and well trained hermaphrodite physician I am not sure I would not send for him—her . . . as likely to combine more excellences than any unisexual individual. . . . Mainly, however, I think the ovarian sex finds its most congenial employment in the office of nurse; and I would give more for a good nurse to take care of me while I was alive than for the best pathologist that ever lived to cut me up after I was dead.[50]

Into his lecture he brings a new argument for his old theme—the importance of clinical teaching; he says that it is at the bedside that the doctor learns psychology and acquires an ability to recognize "neuroses."

Of the importance of his own subject he says that the surgeon must have anatomy at his fingers' ends "or he is likely to be at his wits' ends before he thinks of it." [51] The subject is even more important for the general practitioner who works in the dark; "the language of visceral disease is a kind of ventriloquy. We hardly know where the words come from." [52]

But for all he loved his subject and enjoyed the lectures, he was feeling monotony in the seven months' round. Possibly, too, the woman question, as it turned into a political problem, helped him to make up his mind to retire. The medical faculty, led by the die-hard Bigelow, had been embroiled in an argument with the administration for over a year. The original question—the admission of women—had been lost sight of in the new question of the right of the overseers to legislate for the medical faculty. Holmes's recorded votes are plain enough. He was *for* the admission of women and feels strongly enough to insist, along with Henry Pickering Bowditch, that the minority opinion be noted in the record. In the last stage of the debate, the question became a rider to proposals governing the relations between the faculty and the overseers. Holmes evaded an argument by voting "yes" to the whole and asking that his qualifying remarks be entered in the record.[53]

Meanwhile his publishers and Howells were making tantalizing offers. The combination of this pressure, his sense of the tedium of lecturing, and, possibly, a feeling that the medical faculty should be left entirely to the younger men, prompted him to submit his resignation in 1882. Prevailed upon at least to start out the new term, he did so, making his last appearance on November 28.

Having learned, by hints from friends, that the day was to be an occasion, he hastily prepared a personal farewell address. He had not expected, however, a great bouquet, a silver loving cup, and a tremendous ovation. For once in his life Dr. Holmes found himself too overcome for words; he had to wait until the next day to write a letter expressing his thanks. A biographer who knew him wrote: "If later classes might have teachers equally efficient, no one else was ever to inspire such personal affection as had been felt for Dr. Holmes." [54]

Man of Letters

I wrote in my usual way, dilatorily and hastily.

THE PUBLIC NOTICES of Holmes's retirement had announced that he would now write exclusively for the *Atlantic*. As each of his three predecessors had done, the new editor, Thomas Bailey Aldrich, who had taken the magazine over from Howells in 1881, was begging Holmes for contributions, calling him his "best foot." [1] But Holmes was too busy—as busy as if he had not retired—to do more than supply Aldrich with a few poems and two agreeable prose pieces.

His immediate literary occupation was the editing of his earlier books for reissue, a task begun in 1882. His publishers were taking a practical advantage of the publicity which, since his seventieth birthday, had been showered upon Boston's most accessible celebrity. There was a new market for Holmes. The "Gilded Age," which on one side showed ruthless greed, political corruption, and lively vulgarity, showed on another a fondness for middle-class domesticity and a sentimental morality which the works of Whittier and Holmes, among the living, and Longfellow, among the dead, could satisfy. The publication of "Household" and "Cabinet" editions of the poets' works and the popularity of magazine articles of the author-at-home type are tokens of that domesticity.

The reprinting of Holmes's medical essays was neatly timed to fit in with his reception in New York in April. Besides an affair at the Century Club, there were a dinner at the Astor's, a reception given by the gynecologist Fordyce Barker, and a party at the Lotos Club. The big event was the dinner at Delmonico's given by the medical profession. The whole made a seven-day social orgy in which Manhattanites demonstrated their acceptance of their rival's product, not without showing signs of envy and self-consciously resurrecting their own literary past. The living authors they might have claimed—Whitman and Melville—they ignored.

Souvenir telegram for dinner given to Dr. Holmes by medical profession of New York City. Left to right: Dr. Fordyce Barker, Dr. Holmes, and Gov. Ben Butler—1883.

In Delmonico's banquet-room, some two hundred New York physicians met to pay their respects to the most versatile member of their profession. It was a banquet typical of the period: nine courses, five wines, plush-covered menus, ices served in miniature paraffine skulls, music, potted palms, and—no women. The ladies, banished to the balcony, could watch, if they liked. The room was close and the speeches long, so that one non-medical guest was moved to remind the doctors that the affair was wholly contradictory to the principles of simple living they taught their patients. In the midst of jests, topical allusions, expressions of affection, and

336

compliments proper in after-dinner speeches, occurs one observation worth 'preserving. Whitelaw Reid, editor of the *New York Tribune,* was the speaker for the press. After commenting upon the three generations of Holmeses—the clergyman, the physician, and the jurist, Reid claims the doctor for the press, "For what is an Editor but a man whose business it is to say the word he has to say at the instant, to deal with every new occasion when it comes? Yet here is the Prince of all writers for an occasion—more journalistic in this than the journalist." Reid was hitting the mark.[2]

In his response to the toast to him Holmes shows himself less felicitous than usual, although perhaps his pointed way of reading made the poem sharper, less fuzzy than it seems in print. He is moved at first to apologize for his meter.

> Full well I know the strong heroic line
> Has lost its fashion since I made it mine

but after reflection, all his admiration for the form and those poets who had used it breaks out, and with it some of his scorn for the pretty poets of the day.

> Nor let the rhymester of the hour deride
> The straight-backed measure with its stately stride;
> It gave the mighty voice of Dryden scope;
> It sheathed the steel-bright epigrams of Pope;
> In Goldsmith's verse it learned a sweeter strain;
> Byron and Campbell wore its clanking chain;
> I smile to listen while the critic's scorn
> Flouts the proud purple kings have nobly worn;
> Bid each new rhymer try his dainty skill
> And mould his frozen phrases as he will;
> We thank the artist for his neat device;
> The shape is pleasing, though the stuff is ice.

A few characters appear in the poem: Landlord Porter who:

> Though to belles-lettres he pretended not,
> Lived close to Harvard, so knew what was what.

and Lowell, "lively, not churlish, somewhat free of speech." Dr. Jacob Bigelow is offered, admiringly, as the learned physician whose blind old age is not made empty by a barren mind.

Holmes's modesty compels him to reject praise as a physician, for he had been:

> For nature's servant far too often seen
> A loiterer by the wave of Hippocrene.[3]

The New York ovation did not bring his medical career to a close; one more appearance was scheduled for May. The inadequate facilities of the North Grove Street building had become so apparent by the time of the reform of the medical school that it was decided to put up an entirely new building. A committee, of which Holmes was a member and for which he wrote the official appeal, had worked to raise funds; and during the past year the new building on Boylston Street had gone up. Holmes was to make the dedicatory address. On the morning of the 11th as he sat meditating over his speech, his neighbor Robert C. Winthrop called. The two men went off to admire the building; before evening, it was gutted by fire.[4] There is no evidence to suggest that the fire was set, although Holmes apparently thought so because the blaze started in the new anatomical amphitheater.

At that moment, Governor Ben Butler, political soldier of fortune, was conducting his notorious investigation of the Tewkesbury Almshouse, making a great point of that institution's disposal of bodies to the Harvard Medical School. Doctors and medical students were among the witnesses; all the possibilities for horror were exploited by the unscrupulous Butler, who wore the convenient mask of the humanitarian. Although the disposal of bodies was of small importance compared to the treatment of the living, Butler knew how to play upon the fears and superstitions of the people and did so to such an extent that public attention was focused there instead of on other questions. Allusions to students' buying bodies wholesale and to Dr. Holmes's displaying a piece of tanned human skin to his classes were of a kind to create shudders. Butler played upon the latter detail particularly.[5]

So far as Dr. Holmes was concerned, he could not be personally harmed by references which were designed less to discomfort him than to stir general horror. The Harvard medical faculty, however, was disturbed enough to display a timidity at variance from the traditional boldness of their anatomists. When the new building was repaired and ready for the postponed dedication ceremonies on October 17, it was supposed to be open for public inspection; but one room was carefully locked—the dissecting room. The timid faculty met with a just reproof from the retired professor.

The opening of Holmes's speech was innocuous; he gave a brief history of the important medical discoveries of the century. For this part of his address, Holmes had asked the help of younger men. The surgeon John Collins Warren, namesake and grandson of Holmes's old teacher, son of his Paris friend, had got him up-to-date on surgery. Francis Minot, his former student, had enthusiastically answered his questions about internal medicine, and Henry Pickering Bowditch supplied him with information about physiology. The doctor's historical opening touched upon the most significant developments, acknowledging particularly the latest of them—the germ theory of disease.[6]

After this preamble, Holmes treated his audience to a few shocks. The woman-question, still an issue in the medical school, had recently become the subject of acrimonious debate in the Massachusetts Medical Society. The speaker knew very well the temper of his audience; he knew that most of them were violently opposed to medical education for women and that, of his own acquaintances, only Henry I. Bowditch was prepared to do battle on the side of the women. His unsuspecting audience heard him introduce the subject of nurses and note that their improved training was an important advance; they heard him make his customary allusions to the natural skill of women as nurses. "I have always felt that this was rather the vocation of women than general medical and especially surgical practice." The anti-woman faction applauded vigorously.

But, to their chagrin, the doctor went on:

Yet I myself followed a course of lectures given by the younger Madame Lachapelle in Paris, and if here and there an intrepid woman insists on

339

taking by storm the fortress of medical education, I would have the gate flung open to her as if it were that of the citadel of Orleans and she were Joan of Arc returning from the field of victory.[7]

His talk led him eventually to the new building. Holmes prepared his audience for what they would see: well-lighted, well-ventilated, and well-equipped lecture-rooms and laboratories, more space and equipment than might appear necessary. The doctor explained the necessity for space and equipment. Recalling the old, airless amphitheater in which he had lectured for thirty-three years to weary, word-stuffed, hungry students, he described the physiological experiment that demonstrates what happens to a creature shut up in an airless atmosphere. He continued:

So when the class I was lecturing to was sitting in an atmosphere once breathed already, after I have seen head after head gently declining, and one pair of eyes after another emptying themselves of intelligence, I have said inaudibly, with the considerate restraint of Musidora's rural love, Sleep on, dear youth; this does not mean that you are indolent, or that I am dull; it is the partial coma of commencing asphyxia.[8]

From airy lecture-rooms, he went to laboratories, and enthusiastically described what was new in teaching—the laboratory method—coming finally to his beloved microscopes. The listening audience, hearing the doctor get off on one of his hobbies, relaxed. He was near the end and he had not mentioned the unmentionable. Then unexpectedly the doctor was heard to say: "Among the various apartments destined to special uses, one will rivet your attention; namely, the Anthropotomic Laboratory, known to plainer speech as the Dissecting-room." [9]

And Holmes went on in language that filled his former colleagues with shame for their timidity. In taking up the subject, the doctor's years dropped from him; he spoke with the same fire, the same intense conviction, and the same boldness he had shown in 1843. He was not merely rhetorical; nor was he defensive and apologetic. The study of anatomy had always faced obstacles, and humanity had been the sufferer in consequence. "It is the duty and interest of all intelligent

340

members of the community to defend the anatomist and his place of labor . . . against such inflammatory representations as might be expected to lead to midday mobs or midnight incendiarism." He spoke candidly of the anatomist's work; he admitted that he had had twice in thirty-five years to administer rebukes to students, that no doubt many had shown levity, been unmindful of the proprieties, as young men were likely to be. But, he went on:

> Some of us have encountered Congressional committees attending the remains of distinguished functionaries to their distant place of burial. They generally bore up well under their bereavement. One might have expected . . . to meet the grief-stricken members of the party smileless and sobbing as they sadly paced the corridors of Parker's, before they set off in a mournful . . . procession. It was not so. Candor would have to confess that it was far otherwise . . . Humanity would try to excuse what she could not help witnessing; and, it may be, hoped that a tear would fall from the blind eye of Oblivion, and blot out their hotel bills forever.

Thus giving unscrupulous politicians a scornful dismissal, Holmes went on to give a clear example of the relation between anatomical studies and actual practice. He told the audience of Henry Jacob Bigelow's study of the hip joint which led to his discovery of a means to reduce the extremely painful dislocation of the thigh, and of the experiments which led to a new operation for calculus: "I cannot stop to moan over a scrap of human integument . . . when I remember that for every lifeless body which served for these experiments a hundred or a thousand fellow-creatures have been saved from unutterable anguish, and many of them from premature death." [10]

Some member of the chastened medical faculty got over to the new building to unlock the doors of the dissecting room before the audience was released to make its tour of inspection.

But the doctor was a just man. He had been bold here where younger men were timid, but at the close of his address, he described the new school as "a lasting record of the spirit and

341

confidence of the young men of the medical profession, who led their elders in the brave enterprise." [11]

Although his feeling here was forward-looking, the doctor's mood in this period was mainly reminiscent. The biographical notices of his friends had taken him back into the past. Facing his class for the last time, Dr. Holmes had gone back to his earliest days as a student, summoning up a procession of ghosts and animating them with effective phrases. "It is always the same story," he said, "that old men tell to younger ones." [12]

Something of the same feeling moved him as he still faithfully attended the Saturday Club. Writing Lowell in February, he remarked, "the company is more of ghosts than of flesh and blood for me." [13] The first of the early members to die had been Hawthorne; since then, Agassiz, Motley, Fields, and Peirce had followed; within the last year, Dana, Longfellow, and Emerson had gone. The poem "At the Saturday Club" crystallizes in his favorite form the notion he had expressed to Lowell.

> A month had flitted since The Club had met;
> The day came round; I found the table set, . . .
> I was a full half hour before the rest,
> Alone, the banquet-chamber's single guest.
> So from the table's side a chair I took,
> And having neither company nor book
> To keep me waking, by degrees there crept
> A torpor over me,—in short, I slept.
> Loosed from its chain, along the wreck-strewn track
> Of the dead years my soul goes travelling back;
> My ghosts take on their robes of flesh; it seems
> Dreaming is life; nay, life less life than dreams,
> So real are the shapes that meet my eyes.
> They bring no sense of wonder, nor surprise,
> No hint of other than an earth-born source;
> All seems plain daylight, everything of course. . . .
>
> Here sits our Poet, Laureate, if you will.
> Long has he worn the wreath, and wears it still. . . .

Full-featured, with the bloom that heaven denies
Her children, pinched by cold New England skies. . . .
Kind, soft-voiced, gentle, in his eye there shines
The ray serene that filled Evangeline's.
Modest he seems, not shy; content to wait
Amid the noisy clamor of debate
The looked-for moment when a peaceful word
Smooths the rough ripples louder tongues have stirred.
In every tone I mark his tender grace
And all his poems hinted in his face. . . .

There at the table's further end I see
In his old place our Poet's *vis-à-vis,*
The great Professor, strong, broad-shouldered, square,
In life's rich noontide, joyous, debonair. . . .
That lusty laugh the Puritan forgot,—
What ear has heard it and remembers not? . . .
How does vast Nature lead her living train
In ordered sequence through that spacious brain,
As in the primal hour when Adam named
The new-born tribes that young creation claimed! . . .

But who is he whose massive frame belies
The maiden shyness of his downcast eyes?
Who broods in silence till, by questions pressed,
Some answer struggles from his laboring breast?
An artist Nature meant to dwell apart,
Locked in his studio with a human heart,
Tracking its caverned passions to their lair,
And all its throbbing mysteries laying bare. . . .
So in his page, whatever shape it wear,
The Essex wizard's shadowed self is there,—
The great Romancer, hid beneath his veil
Like the stern preacher of his sombre tale;
Virile in strength, yet bashful as a girl,
Prouder than Hester, sensitive as Pearl.

From his mild throng of worshippers released,
Our Concord Delphi sends its chosen priest. . . .
Why that ethereal spirit's frame describe?
You know the race-marks of the Brahmin tribe,—
The spare, slight form, the sloping shoulders' droop,
The calm scholastic mien, the clerkly stoop,
The lines of thought the sharpened features wear,
Carved by the edge of keen New England air. . . .

> Where in the realm of thought, whose air is song,
> Does he, the Buddha of the West, belong?
> He seems a wingèd Franklin, sweetly wise,
> Born to unlock the secrets of the skies;
> And which the nobler calling,—if 'tis fair
> Terrestrial with celestial to compare,—
> To guide the storm-cloud's elemental flame,
> Or walk the chambers whence the lightning came,
> Amidst the sources of its subtile fire,
> And steal their effluence for his lips and lyre?
> If lost at times in vague aerial flights,
> None treads with firmer footsteps when he lights;
> A soaring nature, ballasted with sense,
> Wisdom without her wrinkles or pretence,
> In every Bible he has faith to read,
> And every altar helps to shape his creed.[14]

The last passage about Emerson is a decided contrast to those sharp thrusts made years ago. Holmes was clearly no convert to the transcendental faith, but he had a new perspective on its greatest figure.

About the time Holmes wrote the poem "At the Saturday Club," he had made up his mind to accept the invitation to write the life of Emerson for the American Men of Letters Series. No choice seemed stranger to those of Emerson's disciples and idolators who still lived; in their recollections Holmes was the satanic materialist who had directed no small part of his wit against the transcendentalists. Yet for the moment Holmes was probably the wisest choice; there was no one who could better play the mediator between Emerson and a scientific generation ready to repudiate him and all his works.

When he first heard that his old acquaintance was going to undertake a biography of Emerson, Henry I. Bowditch was provoked to laughter; he could not "conceive of two men more diametrically opposed in their natural traits." [15] But it was Emerson himself who had observed that Holmes was "really catholic, more catholic even than Lowell." [16] Holmes very nearly justified Emerson's faith. Although he necessarily produced a book useless for the modern student of Emerson, he was able to approach his subject in a way appropriate for the moment, yielding neither to the idolators nor to those who complained that Emerson was overrated and needed to be taken down.

As might be expected, Holmes went at the Emerson book in his own purely personal way. Not unaware of his own limitations, he felt about Emerson as Goethe felt about Spinoza, and he quoted the German poet to describe the feeling. "I cannot say that at any time the complete architecture of his intellectual system has stood clear in view before me. But when I look into him I seem to understand him,—that is, he always appears to me consistent with himself, and I can always gather from him very salutary influences for my own way of feeling and acting." [17] On the plane of metaphysical speculation Holmes could not meet Emerson, for no philosophical reflection not related to science could evoke in him belief, and reflections upon the workings of the human mind had led Holmes to psychology, not to idealism.

With Emerson's prose, Holmes betrays "embarrassment and uneasiness" [18] except where he finds echoes of his own thought on such subjects as reformers, conversation, poetry, politics, reading, borrowing, authoritarian creeds, England. The whole memoir is laced with quotations in which Holmes has seen his own image. But even on the subject of reformers, especially the abolitionists, Holmes's very personal bias does not end in distortion of his subject. Still haunted by recollections of 1855 and his New England Society address, Holmes seems to be thinking more of his own experience than of Emerson's when he says: "It must be remembered that Emerson had never been identified with the abolitionists. But an individual act of wrong sometimes gives a sharp point to a blunt dagger which has been kept in its sheath too long." [19] He goes on to quote Emerson's speeches on Sumner and Kansas. But he does not ignore the fact that Emerson's whole point of view before these events was different from his own. Attacked by reviewers for his comments on Emerson's relation to the abolition movement, Holmes found himself defended by—of all people —Henry I. Bowditch.[20]

The doctor bogs down completely before the essential tenets of the transcendental faith; and in his efforts to anchor Emerson to the planet he himself loves so well, Holmes is led to minimize what is fundamental in his subject. Nevertheless, his attitude is humble here; if his emphasis is wrong, he is right in his feeling that what was good in Emerson might be absurd and dangerous in his imitators.

Holmes could not play the role of disciple here, but he could break down a few barriers in the way of those who felt there was nothing at all to be found in Emerson. On the book's publication, Holmes received more than one letter like that of Charles Francis Adams who had never been able to read a word of Emerson, but now understood why his friends had been so much influenced by the man.[21] The letter of Adams's son, Henry, is revealing, too, of a younger generation's impatience with the Concord religion.

Will you forgive me for writing a few words to say with how much pleasure I have read your volume on Emerson? I fear that Emerson, with all his immortal longings and oneness with nature, would not have returned such a compliment in kind. He had neither the lightness of touch nor the breadth of sympathy that make your work so much superior to anything that we other men, who call ourselves younger, succeed in doing.

As a mere student I could have wished for one chapter more, to be reserved for the dissecting room alone. After studying the scope of any mind, I want as well to study its limitations. The limitations of Napoleon's, of Shakespeare's minds would tell me more than their extensions, so far as relative values are concerned. Emerson's limitations seemed to me very curious and interesting. At one time I had a list of five dicta of his, some of which belonged probably to the narrowed perceptions of his decline. I have forgotten some of them, but they began: No. 1, "There is no music in Shelley." No. 2, "There is no humor in Aristophanes." No. 3, "Photographs give more pleasure than paintings." (i.e., the photograph of a painting gave him more pleasure than the painting itself.) No. 4, "Egypt is uninteresting."

In obtaining extreme sublimation or tenuity of intelligence, I infer that sensuousness must be omitted. If Mr. Emerson was in some respects more than human, he paid for it by being in other respects proportionally less.

. . . If I were daring enough to hint it, I would go so far as to say that however much respect the public may feel for Judge Hoar, Mr. Freeman Clarke and Mr. Alcott, they feel a strong and decided preference for yourself, in the matter of literature; and would be willing to spare no small part of Chapter XV, if by doing so they would correspondingly enlarge Chapter XIV [On poetry].

This is an Art criticism which I ought not to venture; but we un-illumined, although pleased and proud to admire and study Mr. Emerson, must always indulge in a little lick or snort of protest in having Mr. Emerson's echoes make themselves heard. Human nature is but a reed shaken by a breeze. The Concord breeze shakes it sometimes like an east wind.[22]

Henry Adams's reference to the chapter on Emerson's poetry is characteristic of many comments on the book. Written first, before he began to weary of the labor of putting his materials together, and based on a long familiarity with the poems, the chapter is the best section of the book. The lofty impersonal quality of Emerson's prose left Holmes chilled and indifferent except where he could find wit like his own. The metaphysics provoked his scientific bias to criticism; but in the presence of Emerson's poetry, Holmes was free from science and its constant criticism, for his observations were controlled by a sense of a difference between science and poetry. In the poetry, there were no barriers to belief; and here, too, he felt himself in the presence of an approachable personality. Emerson the poet seemed more human to Holmes than Emerson the preacher of transcendentalism. Having grown to love Emerson's poetry, Holmes could override long-established prejudices, quirks of taste, and even sound instincts. The resulting enthusiastic appreciation is real and infectious.

Holmes's personal discovery of Emerson, like his discovery of the English romantics, came late; but the record of his life does not suggest that the discovery was either insincere or incomplete. At the moments when his contemporaries were discovering Wordsworth and Emerson, Holmes was dissecting cadavers, thumping tuberculous chests, reading physiology, and writing prescriptions. When his contemporaries moved from Byron and Scott to Shelley and Coleridge, Holmes moved to Corvisart, Louis, and Schwann. He looked at the *Dial,* but he studied the *Lancet.* Of the whole group, it was Holmes alone who followed the profession—who earned his living— in the field then most remote from literature. He was forty-four when the engagement to do the Lowell lectures led him into the English romantics, forty-eight when the founding of the *Atlantic* and the Saturday Club brought him into any close relationship with his American contemporaries, and over seventy when he undertook to study Emerson. The early immersion in science that enabled him to face with equanimity the tidal wave of discovery in the late nineteenth century had prevented his absorption of the literary influences of the earlier period. When he was exposed to these influences, it was too late for them to do more than make him more dissatisfied than ever with his own poetry; all its defects were painfully apparent to him. But he was still a poet, nevertheless, and able to appreciate what he could not do himself. It is easy to pull out of his chapter on Emerson's poetry passages which reveal the lingering traces of a taste formed early on eighteenth-century models; but what calls for emphasis is his moving well outside the limits of habit. Throughout the chapter, Holmes's delight and excitement in recognizing Emerson's poetry are much more evident than his prejudices, which, in fact, he deliberately pushes aside.

The chapter was based in part upon a lecture given for the Century Club in 1883; the introductory remarks to the lecture show that Holmes was aware of the barriers in the way of an appreciation of Emerson as a poet. Emerson's poetry appeared, after all, to be as eccentric as that of Walt Whitman. The irregularities and infelicities that had disturbed Holmes originally were equally distressing to a generation shaped by the melodies of Longfellow and Tennyson. In the late nineteenth century competent versifiers were not the rarity they had been in the earlier period. Facile poets were plentiful; the individual accents of an Emerson had an even odder sound in the ears of those who could find something smoother and easier in any newspaper, and who were brought up reading the conventional rhythms of Holmes, Whittier, and Longfellow.

When Holmes addressed the gathering of the members of New York's fashionable and semi-literary Century Club, he knew that nearly every member of his audience could turn out fairly decent verse. To prepare for Emerson, he went after his audience, calling them authors of poetry of "most respectable mediocrity. . . . He held up such performances to ridicule so mercilessly, so cleverly, so good naturedly, that those whose toes were the worst crushed led the applause." And he made it plain that he included himself in his strictures, "drawing a comparison which few in his place would have dared to draw between that poetry that touches the many and that which touches the few." [23]

For Holmes personally the book was a tiring job, for it demanded more of him than he quite had to give; yet "I got from it some of those 'vibrations' that Milton speaks of which were impulses, I hope, in the upward direction." [24] To Holmes's friends the book, when it appeared in December 1884, was a surprise; he had done more than they expected of him, shown more understanding than they had imagined possible: so much in fact that even those who disagreed or found more than he were moved to compliment him. Lowell wrote: "There are admirable things in the chapter about Emerson's poetry, many that made me slap my thigh with emphatic enjoyment. . . . I thank you for helping me to a conclusion (or a distinction) I was fumbling for. If Emerson showed no sensuous passion in his verse, at least there is spiritual passion enough and to spare —a paler flame, but quite as intense in its way." [25]

Holmes had said that the book tired him; his weariness was so obvious that one has to conclude that Lowell was being polite when he said he saw no signs of it. Holmes's brother John was wiser and gave the doctor a prescription: "Now do take a turn at novel-reading and have a blow-out on tea, if you won't go anything stronger." [26]

Tired or not, before the Emerson volume was off the press, Holmes had already started work on a third "medicated" novel, *A Mortal Antipathy;* Aldrich had his wish, and, at seventy-five, Holmes was striking out again, opening "The New Portfolio" with a liveliness of spirit which suggests that he was glad to be relieved of a biographer's responsibilities. He admitted it, in fact, describing himself as a horse out of harness, turned loose in the pasture where he wants to roll. He betrayed his age only in his choice of subject-matter for his introductory essay where he recalls the literary world of Boston in 1830—a world dominated by the figure of Nathaniel Parker Willis, who was "something between a remembrance of Count D'Orsay and an anticipation of Oscar Wilde." [27] His reminiscences take him to the founding of the *Atlantic,* to the experience of writing the memoirs of his friends, and to his meditations on Dr. Johnson. "Year by year, and almost month by month, my life has kept pace in this century with his life in the last . . . it was for me a kind of unison between two instruments, both playing that old familiar air, 'Life,'—one a bassoon, if you will, and the other an oaten pipe." [28] But Johnson died in 1784. Holmes was still disgracefully alive and he suspected that he had no business to be so. His seventy-fifth birthday had brought a flood of letters and gifts, and a special number of the *Critic* given up entirely to letters from persons of fame. Holmes felt as if he were "embalmed like Pharaoh, and built over with a pyramid of famous names." [29]

He had lost another kind of landmark in the old Cambridge house, which, sold long since to the university, had now been torn down in spite of the efforts of sentimentalists to save it. Holmes considered it a case of "justifiable domicide" and allowed himself to recall the Cambridge of the early decades of the century when the place was a village. The college, which had for decades "sat still and lifeless as the colossi in the Egyptian desert," had been animated in the post-war era, and now its iron step was everywhere.[30]

Completely relaxed, the doctor enjoyed himself, disporting in "reminiscences and fancies, and vagaries and parentheses," [31] not only in the introduction but throughout the successive

350

numbers of the book. *A Mortal Antipathy* is a "story" only by courtesy.

None of the characters is in the least credible, except the familiar village doctor; they and the village in which they live have a fantastic quality. The village is an idealized Pittsfield-Cambridge showing signs of the infection of the Gilded Age only at the end. For the author's convenience the town has a literary society to which papers are contributed; the papers are the Autocrat's monologues on ocean, river, and lake; on interviewers, on the intellectual humility necessary in a doctor or scientist; on the novelist's exhausting his blood relations as character sources and resorting finally to his mother-in-law. Holmes had found a new outlet for his discursive mind, a "form"—if it can be called that—different from the breakfast-table device, but serving a similar purpose. All that keeps the narrative moving in a straight line is the mystery of the "hero," who, like Elsie and Myrtle, is a psychological case, the victim of a phobia. For the rest, the story wanders speculatively and suggestively around the woman-question.

Lurida, the high-strung feminine intellectual, is the Athena of his idealized village; Euthymia, the strong and beautiful woman, is its Aphrodite. Both girls are exaggerated to the point of absurdity, suggesting in their combined qualities a curious mixture of feminine and masculine traits. Holmes seems to be satirizing not only the advocate of woman's rights but also the opposition, implying that neither party is on the right track. Since the physiological arguments of the opponents of women's rights strike him as fallacious, he gives his thoroughly feminine Euthymia the physical strength and endurance of a man. Finding the intellectual arguments of the suffragette equally limited, he makes his feminist hysterical, dangerously misanthropic, and physically weak.

There is nothing conclusive here; Holmes is being comic and critical. He does, however, reveal the expected bias. He would not have his doctor in the story deny to the voracious mind of Lurida any form of knowledge she might seek, but he plainly regards her as a less normal specimen than Euthymia.

The first is a "Terror," the second a "Wonder." Since he could not be enough of a realist to leave Lurida to the fate he thinks most likely, he marries her off in the last chapter to a young minister lugged in for that purpose.

About his "case," Maurice Kirkland, he is also more suggestive than conclusive: Maurice's antipathy to women is attributed to a violent experience in his early childhood; his physical symptoms when in the presence of the object of his phobia are explained as a complicated chain of reflexes in the nervous system set in motion by the mind's response to the stimulus. Each time Maurice encounters a woman, he automatically re-experiences all the emotions of terror and physical sensations of shock evoked by the original experience. To his contemporary readers Maurice's case was so fantastic that it evoked all the laughter and incredulity Holmes struggled to anticipate; eleven years later, his official biographer's attitude was apologetic. Even Dr. S. Weir Mitchell, Philadelphia neurologist, thought Holmes "daringly medical," although he did not think Maurice's case incredible.

Again the "literary" critics have a point. It is the business of the novelist to make the unbelievable appear "true." Holmes's difficulty is that he selects for realistic treatment materials which his audience could have accepted only if they were treated unrealistically. That dilemma inherent in his choice of subject Holmes never solved; his failure is due not only to his impatience as a craftsman, but also to his tackling problems for which contemporary psychology offered no clues to means of literary treatment. He uses a dream, a written account of the "case" by its victim, a medical journal's paper on the case, and a subjective essay by Maurice, but his own realization that the dream and the essay may have a value as revealing a mental patient's unconscious mind is offset by the admission of ignorance and the superficiality of the two objective reports of the case.

Nor could Holmes get any help from the "realists" of his own day. The naturalism of "unwashed Zola" [32] offered him nothing; he had spent two years in the wards of the Paris hospitals, a year in the Broad Street dispensary. Such photographic realism seemed to him disgusting, pointless, and all too familiar. Privately he thought that it was "time for the decently immoral to interfere with the nauseating realism of Zola and the rest." [33] A Howells could accept Zola because he had started on the trail of socialism; but Holmes who thinks like a doctor, in terms of individual cases, cannot. When he does consider a collection of cases, he becomes "socially conscious" only to the extent of imagining public health projects. His attention is focused on the emotional-physical problems of individuals; other subjects are on the periphery of his consciousness. Van Wyck Brooks is partly justified in claiming that Holmes is paving the way for Freud, but he is off the track in more ways than one when he claims that Holmes paved the way for Marx.

A Mortal Antipathy reveals very plainly Holmes's position on the road that leads to Freud and the road leading from Marx. For the first, that "vicious, kicking brain" he complained of had taken him in so many directions at once that he can only suggest and hint. For the second, he was aware enough to know that there was something wrong somewhere; and he ventured to talk about it in the conclusion of his introductory essay. He had seen American society becoming more noticeably stratified; being what it was, its aristocracy would have to be founded, Holmes thought, on wealth. Holmes's ideal notion of the aristocrat seems to be not unlike that of those wide-eyed Americans in the novels of Henry James, the ideal that leads Isabel Archer to read lessons to Lord Warburton in *The Portrait of a Lady*. Holmes would have the moneyed dynasty emerging in this Gilded Age adopt the European adage *noblesse oblige* as *richesse oblige*.[34]

But this is all by-the-way; he would no more accept or offer a social panacea than he would a medical one; mistrusting "systems" in medical theory and in religion, Holmes would be likely to regard Marx as having much in common with Hahnemann and Calvin. A similar skepticism affects his attitude toward metaphysical speculation; his struggle with Emersonian

353

philosophy obviously accounts for references in *A Mortal
Antipathy* to the questions of space and time. Holmes makes it
plain that he looks to the physicist to provide an answer there.
When the scientist has given us much more knowledge of the
macrocosm and the psychologist has given us more of the
microcosm, then it will be time for metaphysics.

Such hints are a small part of *A Mortal Antipathy;* he was
on the whole doing what he had threatened to do—he was
rolling, being as extravagant as he liked, having obviously a
good time with his novelist's burlesque essay on the troubles
of finding characters, and with his interviewer. In the tale of
the Interviewer and the Literary Celebrity, Holmes made fun
of himself, laughing at the vanity which made him an easy
mark for a skillful reporter. The Interviewer is worsted, however, in his encounter with Holmes's hero. But Holmes implies: what's the use; having no scruples, the reporter will
make up some kind of story anyway. The whole book, in spite
of Holmes's seriousness about the psychological theme, is
light-hearted. The bug-a-boo of Calvinism is conspicuously
missing; its absence accounts in part for the genial freshness
that pervades the whole.

Feeling the loneliness of old age, weary from the ordeal of
writing the Emerson book, suffering a long siege of illness in
the spring of 1885, Holmes can still summon up, from some
inexhaustible source, liveliness and humor. He had still some
rhymes on tap; when he had written Higginson that his rhyming would be for "crowned heads only," he spoke the truth
figuratively. Holmes's private royalty was still well-served; the
scientist Benjamin A. Gould, the class of '29, James Russell
Lowell, his old schoolmate F. H. Hedge, and Harvard's Phi
Beta Kappa Society. One outsider was greeted on his fiftieth
birthday—Mark Twain.

The pressure of correspondence, the burdens of being a celebrity provoked from Holmes "A Cry from the Study." [35]
Unable to be unkind, the doctor apparently hoped to stop the
deluge by appeals to reason and feeling, by describing his
plight. His appeal brought no diminution in the number of

354

callers who besieged him in his pleasant library. He came to think that his kind-heartedness made him something of a hypocrite; it is noticeable that his frequent comments on his flattering but sometimes annoying admirers are touched with acid now and then. In print he dared to be less polite than he was in person. The visitors irritated other members of the family, especially the youngest. Being constantly asked if he too were going to be a poet evoked from the doctor's grandson an expression of independence the doctor respected. The boy declared that he wouldn't read *The Autocrat;* the Autocrat, an individualist himself, told the boy that he was right; he ought not to read it unless he really wanted to.[36]

In spite of the doctor's lamentations, the next batch of letters came from admirers who supposed that, of course, Holmes was not referring to them in his essay. From England came a steady flow of invitations. He had thought often that he would like to see Europe again; his letters to Lowell reflected his sense that his life, always provincial, had perceptibly narrowed. He listened with envy to his children's accounts of their trips abroad. Now in 1886, his family and friends begged him to accept the invitations to visit England. The Judge and his wife would take care of Mrs. Holmes; the doctor's widowed daughter could travel with her father.

Holmes knew that the homage being paid him from all sides was in large part the awed respect man pays to age. On his seventieth birthday, he had observed "everybody looked as pleased as possible to recognize the fact that I had at least reached the natural limit of human existence." [37] Having exceeded that limit by seven years, he was automatically entitled to veneration. It was a state of existence that had disadvantages, but Holmes was grateful for its privileges and quite prepared to accept them, short of being smothered to death by displays of respect and affection. The invitations from England were not the least pleasurable parts of that homage.

By March 21, Holmes had given in to the urgings of his family and friends and was writing Lowell to ask where he should stay in London. On April 29 at six-thirty in the morning, the doctor and his daughter, attended by a retinue of friends, were on the wharf in Boston, ready to board the *Cephalonia*. Judge Hoar provided him with a basket of champagne; others sent grapes and oranges, the latter as much of a luxury then as champagne is today, if not more so; but a half barrel of oysters gave the doctor his greatest pleasure. He did not like "the terrible solitude of the ocean"; the lifeboats evoked no sense of security but rather the reverse.[38] But although Holmes was a nervous ship's passenger, he was a good sailor, able to enjoy some oysters from his barrel at every meal. The going-away present that gave him the greatest pleasure, however, was a new gadget—a safety razor. He was so delighted that when he came to write an account of his trip for the *Atlantic,* he gave the manufacturers two pages of free advertising, and, in London, he showed the razor to the fashionable barbers in the Burlington Arcade, who were probably confirmed in any odd notions they may have had about Americans.[39]

In spite of some pleasures, the trip was for Holmes a very uncomfortable one. The asthma that always troubled him away from home kept him up all night, smoking medicated cigarettes in the vain hope of getting enough sleep; a few hours of relief were the most he could get. Mercifully, the *Cephalonia* took only a quarter of the time to make the crossing that the *Philadelphia* had needed over fifty years before.

Celebrity in England

1886

I was glad to go abroad, and perhaps, glad to come home.

TEN DAYS after its departure from Boston, the *Cephalonia* lay off Liverpool; a deputation of local physicians waited upon the distinguished visitor. They found Dr. Holmes with his small figure muffled in a thick overcoat and blanket, wrapped Indian-wise. Weary from sleepless nights and still shaken with an asthmatic cough, the doctor could be polite, but he begged to be excused from dinners and speeches.[1]

It is not hard to imagine what his feelings had been on May 8 when the ship had come in sight of the Irish coast and taken on mail delivered from Queenstown. The doctor had letters from London, Glasgow, and Edinburgh inviting him to parties or begging him for lectures. Friends who should have known better were all prepared to hire halls, set the old man up on a platform, and let him amuse them for an hour. He had come to England for a vacation, had come on the understanding that he would not lecture. From that resolution, neither his vanity nor good-nature shook him. The letters gave him only a slight inkling of what was in store for him in London; it was just as well that he stopped off for two days in Chester, where he and his daughter "had the blissful security of being unknown." [2]

As a youthful traveler in 1833 and 1834, Holmes had been bored by sight-seeing, moved by what was living in the places he visited rather than by memorials or reminders of antiquity; the railroad train, the Derby, the theaters—all excited him

357

more than ruins or cathedrals (except Salisbury) or historic places. He had not changed; now as then, the immediate present interested him more than the past. What belonged to the past excited him only as he compared his impressions of 1833-34 with those of 1886. The cathedral at Chester seemed to him "particularly mouldy, and in fact too high-flavored with antiquity." He liked the daisy-starred meadows of the countryside, but not the dark old houses of the town. The Duke of Westminster's Eaton Hall, "high-roofed, marble-columned, vast, magnificent . . . is disheartening and uninviting. . . . It is best, perhaps, that one avoid being a duke and living in a palace." The nobleman's stables were a different matter; Holmes got acquainted with the master of the stables, was taken on tour, had his questions answered, and was allowed to admire the famous Derby winner, Bend Or, sire of Ormonde, the Duke's entry for the Derby of 1886. To that classic, Holmes was determined to go.[3]

The next day Holmes and his daughter departed for London; someone had engaged a saloon car for him and filled the train with flowers. The well-groomed landscape and the glowing green of the hedges delighted him. The trees, however, were not respectable, not being big enough to suit the doctor's taste. "Most of those I see are of very moderate dimensions, feathered all the way up their long slender trunks, with a lop-sided mop of leaves at the top, like a wig which has slipped awry." [4] Such was his first impression.

In London, he found his rooms prepared comfortably, with a fire laid and flowers arranged, but the accommodations were not large enough. Amelia's maid Emily, "the most sagacious and untiring little mortal," [5] went out the next morning on a search for an establishment large enough for a party of four. Besides Mrs. Sargent, the doctor, and Emily, there was the pretty Adelaide Bush, the social secretary the doctor had to hire at once, for his arrival had "pulled the string of the social shower-bath" [6] in which he and his daughter came very near drowning. With satisfactory quarters at MacKellar's Hotel, not far from Bond Street and Piccadilly Circus, Holmes was comfortable. Friends were attentive and generous with broughams and victorias. If they had not been so generous with invitations, the doctor might not have been so weary.

Into the first month of the hundred days was crowded every variety of social entertainment the London season, then at its height, could offer. A constant round of breakfasts, luncheons, teas, receptions, and dinners persuaded the doctor that it was a life more suited to a ruminant with several stomachs than a human being with only one.[7] The parties varied from quiet literary dinners given by Lowell and others to great receptions like Lady Rosebery's affair. At Lowell's party Holmes felt himself in the atmosphere of the Saturday Club; he was glad to meet DuMaurier and Tenniel, whom he knew from their drawings, and Leslie Stephen, who was an old acquaintance. Holmes had a long talk with Laurence Oliphant in which the doctor's rationalism and Oliphant's spiritualism must have produced a conversation worth hearing. Other guests were Andrew Lang, Burne-Jones, and, naturally, Henry James.

The two thousand guests at Lady Rosebery's reception were altogether too much for the doctor. He came very near being crushed to death in the jam from which he was happily rescued by a helpful and—more important—tall countryman. Lady Rosebery asked them to stay until the crowd had thinned and have supper, but Amelia, who had dined at No. 10 Downing Street, and the doctor, who had been a guest at Sir William Harcourt's dinner for the officials of his department, were both worn out, and ordered their carriage: "*Ordered our carriage!*

> I can call spirits from the vasty deep. . . .
> But will they come when you do call for them?

The most formidable thing about a London party is getting away from it." It took three-quarters of an hour on this occasion.[8]

But grateful as the doctor was for the hospitality London showed him, the round of parties left only the dimmest impressions. He was an alert and lively guest, amused by Lady Harberton, advocate of the divided skirt; admiring Lady

Stanley, hardened London dowager of eighty; [9] much taken with the political dog who would accept a morsel if given him in Queen Victoria's name, but refuse it if Gladstone was mentioned. The dog he thought was the only passionate politician he met in London. The Englishman's attitude toward his hat fascinated Holmes. "It is a common thing for the Englishman to say his prayers into it, as he sits down in his pew. . . . His hat is as sacred to an Englishman as his beard to a Mussulman." [10]

The many people he met could not be recalled for comment other than to receive the doctor's genuine gratitude. Of the literary figures, Robert Browning had turned up at nearly all the many functions Holmes went to in London. The doctor thought he had "much of Ben Jonson about him." [11] Oscar Wilde, whom he had met in America, he met again at several parties. Edmund Gosse and Locker-Lampson both entertained him at small dinners where he met the ubiquitous Browning and Henry James, as well as less conspicuous men like Walter Pater and Austin Dobson. He had wanted to meet Ruskin, whose notions he had taken exception to in his life of Emerson and about whom Charles Eliot Norton was always talking, but Ruskin was too ill for callers.

He did not forget his profession. One of the first men he had looked for was his old Paris acquaintance Dr. Walter Hale Walshe. Walshe had dedicated a book to him; Holmes was grateful for the compliment, but he called upon Walshe as much to recall his youth as to express his thanks. Dr. Willson Fox gave his professional services free, and Dr. William Priestly and his wife gave Holmes and his daughter the use of their house that they might give a reception and entertain both friends who had been kind to them and professional men to whom Holmes wished to pay his respects. He was glad to meet Sir James Paget, especially, and Sir William Gull, who had been his friend Motley's physician. The doctors in their turn gave Holmes a party at the Royal College of Surgeons.

In this orgy of parties, not much of his time was his own, but he had meant to go to the Derby and go he did. He had made no secret of his excitement about horse-racing; all the papers noted that the American visitor was going to the Derby of 1886 to compare the winner with the famous Plenipotentiary who had won in 1834. But he was not a twenty-five-year-old wandering student; the problem was how to go in reasonable comfort. The machinations of Lord Rosebery and the American Ambassador, Edward John Phelps, made it possible for him to travel in state in the special train of the Prince of Wales. The doctor enjoyed himself thoroughly; it is rather difficult to tell from his account of the affair which he enjoyed the more, the agreeable company or the handsome horses. He thought both equally royal. He thought Prince Albert Edward very natural and cheerful, a person of "lively temperament." He enjoyed a pleasant conversation with Prince Christian, future King of Denmark, and admired the flock of princesses. It amused him to compare his state in 1834, down among the crowd, with that of 1886, up in the royal box.

The day was chilly and the wind piercing; always fearful of catching cold, he wrapped himself in his blanket shawl and told his royal English friends that it was "the more civilized form of the Indian's blanket." He thought of the verses

> Zephyr with Aurora playing
> As he met her once a-Maying,

and decided that "Zephyr ought to have come in an ulster, and offered Aurora a warm petticoat." Holmes shivered and talked while some members of the party went down to inspect the horses as they were shown in the paddock. There had been a preliminary race, but no one was much interested in that.

Finally the horses were brought out, "smooth, shining, fine-drawn, frisky, spirit-stirring to look upon,—most beautiful of all the bay horse Ormonde, who could hardly be restrained, such was his eagerness for action." Holmes's eyes were not so good as they used to be; he could not make out the start, but there was no doubt about the finish:

Two horses have emerged from the ruck, and are sweeping, rushing, storming, toward us, almost side by side. One slides by the other, half a

361

length, a length, a length and a half. Those are Archer's colors, and the beautiful bay Ormonde flashes by the line, winner of the Derby of 1886.[12]

There was some question now as to which was the greatest three-year-old of the century—Plenipotentiary of 1834 or Ormonde of 1886. Holmes ordered a picture of the present winner—a colored affair showing the favorite with the famous jockey Archer, five times winner of the Derby. His sporting gallery would then be complete, Ormonde added to Herring's picture of Plenipotentiary, and Stubbs's engraving of the great Eclipse, eighteenth-century favorite.

Lord Rosebery, whom he had met in America at his friend Winthrop's, had helped him to realize one desire; Lady Harcourt helped him to another. Lady Elizabeth Harcourt was a familiar friend, the daughter of John Lothrop Motley. Her husband, Sir William Harcourt, was Gladstone's party lieutenant and Chancellor of the Exchequer. On the Queen's birthday, he gave a state dinner to his department and invited Dr. Holmes. The doctor had some misgivings about the Chancellor of the Exchequer's dinner; not particularly concerned about conventions of thought, Holmes liked to observe conventions of dress and manner. His host assured him that plain American evening clothes would be all right although the other guests would be in full court dress, knee-breeches and dress uniforms. The doctor was not a shy man, but his vanity had never led him to suppose that he was a person of any great importance, and he looked upon people he regarded as personages with a mixture of intense curiosity and respect. Holmes found Sir William Harcourt glad to answer questions about the persons of note at his table; in fact Holmes thought he might have made a fortune if he had been a reporter. The guest about whom he was most curious was the Prime Minister. Gladstone's face was familiar from pictures, but the doctor could not get used to the sight of him dressed up with epaulets and a rapier. He would a few days later see the minister in action.

About all his coevals Holmes was curious; in England Prime Minister Gladstone and Poet Laureate Tennyson were like Holmes born in 1809. The more interesting of them, Gladstone, who had attempted to retire from public life in 1874, had come back into it almost at once and was now filling his office for the third time in his career. The political issue of the day was the Irish Home Rule Bill, and on the night of June 7, the minister came before Parliament to urge the passage of the bill.

By courtesy of Gladstone himself, Dr. Holmes had a card of admission, entitling him to a seat among "the distinguished guests," but there were so many of them that he was seated finally among the ambassadors. Even there he took up too much room and was ousted from his seat by the minister from Russia, but he speedily settled himself on the stairs. He heard the tail end of the speech of the opposition. When Sir Michael Hicks-Beach had finished and resumed his seat, "there was a hush of expectation, and presently Mr. Gladstone rose to his feet. A great burst of applause welcomed him, lasting more than a minute." But Holmes was no objective reporter and would not encroach upon the prerogatives of the journalists of the day. He left only a brief record of the occasion. His interest in the event did not arise from any reflections on the Irish question or curiosity about English politics. He was absorbed in watching a coeval, measuring perhaps his own vitality and accomplishments against those of the old man whose voice now came to him clearly—pretty clearly; Holmes was getting a little deaf. Gladstone was not in perfect condition either; the doctor observed that he poured something out of a little bottle now and then and drank it. Holmes thought him forcible rather than eloquent, but toward the end Gladstone became "animated and inspiriting, and his closing words were uttered with impressive solemnity: 'Think, I beseech you, think well, think wisely, think not for a moment, but for the years that are to come, before you reject this bill.'"

The doctor stayed for the voting although it was well after midnight. He was not too tired to enjoy the excitement. Presently the announcement was made that a majority of thirty had ruled against a second reading of the bill. "Then arose a tumult of applause from the conservatives and a wild confusion, in the midst of which an Irish member shouted, 'Three cheers for the Grand Old Man!' " Holmes does not say whether he joined in the cheers which were lustily given to the Prime Minister in his defeat; but one suspects that he would want to, if only as a salute to his own generation.

It was two o'clock in the morning when he started home alone on foot. He got lost and had to ask a passing stranger for help; his rescuer, an ex-M.P. escorted him back to 17 Dover Street, where he sought his "bed with a satisfying sense of having done a good day's work and having been well paid for it." [13] He had spent part of the day among the crowded dead in Westminster Abbey. Although he had looked with pride upon the bust of Longfellow, he had found the place oppressive on the whole; the living drama in the House of Commons had been more rewarding than the Abbey, where Macbeth's expression "dusty death" had taken on a new significance.

A few days later Dr. Holmes was on his way to visit another coeval. Departing from Waterloo Station in the midst of one of London's yellow fogs, he found himself before the day was over at Farringford on the Isle of Wight. Respect for the poet's desire for seclusion kept him from telling more of his visit to Tennyson than his wandering under the trees with him.

His quiet visit with Tennyson coincided with the end of the London season. It was not quite the end of the ordeal, for there were three more big events ahead, but there were no more elaborate parties of the kind which required six footmen to usher Dr. Holmes and his daughter into a cavernous palace. Holmes thought that the great houses of England were the legitimate end of the caves of the European troglodytes, as the temporary houses of nomadic Americans were the end of the Indian wigwam. On the whole, the wigwam seemed the more homelike of the two.

The three ordeals ahead were the honorary degrees to be bestowed by Cambridge, Edinburgh, and Oxford. The cheering undergraduates in each university bewildered the doctor. At Cambridge he resisted the shouts for a speech, at Edinburgh he made one, at Oxford he waited to see what John Bright would do. At Cambridge, the young men brought out the too familiar variation on the old song: "Holmes, sweet Holmes," they shouted; the doctor forgave them for the crime he had often committed, the one he had named "verbicide." At Oxford they asked if he came in the "One Hoss Shay."

For the rest, the latter part of June and July was mercifully peaceful as the doctor realized his desire to relax and enjoy his vacation. The English trees were more satisfying on a second look: those on Tennyson's grounds, the oaks on the lawns at Windsor Castle, and a great elm on the grounds of Magdalen College. The last was so large that the doctor insisted on having it measured; someone was sent for a string and under his directions the dimensions of the tree were taped. Holmes was almost as excited as he had been at the Derby; the race was between the Springfield elm in Massachusetts, which he had measured in 1837, and this Oxford tree. The English tree nosed out the American by almost a foot.

Windsor Castle, which Holmes visited early in the season, pleased the poet. Although he heard no nightingales and his eyes were no longer sharp enough to catch the lark rising from Salisbury Plain, his ears did catch the cuckoo's "wandering voice." It was too early in the spring for the double-note to be heard often enough to fit Shakespeare's image of "the skipping king."

> He was heard but as the cuckoo is in June,
> Heard but not regarded.

Holmes felt about the sound as Wordsworth did, quoting the poet:

> that cry
> Which made me look a thousand ways
> In bush, and tree, and sky.

No oak in Windsor Park equaled the one at Beverly, but an English hawthorne tree in full bloom, spreading its "snowy but far from chilling canopy" was a proper tree and not a bush as he had supposed it.[14]

It was for such associations with the poets and his own past

365

that he had come to England, as he explained to the strangers he met at parties. The Englishwoman's opening gambit was nearly always: "It is a long time since you have been in this country, I believe?" When he confessed to the interval's being fifty years and more, the counter-remark was invariably: "You find great changes . . . of course." The changes were not so great; as Holmes told them, the Tower was where he left it.[15]

The doctor and his daughter saved their explorations of London for a later time, and spent the last of June and most of July visiting other parts of England. At Stratford-on-Avon, Holmes found the memorials of Shakespeare altered. On this visit he meditated on the poet, not upon his countryman Irving, as he had in 1834. In Stratford, too, he met Lawson Tait, the English gynecologist, famous for his successful ovariotomies. Again Holmes's record is incomplete; he would not consider medical matters in professional detail proper for the *Atlantic Monthly*. He mentions only his admiration for Tait and, with proper patriotism, notes that it was an American surgeon in the backwoods of Kentucky who first performed the operation in the days before anesthesia—Ephraim McDowell, in 1809. Yet the author of *The Contagiousness of Puerperal Fever* must have had a good deal to say to the surgeon who was also known for his opposition to the hygienic practices of his contemporary Lister, for Holmes's recommendations for gynecologists anticipated those of Lister for surgeons. Surely he would have discussed asepsis with Lawson Tait.

His old essay was in the doctor's mind at any rate when he asked about the relative value of the living surgeon's work and the dead playwright's. It was just a question, he added hastily, warning his readers not to deluge him with letters asking him what he thinks.

From Stratford-on-Avon, he and his daughter went on to Great Malvern. When the doctor got to his room at the hotel and looked out of his window, he found himself staring into an apothecary's shop. His eyesight was not so bad that he did not recognize the bust in the window; the plaster face that looked up at him was that of the founder of homeopathy, Samuel Hahnemann. He asked for another room.

In Great Malvern Amelia and her father were "deliciously idle," walking and driving as they pleased. One expedition into the hills was a matter of course; they hired a four-wheeler and made the perilous ascent of the Beacon, an adventure that made Holmes think of Mark Twain and the Riffelberg. The gale at the top was too much for a man his passport described as being seventy-six years old and only five feet, four inches tall.[16] Amelia noted in her diary that her father "nearly blew off from the top of the mountain." [17]

His pilgrimage was leading him back to Salisbury Cathedral, his first love of 1834, but they stopped first at Bath where the window-shopping doctor found amusement. At Salisbury, his traveling host had taken a whole house inside the cathedral close; for a week Holmes lived under the shadow of the great spire.

From these comfortable quarters, he made sentimental journeys into the surrounding countryside to all the places he and Bob Hooper had gone. The doctor's mood was not one of self-pity and sighings for his lost youth. The amateur psychologist was making a study of memory; he liked to check his memory against the actuality, to compare what had struck him then with what attracted him now. At Longford Castle on his first visit, a Claude Lorraine landscape had pleased him; now it was Holbein's portrait of Erasmus. At Wilton House, seat of the Earl of Pembroke, thoughts of Sir Philip Sidney, who had written his *Arcadia* there, were natural to both the young man and the old one, but only the second would visit Bemerton where George Herbert had lived and preached. Holmes's thoughts had always three focal points: his own feelings, the personality belonging to the place he was visiting, and some remembered friend from home. At Bemerton, Holmes kept company with Herbert and Emerson; if he had believed in metempsychosis, he would have thought the English poet of the seventeenth century had reappeared in the American one of the nineteenth.

In this region, he had to visit Stonehenge again. No line of thought could bring the unchanged broken ring of stones into a real relation with anything in Holmes's imagination. "Nothing dwarfs an individual life like one of these massive, almost unchanging monuments of an antiquity which refuses to be measured." [18] It was a *tour de force* of a mind uncomfortable in the presence of these Sphinxlike stones that led him to use them as an image for a class poem.[19] He mitigated their effect too by working out the simple mechanics by which they might have been erected.

Holmes had come to Salisbury via Bath, the famous watering-place of the eighteenth century; he left it to go to the nineteenth-century resort Brighton. Here he simply rested for a week at the home of friends until, on July 29, he and his daughter thought themselves ready for London again. A mere week of sight-seeing in the city was not likely to leave many impressions; Holmes told his readers that he was showing them how not to do it. He did, however, make the pilgrimages he liked, going to Chelsea to try to conjure from his grave the man he wished that he had met—Thomas Carlyle, to Fleet Street and Bolt Court to look for Dr. Johnson, and to the Temple Church to see Goldsmith's grave. The images of Johnson and Goldsmith, Holmes could easily evoke, but Carlyle eluded him, although he went twice to Chelsea.

London had changed, of course, but Holmes was delighted to find Prout's still standing where he left it; he had bought brushes there in 1834 and had to buy them again in 1886. To a new shop he paid a visit restricted carefully to ten minutes; he was apparently afraid for his pocketbook. Something of a book collector, trying to confine himself to medical volumes although tempted by other treasures, Holmes wanted to call at the establishment of the famous book-seller Bernard Quaritch. His ten minutes were very satisfying, for while he was there his namesake, the Queen's librarian, Richard Holmes, came in.

His daughter, meanwhile, had been shopping in London and was easily persuaded to continue the process in Paris. On

August 5, they made the Folkestone-Boulogne crossing and were in Paris by six p.m. The doctor carried no letters of introduction and knew no one now in Paris; while his daughter shopped, he visited alone the familiar places—the rue Monsieur-le-Prince, St.-Étienne-du-Mont, the Panthéon. It was the Café Procope that drew him most; he found it renovated and labeled with an inscription telling the date of its founding, 1689. Here he spent five sous for a cup of coffee and indulged in sentimental recollections. "If there is a river of *mnēmē* as a counterpart of the river of *lēthē*, my cup of coffee must have got its water from that stream. . . ." [20]

As always, along with memories of the past went awareness of the present. Dr. Holmes had one call he wanted to make. He might have had a letter of introduction, but he went without it to the busy courtyard in rue Vauquelin. He sent in his card, and presently the man he wanted to see—Louis Pasteur— came to greet him. For Holmes, Pasteur was "one of the greatest experimenters that ever lived, one of the truest benefactors of his race." [21] Royalty was all very well in its way, good company at the races, but a scientific discoverer was someone to be treated with reverence.

After Paris, the hurried return to London and the last week there could not be recalled. Dr. Holmes had planned to stay longer in Europe, but a message had come that his wife was ill; father and daughter hurriedly changed their plans, said good-bye to some of their English friends, and departed for Liverpool. Remembering his welcome there on his arrival and his inability to respond to it, Holmes remained a day in Liverpool, giving a farewell reception and being banqueted by the Philomathean Society. On August 21, he went aboard the *Aurania*. The eight-day voyage to New York was no more comfortable than the outward-bound journey had been, but he took part in a ship's entertainment given for charity, reading some of his poems. On August 28, the ship crept through the fog toward the harbor.

On August 29, his seventy-seventh birthday, he arrived at New York. A birthday bouquet from his former demonstrator,

Dr. Beach, had been carefully preserved during the whole trip, and the ship provided an enormous cake in which years were marked off in a ring of raisins, which made him feel like Methuselah. After a night in the Fifth Avenue Hotel, Dr. Holmes and his daughter took the train for Boston to sleep at last in their own beds.

He found many birthday letters waiting for him, but of the few he saved, perhaps the one from his successor as Parkman Professor meant the most. Welcoming the doctor home, Thomas Dwight reminded him that the present generation of students had not heard him and he asked if the doctor would give a lecture or two for them.[22] Holmes could not complain that his one hundred days in Europe had brought exile as their aftermath.

Last Leaf

1886–1894

*There passed not a minute, I believe, between
health and death.*

He was no sooner home than he had to perform for
Harvard's two hundred and fiftieth anniversary in November.
Harvard had called upon her two poets, Lowell for an address
and Holmes for a poem; neither gave the satisfaction expected
of him. At the time both speakers were criticized, Lowell for
calling the university's educational policies in question and
Holmes for his fulsome praise of Harvard as the leader in
bringing the colleges out of the dark ages of an old-fashioned
theology. One insulted listener, the president of Princeton
University, Dr. James McCosh, mistaking Holmes's sharp allusion to Andover as further comment on Princeton, walked out
in indignation.[1] Most of the poem is too topical for the twentieth century; but in speculating on the future, the doctor takes
a sympathetic look at the underpaid teacher, the alleviation of
whose plight he thinks may be too long delayed:

> I see gray teachers,—on their work intent,
> Their lavished lives in endless labor spent,
> Had closed at last in age and penury wrecked,
> Martyrs, not burned, but frozen in neglect. . . .[2]

In spite of flashes of this kind, his long poem shows his weariness and suggests that the ordeal of his trip, exciting as he had
found it, and the sadness of his wife's illness were having their
effects. The geniality and liveliness, for which he was so well
known, depended a great deal on outward circumstances,
which were now not particularly happy. He was glad that the

cloud that had fallen on his wife's mind did not cause suffering or change her gentleness, but her constant care and com-
panionship had always meant a great deal to him.[3] The long
and turgid poem has more melancholy than life in it; he was
led on by an endless chain of rhymes rather than by any energy
he could bring to the moment.

Moreover, Holmes would not have thought it fitting to
show on this occasion the "happy audacity" [4] of 1836, when,
for Harvard's two hundredth anniversary, he had climbed on
a table and sung some funny verses; now the "monumental
pomp of old age" required him to be dignified. The college,
too, although it had abandoned the traditional Latin, had put
on pomp; its commencements and celebrations were sedate,
formal, and non-alcoholic—in public at any rate. Street-fights,
side shows, picnics in the cemetery, and military parades had
given a carnival spirit to the literary festivals of the early part
of the century. "Nowadays our celebrations smack of the Sun-
day-school more than the dancing-hall. The aroma of the
punch-bowl has given way to the milder flavor of lemonade
and the cooling virtues of ice-cream. . . . Let us be thankful
that the vicious picturesque is only a remembrance, and the
virtuous commonplace a reality of today." [5] But Holmes liked
the picturesque; and his pious prayer was probably half-ironic.
He might have observed, too, that the perfunctory addresses of
the present were very different from the six hours of learning
undergraduates had displayed in the old ceremonies. In 1886,
both the idealistic Lowell and the convivial Holmes were
anachronisms.

They were both in demand, however, for a new kind of
entertainment, invented for the purpose of raising money for
charities but seeming to one of its victims to be a new form of
torture. Dr. Holmes took more willingly than Lowell to the
business of giving author's readings. Giving readings, providing one or two occasional poems, and writing up his account
of the one hundred days in Europe kept Holmes busy so that
he had little time for his correspondence.

Nor had he eyes for it; a few years earlier he had been

obliged to abandon all work with the microscope. Now he began to employ a secretary. Many correspondents had to be content with a regretful, printed notice explaining his condition. Writing an English friend, the doctor, in spite of his infirmities, was gallant and gay, succumbing to his favorite vice. "My eyes are getting dreadfully dim, and I should hardly know your beautiful face across the street. One of them has, I fear, though I don't quite know—a cataract in the kitten state of development." [6] He was very nearly a candidate for his own asylum for aged and decayed punsters.

He had just begun to recover his health and spirits enough to begin a new series of papers in the *Atlantic,* one number of *Over the Teacups* reaching the printer early in 1887, when in the space of a few months, he lost his wife and his closest friend, James Freeman Clarke. The new series of papers was abandoned.

The death of Clarke led the doctor to write his last poem for his classmates. Only six of them could gather for the regular meeting in January 1889, stoically refusing to be melancholy; it was the next to the last regular meeting they would hold. If Holmes with his poems had made the class known as a group and the faithful May had preserved in detail its records, it was apparently Clarke's spirit that held together men who, so long ago as undergraduates, had been split into many factions.

In the meanwhile, his widowed daughter, Amelia Sargent, came to live with him, rejuvenating his household and encouraging him to start "a new life—a fragment of life." [7] With his daughter's coming, his mind recovered its tone, and he was able to perform his old function as occasional poet and speaker with some of his old felicity.

On January 29, he presented his medical library of nearly a thousand volumes to the Boston Medical Library Association. All his old enthusiasms were re-expressed. He was giving away his handsome anatomical volumes, but not without words of appreciation. He could not help commenting particularly upon the plates in his Spigelius, upon the "grace and beauty of the females who display their viscera as if they were their jewels and laces." Of the unorthodox books in his library, he said:

> The débris of broken systems and exploded dogmas form a great mound—a *Monte Testaccio* of the shards and remnants of old vessels which once held human beliefs. If you take the trouble to climb to the top of it, you will find your horizon; and in these days of specialized knowledge, your horizon is not likely to be very wide.

He kept out a few favorites which he could not give up immediately, among them the Hippocrates, edited by Rabelais, which he had bought long ago in Lyons.[8]

The same spirit had informed his verses for the dedication of the new City Library in November 1888. As an occasional piece, the Public Library poem is one of his best. Unerringly, Holmes achieved just the right blend of the three sentiments appropriate for the moment—civic pride, democratic fervor, and a love of learning. Simple and clear, the lines of the poem are sharply turned with none of the verbosity that makes his Harvard poem of 1886 hard going. The Public Library poem shows the quality Emerson had noted in his journal:

> Wendell Holmes hits right . . . by his instinct at obeying a just perception of what *is* important, instead of feeling about how he shall get some verses together on the subject.[9]

For a very different kind of occasion on February 22, 1889, Holmes again hit the right note. The occasion was a birthday party for Lowell, given at the Tavern Club. Lowell was seventy; Holmes was within sight of his eightieth birthday, but so felicitous were his lines for the "younger" poet, that Charles Eliot Norton, begging the manuscript for the club records, addressed the doctor as "My dear young friend." [10]

The poem pays its warm but unsentimental compliments to its subject as critic, poet, and politician. To make his point that Lowell is the best type of each, the doctor exposes the worst. For these satiric passages, the heroic form is right; and Holmes handles his couplets with all the old dexterity, blasting the false critic with indignant lines, mocking the fashionable poets, and scorning the corrupt politician. It must be admitted that the poem is best on its negative side. Agreeing

or not with his thrust at Whitman, a reader has to credit him
with good lines:

> Or is it he whose random venture throws
> His lawless whimseys into moonstruck prose,
> Where they who worship the barbarian's creed
> Will find a rhythmic cadence as they read.

No one can disagree, however, with his attack on the corrupt
politician.

> He who deftly bends
> To every shift that serves his private ends,
> His face all smiling while his conscience squirms,
> His back as limber as a canker worm's;
> Who sees his country floundering through a drift,
> Nor stirs a hand the laboring wheel to lift,
> But trusts to Nature's leisure-loving law,
> And waits with patience for the snow to thaw.[11]

Lowell, however, could not have been exactly pleased when
Holmes in excess of affection looked forward to his subject's
eightieth year and drew an analogy between him and Gladstone, for Lowell's opinion of Gladstone is neatly expressed in
his epigram:

> His greatness not so much in genius lies
> As in adroitness, when occasions rise,
> Lifelong convictions to extemporize.[12]

If Holmes did not see Gladstone as his friend did, he appreciated the fact that Lowell's convictions were real and not
assumed. With Lowell's political work in mind, Holmes wrote
that he was one:

> Who touches lightly with Ithuriel spear
> The toad close squatting at the people's ear,
> And bids the laughing, scornful world descry
> The masking demon, the incarnate lie.[13]

The short winter of rejuvenation that had brought forth
these lines came speedily to an end. Early in the spring, Amelia
Sargent, seriously ill, recovered for a short interval; but the
doctor hardly dared to be encouraged.[14] A few weeks later

came the inevitable relapse, and on April 4, his daughter died. The doctor had lost his younger son in 1884; the elder, now Justice of the Supreme Judicial Court of Massachusetts, and his wife came to live with him. "Mrs. Judge" or the "embroideress," as Holmes called Fanny Dixwell, ran his house smoothly and made him comfortable. "A helpful, hopeful, powerful as well as brilliant woman," [15] she had the doctor's gratitude and admiration.

He was now eighty years old; on his birthday he wrote to Whittier, his senior by two years: "Here I am at your side among the octogenarians. At seventy we are objects of veneration, at eighty of curiosity, at ninety of wonder; and if we reach a hundred we are candidates for a sideshow attached to Barnum's great exhibition." [16] A few years later, he wrote to the same correspondent: "I have just been looking over the headstones in Mr. Griswold's cemetery entitled 'The Poets and Poetry of America.' " [17]

Holmes was not yet ready for a headstone; he had found one more book in the pasture beyond the eight-barred gate. The series he had abandoned at the time of his wife's death, he returned to in the fall of 1889. For each successive editor of the *Atlantic Monthly*, Holmes had produced a series; the new editor, Horace E. Scudder, was not to be disappointed. Although *Over the Teacups* is in part a study of old age—the doctor was still subjecting himself to psychological scrutiny—there is no sign that he had retreated wholly into those daydreams of the past which, as he said, are often more real to an old man than the immediate present.

He expected to repeat himself:

The area of consciousness is covered by layers of habitual thoughts, as a sea-beach is covered with wave-worn, rounded pebbles, shaped, smoothed, and polished by long attrition against each other. . . . When we think we are thinking, we are for the most part only listening to the sound of attrition between these inert elements of our intelligence. They shift their places a little, they change their relations to each other, they roll over and turn up new surfaces. Now and then a new fragment is cast among them, to be worn and rounded and take its place with the others, but the pebbled floor of the consciousness is almost as stationary as the pavement of a city thoroughfare.[18]

The old pebbles are there—homeopathy in the form of the "Hahnemaniac . . . [who] had cultivated symptoms as other people cultivate roses";[19] unconscious plagiarism, pathological piety; the dangers of over-specialization, amusingly demonstrated and expanded with a not unjust criticism of modern medical terminology. In this last he was objecting to the multiplication of names for variants of diseases essentially similar, as well as to the substitution of "fancy" names for plain terms already accepted. Emerson had noted in Holmes "a sharp taste for a fact instead of a blur of a word," [20] apparently referring to Holmes's dislike of words fuzzily used without regard for the realities they were supposed to symbolize. As Hayakawa has observed, Dr. Holmes anticipated the modern student of semantics in many of his observations.

Already in 1890, although he did not profess to be keeping up his old professional interests, Holmes was delighted to find his former student, William James, carrying out studies he had thought necessary. The doctor's notions about "I-My-Self & Co." had passed out of the hands of the speculative poet into those of the scientific investigator. But he had a new speculation to offer. It was actually an old one, one he had noted from time to time but never pulled out of his manuscript into print, apparently fearing misunderstanding and ridicule. Since he had seen by the papers that legitimate scholars, among them Josiah Royce, had met to discuss the matter scientifically, he was encouraged to bring up the subject of mental telepathy. He invented a word of his own, however, not liking the fact that the common phrase is, as he said, "polarized" by its association with spiritualism. His own word "cerebricity," by analogy with electricity, suited him better.[21]

Such reflections come from the Dictator, the Professor, or the Doctor, all three of whom speak with the caution and dignity proper to their stations; for his eccentric notions and his emotional outbursts, Holmes uses a fourth *alter ego*, Number Seven, the crank. Knowing that on the subject of religion he has the reputation of being a "crank," Holmes allows Number Seven to let out a blast against that form of contemporary hypocrisy which leaves written into any religious creed principles its adherents profess to disavow. The amateur student of semantics has a legitimate fear of the paralyzing magic of polarized words. Number Seven may be a cracked teacup, may have a "squinting brain," may even have his "idiotic area" (by analogy with the blind spot in vision), but Holmes implies that everyone has such defects and all cranks are worth listening to. Number Seven (Holmes's safety valve, like Little Boston) is allowed on this basis to burst into an enthusiastic toast to the roasted crank, Giordano Bruno, "a murdered heretic in the beginning of the seventeenth century, a hero of knowledge in the nineteenth." [22]

Other reflections are expressed by Number Five, a feminine character, who, in spite of three younger rivals, commands the most affection among the guests at the tea-table. In the third paper she gives an account of a dream in which she has a view of the world, of the moon, and of Saturn. By means of Number Five's narrative, Holmes lets loose some political opinions. On Saturn lives a race which claims to be the only truly republican group in the solar system, living by a creed which proclaims that all are "born equal, live equal, and die equal." They are all free—"free to obey the rules laid down for the regulation of their conduct, pursuits, and opinions, free to be married to the person selected for them by the physiological section of the government, and free to die at such proper period of life as may best suit the convenience and general welfare of the community." Since the establishment of this new order, there had been but one serious uprising; the abolition of plates, regarded as effete, and the substitution of troughs designed for twelve persons had started a movement for partitions which would divide the troughs into individual compartments. This aristocratic movement was put down by the Saturnians, who loathed nothing so much as inequality.

There were, however, two reform groups in this community, the Orthobrachians, who objected to the inequality of the left arm and hand, and the Isopodians, who protested the inequality of the upper and lower limbs. "If you can believe it, they actually practise going on all fours,—generally in a private way, a few of them together, but hoping to bring the world round to them in the near future." The inhabitants of this equalitarian community suffer from an endemic disease of prolonged yawning, which brings about anchylosis of the lower jaw; their chief recreations are intoxication and suicide.

Commenting on the dream, the Dictator expresses a mild objection to contemporary social philosophers, claiming that they treat the world of human beings as if "they were playing solitaire," but he allows each of the guests at his tea-table to express his opinion of the dream. The younger generation finds it too hard on reformers who wish to cure the evils of over-crowding and competition; Number Five says it was evoked by reading some Utopias which seemed to her pretty but dull; Number Seven says he had a scheme of his own but had been shown by the Counsellor that it would take one policemen to every two citizens to carry it out. The Counsellor, showing a lawyer's discretion, ventures no positive comment on Number Five's dream.[23]

Of all the tea-table company, it is the lawyer who is treated with the greatest caution. In spite of the author's almost querulous insistence that none of the characters have real counterparts, the Counsellor's age, war record, and reputation for eloquence leave no doubt of his identity. Of his son's reputation as an orator, Dr. Holmes was especially proud. As he had written in 1885, "Perhaps I have shown more lively sympathy with your triumphs in a field with which I was more familiar than with those abstruse and profound professional labors which I could admire as an outside looker-on but not enter into so completely as I could into the spirit and form of these address[es] which I look upon as master-pieces of American eloquence—in simplicity, grace, and true feeling." [24] Praising particularly two addresses given by the younger Holmes in 1884, the doctor had advised his son to consider himself a *"star"* and to be chary of displaying his talents.[25] In

Over the Teacups, Dr. Holmes is mindful of the Judge's dignity; as his "Honor's most humble and most obedient parent,"[26] he treats the Counsellor with great respect and deference, making his character much more taciturn than the original. A few of the observations the Counsellor makes appear, however, to come straight from the Judge's mouth.

He is made to remark that he would have no objection to living to an advanced age. Some of his father's advice on how to attain that end he had, of course, unintentionally taken already. That advice the elder Holmes gives in answer to those "brain-tappers" who want an octogenarian's opinion on everything from religion to the nutritive value of oatmeal. He mixes nonsense and wisdom neatly, beginning: "The first thing to be done is, some years before birth to advertise for a couple of parents both belonging to long-lived families." The advice to be cheerful he gives for what it is worth as he would recommend anyone to be six feet tall. Before he has done with the question he exposes its absurdity, for he suggests that the surest way to live a long time is to "become the subject of a mortal disease," the kind you think you have but which no doctor can name.[27] The "brain-tappers" did not make Holmes peevish, but he let them know what he thought of them.

One set of questions, however, he treated seriously. They were addressed to him and to others and were printed in the *American Hebrew* for April 4, 1890. The questions asked individuals to account for their racial prejudice and to suggest ways to dispel it. Holmes's answers are worth reading. Free of cant and self-righteousness, always honest and personal, he replied from his own experience. "I shared more or less the prevailing prejudices against the persecuted race." He traced that prejudice to Christian teaching and, in his own case, to puritan exclusiveness.

It was against the most adverse influences of legislation, of religious feeling, of social repugnance, that the great names of Jewish origin made themselves illustrious; that the philosophers, the musicians, the financiers, the statesmen, of the last centuries forced the world to recognize and accept them. . . . Christians, as they called themselves, have insulted, calumniated, oppressed, abased and outraged "the chosen race" during the succession of centuries since the Jewish contemporaries of the Founder of Christianity made up their minds that he did not meet the conditions of their Scriptures. . . .

It seems as if there should be certain laws of etiquette regulating the relation of different religions to each other. Still more, there should be something like politeness in the bearing of Christian sects toward each other, and of believers in the new dispensation toward those who still adhere to the old. . . . I doubt if a convert to the religion of Mahomet was ever made by calling a man a Christian dog. I doubt if a Hebrew ever became a good Christian if the baptismal rite was performed by spitting on his Jewish gabardine. . . .

The religion we profess is not self-evident. It did not convince the people to whom it was sent. We have no claim to take it for granted that we are all right, and they are all wrong. And, therefore, in the midst of all the triumphs of Christianity, it is well that the stately synagogue should lift its walls by the side of the aspiring cathedral, a perpetual reminder that there are many mansions in the Father's earthly house as well as in the heavenly one; that civilized humanity, longer in time and broader in space than any historical form of belief, is mightier than any one institution or organization it includes.[28]

For his readers in 1890, however, the greatest delight and surprise came from a poem at the end of the ninth paper. In 1857, it was the "Deacon's Masterpiece" that brought down the house. Now at eighty, the doctor had done it again with "The Broomstick Train; or, the Return of the Witches." [29] In lively tetrameters he tells his yarn of the witches released from hell to return to the world where they are metamorphosed into the century's latest mechanical contraption—the electric trolley car. Holmes called the book the "wintry products of my freezing wits," [30] but, after reading these verses Lowell wrote him that it was "a serious thing to have 'eclipsed the gayety of nations.'" [31]

Holmes was somewhat less gay than his poem; as he had written Lowell, his life had become "as mechanical and simple as if I had been sawed out of a board and was worked with a string." [32] His readers might want "The Broomstick Train"; he himself wanted to read Matthew Arnold's "Oberman" and "Oberman Once More," which had for him, then, a "melancholy charm . . . hardly any other verse possessed." [33] He could find his own thoughts and feelings in some of Arnold's stanzas. Aware of the limitations of his own verse, he would surely hit upon the following lines:

> Too fast we live, too much are tried,
> Too harass'd, to attain
> Wordsworth's sweet calm, or Goethe's wide
> And luminous view to gain. . . .

Holmes's melancholy showed chiefly in his notes to Annie Fields, whose company on drives and at tea he valued, and his letters to Whittier. The death of Lowell in 1891 had followed hard upon the death of Henry Jacob Bigelow; bereft of the two friends of his two professions, Holmes looked to the Quaker poet; their raft, he said, had dwindled to a spar.[34] But a year later Whittier, too, was dead, his last poem some lines for Dr. Holmes's eighty-third birthday.

His classmates, Samuel May and S. F. Smith, dined with him once a year; there were no more verses, but the three old men enjoyed each other's company. These two old friends were with him at his last public appearance in November 1893, when he gave a poem for the Young Men's Christian Union. Occasionally one or the other of them came to spend a day at his summer home in Beverly Farms. Holmes seems to have occupied his time in attempting to turn Smith, an orthodox Baptist preacher, into a Unitarian; he thought he might have succeeded if his classmate hadn't been so deaf.[35]

At Beverly Farms during the summer months, one of his greatest pleasures was to take long drives into the surrounding country which, in spite of its string of factory towns, was still a rural landscape with rolling, wooded hills, broken by open fields marked off by rough stone walls and laced with ponds and streams. The connoisseur of trees liked particularly the neighborhood of Topsfield and Boxford, where near the town line in a grove of straight pines grew five royal oaks, centuries old. Their thick trunks and the long horizontal reach of their great branches testified to the fact that they had stood there before the first settlers came to America; three of them stand there now.

Dr. Oliver Wendell Holmes—c. 1865

Dr. Holmes in front of the big rock at Beverly Farms—
c. 1890

His social life had narrowed to tea parties, a rare dinner, drives, and expeditions to the symphony rehearsals. He was still a faithful member of the Saturday Club, but he knew that he and his few fellow-ancients were getting, to say the least, a little repetitious. He did not write a great deal in these last few years—a few poems, an introduction or two for other people's books. His major literary labors were writing new prefaces and reading proof for the Riverside Edition of his works. Toward the end he spent some time dictating his reminiscences to his secretary, apparently more for the pleasure they gave him than for any serious intention to publish. Yet the insatiable *Atlantic Monthly* was still at him; as late as 1893, Horace Scudder made several entries in his notebook about getting the doctor's autobiography, including one reminder to see the judge about it.[36]

In *Over the Teacups,* Holmes is so firm about an octogenarian's dislike of pitying kindness that it seems false here to dwell too long on the melancholy aspects of his last few years. Outwardly he showed the old sparkle of his convivial spirit. His infirmities he could ease with a joke—"the buckets of the Danaids are nothing to my memory in the way of leakage." [37] When he forgot his sittings for the portrait Mrs. Whitman was doing of him for the Philadelphia College of Physicians, he wrote verses to the painter to announce his coming for the postponed sitting:

> Some in rags
> Some in tags
> And one in an Oxford gown.[38]

Nor was Dr. Holmes beyond gallantry. When the actress Ellen Terry came to town in 1894, Holmes sent her a note:

> *Sur la scène*
> *Toujours la Reine;*
> *Sans diadème*
> *Encore la même.*[39]

But in the spring of 1894, he went through a long siege of illness, the second within a year. The judge and Mrs. Holmes carefully kept the news of his health from getting out lest the ravenous journalists start camping on the doorstep.[40] Holmes himself had become weary of batteries of strangers; as he remarked, the sensibilities of an old man become somewhat dull so that he cannot respond as willingly as he might wish. In his last years, he was often bothered by doting admirers, who followed him home from church and pursued him even into the house. An anecdote has it that on one such occasion, after trying to elude his pursuers by taking back alleys, he found them still on his trail as he neared 296 Beacon Street. Gathering energy in his need, he ran up the brownstone stairs, got the door open, and then turned to look down at the group hurrying toward the stairs. He raised his voice: "Don't come in; it's catching and I've got it."

He was still enough of a doctor to know what his illnesses meant. In June, meeting a friend who inquired about his health, he answered, "Thank you. My house is tottering, but I am well." [41] Back in town after his summer at Beverly Farms, Holmes went about his usual business, attending a symphony rehearsal, going to the Club, and calling at his publisher's. Here he told young Garrison, grandson of the abolitionist, that he felt like Hamlet, "fat and short of breath." [42]

A week later on Sunday, October 7, 1894, he sat in his library, talking with his son. "He simply ceased to breathe," [43] wrote the judge to Samuel May the next day. And on October 11, May entered in the Class Book: "Probably the only meeting this year was that on October 10 when Smith and May sat together in a pew, at King's Chapel, at the funeral services of our dear Dr. Holmes." [44]

"Life is a fatal complaint and an eminently contagious one," wrote the doctor in 1872.[45] Extremely susceptible to the contagion of life, he could not withdraw from it into what he called a thinking-cell. Ruefully he had described the kind of thinking-cell he would require—something modeled on a hen's egg might suit. "Build me an oval with a smooth, translucent wall, and put me in the center of it with Newton's 'Principia' or Kant's 'Kritik,' and I think I shall develop 'an eye for an equation' . . . and a capacity for abstraction." [46]

He could not spend hours upon such labor as the translating of Dante as Longfellow had done, upon such specialized scientific study as Agassiz, upon such digging in the archives of history as Motley. Able to read only *in* books, not through them as Lowell did, Holmes found comfort in Dr. Johnson's admissions that he had read only two books through and wished only one book, *Don Quixote,* longer.[47] The books he himself chose to come back to are revealing; he was attracted to the discursive and the personal: Montaigne's *Essays,* Pascal's *Pensées,* Burton's *Anatomy of Melancholy,* Boswell's *Life of Johnson;* even Mather's *Magnalia,* in spite of his horror of the writer's theology, had a similar fascination. Writers of another age were free to range as widely as they pleased, but in the nineteenth century, living in the Boston atmosphere of moral earnestness, Holmes could not enjoy the same license without evoking criticism.

Since that day in 1846 when a very young and earnest James Russell Lowell had written to rebuke Holmes for being less earnest than he, Holmes had been constantly scolded and criticized. He responded to these attempts on the part of his well-meaning critics to recreate him in their own images, but he never let himself be entirely made over. Instead he was led to self-examination and self-revelation. With that candor that frequently embarrassed his friends, he admitted, "I am intensely interested in my own personality." [48]

Remembering that he had been criticized for speaking of subjects which he had not properly studied, for borrowing so freely from others, for not being original (as his age conceived of originality) and for always talking of himself, Holmes could not help but take delight in such writers as Montaigne. Not surprisingly, he made a special note of the essay on "Bookes." [49] There Holmes found lines he might have written of himself: "I make no doubt but it shall often befall me to speake of

385

things which are better, and with more truth, handled by such as are their crafts-masters. . . . He that shall search after knowledge, let him seek it where it is; there is nothing I professe lesse. These are but my fantasies by which I endevour not to make things known, but my selfe."

Notes

THE CHIEF SOURCE of manuscript material is the Holmes collection given to the Houghton Library, Harvard University, by Mr. Edward Jackson Holmes. The particular manuscripts used in this biography are described in the notes, but perhaps a word about the collection as a whole is needed. The most important items are medical lecture notes taken when Holmes was a student in Boston and Paris, medical casebooks, a bound volume of manuscripts (of which about a third are unpublished), a bound volume of letters (chiefly those written to his parents from Paris), notebooks for his major books after *The Autocrat* and *The Professor*, indexes to periodicals, and four miscellaneous notebooks.

Holmes was not a journal-keeper. The nearest thing to a journal is a small black notebook in which the entries range in date from 1843 to 1894 and in subject from notes in French on Pascal to the date when he took off his winter flannels. The original intention was apparently to keep notes of his reading, arranged under general subject headings; most of the entries, made in the 1860's, are of this kind. Somehow the records of trotters, personal data, addresses, and other odds and ends got in too, so that as a whole the notebook is typical of Holmes in its combination of the trivial and the erudite, its juxtaposition of trotters and theology.

The indexes to periodicals are of some interest; there are three made between 1837 and 1856. The first is an index for the major medical journals: *Encyclographie des sciences médicales, British and Foreign Medical Review,* and *American Journal of the Medical Sciences*. The second takes care of the American editions of the four heavy British reviews: the *Edinburgh, Quarterly, Westminster,* and *Foreign Quarterly*.

The third indexes the *North American Review*. The material is classified under general subject headings; occasionally a title is marked. It is no surprise to find checked an article on trees or one defending mechanical philosophy; it is less expected to find a check against an item on the Bank of the United States. Significantly the majority of the articles checked are theological. Holmes's reading was likely to be on scientific and theological subjects rather than literary ones, as information in the notes to follow will suggest.

The collection in Houghton does not include books from Holmes's library, which is now scattered. His medical books he gave to the Boston Medical Library; other books remained in the possession of his son until 1935 when Mr. Justice Holmes's books went to the Library of Congress. Other volumes are in the Berkshire Athenaeum, the library of the Phillips Academy at Andover, and the private library of Mr. Edward Jackson Holmes.

This brief accounting and the notes to follow make a separate bibliography unnecessary. In the American Book Company's edition of Holmes selections, edited by S. I. Hayakawa and H. M. Jones, there is a good bibliography of books and articles on the subject. And it is assumed that Thomas Franklin Currier's projected bibliography of Holmes will be completed sometime in the near future.

Expecting also that Miss Miriam Small's edition of Holmes's letters will be published, I have throughout used excerpts from letters without giving the full context. Miss Small's edition of the complete letters will provide the necessary check.

THE FOLLOWING ABBREVIATIONS ARE USED:

A.l.	Autograph letter
AJMS	*American Journal of the Medical Sciences*
AM	*Atlantic Monthly*
AMA	American Medical Association
BAT	Boston Athenaeum
BDA	*Boston Daily Advertiser*
BET	*Boston Evening Transcript*
BML	Boston Medical Library
BMSJ	*Boston Medical and Surgical Journal*

BPL   Boston Public Library
BSMI Boston Society for Medical Improvement
HC   Holmes collection, Houghton Library, Harvard University
MS.BK. versity
HUa   Harvard University Archives
HUh   Harvard University, Houghton Library
HUm   Harvard University, Medical School Library
L.BK. See Chap. 2, n. 50, p. 392.
LC   Library of Congress
MHS   Massachusetts Historical Society
MMS   Massachusetts Medical Society
MS.BK. See Chap. 1, n. 5, p. 389.
NYPL New York Public Library

CHAPTER 1.   *MINISTER'S SON*

1 John T. Morse, Jr., *Life and Letters of Oliver Wendell Holmes* (Boston, 1897), I, 16. Miss N. W. is Nancy Williams, see *Publications of the Cambridge Historical Society*, I, (1906), 49.

2 *The Writings of Oliver Wendell Holmes* (Riverside Edition; Boston, 1891), VIII, 158. (These volumes will be hereafter referred to as *Works*. This is the edition in which the poems appear in Vols. XI-XIII and the lives of Motley and Emerson in Vol. XIV.)

3 *Works,* III, 10ff., and VII, 22ff.

4 *Ibid.*, III, 24.

5 Text for readings of his poems, n.d., [1878-9] in *Lectures, Memoirs, Prefaces, and Miscellaneous Manuscripts*, bound volume of mss., p. 911, HC. The mss. range in date from 1841-1891; the pagination and table of contents were added by T. F. Currier; the selection, arrangement, and binding were done after Holmes's death, apparently by his son. Hereafter this volume will be referred to as MS.BK.

This room affected Holmes's imagination enough to be recalled on several occasions, notably in the heroine's nightmare in *The Guardian Angel* (*Works*, VI, 182-6), where a pair of portraits and an intricately carved chair provide the background of the dream. Holmes was nine years old when the "aged owner," Judge Wendell, died.

6 *Works,* I, 23.

7 Letter, Nov. 13, 1880, in *Brooklyn Union*, Nov. 17, 1880.

8 Harvard Library, Records of withdrawals, 1828-9, ms., HUa.

9 Morse, I, 41, from autobiographical notes.

10 *Works*, III, 26.

11 Text for readings, MS.BK., pp. 895-6.

12 Morse, I, 39-42, from autobiographical notes.

13 *Works*, III, 26-7.

14 Morse, I, 27.

15 Ms., July 24, 1822, in Abiel Holmes's hand, endorsed by O. W.

Holmes, June 27, 1871, HC. See Miriam R. Small, "First and Last Surviving Poems of Dr. Oliver Wendell Holmes," *American Literature*, 15 (Jan. 1944), 416-420.

16 (Abiel Holmes and others), *A Family Tablet* (Boston, 1796), p. v.

17 *Ibid.*, p. [63].

18 Morse, I, 47-8.

19 *Works*, VI, 275.

20 A.l., Feb. 21, 1838, O. W. Holmes to Rev. William Jenks, Henry W. and Albert A. Berg Collection, NYPL.

21 Anonymous, *Controversy Between the First Parish in Cambridge and the Rev. Dr. Holmes,* Published by the Parish Committee (Cambridge, 1829), p. 75.

22 Morse, I, 35-6.

23 *Works*, III, 17.

24 John F. W. Ware, *A Discourse Delivered in the Cambridgeport Parish* (Cambridge, 1864), p. 11.

25 Morse, I, 38.

26 *Works*, VIII, 147-8.

27 Text for readings, MS.BK., p. 897.

28 The primers of the early nineteenth century apparently did not print Cotton's catechism, but it seems safe to assume that Abiel Holmes would have possessed one of the earlier editions (1777 or 1782, for example). The shorter Westminster catechism, in answer to the nineteenth question, called for a similar, if less personal answer: "All mankind by the fall lost communion with God, are under his wrath and curse, & so made liable to the miseries of this life, & to the pains of Hell forever."

29 Stephen P. Sharples, ed., *Records of the Church of Christ at Cambridge, 1632-1830* (Boston, 1906), p. 462. The youngest daughter in the household, Sarah Lathrop, died November 6, 1812, a few weeks before her seventh birthday.

30 *Works*, IV, 247. See also letters to Harriet Beecher Stowe, Morse, II, 223-255.

31 Morse, II, 230.

32 *Works*, IV, 246-7.

33 Morse, I, 37.

34 *Ibid.*, I, 12.

35 *Albany Evening Journal*, Nov. 25 and Dec. 2, 1854. See also "The Hudson, After a Lecture at Albany" in *The Complete Poetical Works of Oliver Wendell Holmes* (Cambridge Edition; Boston, 1891), p. 94. (This volume will be hereafter referred to as *Poems*.)

36 *Works*, IX, 337.

37 Alexander McKenzie, *Lectures on the History of the First Church in Cambridge* (Boston, 1873), pp. 186-7.

38 Abiel Holmes, ms. account book, HC.

39 "The Opening of the Piano," *Poems*, p. 166.

40 *Works*, III, 96-7.

CHAPTER 2. *SCHOOLBOY*

1 *Works,* III, 186-9.
2 *Ibid.,* I, 204-5.
3 *Ibid.,* VIII, 148.
4 *Ibid.,* VIII, 150.
5 *Ibid.,* VII, 23-4
6 *Ibid.,* III, 22-3.
7 Autobiographical notes, ms., n.d. (late), HC. (These are not the notes used by Morse.)
8 Morse, I, 34.
9 *Works,* I, 200.
10 Morse, I, 30.
11 *Works,* VIII, 163-4.
12 Holmes, "One of my early writing-books," ms., 1817-8, HC.
13 Holmes, "Address," *The New Century and the New Building of the Harvard Medical School* (Cambridge, 1884), p. 5.
14 *Works,* IX, 387.
15 James Russell Lowell, "Cambridge Thirty Years Since," *Writings* (Riverside Edition; Boston, 1890), I, 94-5.
16 *Ibid.,* p. 53 ff. Other accounts of commencement are those of Holmes in *Works,* VIII, 159-60, and IV, 260; and of his brother John, in *The Harvard Book,* ed. by F. O. Vaille and H. A. Clark (Cambridge, 1875), II, 18 ff.
17 *Works,* VIII, 159.
18 Morse, I, 36.
19 "One of my early writing books."
20 *Works,* I, 177-8.
21 Frederick Henry Hedge, *Christian Register,* 62 (June 7, 1883), 360.
22 Autobiographical notes, ms.
23 Harvard College, *Catalogue for 1825,* p. [3].
24 A.l., Sept. 29, 1822, Harvard Law School. Mary Jackson Holmes married Dr. Usher Parsons on Sept. 23.
25 A.l., Mar. 2, 1894, Furness to Holmes, LC.
26 A.l., Sept. 29, 1822. Mary Parson's learning is remarked upon by George Otis, Harvard Tutor; in his diary (ms. 1824-25, LC). He says: "Her taste was a treasure. Her acquirements were rapid and unusual. She rose with the finest genius in our literature, and her cultivation bore her to European fields of learning."
27 *Works,* VIII, 241-3. He spoke of his jealousy to the Rev. Hugh R. Haweis; see the latter's *Travel and Talk,* (London, 1896), I, 29.
28 *Works,* VIII, 243-4.
29 *Ibid.,* XIV, 36. Gourdin is mentioned by young Holmes in his letter of Sept. 29, 1822 (see note 24), where he is described as one of Mary's "old admirers."

30 *Controversy Between the Parish . . . and the Rev. Dr. Holmes,* p. 70.

31 J. F. W. Ware, *op cit.,* p. 9.

32 Abiel Holmes, *The Annals of America* (2nd ed., Cambridge, 1829), I, 438.

33 George Otis, ms. diary, entry for Sept. 2-5, 1824.

34 Works, VIII, 245, and a.l., Mar. 14, 1893, Mrs. Richardson (née Ann Murdock) to Holmes, HC.

35 *Works,* VIII, 247.

36 A.l., Mar. 14, 1893, Mrs. Richardson to Holmes.

37 A.l., Sept. 12, 1824, Holmes to his mother, Harvard Law School.

38 A.l., Dec. 28, 1868, Holmes to Phinehas Barnes, privately owned, printed with omissions in Morse, I, 24. See also ms. Records of the Class of '29 (hereafter referred to as Class BK.) p. 221, HUa. Holmes refers to the one man he hates in "The Autocrat of the Breakfast-Table," No. 1, *The New England Magazine,* 1 (Nov. 1831), 430, reprinted in *Oliver Wendell Holmes,* ed., S. I. Hayakawa and H. M. Jones, (New York, 1939), p. 439.

39 *Poems,* p. 321, and *Works,* VIII, 247.

40 "Records of the Proceedings of the Social Fraternity," Vol. II, ms. Oliver Wendell Holmes Library, Phillips Academy, Andover, and A.l., Jan. 11, 1885, Holmes to Mrs. Martin (daughter of Phinehas Barnes), privately owned.

The debate with Crocker was on May 3, 1825; the debate with Barnes, on Aug. 10.

41 *Works,* VIII, 253.

42 A.ll., June and Sept., 1828, Barnes to Holmes, HC. Aug. 15, 1828, Morse, I, 57, Holmes to Barnes.

43 A.l., Mar. 14, 1893, Mrs. Richardson to Holmes.

44 Letter, May 24, 1875, *Semi-Centennial of the Philomathean Society,* Phillips Academy, (Hyde Park, 1875), pp. 73-5. See also Holmes's sketches of Dr. Woods and Dr. Porter in *Works,* VIII, 249-50.

45 A.l., Sept. 1828, Barnes to Holmes, HC.

46 *Works,* VIII, 251-2, and Class BK., p. 287. In the Class BK., Francis Crocker, who with Holmes went from Andover to Harvard, speaks of being one of three who were unmoved by the revival; I am assuming on the basis of Holmes's letters to Barnes that he and Barnes were the other two.

47 *Works,* VIII, 247.

48 Dec. 1828, Morse, I, 59; Morse has blanked out the name. (The original letter exists, but the owner of it can't at the present writing find it.) Holmes may have been referring to Clement.

49 *Works,* VIII, 248.

50 A.l., Mar. 25, 1825, Abiel Holmes to his son, third letter in bound volume of letters (hereafter referred to as L.BK.), HC. See also letter of Jan. 5, 1825, in Morse, I, 26. In 1865, in a conversation with John Murray Forbes, Holmes apparently cited his Andover experiences in defense of his unorthodox religious beliefs, about which his friend Forbes was

alarmed. In a letter written the next day (a.l., Feb. 26, 1865, HC), Forbes referred to the conversation and admitted that such experiences might have been chilling and blinding and might make evangelical Christians appear unlovable.

The death of his sister, Mary Parsons, in June 1825, would add to Holmes's unhappiness at Andover. Tutor Otis describes Mary in his diary in words of lavish praise, speaking of her "generous, open, affectionate, confiding heart. . . . She spoke as a friend, where she knew herself to be an idol. . . ." See note 26.

51 May 29, 1869, to Mrs. Stowe, Morse, II, 226.

CHAPTER 3. *HARVARD STUDENT*

1 Harvard, Records of the College Faculty, Vol. X, 1822-29, p. 116, ms., HUa.

2 *Ibid.*, p. 117.

3 Harvard, College Records, Vol. VI, 1819-1827, p. 29, ms. HUa.

4 A.l., Oct. 22, 1825, Benjamin Peirce to his mother, Peirce papers, HUa.

5 Vincent Y. Bowditch, *Life and Correspondence of Henry Ingersoll Bowditch* (Boston, 1902), II, 295.

6 Edward Everett Hale, ed., *James Freeman Clarke* (Boston, 1891), pp. 34-6.

7 "To the Faculty of Harvard University," ms., Berg Collection, NYPL.

8 Class BK., p. 13.

9 E. E. Hale, *op. cit.*, p. 33.

10 Class BK., p. 13.

11 Morse, I, 52. The letter is misdated Jan. 31, 1828; it should be 1829 obviously; the error is Holmes's (original letter privately owned).

12 A.l., June 1828, Barnes to Holmes, HC.

13 Records of the Faculty, X, 153. The book Holmes received is owned by his grandson, Edward Jackson Holmes.

14 Rank lists, HUa.

15 Aug. 15, 1828, Morse, I, 56.

16 A.ll., v.d., Barnes to Holmes, H.C.

17 A.l., Nov. 2, 1827, Ticknor Letters, p. 83, HUa. Ticknor's report of March 26, 1827, is at p. 74. The letter of Nov. 2 also named Holmes as one of eight juniors who were "far advanced" in French.

18 A.l., March 21, 1828, Ticknor Letters, p. 92-4. Rank list, April 1828; his lowest grade was in mathematics; he was eighth in his class.

19 Rank lists, July and Dec. 1828.

20 Dec. 1828, Morse, I, 60.

21 Henry Adams, *The Education* (Boston, 1918), p. 69.

22 Records of the Faculty, X, 112. The gravel pit is vouched for by Lowell, *op. cit.*, p. 57.

23 Letter, Aug. 29, 1889, Samuel Devens, *BDA*.

24 Samuel May, ms., Class of '29 papers. HUa.

25 Edward Tyrell Channing, Review of *Two Years Before the Mast*, *North American Review*, 52 (Jan. 1941), 61.

26 A.l., Dec. 6, 1877, Edward Cunningham to Samuel May, Class BK., p. 209.

27 *Works*, XIV, 19.

28 Morse, I, 55. This letter is incorrectly dated by Morse; it should be March 28, 1829, not 1828. See p. 396 for a further note on this letter.

29 Harvard Library, Records of withdrawals, 1825.

30 "Introductory—Sept. 26th, 1879," MS. BK., pp. 213-4.

31 *Works*, I, 75.

32 Anonymous, *An Account of the Controversy in the First Parish in Cambridge,* published pursuant to a vote of the church (Boston, 1829), pp. 4-6.

33 *Controversy Between the First Parish . . . and the Rev. Dr. Holmes,* p. 77. (See p. 390.)

34 Susanna Willard, "Extracts from the Letters of the Reverend Joseph Willard, President of Harvard College and of Some of His Children, 1794-1830," *Publications of the Cambridge Historical Society*, XI, 1920, 30. The letter is dated Oct. 1828, from Lucinda Willard to her brother Joseph.

Letters from "Firmness" and "A Well-Meaning Parishioner," in the *New England Galaxy* for Aug. 8 and 15, suggest the temper of the militant liberals in the town. By 1828, Abiel Holmes had been a resident of Cambridge for twenty-seven years, but some of his disaffected parishioners seem to have thought his Connecticut origin and southern pastorate put him in the category of a foreigner. But in these letters, as in an article in the *Christian Register* (Aug. 30, 1828), entitled "Calvinistic Interlopers," the feeling of the liberals seems to have been directed chiefly against "two or three of the (imported) leading clergymen of orthodox persuasion who have been so officious in causing divisions and animosities in the societies of the towns around us." The article went on to suggest that Abiel Holmes was under the "baneful influence" of these interlopers.

The tone of the orthodox is suggested in the *Boston Recorder*'s quotation from a lecture on the general subject of the "Unfaithful Minister," whom the speaker had described as worse than a murderer or a thief; "the lowest depths in the prison of despair are occupied by unprincipled, unfaithful ministers"; *i.e.,* any ministers who gave aid to the Unitarian enemy in any way. These cheerful sentiments appeared on Aug. 29, 1828, and doubtless made happy birthday reading for young Wendell Holmes.

35 Willard, *op. cit.*, p. 29.

36 *An Account of the Controversy in the First Parish in Cambridge,* p. 47.

37 McKenzie, *op. cit.*, pp. 198-9.

38 *Christian Register*, 9 (Dec. 19, 1829), 202.

39 McKenzie, *op. cit.*, p. 222.

40 A.l. Oct. 29 or 30, 1829, Barnes to Holmes, HC., and Morse, I, 57.

41 A.l., Oct. 1828, Holmes to Barnes, privately owned. (Part of the letter is in Morse, I, 58.)

Not until 1886, for the 250th anniversary of the First Church, did the split parish meet together again. At the ceremonies, three generations of the Holmes family were represented. Hymns by Abiel Holmes and his son were sung; and Oliver Wendell Holmes, Jr., made a speech.

CHAPTER 4.   *POET OF THE CLASS OF '29*

1 Aug. 15, 1828, Morse, I, 56. In the same letter he says he ranks seventeenth in his class; the lists put him at eighth place in April and at fourteenth in December.

2 Morse, I, 55. (The letter is misdated; it should be March 28, 1829.)

3 Records of the Hasty Pudding Club, Vol. VIII, entry of October 31, 1828, ms., on deposit, HUa.

4 Samuel May, ms., Class of '29 papers, HUa.

5 Dec. 1828, Morse, I, 59.

6 Class BK., p. 11; see also Hale, *op cit.*, p. 35.

7 Hale, *op. cit.*, p. 35.

8 Records of the Hasty Pudding Club, VIII, 100-9. The secretaries were apparently supposed to be as "clever" as possible; they all show the strain.

9 *Ibid.*, May 2, 1828.

10 *Ibid.*, June 2, 1828.

11 *Ibid.*, Sept. 5, 1828.

12 *Ibid.*, Vol. IX, Mar. 27, 1829.

13 *Ibid.*, Vol. VIII, Feb. 19, 1829.

14 *Ibid.*, Dec. 5, 1828.

15 *Ibid.*, Feb. 22, 1828.

16 Oct.[23] 1828, Morse, I, 58-9.

17 Holmes, "Forgotten Ages," ms., in collection of Harvard exhibition and commencement parts, HUa.

18 Morse, I, 51, from autobiographical notes.

19 Dec. 1828, Morse, I, 60-61. This society had not yet fallen into disrepute.

20 Class BK., p. 17.

21 James Russell Lowell, "Class-Day," *Harvard Book*, II, 165, quoting the Reverend Frederick Whitney's diary.

22 Maria Sophia Quincy, "Journal," *Harvard Graduate's Magazine*, 26 (June 1918), 576.

23 *Ibid.*, p. 575.

24 Holmes, "A Poem," ms., in collection of Harvard . . . commencement parts.

25 Maria Quincy, *op. cit.*, p. 577.

26 *Ibid.*, p. 577. She calls Holmes's poem "amusing," p. 578.

27 "Order of Exercises for Commencement," 1829; both programs referred to are privately owned.

28 *New England Palladium*, August 28, 1829.

29 Holmes, "A Poem."

30 Class BK., p. 18.

31 Morse, I, 55. The letter (March 28), misdated 1828 instead of 1829, indicates that Holmes had already appeared in print. He says: "I . . . have written poetry for an Annual, and seen my literary bantlings swathed in green silk, and reposing in the drawing-room." For some forty years, accepting Morse's date, collectors and dealers have searched diligently for the wrong annual bound in green silk. Ironically, knowing the right date has been no more fruitful. When the original search was made (1939) and eight libraries canvassed for their gift books, no 1829 annual in green silk was found; since then, both *The Token* and *The Offering* for that year have turned up in the desired binding, but of the few poems whose authorship is still unknown, not one could be confidently claimed, on internal evidence alone, as being by Holmes.

Holmes himself consistently put his first appearance in print in 1830, admitting no earlier publication, except in a letter of July 15, 1889, in which he says, "I think it was in some newspaper that my first published lines appeared, but the first periodical in which I wrote was 'The Collegian' . . . in the year 1830." The letter, unfortunately, is a forgery; and, although the perpetrator is known to be a free-hand forger, who rarely works without an original in front of him, the late date—supposing such an original to have existed—makes Holmes's statement of doubtful value, for by then he was not even sure of when he wrote "Old Ironsides." The mystery is made the more obscure not only because of Holmes's subsequent silence but also because of the facts that the particular letter to Barnes is one of three not yet located and that Barnes's answer to the letter was apparently not preserved.

Yet there can be no doubt that as an undergraduate, Holmes somewhere appeared in print. Since he contributed nothing to the *Harvard Register,* his membership in the club called *Diaphemizomenoi*—a temporary club apparently founded by Clarke and Holmes—suggests that he had been published elsewhere. The founders of the club may, of course, have meant the word to indicate only that they made themselves known by recitation, by writing; but Clarke and Curtis both had appeared in print, so that it seems likely that the third known member had done so, too. What and where must remain a mystery until someone has the patience to wade through the annuals a second time.

32 A.l., Feb. 16, 1829, Barnes to Holmes, HC.

33 Morse, I, 62. The original letter is dated "Sept. *je ne sçais pas quoi,* 1829," but it is surcharged Oct. 20.

34 A.l., January 13 [1830], Holmes to Barnes, privately owned. This is the letter Morse prints, I, 64-5, but the reference here is to a passage deleted. Holmes identifies the subject of the first poem and quotes two stanzas. The "S.L." to whom the lines were addressed was "Sukey Len-

nox," a "brunette of the darkest complexion with locks of that peculiarly intricate curl which distinguishes the daughters of Nubia."

35 *The Collegian*, six numbers, February-June, 1830. The Club members were Sargent ("Sherry" and "Hock"), Theodore Snow '30 ("La Touche"), William Simmons '31 ("Lockfast"), Robert Habersham '31 ("Airy"), and Frederick W. Brune '31 ("Templeton").

36 *New England Galaxy*, Feb. 26, 1830.

37 *Ibid.*, April 9, 1830.

38 Morse I, 67-9 (The original letter, privately owned, is dated May 6, 1830).

39 *New England Galaxy*, June 16, 1830.

40 Morse, I, 145.

41 (O. W. Holmes, John O. Sargent, and Epes Sargent), *Illustrations of the Athenaeum Gallery*, (Boston, 1830). Two copies initialed by Holmes exist, HC and LC. The verses are similar to those written to go with the engravings in the literary annuals of the day.

42 *Amateur*, July 17, 1830; *Poems*, pp. 328-9.

43 *Amateur, loc. cit.; Poems*, pp. 329-30. He called these early poems "barbarisms" in a letter to Sarah J. Hale, March 23, 1844, Huntington Library.

44 *Knickerbocker Magazine*, 19 (March 1848), 270-1.

45 A.l. to Mrs. Dubois, Feb. 13, 1886, privately owned.

46 Only one of the five was ever collected.

47 *Works*, VII, 5-7. Snelling was editing the *Amateur* when Holmes was a regular contributor to it in 1830.

48 *Ibid.*, IX, 424.

CHAPTER 5. *MEDICAL STUDENT*

1 Mar. (1831), Morse, I, 69-72.

2 July 14, 1831; Feb. 22, 1832, *Ibid.*, 72, 74.

3 *Ibid.*, 81-2, see also *Works*, IX, 424.

4 Edward Warren, *The Life of John Collins Warren* (Boston, 1860), I, 419; see also p. 404. An exchange of letters between Holmes and Dr. Elisha Bartlett in 1838 shows how the problem of the anatomist continued after the passage of the Anatomy Act. (A.ll., Nov. 21, 1838, Holmes to Bartlett, Brown University and Dec. 3, Bartlett to Holmes, HC.) A letter of Oct. 25, 1854, from Holmes (HUm) indicates that there had been little improvement even by that late date. Holmes was extremely circumspect, referring to "certain incidental advantages" and asking for an interview with his correspondent, who was obviously connected with either the Tewksbury Almshouse or the Bridgewater State Hospital. Holmes apparently preferred not to state his business too plainly in writing. The incidents of 1883 are described here in Chap. 22, pp. 338-341.

5 See Harvard Catalogues, 1830 *et passim;* Dr. Lewis was not recognized as a member of the faculty, however; See College Records, Vol. VI, Sept. 22, 1832.

6 Holmes, "Lectures on the Theory and Practice of Medicine by James Jackson, M.D. 1831-2," ms. notebook, containing notes of both regular and clinical lectures; references hereafter will be made to Jackson I, L or C. The second notebook for Jackson's clinical lectures, 1832-33, has no title; the notes are for clinical lectures only. Reference will be made to Jackson II. Both are in HC.

7 Jackson II, p. 33, Nov. 15, 1832. Holmes's note includes: "The case is remarkable from its having proved fatal without severe local affection."

8 James Jackson, and Henry I. Bowditch, *Memoir of James Jackson, Jr., M.D.* (Boston, 1836), p. 316, letter, Nov. 4, 1834, Holmes to Jackson, Sr., on death of the latter's son.

9 *Works*, IX, 305, 307-8.

10 Jackson I, L., p. 89, Feb. 6, 1832.

11 Jackson II, p. 24, Nov. 5, 1832.

12 Jackson II, p. 47, Dec. 13, 1832. Jackson recognized no distinction between typhoid and typhus fever, lumping most types of "fever" together; occasionally he used the term "synochus" and spoke of a fever as having a "typhoid character."

13 Jackson I, L., p. 23, Dec. 9, 1831; also I, Cl., p. 4, Oct. 20, 1831.

14 *Works*, IX, 306.

15 Jackson I, L., p. 42, Dec. 30, 1831.

16 *Ibid.*, p. 7, Nov. 22, 1831.

17 *Ibid.*, p. 10, Nov. 25, 1831.

18 *Works*, IX, 306.

19 *Poems*, p. 59.

20 Feb. 22, 1832, Morse, I, 73-5.

21 Jackson, *Memoir*, p. 346.

CHAPTER 6. *TRAVELER IN EUROPE*

1 "Cranks," MS. BK., p. 1097. Holmes does not name the fellow-boarder, but describes him as a member "of a famous family"; Dana's is the only possible name listed at that address in contemporary Boston directories.

2 A.l., Mar. 30, 1833, Holmes to his parents, L.BK. 5. Some of the letters to be referred to in the notes which follow are printed as a whole or in part in Morse, I, 98-156, and 83 *et passim*. Wherever all that is used is in print, the reference will be made to Morse; where any part of what is used has been omitted by Morse, reference will be made to the original. Since there is no pagination in the bound volume and some of the letters are bound out of order, the reference will give the number of the letter as well as the date. Except for paragraphing, the text of each letter quoted is that of the original.

3 Susan Hale, ed., *Life and Letters of Thomas Gold Appleton* (New York, 1885), pp. 84-6.

4 *Ibid.*, pp. 91-2.

5 *Ibid.*, pp. 86-7.

6 *Ibid.*, pp. 92-3.

7 Robert William Hooper, "Voyage from New York to England, Apr. 1833," entry for April 24, 1833, ms. Diary 1, privately owned.

8 *Works*, X, 200; Hooper Diary 1, April 19, 1833; Holmes, ms. outline of trip, tipped in black notebook (see introduction to Notes, p. 387), HC.

9 S. Hale, *op. cit.*, p. 93.

10 *Ibid.*, p. 86.

11 *Ibid.*, p. 99.

12 May 14, 1833, L.BK. 8.

13 *Works*, X, 117.

14 May 2, 1833, L.BK. 7.

15 *Works*, X, 127.

16 Hooper, Diary 1, April 27, 1833.

17 *Ibid.*, May 4, 1833.

18 April 26, 1833, L.BK. 6.

19 May 14, 1833, L.BK. 8.

20 Hooper, Diary 1, May 6, 1833.

21 *Works*, X, 174.

22 May 14, 1833, L.BK. 8.

23 May 21, 1833, L.BK. 9.

24 May 31, 1833, L.BK. 10, and Hooper Diary 1.

25 May 21, 1833, L.BK. 9, and Hooper Diary 1.

26 Howard Payson Arnold, *Memoir of Jonathan Mason Warren*, (Boston, 1886), p. 73.

27 May 31, 1833, L.BK. 10.

28 May 21, 1833, L.BK. 9.

29 Aug. 13, 1833, Morse, I, 107.

30 May 21, 1833, L.BK. 9.

31 Hooper, Diary 1, May 15, 1833; see Morse, I, 87.

32 June 29, 1833, Morse, I, 103.

33 Aug. 13, 1833, *ibid.*, I, 109.

34 V. Y. Bowditch, *op. cit.*, I, 49.

35 May 21, 1833, L.BK. 9.

36 July 29, 1833, L.BK. 16.

37 Aug. 30, 1833, Morse, I, 110-1.

38 July 14, 1833, *ibid.*, I, 105.

39 July 29, 1833, L.BK. 16.

40 June 14, 1833, Morse, I, 98-99. Appleton vouches for Holmes's fondness for Titian, a.l., n.d. [Spring, 1875], to Holmes, HUh.

41 June 6, 1833, L.BK. 11; Oct. 30, 1833, Morse, I, 119; and S. Hale, *op. cit.*, pp. 131-2.

42 Aug. 13, 1833, Morse, I, 109.

43 Dec. 13, 1833, Morse, I, 122.

44 May 31, 1833, L.BK. 10.

45 June 14, 1833, Morse, I, 99.

46 Oct. 14, 1833, L.BK. 20.

47 Arnold, *op cit.*, p. 48. The elder Warren sent his son off to Paris with a large, black notebook in which he listed a miscellany of moral advice and medical questions; in this catalogue he included a similar exhortation.

48 Oct. 30, 1833, Morse, I, 120.

49 Dec. 13, 1833, *ibid.*, I, 124.

50 Sept. 28, 1833, *ibid.*, I, 113.

51 Dec. 13, 1833, *ibid.*, I, 123-4. Holmes's letter of Sept. 28, with its graphic account of how a stranger can be extravagant in a foreign country at first, had apparently provoked admonishments from his parents to which the letter of Dec. 13 was his answer.

52 Aug. 13, 1833, *ibid.*, I, 107.

CHAPTER 7.   *SCHOLAR IN PARIS*

1 V. Y. Bowditch, *op. cit.*, I, 49, quoting a letter of May 12, 1833. See also *BMSJ*, 127 (Aug. 25, 1892), 183, where, in a letter for the memorial meeting for Bowditch (Suffolk County Medical Society), Holmes recalled this episode and admitted: "He was right and I was wrong."

2 June 21, 1833, Morse, I, 102.

3 V. Y. Bowditch, *op. cit.*, I, 37.

4 Aug. 13, 1833, Morse, I, 108-9.

5 Nov. 14, 1833, Morse, I, 89-90.

6 Oct. 22, 1833, L.BK. 57.

7 June 21, 1833, L.BK. 13, (in Morse, I, 100, except for deletion of the name of the horrible example).

8 Nov. 29, 1833, Morse, I, 121. The blanks are in the original.

9 Apr. 4, 1856, Holmes to Emerson, L.BK. 65. Holmes had heard Emerson's lecture on France the evening before and been shocked to hear him use Louis as an example of the French love of effect. Holmes assured Emerson that Louis was the "most genuine and untheatrical of men." The anecdote Emerson (quoting his brother-in-law, Dr. Charles T. Jackson) had used was one Holmes would not believe if it were "sworn to by the four Evangelists and counter-signed by the apostle Thomas."

10 E. Warren, *op cit.*, I, 334, quoting a letter of Dec. 30, 1837.

11 Apr. 4, 1856, L.BK. 65.

12 V. Y. Bowditch, *op. cit.*, I, 37, quoting a letter of Jan. 27, 1833.

13 Apr. 4, 1856, L.BK. 65. See Arnold, *op cit.*, p. 108 for the younger Warren's comment on Louis.

14 Aug. 13, 1833, Morse, I, 109.

15 Nov. 14, 1833, *ibid.*, I, 89.

16 V. Y. Bowditch, *op. cit.*, I, 50, 62-3.

17 *Ibid.*, II, 275. The original reads: *"Il y a quelque chose de plus rare que l'esprit de discernement; c'est le besoin de la vérité, cet état de*

l'âme qui nous permet pas de nous arrêter dans les travaux scientifiques à ce qui n'est que vraisemblable mais nous oblige à continuer nos recherches jusqu'à ce que nous soyons arrivés à l'évidence."

18 *Ibid.*, II, 272.

19 Aug. 13, 1833, Morse, I, 109.

20 J. Jackson, *Memoir of James Jackson, Jr.*, p. 129, quoting letter of Mar. 20, 1832.

21 Nov. 14, 1833, L.BK. 22.

22 Holmes's program can be compared with that of Jackson, *Memoir*, pp. 23-4.

23 *Works*, IX, 429-30; Henry Ingersoll Bowditch, *Brief Memories of Louis and Some of his Contemporaries*, (Boston, 1872), pp. 23-4.

24 Arturo Castiglioni, *A History of Medicine*, tr. and ed., E. B. Krumbhaar (New York, 1941), pp. 699-700.

25 J. Jackson, *Memoir*, p. 163.

26 Holmes, "Internal Pathology," pp. [1-6], Nov. 6, 1833; ms. notes on Andral's lectures, Nov. 6, 1833-[Mar. 26, 1834], H.C. These notes are in English.

27 *Ibid., passim.*

28 *Ibid.*, pp. [145-7], [Mar. 19, 21, 1835].

29 H. I. Bowditch, *Brief Memories of Louis*, p. 31.

30 "Internal Pathology," p. [91], Jan. 27, [1834].

31 Holmes, ["Medical Characters in Paris"], n.d., MS.BK., p. 6. This is apparently the ms. for a talk given before the Boston Society for Medical Improvement, Nov. 8, 1841, Records of BSMI, VI, 117, ms., BML.

32 Holmes, Notes on Marjolin's lectures, p. [31] [Dec. 10, 1833], ms., Nov. 14, [1833-March 22, 1834], HC. These notes are in English.

33 Arnold, *op. cit.*, p. 105. Warren describes Marjolin as gay, having a penchant for "camaraderie."

34 Notes on Marjolin, *passim.*

35 ["Medical Characters in Paris"], MS.BK., p. 9. Holmes did not save his notes on Biett's lectures, possibly because the dermatologist's major work was already available in English.

36 Mar. 6, 1834, L.BK. 28.

37 May 14, 1835, Morse, I, 151.

38 Dec. 13, 1833, *ibid.*, I, 122.

39 Dec. 29, 1833, *ibid.*, I, 125.

40 June 6, 1833, L.BK. 11.

41 Nov. 29, 1833, L.BK. 23.

42 Feb. 14, 1834, Morse, I, 127-30.

43 Apr. 13, 1834, L.BK. 29.

44 Arnold, *op. cit.*, pp. 173-4, quoting letter of Apr. 15, 1834.

45 Apr. 30, 1834, L.BK. 30.

46 R. W. Hooper, "Journals of visit to Holland in 1834 O. W. Holmes, Mason Warren & Self," ms. Diary 2, privately owned.

47 May 21, 1834, [from London], L.BK. 32, and Hooper, Diary 2, May 3, 1834.

48 May 21, 1834, L.BK. 32.

49 Hooper, Diary 2, May 4, 1834.

50 May 21, 1834, L.BK. 32.

51 May [late] 1834, L.BK. 31. (Although bound before the letter of May 21, this letter was clearly written later.)

52 Hooper, Diary 2, May 8, 1834.

53 June 7, 1834, L.BK. 33.

54 July 5, 1834, Morse, I, 136, where it is misdated July 25. The letter was started apparently on June 29th; the date, partly crossed out; and July 5th, written over it, L. Bk. 37.

55 Arnold, *op. cit.*, p. 177.

56 May 21, 1834, L.BK. 32.

57 June 13, 1834, Morse, I, 132.

58 May 21, and May [late] 1834, L.BK. 32, 31.

59 June 13, 1834, Morse, I, 133.

60 May 21, 1834, L.BK. 32, and J. Jackson, *Memoir,* p. 314-6.

61 Jane M. Oppenheimer gives the story of these manuscripts in her *New Aspects of John and William Hunter* (New York, 1946).

62 June 13, 1834, Morse, I, 133, and Arnold, *op. cit.*, p. 181.

63 June 21, 1834, Morse, I, 134. The same thought was expressed by Warren in a letter to his father, June 20, 1834, Warren papers, MHS.

64 V. Y. Bowditch, *op. cit.*, I, 62.

65 June 21, 1834, Morse, I, 134-5; see also *Works*, X, 5.

66 *Works*, X, 32-3.

67 July 14, 1834, L.BK. 36.

68 Hooper, Diary 2, July 13, 1834.

69 Aug. 13, 1834, L.BK. 38.

70 Sept. 3, 1834, Morse, I, 139.

71 Aug. 15 postscripts to Aug. 13, 1834, L.BK. 38.

72 Sept. 3-4, 1834, L.BK. 39.

73 *BET*, Dec. 11, 1839. See note 9, p. 400, for the letter to Emerson.

74 Sept. 19, 1834, L.BK. 40.

CHAPTER 8. *MEDICAL DISCIPLE*

1 La Société médicale d'observation, Cahier des signatures de présence, ms., Bibliothèque de l'École de medécine. As *étranger*, Holmes signed the book ten times between Dec. 7, 1833, and Sept. 6, 1834. As *membre titulaire,* he missed only three meetings from Sept. 20, 1834-July 18, 1835.

2 *Works*, I, 2, note a. "Select corps" is James Jackson, Jr.'s phrase; see *Memoir*, p. 137.

3 P. Ch. A. Louis, *Memoires de société médicale d'observation,* Paris, 1837, I, xii.

4 V. Y. Bowditch, *op. cit.*, I, 38, quoting letter of Jan. 27, 1833.

5 J. Jackson, *Memoir,* p. 137.

6 Louis, *op. cit.*, I, [xi]-x. The original reads: "*Frappés . . . de*

l'incertitude des connaissances médicales: persuadés que cette incertitude tient à la fois à une observation imparfaite des faits particuliers, et à la manière non moins imparfaite dont ceux-ci sont étudiés . . . une association qui aurait pour but de faire voir ces difficultés à ceux qui en feraient partie, de leur apprendre à les vaincre, de rendre observation vraiment utile en la rendant exacte et précise, puis de montrer comment on peut s'élever avec sécurité des faits particuliers aux faits généraux. . . ."

7. *Société médicale d'observation . . . règlements,* n.p., n.d., printed leaflet with ms. notes, HC.

8 Nov. 2, 1834, Morse, I, 145. R. W. Hooper, "Return to Paris for the winter of 1844-5," ms. Diary 4, privately owned. Holmes, as one of "our Boston group," probably went to a few of the parties Hooper notes. He and Holmes spent Christmas day together and made themselves "cozy" over their pipes. The Sunday dinner at the Trois Frères had become a tradition so that any breach of it had special notice in Hooper's diary.

9 J. Jackson, *Memoir,* p. 137, and V. Y. Bowditch, *op. cit.,* I, 47-48. The phrase is Jackson Jr.'s. Bowditch observed of the criticism: "generally the rod is applied with great severity and yet all is harmony," (Jackson, *Memoir,* p. 209).

10 Oct. 6, 1834, Morse, I, 142-3.

11 Holmes, "Marshall Hall," *BMSJ,* 56 (Mar. 12, 1857), 121-2.

12 Dec. 28, 1834, L.BK. 44.

13 Nov. 4, 1834, Jackson, *Memoir,* p. 316.

14 Jackson, *Memoir,* p. 80.

15 Holmes, "Aphorisms Louis Chomel," bound volume of ms. notes, (c.1835), entries in English. "Leçons de M. Chomel," Nov. [1833?], Mar. 1835, ms.; the Nov. notes are in English; those for Mar. are in French. Both volumes are in HC.

16 *Works,* IX, 42-8.

17 ["Medical Characters in Paris"] MS.BK., p. 5.

18 Holmes, "Leçons Cliniques de M. Velpeau," p. [54] July 6, 1835; ms. notes, Nov. 8, 1934-July 15, 1835, HC. The original reads:
"—Remarques sur la conduite de certaines personnes—qui s'appliquent à merveille à M. Bouillaud et dans lesquelles il fait des reflections assèz[sic] sévère sur ceux qui accusent leurs confrères de tuer leurs malades.—Du reste les idées de M. V. sur le puissances de la saignée . . ...s'accordent fort bien avec ceux de M. Louis."

19 *Ibid.,* pp. [6-11], Nov. 14, 1834; the ms. includes a drawing.

20 A.l., Mar. 22, 1835, J. M. Warren to his father, Warren papers, MHS. A letter of Jan. 4, 1835, speaks of the French surgeons as being behind the English and American.

21 ["Medical Characters in Paris"], MS.BK., p. 5.

22 *Ibid.,* p. 1.

23 Arnold, *op. cit.,* p. 93.

24 Holmes, "Leçons de M. Lisfranc," p. [1], Nov. 15, 1834; ms. notes, Nov. 15-Dec. 26, 1834, HC. The original reads "(*cette bêtise me semblable inconcevable—mais la voilà—*)"

25 Arnold, *op cit.,* p. 101.

26 ["Medical Characters in Paris"], MS.BK., p. 1.

27 *Ibid.,* p. 2; see also *Works,* IX, 428.

28 *Works,* IX, 428.

29 ["Medical Characters in Paris"], MS.BK., p. 6.

30 Holmes, "Leçons de M. Roux," p. [10], Jan. 7, [1835]; ms. notes, Jan. 5-Mar. 26, 1835, HC.

The original reads: " 'Subitement, (et quand je dis subitement, &c. &c.—) ((suit une parenthèse enorme et compliquée.—)) Subitement la peau devient bleuâtre &c &c.' "

31 ["Medical Characters in Paris"], MS.BK., p. 7. Holmes seems to have observed Civiale, Breschet (to whom he had a letter of introduction), and Trousseau but never to have attended them regularly. Trousseau he saw perform two unsuccessful tracheotomies, which, as a practitioner, he had reason to recall when he and his fellow-members of the Boston Society for Medical Improvement discussed "croup" (diphtheria), BSMI records, III, 144, BML.

32 May 14, 1835, Morse, I, 151-2.

33 ["Medical Characters in Paris"], MS.BK., p. 9.

34 Holmes was as pleased with this phrase as medical historians have been; he used it first in his review of James Jackson's *Letters to a Young Physician, BMSJ,* 53 (Oct. 4, 1855), 199.

35 *Works,* IX, 437.

36 ["Medical Characters in Paris"], MS.BK., pp. 7-9. Warren speaks of Ricord's willingness to talk to students and to discuss cases with them (a.l., Oct. 26, 1834, to his father, Warren papers, MHS.)

37 Hooper, Diary 4.

38 April 13, 1835, L.BK. 49; see also letter of Jan. 14, 1835, L.BK. 35.

39 Feb. 6, 1835, L.BK. 46, and April 13, 1835, L.BK. 49.

40 Mar. 6, 1835, L.BK. 47.

41 Jan. 14, 1835, L.BK. 45.

42 April 13, 1835, L.BK. 49.

43 There had been a further exchange of letters in the interval. Holmes was obviously torn between desire to stay and anxiety about his family. "I hope I have convinced you that I acted right in not quitting my studies abruptly on account of a desponding letter—I did what I thought my duty." May 14, 1835, L.BK. 52.

"You see I write cheerfully—it is self-defence. . . . Have I not done better than when I first found myself away from home—at Andover—when I refused to be comforted because I was so far away from my own fireside?" June 28, 1835, L.BK. 35.

44 July 4, 1835, L.BK. 59.

45 Aug. 16, 1835, [from Milan], Morse, I, 153-4.

46 Sept. 8, 12, 1835, [from Rome], *Ibid.,* I, 154-6.

47 Holmes, "Address before the Medical Library Association," *BMSJ,* 120 (Feb. 7, 1889), 129-30.

48 *Works,* IX, 87. John Williams is the quack referred to.

49 Holmes, *Acute Pericarditis* (Boston, 1937). (The ms. is in BML.)
50 College Records, VII, 414.
51 Ms. notice of admission, HC.

CHAPTER 9. *DOCTOR*

1 Nov. 2, 1834, Morse, I, 145-48.
2 *New England Magazine*, 5 (Oct. 1835), 305-6.
3 *Poems*, p. 331; *American Monthly Magazine*, 1 (Feb. 1836), 185.
4 *Poems*, p. 15; *American Monthly Magazine*, 1 (Apr. 1835), 372.
5 May 11, 1836, Morse, II, 269-72.
6 *Poems*, p. 3. The Phi Beta Kappa poem was given Sept. 1. Cornelius Felton, in the society's records (HUa), labelled it "brilliant." The centennial song, Sept. 8, is in *Poems*, p. 30.
7 *Poems*, pp. 15, 24-25.
8 R. W. Emerson, *Letters*, ed., R. L. Rusk (New York, 1939), II, 39.
9 *North American Review*, 44 (Jan. 1837), 27.
10 A.l., Jan. 24, 1836 [*sic*, the surcharge is 1837], to Lydia Huntley Sigourney, Connecticut Historical Society. The poem referred to is "The Only Daughter," which appeared in *The Token* for 1837, see *Poems*, p. 32.
11 A.l., Mar. 23, 1844, to Sarah J. Hale, Henry E. Huntington Library.
12 March 17, 1838, Morse, I, 272-3.
13 Holmes, *At Dartmouth*, with introduction by E. M. Tilton, (New York, 1940), p. 18 and n. 53.
14 *Library of Practical Medicine* (Boston, 1836), Vol. VII. Holmes's essay appears at pp. [189]-288. Holmes was announced as the prize-winner in *BMSJ*, 15 (Aug. 24, 1836), 50.
Dr. Shattuck himself sent a copy of the volume to Holmes's father, whose old-fashioned note of thanks is dated Oct. 25 (Shattuck papers, MHS). The volume, then, came out before Holmes's *Poems* (preface, Nov. 1), but the two books were near enough together to put Holmes's name almost simultaneously before two different audiences.
15 A.l., n.d., Jacob Bigelow, and A.l., Sept. 3, John Collins Warren, Boston Dispensary.
16 *The Boston Almanac for the year 1838*, (Boston, [1837]), p. 92. He was "not required to attend the intemperate or vicious."
17 *Works*, IX, 203.
18 Oct. 16, 1837, *History of the Boston Dispensary*, (Boston, 1859), pp. 138-141.
19 MMS, *Medical Communications*, Vol. V, Appendix, p. 123. The committee of 1834 reported its failure in Feb. 1836.
20 Holmes *Boylston Prize Dissertations for the Years 1836-7*, (Boston, 1838), p. 17. The letters to Holmes on the subject are in HC.
21 *Ibid.*, p. viii.
22 *Ibid.*, p. 132.

23 *Ibid.*, p. 10, and Abiel Holmes, *An Address Delivered Before the American Antiquarian Society*, (Boston, 1814), p. 14. O. W. Holmes used lines from the description of Satan's journey through chaos; his father used a passage from the description of the fallen angels' exploration of Hell.

24 *Boylston Prize Dissertations*, p. viii.

25 *BMSJ*, 16 (May 24, 1837), 258.

26 *Ibid.*, 17 (Aug. 23, 1837), 258.

27 *Ibid.*, 17 (Jan. 31, 1838), 417.

28 *AJMS*, 22 (May 1838), 163-5.

29 Erwin H. Ackerknecht, *Malaria in the Upper Mississippi Valley*, Supplement to the *Bulletin of the History of Medicine*, No. 4 (Baltimore, 1945), p. 55.

30 McKenzie, *op. cit.*, p. 214. Abiel Holmes died June 4.

31 William R. Thayer, ed., "Journal of Benjamin Waterhouse," *Publications of the Cambridge Historical Society*, IV, 1909, 20-30.

32 A.l., Feb. 21, 1838, to the Reverend William Jenks, Berg Collection, NYPL.

33 A.l., April 9, 1838, to Jenks, American Autograph Shop, Catalogue for July, 1938, p. 258.

34 See announcements of the Tremont Medical School in *BMSJ*, *passim*, and the catalogues (HUm).

35 BMSI Records, Vol. II ff., ms., BML.

36 BMSI Records, III, 16, Dec. 12, 1836.

37 *Ibid.*, III, 72, Dec. 25, 1837.

38 *Ibid.*, III, 257-8, Nov. 11, 1839.

39 *Ibid.*, III, 25, Feb. 13, 1837.

40 *Ibid.*, III, 82, Feb. 7, 1838. Holmes's reports are at pp. 74-173 of this volume. His poem is described in *BMSJ*, 18 (Feb. 21, 1838), 50, as being "conceived in a spirit of playful satire." The poem was written at the last minute obviously; see his letter to Barnes, Feb. 3, 1838, Morse I, 168.

41 A.l., Apr. 3, 1837, HC (intermittent fever file).

42 A.l., Feb. 8, 1837, HC (intermittent fever file).

43 The whole poem has apparently never been printed; the facetious lines restored in the appendix of *Poems* (p. 338) are not complete. Thomas Wentworth Higginson gives as part of the poem the verses:

"One hundred Marys and that only one
        Whose smile awaits me when my task is done."

Higginson identifies the Mary as Mary Benjamin, but by September 1836, she was probably already engaged to John Lothrop Motley, whom she married in March 1837. [Higginson and H. W. Boynton, *A Reader's History of American Literature* (Boston, 1903), pp. 105-6.]

44 Feb. 3, 1838, Morse, I, 168-9.

45 Henry and Mary Lee, *Letters and Journals . . . 1802-1860*, ed., F. R. Morse, (Boston, 1926), pp. 269-270.

46 Holmes, *At Dartmouth*, p. 6 and nn. 7 and 8.

47 *Ibid.*, pp. 6-7 and n. 10.

48 *Ibid.*, pp. 10-11, and nn. 25-31.

49 *Ibid.*, p. 11 and nn. 32-34. The text of Jackson's letter was misread; the reading here is correct.

50 *Ibid.*, pp. 11-12 and n. 35.

51 *Ibid.*, p. 12 and n. 37.

52 *Ibid.*, p. 15 and n. 47.

53 *Ibid.*, pp. 1-2.

54 *Ibid.*, pp. 16-17.

55 *Ibid.*, p. 24.

56 *Ibid.*, p. 14, where it is incorrectly stated that no part of the poem had ever been printed.

CHAPTER 10. *MEDICAL REFORMER*

1 Holmes, "Hanover—1st Introductory—Aug. 1839," ms., HC.

2 Holmes, Review of the first American edition of John Elliotson's *Principles and Practices of Medicine, BMSJ,* 29 (Dec. 13, 1843), 375-6. He included in his censure the American editor of this volume only as he included himself; the editor, after all, was his old friend, Stewardson.

3 A.ll., Jan. 15, 17, Apr. 21, Jan. 14, 1837, HC (intermittent fever file).

4 *Works,* XIV, 134, 302. The allusion (301-2) to the lawyer who turned Emerson over to his daughters is probably an allusion to Judge Charles Jackson, one of whose daughters married Holmes.

Holmes owned the Divinity School Address and *The American Scholar* (Holmes Library, LC), but he may not have bought them at the time.

In 1838, Holmes confessed to James Freeman Clarke (Morse, II, 275): "No graduate of Harvard—or at least very few—had ever read less at my age than myself. . . . Now for the first time in my life I find the true desire for knowledge growing up in my mind."

5 Public Notice, *BET,* Dec. 7, 1837, announces a lecture for that evening. Holmes's "Index-Memoranda" (ms., HC), lists "Cities—Boston Lyceum" on inner front cover in a list made about 1848. The black notebook, p. 109, has an entry: "From my old Lecture on Cities," and briefly notes two anecdotes used.

6 Public Notice, *BET,* Dec. 19, 1837, (also listed in "Index-Memoranda") and *Baltimore Sun,* Dec. 28, 1841. *BET,* Dec. 6, 1838, indicates that Holmes repeated this lecture for the Boston Lyceum. The black notebook, p. 108, notes that Holmes lectured 8 times in 1838, probably giving this same lecture or alternating it with "Cities."

7 *BET,* report of Lowell Institute Lecture on Tennyson and Browning, April 20, 1853. See S. I. Hayakawa, "Holmes's Lowell Institute Lectures," *American Literature,* 8 (Nov. 1936), 288.

8 Holmes, Tribute to Metcalf, MS.BK., p. 707.

9 June 8, 1840, King's Chapel Archives.

10 Claire McGlinchee, *The First Decade of the Boston Museum,*

(Boston, 1940), p. 12. The house was torn down after the Holmes family moved in 1857; the street is now called Bosworth Street, connecting Tremont and Province Streets, between School and Bromfield. Central Court, where Holmes boarded, no longer exists.

11 A.l., Sept. 15, 1842, Waldo Higginson to Henry Lee, Jr., privately owned.

12 A.l., Dec. 23, 1842, Higginson to Lee, privately owned.

13 A.l. July 28, 1842, Catherine Cabot to Lee, privately owned.

14 Mar. 9, 1841, to Mrs. Charles Wentworth Upham, HUh. (Part of the letter is in Morse, I, 322.)

15 Two ms. Pencil scraps in Dr. Holmes's hand in a Scrapbook compiled by O. W. Holmes, Jr. (c. 1862), HC.

16 Holmes, Casebook II, p. 125. There are four casebooks as follows: I Records of cases, June 11, 1838-Dec. 28, 1842, with index, five pp. of non-medical notes, and five pp. of notes on personal health for Nov. 29, 1842-Oct. 24, 1845. II Records of cases, Jan. 3, 1843-Mar. 15, 1844, with index and 1 p. of notes on expenses. III Records of cases, Jan. 1, 1844-Jan. 13, 1846, with index. IV Records of cases [Jan.] 1846-Dec. 29, 1848. The active record stops in March 1847; the few entries thereafter are of cases seen in consultation. HC.

A few entries from these casebooks are printed by Dr. Clement L. Poston in his privately printed *Dr. Oliver Wendell Holmes. Some Unpublished Medical Case Records*, n.p., n.d.

17 A.l., Oct. 29, 1843, privately owned.

18 Casebooks, I-IV, *passim*.

19 Given Dec. 9, 1839 for Franklin Institute Series, reported *BET*, Dec. 11, 1839. Listed in "Index-Memoranda." The black notebook, p. 108, notes 10 lectures for 1839. A broadside of Jan. 20, 1840, announces Holmes as one of the volunteer lecturers in a series to be given in Cambridge to raise money for a Lyceum Hall; he probably gave this lecture.

20 Given Dec. 10, 1840, for the Boston Lyceum, reported *Boston Courier*, Dec. 12, 1840. Black notebook, p. 108, notes 8 lectures for 1840.

This lecture was repeated on Dec. 23 for the Warren Street Chapel series.

BET, Dec. 11, has a report of the lecture, too, but that in the *Courier* is fuller. Hereafter the references to newspaper reports of Holmes's lectures will be made to the one which is the most complete; if of two reports, one has a full report; and the other, apparent fidelity to the speaker's language, both will be referred to.

21 The first survives in ms., MS.BK., pp. 77-125. The published essay is collected in *Works*, IX, 1-102. The newspaper announcements appear in several newspapers in several issues. An error in *BET*, Oct. 13, 1841, corrected in the *Atlas*, Oct. 14, lists these three as for the Boston Lyceum. His lectures for the Lyceum, Oct. 14, 21, 28, 1841, were on the subject "The Physical History of Mankind"; no reports of these lectures have been found. In "Index-Memoranda" occurs the entry:

"Races: Last of 3 at Boston Lyceum," possibly one of this series, although there is evidence that Holmes lectured on this subject in 1849 and again in 1850. Except that he was handsomely (for the times) paid for these lectures, $90 for the three of them (a.l., June 21, 1841, J. T. Bigelow to Holmes, HC), no further facts have emerged; for that reason, this series has not been mentioned in the text. It is to be observed, however, that the subject for this series is, as it is for others in the period, scientific.

22 *Boston Post,* April 12, 1842.

23 *Works,* IX, 17.

24 *Ibid.,* IX, 22.

25 *Ibid.,* IX, 33.

26 *Ibid.,* IX, 70-71.

27 *Ibid.,* IX, 76-77.

28 Robert Wesselhoeft, *Some Remarks on Dr. O. W. Holmes's Lectures on Homeopathy and Its Kindred Delusions* (Boston, 1842). The first two attacks were those of A. H. Okie, and Charles Neidhard upon which *BMSJ,* 26 (Aug. 3, 1842), 417, commented: "Poor Dr. Holmes, thus far, is between two fires—but there is hope for him yet, if the besiegers give him nothing but homeopathic doses."

29 *Quarto Boston Notion,* Feb. 19, 1842, p. 315

30 *BMSJ,* 26 (Apr. 27, 1842), 191.

31 BSMI Record, III, 268, Feb. 6, 1840.

32 *Ibid.,* IV, 117, Nov. 8, 1841. The manuscript for part of this talk has been quoted in Chapters 7 and 8; it appears in MS.BK pp. 1-9. That the ms. is of this date is indicated by the allusions to the deaths of Biett (1840) and Alibert (1837).

33 BSMI Records, IV, 28, Jan. 25, 1841.

34 A.l., June 28, 1843, Harriet Jackson Lee to Henry Lee, Jr., privately owned.

35 BSMI Records, IV, 167-8, June 27, 1842.

36 *Ibid.,* IV, 205.

37 *Ibid.,* IV, 190. Fisher's report is quoted by Dr. Henry R. Viets in "A Mind Prepared," *Bulletin of the Medical Library Association,* 31 (Oct. 1943), 322-3. Laid in Holmes's medical casebook II are mss. (3 folio pp.) tabulating twenty-nine "Cases of Dissection Wounds," of which twelve were fatal. The handwriting and their being in his casebook for 1843-44 puts the mss. about this time. The tables are set up à la Louis, but Holmes apparently never did anything further with this material.

38 *Quarterly Summary of the Transactions of the College of Physicians of Philadelphia,* 1 (May, June, July, 1842), 50-61.

39 Charles D. Meigs, *Medical Examiner* (Philadelphia), 6 (Jan. 21, 1843), 3.

40 BAT Records, Dec. 12, 1842.

41 Casebook II, pp. 11-12, Jan. 9, 1843.

42 BSMI Records, IV, 217, 218. See Viets, *op cit.,* p. 324.

43 BSMI Records, IV, 221.

44 BAT Records, Jan. 30-Feb. 8, 1843.

45 *Works*, IX, xvi.

46 BSMI Records, IV, 223, Feb. 13, 1843.

47 *Works*, IX, 128-9.

48 *Ibid.*, IX, 167.

49. *Ibid.*, IX, 169.

50 Holmes refers to these authors in his essay. See also Claude Edwin Heaton, "Control of Puerperal Infection in the United States," *American Journal of Obstetrics and Gynecology*, 46 (Oct. 1943), 479-486.

51 *AJMS*, 6, n.s. (July, 1843), 260-2.

52 *Ibid.*, 11, n.s. (Jan. 1846) 45-63. Kneeland subsequently became Holmes's demonstrator at the Harvard Medical School.

53 Holmes ["Medical Statistics"], pp. [6-7] ms., n.d., HC. BSMI Records, v. 184, May 11, 1846. Pp. 1041-1052 of MS. BK. are also on the subject of medical statistics; probably the two mss. belong together.

Holmes showed his feelings, however, in indirect ways; in his review of Stewardson's edition of Elliotson (see n. 2, p. 407) he could not resist an allusion to Philadelphia's ignorance of Boston productions. Stewardson had failed to mention Dr. John Ware's classic essay on *Delirium Tremens* (1832); Holmes remarked that the essay could have been had via Europe "if the scientific highways between Boston and Philadelphia are impassable."

54 BSMI Records, V, 329, Mar. 11, 1844.

55 *BSMJ*, 40 (May 9, 1849), 274-5.

56 Meigs, *Obstetrics* (2nd ed., Philadelphia, 1852), p. 631. The same passage is repeated in subsequent editions. In the first edition (1849, p. 567) Meigs expresses the opinion that Asiatic cholera, measles, and scarlatina (scarlet fever) are *not* contagious.

57 Meigs, *On the Nature . . . of Childbed Fevers* (Philadelphia, 1854), Letter IV, p. 113. The whole letter (pp. 85-114) was directed against Holmes, but Meigs carefully refrained from mentioning Holmes's name any more than he had to and never gave the title of the essay; he apparently did not want to give the "sophomore writer" any more advertising than he could help.

58 A.l., Dec. 3, 1852, Bartlett to Holmes, HC.

59 *Works*, IX, 106.

60 *Ibid.*, IX, 126-7.

61 *Ibid.*, IX, 127-8.

62 *AJMS*, 29, n.s. (Apr. 1855), 459-62.

63 *BMSJ*, 54 (Feb. 28, 1856), 81. Channing's article is in *BMSJ*, 52 (May 17, 1855), 293-9.

64 AMA, *Transactions*, IX, 1856, 372.

65 *BMSJ*, 55 (Jan. 15, 1857), 490.

CHAPTER 11. *OCCASIONAL POET*

1 A.l., May 24, 1843, Joseph Lovering to Holmes, HC.

2 *Poems,* p. 54.

3 *Ibid.,* p. 57. The immediately preceding lines contain a specific allusion to Emerson's "Sphinx." Holmes's poem was printed in *Graham's Magazine* (24, Jan. 1844, 10-11) under the title, "Terpsichore." The letter to Rufus Griswold (Sept. 1, 1843), in which he offered the poem for publication, recognized the likelihood of criticism: "Are you afraid of a hint of repudiation in it?" he asked. (*Correspondence and Other Papers of Rufus Griswold* (Cambridge, 1898), p. 146.)

4 A.l., Jan. 18, 1846, L.BK. 62.

5 *Poems,* p. 38.

6 R. W. Emerson, *Journals* (Boston, 1912), X, 218. The entry is put under the date 1867, but Grattan died in 1864. He was, however, consul in 1842, when Dickens made his first visit to America.

7 *Poems,* pp. 42, 43.

8 *Ibid.,* pp. 49-50.

9 *Ibid.,* p. 52.

10 Nov. 29, 1846, Morse, I, 295.

11 *Ibid.,* I, 296. See the younger Holmes's *Speeches* (Boston, 1934), p. 63. The observations there on dueling can be found in the elder Holmes's writing, too; see *Works* I, 259-60, a passage which modifies what Dr. Holmes had said in the second of two lectures on "The Americanized European," reported in the *Cambridge Chronicle,* Nov. 11, 1854.

12 Morse, I, 297-99.

13 A.l., Mar. 14, 1847, printed in catalogue of Thomas Madigan, Inc., 1939, p. 16, where it is incorrectly described as being addressed to E. E. Hale.

14 A.l., May 20, 1845, privately owned.

15 John Lothrop Motley, *Correspondence,* ed., George W. Curtis (London, 1889), II, 362, letter of Jan. 26, 1873.

16 Holmes, "The Positions and Prospects of the Medical Student," Jan. 12, 1844, *Currents and Counter-Currents in Medical Science* (Boston, 1861), p. 315.

17 *Ibid.,* p. 320.

18 *BET,* Feb. 9, 1846.

19 Henry Jacob Bigelow, *Surgical Anaesthesia and Other Papers* (Boston, 1900), p. 203; and (R. M. Hodges) *A Memoir of Henry Jacob Bigelow* (Boston, 1894), pp. 201-6.

Bigelow had studied under Holmes both at the Tremont School and at Dartmouth; he had, while in Europe, helped Holmes by checking for him the stand of the French physicians on homeopathy and by collecting printed material. His interests were in some ways like those of Holmes. He was something of a wit; he loved mechanical contrivances; and his curiosity was eclectic.

20 Edward Warren, *Some Account of the Letheon* (2nd ed., Boston, 1847), p. 79. This is the first application of these terms to ether surgery. The editors of the Oxford English Dictionary credit Holmes with proposing the terms, but do so second-hand, for the pamphlet is now extremely rare. The letter does not appear in the first edition. Bigelow's use of the terms in his articles on ether surgery probably served to fix them in the language.

Holmes's use of the word is not, however, the first application of the term to signify insensibility to pain in surgery. See John B. Quistorp, *De Anaesthesia* (Rostock, 1718), and John Elliotson, Harveian Oration, June 27, 1846. The latter, Holmes may have seen.

21 Jan. 30, 1849, United States House of Representatives, Report No. 114, Feb. 28, 1849, pp. 97-8.

22 A.l., Dec. 7, 1857, Holmes to R. H. Dana, Dana papers, MHS.

23 *BMSJ*, 36 (Apr. 7, 1847), 206.

24 A.l., Apr. 9, 1847, Edward Everett to Holmes, HC. Holmes's letter of acceptance, April 18, 1847, is in College Papers, Second Series, XIV, 324, ms., HUa.

25 A.l., Apr. 29, 1847, to Everett, *ibid.*, XIV, 331.

CHAPTER 12. *DEAN OF THE MEDICAL SCHOOL*

1 Thomas Francis Harrington, *The Harvard Medical School*, ed. by J. G. Mumford, (Boston, 1905), II, 511-16. And College Records, Vols. VIII and IX, *passim*.

2 College Records, IX, 118-121.

3 A.l., Dec. 11, 1847, Holmes to Everett, College Papers, 2d.s., XV, 239. Miss Hunt's letter, written at Holmes's suggestion, appears at p. 240. Everett's answer (College Letters, Everett, I, 416, HUa), observes that the overseers have a decided feeling "against the promiscuous attendance of the Sexes on the anatomical lectures."

4 "Introductory—Sept. 26th 1879," MS.BK., p. 181.

5 A.l., Nov. 15, 1847, L.BK. 87. The letter does not indicate which Channing is referred to; Holmes's classmate, Henry Channing, may be meant.

6 Holmes, *An Introductory Lecture*, Nov. 3, 1847, (Boston, 1847).

7 Holmes, *Report of the Committee on Medical Literature*, offprint from AMA *Transactions*, Vol. I (1848), pp. 39, 8.

8 *An Introductory Lecture*, p. 33.

9 J. B. S. Jackson, *A Descriptive Catalogue of the Warren Anatomical Museum* (Boston, 1870), *passim*. At p. iv, Jackson records: "Prof. O. W. Holmes has made a great many valuable preparations to illustrate his department of healthy anatomy; and has also, independently of the Museum, a large number of microscopical preparations either made by himself or obtained by correspondence. . . ."

10 Holmes, "The Medical School," *The Harvard Book*, I, 247.

11 *Works*, IX, 210, 425-6.

12 *Poems*, pp. 101-2.

13 A.l., Feb. 19, 1874, to Winslow Lewis, HUh.

14 *BMSJ*, 131 (Oct. 11, Dec. 13, 1894), 375-80, 580-90; and Thomas Dwight, "Reminiscences of Dr. Holmes," *Scribner's Magazine*, 17 (Jan. 1895), 121.

A student's sketchy notes (undated and unsigned ms. HUm), contain a note on Holmes's lecture on the cranium which suggests that he rode his hobbies in the classroom as well as in his books. The note reads "annihilation of phrenologists."

15 James Clarke White, *Sketches from my Life* (Cambridge, 1913), p. 61, diary entry for Sept. 1853.

16 *Ibid.*, p. 66.

17 *BMSJ.*, 131 (Dec. 13, 1894), 585.

18 Hjalmar O. Lokensgard, "Holmes Quizzes the Professors," *American Literature*, 13 (May, 1941), 158-162. The original ms. is in the Oliver Wendell Holmes Library, Phillips Academy, Andover.

Mr. Lokensgard does not attempt to date the poem, suggesting that it may have been written when Holmes was Dean (1847-53), or when he came up for his examination (1836). The internal evidence, however, is plain. The poem must have been written in 1858-9, probably, considering the subject, for the monthly levee just before the examinations—in Feb. 1859, that is.

The allusions to the stylish professor of surgery and the zealous curator of the museum date the poem as after the appointments of Bigelow (1849) and Jackson (1848); the obstetrical dean, then, must be Storer who held the office from 1855-1864. The poem also refers to *two* professors who dispense pills; the two are George Cheyne Shattuck and Edward Hamilton Clarke, professors of clinical medicine and materia medica, respectively. There is no allusion to a professor of theory and practice so that the poem must have been written after John Ware's retirement and before Henry I. Bowditch's appointment, during the 1858-9 term when the chair of theory and practice was vacant.

19 This criticism of the caliber of the students is a commonplace of the period; see the annual reports of the Committee on Medical Education in AMA, *Transactions*. See also White, *op. cit.*, pp. 53-4, 60.

White remarks, however, that "the character of the instruction at the Tremont School was excellent." In 1869 White was the leader of the reform movement within the Harvard Faculty; his evaluation of the Tremont School, which was run by men *opposed* to reform, cannot be said to be prejudiced in their favor.

20 A.l., June 12, 1851, Ware to Holmes, HC.

21 See, for instance AMA, *Transactions*, II (1849), 353, where appears a letter from Harvard's delegates (Jacob Bigelow, John Ware, and Holmes), dissenting from the report of the Committee on Medical Education (the report is at p. 257).

22 Harrington, *op cit.*, II, 640. *The Trial of Prof. John W. Webster*

(Boston, 1850), is the chief source of information here. Holmes's testimony appears at pp. 15 and 40.

23 Harvard College Papers, 2d.s., XVII, 146. Holmes's letter to Sparks (Dec. 12, 1849), notes carefully: "It is, of course, understood that only a temporary substitute is wished for in the emergency." J. P. Cooke received the permanent appointment after Webster's conviction.

24 Harrington, *op. cit.*, II, 640.

25 John Forster, *The Life of Dickens* (Boston, n.d.), III, 368-9, and Edward Payne, *Dickens's Days in Boston* (Boston, 1927), p. 211.

26 Bliss Perry, *And Gladly Teach* (Boston, 1935), p. 14.

CHAPTER 13. *LYCEUM LECTURER*

1 A.l., Jan. 1, 1849, to patient.

2 *BMSJ*, 128 (Apr. 6, 1892), 352.

3 "Lectures and Lecturing," *Cambridge Chronicle*, Dec. 18, 1852 (see Chap. 10, n. 20, p. 408); *Portland Transcript*, Mar. 27, 1852. At the end of the notes (pp. 438-441) appears Holmes's itinerary for the season of 1851-2, representative for this whole period. With this is a chronological list of all recorded Holmes lectures with the source of the fullest report found for each.

4 Holmes, Schedule of lectures, 1851-2, 1852-3, 1853-4, MS.BK., pp. 1055-57; *Old Farmer's Almanac*, 1852, and *Brown's Almanac* for 1855, both with ms. notes by Holmes, HC. Other sources are the newspapers and letters.

5 *Works*, I, 43-44; XIV, 290-292.

6 *Ibid.*, I, 142. For this passage Holmes is borrowing from his lecture, see n. 3.

7 Haweis, *op. cit.*, I, 32-33.

8 "Lectures and Lecturing," *Cambridge Chronicle*.

9 *Lawrence Courier*, Jan. 17, 1852.

10 "Lectures and Lecturing," *Cambridge Chronicle*.

11 *Cincinnati Daily Enquirer*, Sept. 4, 1855.

12 *The Correspondence of Thomas Carlyle and Ralph Waldo Emerson* (Boston, 1883), I, 345.

13 Emerson, *Journals*, VIII, 424.

14 Schedule of lectures and *Old Farmer's Almanac*.

15 "Love of Nature," *Cambridge Chronicle*, Jan. 24, 1852. The passage sketched an institution for the training of those deficient in an appreciation of nature. Holmes used the same basic notion again for a different purpose in his "A Visit to the Asylum for Aged and Decayed Punsters." *AM*, 7 (Jan. 1861), 113-117.

16 The *Boston Journal*, Feb. 26, 1852, briefly reporting the lecture, as it was given before the Boston Mercantile Library Association (Feb. 25), notes Holmes's allusion to the fact that he had given the same lecture four years earlier for the same organization. The best report is that of the *Boston Post*, Dec. 9, 1848.

17 *Louisville Daily Courier,* Sept. 13, 1855.

18 The first and third quotations are from the report in the *Commonwealth,* Jan. 1, 1852; the second is from the *Cambridge Chronicle.*

19 Both these lectures were popular ones; the reports of the first have been noted. For the second, see *Cambridge Chronicle,* Dec. 10, 1853, and *New York Herald,* Dec. 2, 1853. Note also *Works,* I, 140-142.

20 "Lectures and Lecturing," *Portland Transcript.*

21 *Old Farmer's Almanac,* ms. entries for Jan. 1, Feb. 2, and Mar. 1, 1852.

22 A.l., June 8, 1851, Huntington Library. Holmes has in mind a review of his poem, "Astrea." See Chap. 14, p. 222, and notes.

23 *Portland Transcript,* Mar. 27, 1852; *Albany Evening Journal,* Nov. 25, Dec. 2, 1854.

24 *Louisville Daily Courier,* Sept. 10, 1855.

25 *Ibid.,* Sept. 13, 1855.

26 "Lectures and Lecturing," *Cambridge Chronicle.*

27 *Ibid., Portland Transcript.*

28 *Works,* I, 138-9.

29 The schedule of lectures is not clear; the letter A, B, or C appears before the name of each town. The symbol obviously does not refer to the fee he received (this can be checked against data in the almanacs). I have assumed that the lettering may refer to different versions.

30 Casebook I, pp. (125-130).

31 See Chap. 10, n. 4, p. 407. In the Holmes Library (LC), there is a volume of Byron presented to Holmes by Park Benjamin in 1933 (going-away present apparently). An 1835 edition of Coleridge's works has Amelia Lee Jackson's name in it and the date June 1840, apparently a wedding present. Editions of Keats (1847), Shelley (1852), and Scott (1845) all carry a note in Justice Holmes's hand indicating that they were among "the few books of poetry" in his father's library. The note in the Shelley reads: "One of the few books of poetry which my father had when I was a boy. He bought it I think for his Lowell lectures. . . ." There is also an 1849 edition of Wordsworth. Holmes apparently acquired a Spenser on his own account; there is an 1839 edition in the library. See a.l., Aug. 25, 1852, to Folsom, BPL, cited here p. 212.

This is perhaps the place to remark that Dr. Holmes did not mark books; he occasionally made a neat typographical correction or noted on the rear end-paper a page reference or two. The only books with extensive markings by Dr. Holmes are an 1833 edition (10 vols.) of Boswell's Johnson (LC) and the first edition of Cotton Mather's *Magnalia.* The *Magnalia* had already been well marked by Abiel Holmes; Dr. Holmes has added a page of pencil notes at the end. The volume is now owned by Edward Jackson Holmes.

32 A.l., Apr. 9, 1851, To Hawthorne, Berg Collection, NYPL.

33 "Wordsworth," *Louisville Daily Courier,* Sept. 13, 1855. For his Louisville audience, Holmes prepared a special introduction explaining the origin of the lectures.

On Jan. 5, 1853, Holmes gave a special lecture for the American Academy of Arts and Sciences. His subject was "The Relations between Science and Poetry"; regrettably, no report of the lecture has been found. He repeated the speech, as a Phi Beta Kappa address, at Dartmouth, July 28, 1858, when at the last minute he had to substitute for Rufus Choate.

34 *Saturday Evening Gazette,* Mar. 26, 1853.

35 *BET,* Mar. 23, 1853.

36 *Commonwealth,* Mar. 25, 1853. The reporter for the *Commonwealth* was apparently Julia Ward Howe, who with her husband, Samuel Gridley Howe, edited the paper, founded by them as an antislavery paper. In 1854, moved by some agreeable birthday verses addressed by Dr. Holmes to her as "O Minstrel Wild," Mrs. Howe confessed in a poem, "A Vision of Montgomery Place": "I was the saucy *Commonwealth.* . . . " Laura E. Richards and Maude Howe Elliott, *Julia Ward Howe* (Boston, 1916), I, 142.

37 *Ibid.,* Mar. 30, 1853.

38 He was thankful that he never thought of printing them, as he told Edmund Gosse when he received the latter's edition of lectures given on the same subject for the same group. The letter, Oct. 29, 1885, privately owned, reads:

"But what were they? Written in haste—going from hand to mouth . . . from hasty thought to hurried page and then to immediate delivery. They were the skimming of my instinctive judgments—nothing more,— no scholarship, no long maturing thought, but after all I suspect they had the cream of what I might have to say if I had taken more time about them. . . ."

39 *BET,* May 2, 1853. See Hayakawa, "Holmes's Lowell Institute Lectures," p. 289.

40 *New York Evening Post,* Nov. 19, 1853. The much quoted jest, of which this is the first record, appears in a slightly different version in the *Louisville Daily Courier,* Sept. 19, 1855.

The passage is a good example of the bad taste Holmes, who must have known better, shows in these lectures.

41. In the lecture on Scott and Macaulay, Mar. 29, 1853, repeated in New York, Nov. 25. The New York papers, *Post,* Nov. 26, and *Tribune,* Nov. 28, have the fullest reports. For Holmes on Carlyle, see *Works,* III, 255-6; X, 136-7; and XIV, *passim.*

42 *Commonwealth,* Apr. 1, 1853. Holmes's analogies between physical constitution and character gave particular offense. The *Transcript* and *Traveller* (Mar. 30, 1853) approved his strictures.

43 *Commonwealth,* Apr. 20, 1853; *BET,* Apr. 16.

44 *New York Evening Post,* Nov. 5, 1853.

45 *New York Herald,* Oct. 30, 1853.

46 *Boston Evening Traveller,* Apr. 6, 1853.

47. *New York Tribune,* Nov. 19, 1853. The *Commonwealth* (Apr. 12) thought Holmes spoke of Keats with "more admiration than dis-

crimination"; the *Traveller* (Apr. 11), that "Dr. Holmes ranked Keats too high."

48 A.l., Nov. 20, 1853, J. L. Motley to Holmes, HC.

CHAPTER 14. *SUMMER RESIDENT*

1 A.l., June 21, 1851, Dr. John Ware to Holmes, HC.

2 A.l., Aug. 23, 1854, to Isaac Morse, privately owned.

3 Luther Stearns Mansfield, "Glimpses of Herman Melville's Life in Pittsfield," *American Literature*, 9 (Mar. 1937), 29, quoting letter of Aug. 6, 1850, Evart Duyckinck to his wife; Hawthorne, *American Note-books*, ed., Randall Stewart (New Haven, 1932), p. 131.

4 [Cornelius Matthews] "Several Days in the Berkshires," II, *Literary World*, 7 (Aug. 31, 1850), 166. Matthews disguises all his characters: James T. Fields as "Mr. Greenfield," Hawthorne as "Noble Melancholy," Duyckinck as "Silver Pen," and Melville as "New Neptune."

5 Mansfield, *op cit.*, p. 30.

6 [Matthews], *op cit.*, p. 166.

7 Mansfield, p. 30.

8 [Matthews], p. 166.

9 Mansfield, p. 30.

10 [Matthews], p. 166.

11 [Matthews?], Review of *Astrea*, *Literary World*, 7 (Oct. 26, 1850), 330-1. The passage which offended the reviewer is banished to the appendix of Holmes's *Poems*, p. 336-7; "The Moral Bully" appears at p. 87.

12 Nov. 9, 1850, Holmes to Duyckinck, *Bulletin of the New York Public Library*, 4 (Nov. 1900), 357.

13 A.l., Apr. 9, 1851, Berg Collection, NYPL.

14 A.l., Aug. 5, 1853, privately owned. Whipple had apparently suggested that Holmes lecture in Cincinnati, but the doctor pointed out that the dates conflicted with his medical lectures; two years later he accepted an invitation to lecture in Ohio, the series being scheduled for September.

15 He had a pair of lectures on this subject, but the second was given only once, in Cambridge, Nov. 8, 1854, reported in the *Chronicle* of Nov. 11. The first lecture of that title was apparently popular; he gave it fifty-two times in one season. It survives in manuscript (MS.BK., pp. 13-75). The essay of the same title in *AM*, 35, Jan. 1875, 75-86), resembles the lecture only in its general subject.

16 "Literary Tribunals," *Boston Journal*, Feb. 16, 1854. This lecture was later called "Critics and Criticism"; *BET*, Feb. 16, 1854, gives the title "The Literary Ordeal."

17 Holmes, notes for poem, "Agnes," with a few for this address, ms. fragment, HC. Holmes owned the Seventh of March speech, Holmes Library, LC.

18 A.l., July 13, 1855, Morse to Holmes, HC.

19 *Louisville Daily Courier,* Sept. 8, 1855.

20 A.l., April 1, 1856, to Parker, L.BK. 76.

21 See *Exeter* [N.H.] *News Letter,* Mar. 3, 10, 17, 1856. The last prints a letter of Mar. 13 by Holmes. Holmes's "Ode for Washington's Birthday" (1856, *Poems,* p. 98), written for The Boston Mercantile Library Association, also provoked unfavorable comment, comment that would probably never have been made if the New England Society address had not already had its prejudicial effect. One stanza, paraphrasing Washington's *Farewell Address,* read in its original version:

"Doubt the patriot whose suggestions
Whisper that its [the Union's] props may slide!"

The lines were taken to be a specific allusion to Governor Nathaniel Banks, who in the summer of '55 had declared himself willing to "let the Union slide" rather than support the institution of slavery. By 1861 Holmes had amended the final line to read "Strive a nation to divide."

22 A.l., Apr. 1, 1856, to Parker.

23 *Ibid.*

24 A.l., Dec. 28, 1855, Holmes to Sumner, Sumner papers, XXXIII, 135, HUh.

25 A.l., Mar. 26, 1856, Holmes to Emerson, L.BK. 64.

26 A.l., Apr. 1, 1856.

27 A.l., Mar. 26, 1856.

28 A.l., Mar. 8, 1864, to John A. McAllister, Library Company of Philadelphia, Ridgeway Branch.

29 *Poems,* pp. 189-90. "Beni- Israel" is the title of the poem when first printed, *Gifts of Genius* (Boston, 1859), pp. 260-263. See *Boston Journal,* Jan. 16, 1857, for a report of the lecture which gives the title of the poem as "A Hebrew Tale."

30 Holmes, "Fragments of a poem as originally written," ms., (1856), HC. The ms. is complete, on scraps in an envelope.

31 Emerson, *Journals,* IX, 464. See Holmes's use (1858) of the same image, *Works,* I, pp. 82-3. Emerson credits Thoreau with the image.

32 *BMSJ,* 40 (Sept. 18, 1856), 149.

33 A.l., May 3, 1857, Motley to Holmes (part in *Correspondence,* I, 199), HC. Holmes had sent to Motley a private printing of this verse lyceum lecture, "The Heart's Own Secret," first given for the Boston Mercantile Library Association, Nov. 14, 1855. (See *Poems,* pp. 307-320, for final versions of parts of this poem, never completely collected by Holmes. Mss. for these revisions are in MS. BK. pp. 943-5, 959, 961, 966-8, 969-73. See also George B. Ives, *A Bibliography of Oliver Wendell Holmes* (Boston, 1907), pp. 20-24.)

The copy sent to Motley with his marginal notes and Holmes's emendations is in HC. Any discussion of the lecture would be out of proportion here; it will be treated in a separate article.

Motley's letter was actually a more dangerous kind of flattery, though not intended as such, than the public's applause, for he was lyrical about what he thought his friend could do and might do in the future rather than sharp in his criticism of what Holmes had actually produced.

34 *Works*, I, 39.

35 A.l., July 17, 1856, Holmes to David Wells, Public Library, Springfield, Mass.

CHAPTER 15. *AUTOCRAT OF THE BREAKFAST-TABLE*

1 Horace E. Scudder, *James Russell Lowell* (Boston, 1901), I, 410-412.

2 *Ibid.*, I, 353.

3 Dec. 28, 1884, Lowell, *Letters*, ed., C. E. Norton (New York, 1894), II, 292-3.

4 Scudder, *op. cit.*, I, 424.

5 *Ibid.*, I, 416.

6 Motley, *Correspondence*, I, 226.

7 *Works*, I, 25.

8 The letters began to come almost at once apparently; Holmes in a letter to Dana (Dana papers, MHS) on Dec. 7, 1857, spoke of being swamped by a "comber" of communications.

9 *New England Magazine*, 1 (Nov. 1, 1831), 428-431, signed "O.W. H.," and 2 (Feb. 1832), 134-8, unsigned; reprinted in part in Hayakawa and Jones, *op cit.*, pp. 433-447.

10 A.l., Sept. 29, 1857, Swain to Holmes, HC. The "Governor" approved of Holmes's poem ("Sun and Shadow," *Poems*, p. 150), and said he knew that Holmes would not abuse his privileges as N. P. Willis had done in his published account of a visit to the island.

11 May 17, 1858, Motley, *Correspondence*, I, 22. *Works*, I, 125. Oscar Wilde and Frank Harris also borrowed the witticism.

12 *Works*, I, 3.

13 Sept. 16, 1857, Motley, *Correspondence*, I, 204.

14 A.l., Oct. 28, 1857, Benjamin Peirce to Holmes, LC.

15 Edward W. Emerson, *Early Years of the Saturday Club* (Boston 1918), p. 23.

16 *Ibid.*, p. [124].

17 *Works*, I, 63, 64.

18 Amos Bronson Alcott, *Journals*, ed., Odell Shepard (Boston, 1938), p. 304.

19 Edward W. Emerson, *op. cit.*, pp. 91-2.

20 Scudder, *op. cit.*, I, 448.

21 *Works*, I, 50.

22 *Ibid.*, I, 83-4.

23 It is traditional to regard this poem as an intentional attack on Calvinism, although its context in *The Autocrat* and the headnote in *Poems* (p. 158) do not warrant so limited an interpretation. The poem applies quite as well to any "system," that of the homeopathist

Hahnemann, for instance. In tracking down the source of this common interpretation, the late T. F. Currier traced it to Barrett Wendell. A letter by Justice Holmes to a correspondent who inquired about the verses, says that he never heard his father give them such a meaning (a. l., Jan. 31, 1930, privately owned).

A letter about the poem to Theodore Parker (Sept. 13, 1858, L.BK. 78), in which Holmes does *not* mention the poem's being anti-Calvinistic, might be relevant here if it were not for the fact that Holmes was intent upon correcting Parker's medical delusions. Parker's letter (same date, LC), commenting upon the poem with somewhat heavy-handed humor, treats it simply as an hilarious piece and blames his sore throat on the laughter it provoked. Holmes's answer picks up the medical motif and offers two mock prescriptions, one "allopathic" and the other homeopathic, for he knew that Parker had at one time been exposed to the "dangerous influences" of homeopathy (a.l. Mar. 14, 1857, Holmes to Parker, L.BK. 79).

24 "Dr. Holmes's Reminiscences," *AM*, 45 (Feb. 1880), Supplement, 5.

25 Holmes, "A Visit to the Autocrat's Landlady," *Soundings from the Atlantic* (Boston, 1863), pp. 334-5.

26 *BET*, Nov. 24, Dec. 30, 1858.

27 A.l., Sept. 28, 1858, W. O. Bartlett to Holmes, LC; Oct. 5, 1858, Holmes to J. T. Fields, Huntington Library; Oct. 18, 1858, Holmes to Bonner, privately owned.

CHAPTER 16. *PROFESSOR AT THE BREAKFAST-TABLE*

1 *Works*, I, 59.

2 *Ibid.*, I, 37.

3 Holmes's interest in deviations from the normal physical structure has already been indicated; see Chap. 10, p. 169. See also his article "A Case of Malformation," *BMSJ*, 34 (Mar. 3, 1847), 92-96. The records of BSMI (III, 226, June 24, 1939), note an argument between the pathologist J. B. S Jackson and Holmes on the causes of such malformations. Holmes argued for the theories of the "transcendental anatomists," apparently supporting in part the theories of Johann Friedrich Meckel (1781-1833) whose views anticipated in some respects those of Darwin. Holmes's "Hanover—1st Introductory—Aug. 1839" contains a reference to Meckel.

A more immediate source for Little Boston was a visitor to the city in Dec. 1858. On the 7th, there was a special meeting of BSMI to study the deformity of Eugene Groux; Holmes, J. B. S. Jackson and H. I. Bowditch were appointed a special committee to investigate Groux's case (*BMSJ*, 59 (Dec. 23, 1858), pp. 422-3). Groux also appeared before Dr. Holmes's classes (*BET*, Dec. 9, 1858). Probably these experiences contributed something to the passage in the eleventh paper (*Works*, II,

263-4) in which Holmes makes his deformed character exclaim: "I don't doubt I was a *remarkable case*," and has him protest against the "rapacity of science," which would make a show of him.

4 *Works*, II, 18.

5 Hayakawa and Jones, *op. cit.*, p. cix.

6 The scrapbook, containing clippings, mss., and leaflets, and annotated by Holmes was presented by Harlan Ballard to the Oliver Wendell Holmes Library, Phillips Academy, Andover. The presence of notes in Holmes's hand and the early dates of many of the items make it certain that the scrapbook was of Holmes's own making. The volume will be hereafter referred to as Scrapbook A.

7 "The Chief End of Man," *Cambridge Chronicle*, Dec. 2, 1858, an unidentified clipping in Scrapbook A. Holmes's lecture for the preceding season of 1857-58 was "Our Second Selves" (*Boston Journal*, Dec. 24, 1857), which develops a variation (not to the advantage of the idea) of the famous "three Johns" passage in *The Autocrat, Works*, I, 53. The lecture is chiefly topical, having its main point of reference the contemporary financial depression.

8 *Works*, II, 120.

9 *Ibid.*, II, 103, 108.

10 T. W. Higginson, in *Publications of the Cambridge Historical Society*, IV, (1909), 44.

11 *Works*, II, 103-4.

12 Higginson, *op. cit.*, p. 45.

13 Unidentified clipping in Scrapbook A.

14 *Works*, II, 202-3, and *Poems*, p. 166. The same paper (*Works*, II, 195 ff.), contains a lecture on phrenology. Holmes's own chart, dated July 1, 1859, appears in Scrapbook A.

15 *Works*, II, 207.

16 Morse, I, 39-40.

17 *Works*, I, 86. This image, used in other ways, is a favorite with Holmes.

18 *Ibid.*, II, 13.

19 *Ibid.*, IX, 180-1.

20 *Ibid.*, IX, 193.

21 *Ibid.*, IX, 195.

22 *Ibid.*, IX, 202-3, see note, pp. 443-45. In 1838 Holmes was speaking out against the excessive use of antimony (BSMI Records, III, 105).

23 Holmes, *Currents and Counter-Currents in Medical Science*, p. vi.

24 On Oct. 3, 1860, at a meeting of the Councillors of MMS, a letter from Dr. James Jackson was read. Jackson proposed a resolution to recall the vote against Holmes, pointing out that it had been passed hastily and under some excitement. "If he availed himself of a poet's license, let us take and swallow the wholesome morsels which he offers to us, and not cry out that they are too hot and that they burn our mouths." After much discussion, one of the doctors who had voted for the original resolution moved that it now be reconsidered; the subse-

quent vote was 27-17 in favor of reconsideration. (The original vote had been 9-7). *BMSJ*, 43 (Oct. 11, 1860), 225; and MMS, *Medical Communications*, IX, Appendix, 148.

25 *Works*, I, 89.

26 Holmes, Notebook for *The Guardian Angel*, p. 14, ms., HC. The remark was made in an after-dinner speech before the MMS, June 5, 1867; the portion from which this quotation comes was not printed in the newspapers or in *BMSJ*, as Holmes notes.

27 All these notices Holmes preserved in Scrapbook A. One of the most abusive he recalled thirty years later when in *Over the Teacups* (*Works*, IV, 248) he refers to an attack entitled "A Moral Parricide," (unidentified clipping, New England paper, c. Jan.-Feb. 1861). The tirade was provoked by a passage in Chapter XXVI of *Elsie Venner* (*Works*, V, 392), in which Holmes describes the effects of orthodox religious training upon children, particularly the children of professional theologians. The article reads in part as follows:

"Parricide has ever been accounted the most unnatural of crimes. Among the horrible pictures of heathenism none is more revolting than the exposure of aged, sick, or infirm parents to die by the wayside, or their destruction by the hand of violence when their support has become a burden to their children. There are limits, however, to the cruelties of heathenism, and we do not remember that the Fijis, in the days of their cannibalism, ever devoured their own fathers. . . .

"But worse even than the overt act of parricide—because, more refined, deliberate, and exceptional in the manner of it—is the stabbing of the memory of a father with sneers and objurgations;—the attempt to justify one's own departure from the standard of a father's character and faith, by exposing that father's pious training of his household to the ridicule of the world.

"The author of the 'Professor's Story,' in *The Atlantic Monthly*, is known as the son of a divine whose learning, piety, and pastoral fidelity are yet fragrant in the memory of Massachusetts churches. That son has seen fit to depart widely, essentially, from the faith in which he was trained. . . . We do not now criticize either the fact or the manner of his change of faith. . . . But in the name of all reverence and propriety, we insist that he should not defile the pages of a literary and household magazine with unfilial sneers at his own father's domestic nurture. . . .

"We have a right to protest against this wanton insult to a profession to which literature, religion, and the state are alike indebted for the noblest advocacy of freedom in the truth. We have a right to protest against this weak and wicked caricature of that household training which has made New England the nursery of great minds for the nation. . . . The proprieties of life, the sanctity of home, the filial sentiment, forbid that a literary anatomist should dissect before the world the character and memory of his father, and hold these up with gibe and sneer. Let him 'tear off the holy compresses,' if he will, but we cannot suffer him thus wantonly to mutilate the hands that bound them about his infant head."

28 Clarence P. Oberndorf, *The Psychiatric Novels of Oliver Wendell Holmes* (2nd ed., New York, 1946), p. 84.

Described by Holmes "as essentially imaginary" (a.l., Sept. 10, 1860, HUh), Elsie may owe something, nevertheless, to a case reported in *BMSJ* 35, (Oct. 21, 1846), 235. This "Case of Destitution of the Moral Feelings" is described as having snake-like characteristics: unusual flexibility of the muscles, cold skin, and low pulse. See also *BMSJ*, 20 (Mar. 20, 1899), 98-9, about a snake-boy.

The question of pre-natal influence was discussed at a BSMI meeting in Aug. 1856 when an instance of a pregnant woman's being frightened by a rattlesnake was cited; the child was born with a snake-like birthmark on its back [*BMSJ* 17 (Aug. 20, 1856), 57]. In inventing Elsie, Holmes probably recalled, too, the patient he had once described at a BSMI meeting. The patient had tendencies toward suicide and murder, inclinations which came upon him most powerfully in hot weather (BSMI Records, V, 114-5).

Holmes was only an amateur herpetologist, but he had made some personal observations (1854) of a rattlesnake, which he had kept for some time in a cage in the basement of the medical school. In *Yankee from Olympus,* Catherine Drinker Bowen's over-elaborate efforts to belittle the doctor lead her to change the rattlesnake into a "harmless garter snake" and to imply that the doctor was only faking about the creature's being dangerous—a rather foolish distortion of the facts since the same source that confirms the rattlesnake also indicates that the doctor wasn't exactly lion-hearted in handling the snake (James Clarke White, *op. cit.*, p. 73).

29 *Works,* V, 228.

30 *Ibid.,* V, 76.

31 *Ibid.,* V, 227.

32 A.l., Mar. 4 (1861), Bigelow to Holmes, HC.

CHAPTER 17. *PATRIOTIC ORATOR*

1 Class BK., p. 318, report of meeting, Jan. 3, 1861.

2 *Poems,* p. 121.

3 "A Word for the Poets in This Weak Piping Time of Peace," *Boston Courier,* Feb. 21, 1861. Holmes clipped the poem and put it in his Civil War scrapbook (HC, hereafter Scrapbook H) at p. 20, identifying the author as T. W. Parsons. The poem begins "Set not the pine against the palm."

4 A.l., Apr. 23, 1861, Felton to Holmes, copy in College Letters, IV, 144, HUa.

5 A.l., Jan. 17, 1861, *loc. cit.,* p. 108.

6 A.l., Apr. 23, 1861.

7 M. A. DeWolfe Howe, *Holmes of the Breakfast-Table* (New York, 1939), p. 102.

8 *Ibid.,* p. 101.

9 Catherine Drinker Bowen, *Yankee from Olympus* (New York, 1944), p. 144. For his class book the elder Holmes wrote a somewhat less affected autobiographical note.

10 A.l., July 20, 1861, Felton to Holmes, College Letters, IV, 201. It is to be emphasized here that Felton was the aggressor in this correspondence. Holmes's letter (Howe, *Holmes of the Breakfast-Table*, pp. 102-104) was an answer to Felton's; the doctor "did not mean to speak of this matter, except incidentally, so infinitely insignificant does it appear to the interests in which my son with all of us is now involved."

11 A.l., Jan. 8, 1861, Holmes to the Secretary of the American Academy of Arts and Sciences, Berg collection, NYPL. The argument between Bowen and Holmes was apparently a metaphysical one, on the nature of force. Nine years later Holmes still remembered his argument with Bowen; referring to his Harvard ΦBK address of June 29, 1870, "Mechanism in Thought and Morals," Holmes wrote to Underwood (a.l. July 9, 1870, Goodspeed's), "Even Bowen could not pick a quarrel with me." Bowen was likely to be excitable and emotional in an argument, see *DAB*.

12 Motley, *Correspondence*, II, 11.

13 A.l., July 10, 1861, A. J. Browne to Col. Wm. R. Lee, Andrew papers, MHS.

14 *Poems*, pp. 196-8.

15 *Ibid.*, p. 72.

16 *Works*, VIII, 2-15.

17 *BMSJ*, 20 (Feb. 20, 1862), 180. In view of Holmes's satire on reports of this kind in *Elsie Venner* (*Works*, V, 167), it is hard not to suspect that Hitchcock's literary style was more than a little influenced by the Parkman Professor.

In Aug. 1862, Holmes was one of eight doctors in Suffolk County, appointed by the Governor, from whom certificates of disability had to be obtained for release from the draft [*BMSJ*, 67 (Aug. 30, 1862), p. 102]. The active worker in the family, however, was Mrs. Holmes. As president of the Industrial Association (U. S. Sanitary Commission) she was so indefatigable that her husband became worried about her health and tried to curtail her labors (Susan and St. John Mildmay, *John Lothrop Motley and his Family* (London, 1910), p. 187, quoting Dr. Holmes's letter of Aug. 28, 1863, to Lady Harcourt—Motley's daughter.)

18 *Works*, IX, 211.

19 *Ibid.*, IX, p. 245.

20 Holmes, Black notebook, pp. 105-6, has notes on George Henry Lewes's *History of Philosophy;* the BAT Records show that it was charged to Holmes in Aug. 1860.

21 *Works*, IX, pp. 245-6. He had been reading, also, Hobbes, and David Hartley (BAT Records) and an article by Laycock on "The Reflex Action of the Brain" (black notebook, p. 106).

22 E. E. Hale, *op. cit.*, p. 273, quoting an entry from Clarke's diary.

23 O. W. Holmes, Jr., *Touched with Fire*, ed., Mark DeW. Howe,

(Cambridge, 1946), pp. 13-19, prints young Holmes's letter of Oct. 23, written two days after the battle; see also *ibid.*, p. 19, n. 12, and Morse, II, 158. Mrs. Bowen's account of the family anxiety is dramatic and touching, but unreliable.

24 M. A. DeWolfe Howe, *Holmes of the Breakfast-Table,* pp. 105-6.

25 Apr. 26, 1862, Holmes to Motley, *Correspondence,* II, 72.

26 Feb. 2, 1862, Morse, II, 163, 161.

27 Dec. 15, 1862, *ibid.,* II, 169.

28 Aug. 29, 1862, *ibid.,* II, 167, 166, 165. The letter from Locker (Locker-Lampson) is dated Aug. 6, 1862, LC.

29 *Works,* VIII, 18. See M. A. DeWolfe Howe, *Holmes of the Break-fast-Table,* pp. 106-109 and Holmes, *Touched with Fire,* pp. 64-68, for the captain's story. On the whole, one is obliged to conclude that both father and son had a good time, the one satisfying his curiosity and the other languishing among the ladies.

30 Scrapbook H.

31 Nov. 29, 1861, Morse, II, 158, à propos the hero's first con-valescence.

32 A.l., July 8, 1862, Hoar to Holmes, LC.

33 *Works,* VIII, 6.

34 *Ibid.,* VIII, 90.

35 *Ibid.,* VIII, 83.

36 *Ibid.,* VIII, 112, 111.

37 A.l., Nov. 2, 1862, Motley to Holmes, HC (deleted from *Correspondence,* II, 98).

38 This lecture exists in a privately printed edition with the title "Lecture-1863"; HUh has a copy. It appears, considerably revised, as "Our Progressive Independence" in *AM,* 13 (April 1864), 497-512. The revisions are changes designed to cut out the oratorical flourishes and to alter the tone.

A similar falling off of confidence in American talent came out in a letter to Agassiz, Oct. 20, 1863, HUh. Holmes wrote:

"I look with ever-increasing admiration on the work you are perform-ing for our civilization. It very rarely happens that the same person can take the largest and deepest scientific view and come down without ap-parent effort to the level of popular intelligence. This is what singularly fits you for our country, which having established the best *average* of knowledge is ready to push the development of science in all its forms to the *maximum* in each department, so far as the genius of its people is adapted to the pursuit of knowledge for its own sake and not as a trade. . . ."

39 The lecture exists in two privately printed versions; HUh has both. A copy in HC has been further revised by Holmes (1865).

40 A.l., June 17, 1864, to Ticknor and Fields, Huntington Library.

41 David Cheever, Report to Holmes, 1863, ms., HC.

42 It was about 1860 that Holmes invented the "American Stereo-scope," as it was called. His rough model of the invention is preserved in

the Oliver Wendell Holmes Library, Phillips Academy, Andover. He tells the story of the invention in a letter of Nov. 25, 1868, to the *Philadelphia Photographer* [6 (Jan. 1869), 1-9]. Joseph Bates, the Boston photographer to whom Holmes gave the design, reprinted the letter in an elusive advertising pamphlet; MHS has two copies.

CHAPTER 18. *NOVELIST*

1 Emerson, *Journals,* IX, 466.

2 Emerson, *Letters,* V, 305, a letter of Jan. 4, 1863. Emerson observed that Holmes had broken "his rule"; see *Works* VIII, 19, where Holmes speaks of the nuisances who talk too much on trains; Emerson had recently read the passage in the *Atlantic.*

3 A.l., Nov. 8, 1864, Holmes to George Bancroft, Bancroft papers, MHS.

4 A.l., Dec. 19, 1863, Holmes to Childs, NYPL.

5 A.l., Nov. 8, n.y., Holmes to Lowell. The woman was Ann M. Hoyt, whose "Ghost of Little Jacques" appeared in the *Atlantic* in 1863.

6 Annie Fields, *Authors and Friends* (Boston, 1897), p. 131.

7 Scudder, *op. cit.,* II, 83.

8 *Poems,* p. 204.

9 Edward Emerson, *op. cit.,* p. 413.

10 Oct. 10, 1865, to Motley, Morse, II, 175-7.

11 A.l., May 3, 1864, Lowell papers, HUh.

12 Emerson, *Journals,* X, 39. See also, Holmes, "Hawthorne," *AM,* 14 (July 1864), 98-101.

13 Oct. 10, 1865, to Motley, Morse, II, 177.

14 A.l., Nov. 13, 1865, HUh. In another letter (n.d., endorsed "1863," HUh) Holmes diagnosed Aldrich as being in danger of becoming a "verbal voluptuary," the end of which is "rhythmical gout, an incurable poetic disorder." It is a diagnosis he would, I think, have been willing to make of himself.

15 A.ll., May 9 and 10, 1865, privately owned.

16 *AM,* 15 (May, 1865), 589-591.

17 A.l., May 6, 1865, L.BK. 70.

18 Holmes, "Lecture-1865," privately printed, p. 9. Huntington Library has a copy. Some of the raw materials for this lecture are in Scrapbook H.

19 "Lecture-1865," p. 31.

20 A.l., Mar. 13, 1865, privately owned.

21 "Lecture-1865," p. 9.

22 *Ibid.,* p. 10.

23 *Ibid.,* p. 11.

24 *Ibid.,* p. 35.

25 Hamilton Vaughan Bail, "Harvard's Commemoration Day," *New England Quarterly,* 15 (June, 1942), 276-277.

26 *Ibid.,* p. 273.

27 The two major collections of letters to Holmes are in LC and HC; the collection in LC was given to the library by Justice Holmes, who apparently chose the letters for their interest as individual pieces so that he occasionally split a consecutive correspondence; T. F. Currier has added to HC films of the LC letters. Holmes's answers to the letters of Charlotte Dana (Dana papers, MHS) are of some interest in comparison with those to Harriet Beecher Stowe (Morse); to Miss Dana he wrote more calmly and less personally than to Mrs. Stowe. The letter from Dr. Kellogg with its enclosure is in HC.

28 A.l., Jan. 4, 1866, HC.

29 M. A. DeWolfe Howe, "Dr. Holmes, the Friend and Neighbor," *Yale Review*, n.s., 7 (April 1918), 567-8.

30 Ms. Receipt, privately owned.

31 Edward Emerson, *op. cit.*, p. 380.

32 M. A. DeWolfe Howe, "Dr. Holmes, the Friend and Neighbor," pp. 568-9.

33 Holmes, Notebook for *The Guardian Angel*, ms. HC. He began the book on Aug. 6, 1866.

34 Black notebook, pp. 92-3.

35 Nov. 17, 1867, Morse, II, 224. The letter contains an allusion to Nehemiah Adams.

36 Notebook for *The Guardian Angel*, p. 14. See Chapter 16, n. 26, p. 422.

37 Myrtle, like her predecessor Elsie, owes something to the medical journals and the doctor's casebook. The hysteria of adolescent girls had been a common subject of discussion among the members of the Boston Society for Medical Improvement. Although it was recognized that the ailment was not peculiar to young girls, Sydenham's case of male hysteria being the classic example to the contrary, both general medical texts and special treatments of the subject nearly always discussed hysteria as if it were exclusively a manifestation of female adolescence. Holmes shows no such limited conception, for he offers Mrs. Stoker, the bed-ridden wife of the philandering preacher, as an hysteric, and explains her invalidism as a flight from the unpleasant reality.

38 *Works*, VI, 180-1.

39 Henry Maudsley, *The Physiology and Pathology of the Mind* (New York, 1867); *Body and Mind* (London, 1870); third edition of the first, London, 1876, Vols. I and II. The quote is from the last, I, 369, 371-2.

40 *Works*, VI, viii.

41 Nov. 17, 1867, Morse, II, 223.

42 A.l., Mar. 5, 1867, privately owned.

43 C. Hartley Grattan, "Oliver Wendell Holmes," *American Mercury*, 4 (Jan. 1925), 37-41.

44 *Nation*, 5 (May 30, 1867), 432.

45 A.l., Nov. 14, 1867, HUh.

46 A.l., Dec. 9, 1867, to Coleman Sellers, Library of American Philosophical Society.

CHAPTER 19. *MEMBER OF THE OPPOSITION*

1 A.l., Mar. 5, 1867, to H. H. Brownell, privately owned.

2 *Works,* IX, 277.

3 *Ibid.,* IX, 298.

4 *Ibid.,* IX, 292.

5 *Ibid.,* IX, 299.

6 College Records, XI, 64-68.

7 July 7, 1868, *Harvard Medical School Alumni Bulletin,* 17 (Jan. 1943), 33-35.

8 Apr. 3, 1870, Morse, II, 187-8. See Eliot's articles on "The New Education, Its Organization," *AM,* 23 (Feb., Mar. 1869), 203-22, 358-67. Not all the alarm about Eliot arose from a fear that he would be too radical; see Peirce papers (HUa) for letters by professors in the Lawrence Scientific School who expected him to be too conservative. The alarm seemed to come primarily from a fear that they would lose their independence.

9 J. C. White, *op. cit.,* pp. 131, 142-4, 151.

10 Holmes and the older members of the Harvard faculty were not the only ones in their profession who suffered from a kind of fixation, brought about by the ticket-selling system of financing medical schools. Other medical schools in the country were similarly handicapped. The country-wide pressure for reform had brought about in 1867 a special meeting of medical teachers called by the American Medical Association. At that meeting a series of reforms, relatively more drastic than any brought forward before, were proposed; such as, entrance examinations, three regular annual courses of five months each (instead of the traditional two of four months each), and gradation of these courses. In the discussion which followed, the majority were willing to go further and proposed a four-year program, a six-months course, and the institution of annual examinations. But on the agenda was the proposal to abolish the ticket-selling system, and that proposal was promptly tabled. [*BMSJ,* 76 (May 16, 1867), 313; and *AMA Transactions,* XVIII (1867), 363-68, 371-73.]

In all the discussion of medical school reforms, criticism of the financial system that effectively strangled any attempts to achieve these reforms had seldom been made and, then, only by the way, until Eliot turned Harvard College and its satellite professional schools upside down. The bogeyman of financial ruin, raised within Harvard's own medical faculty by Bigelow, was finally brought clear into the open, and other medical schools were obliged to face it. It is noticeable that these other medical schools, whether approving the reform or not, whether prophesying ruin or not, waited discreetly until the financial returns on the Harvard experiment were in.

The reforms were put into effect in 1871 (College Records, XI, 284, Overseers meeting of April 11); for a Harvard medical degree now, a student must spend three full years attending a nine-months course of lectures, laboratory and clinical work; his program was arranged in graded order, and he had to pass annual written examinations in all subjects. The elective system gave choices among specialties in his senior year.

11 "Introductory . . . 1879," MS.BK., p. 221; letter to Motley, Dec. 22, 1871, Morse, II, 190; College Records, XI, 291, 341.

The caliber of the students did not improve overnight. In 1874, on the occasion of the expulsion of some students, Holmes was moved to address his class on the subject of the "painful occurrence"; although not in the habit of writing out his lectures, he did on this occasion prepare a written speech of censure and exhortation, writing it out, as he explained, to keep his indignation from getting the better of his sense of justice. For its purpose, the speech is excellent, with that kind of wholeness that makes it impossible to quote a fragment of it (undated, untitled ms. in MS.BK. pp. 437-449; an allusion to Sumner's funeral gives the date 1874).

Holmes's title was changed in 1871 from Parkman Professor of Anatomy and Physiology to Parkman Professor of Anatomy; he held the same position in the Dental School. No full professor of physiology was appointed until 1876 when Henry Pickering Bowditch, assistant since 1871, was raised to that rank. Before 1871, Joseph Stickney Lombard, William T. Lusk, and Robert Amory had been special lecturers on the subject; from 1866-70, Lombard had been Assistant Professor of Physiology. In 1870, Holmes had written Lusk, remarking on the inadequate physiology that had been taught (a.l., Aug. 19, 1870, N. Y. Academy of Medicine).

12 Dec. 22, 1871, Morse, II, 191.

13 "Introductory . . . 1879," MS.BK., p. 229.

14 *Works,* IX, (312).

15 *Ibid.,* IX, 367,368.

16 In some instances, there can be no doubt about whether father or son withdrew a book; in 1870, for instance, it was certainly the son who took out May's *Constitutional History of England* and the father who took Bain's *Emotions and Will* and *Senses and Intellect.* As for Mill's *Analysis of the Human Mind,* either may have taken it out and both may have read it. (BAT records, 1870.) Mrs. Bowen is exaggerating when she implies that the father took out only "*belles-lettres* and text-books of anatomy" (the Parkman Professor's textbooks of anatomy were in his head, of course), and the son, only weighty volumes of contemporary philosophy. The 1862-3 records, which she was using for this passage (*Yankee from Olympus,* p. 189), suggest no such violent contrast. While his son was away, Dr. Holmes had withdrawn DeToqueville, Faraday, and Plato, and they were both home when someone in the family wanted to read *The Romance of Héloise and Abelard.* As for the volumes of Spencer and Mill (both James and John Stuart) it is more than likely that they were withdrawn by the son; in fact, on Oct. 14, 1862, a few weeks after he had been brought home wounded, the captain received J. S. Mill's *Considerations,* a present "from father" (Holmes Library, LC). But Dr. Holmes refers to Mill and quotes Spencer in his address, July 4, 1863, and there are notes (few) on Mill in his black notebook. It seems safe to conclude that in 1863 Captain Holmes read *through* the books, and Dr. Holmes, after his

fashion, read *in* them. In 1873, however, Dr. Holmes must have read through Spencer's *The Study of Sociology*, for he reviewed it in *BMSJ*, 89 (Dec. 11, 1873), 587-9.

17 *Works*, VIII, 311.

18 *Ibid.*, VIII, 282.

19 *Ibid.*, VIII, 306-7.

20 *Ibid.*, VIII, 273. His tabulations are in MS.BK., pp. 1059-1065, dated May 14-16, 1868; and pp. 1069-1071, dated June 8-10-13, 1870; the last set of experiments was obviously made especially for the address, given June 29.

21 S. Freud, *Basic Writings*, Modern Library Edition, tr. and ed., A. A. Brill (New York, 1938), p. 951.

CHAPTER 20. *POET AT THE BREAKFAST-TABLE*

1 Ms. notes, a.ll., and clipping (*BDA*, Nov. 9, 1869), HC.

2 *King's Handbook of Boston* (Cambridge, 1878), pp. 25-6.

3 Edward Jackson Holmes.

4 A.l., Jan. 31, 1930, Justice Holmes to J. Colby Bassett, privately owned. See also the younger Holmes's letter to Sumner recommending his brother for the position of Sumner's secretary, Aug. 5, 1869, Sumner letters, XCIV, 168, HUh.

5 A.l., Oct. 1, 1870, to Mrs. C. W. Upham, HUh.

6 A.l., Mar 11, 1872, to Mrs. Upham, HUh; Amelia's engagement he announces to Motley (*Correspondence*, II, 135).

7 Class BK., p. 180.

8 A.l., June 29, 1865, to H. H. Brownell, privately owned, and *Works*, VIII, p. 149-50.

9 Letter of Aug. 16, 1871 (incorrectly dated, the date should be 1870), John Holmes to Charles Eliot Ware, John Holmes, *Letters*, ed., W. R. Thayer with an introduction by Alice M. Longfellow (Boston, 1917), p. 81.

10 *Ibid.*, p. xxxii.

11 *Ibid.*, p. xliv.

12 Feb. 19, 1875, Morse, II, 235.

13 *The Later Years of the Saturday Club*, ed., M. A. DeWolfe Howe, (Boston, 1927), p. 105.

14 Sept. 26, 1869, Morse, II, 185.

15 Apr. 3, 1870, *ibid.*, II, 187.

16 Patrick S. Gilmore, *History of the National Peace Jubilee* (Boston, 1871), pp. 291-5.

17 Dec. 22, 1871, Morse, II, 190.

18 Louisa May Alcott, *Life, Letters and Journals*, ed., Ednah Cheney, (Boston, 1925), p. 261.

19 Dec. 22, 1871, Morse, II, 192.

20 Feb. 7, 1870, *ibid.*, I, 219.

21 Aug. 18, 1870, *ibid.*, I, 220.

22 A.l., Oct. 18, 1871, HUh.

23 *Poems*, p. 174-5.

24 M. A. DeWolfe Howe, "Dr. Holmes, Friend and Neighbor," p. 576. The conversation took place Oct. 11, 1873.

25 The book is the Holmes Library, LC. Abiel Holmes's entry appears in the table of contents and refers to his ms. notes interleaved at the end of the volume; it reads: *Vide dua folia in Indice apud finem.* Dr. Holmes's entry reads: "*In locem reposita cura filii.* O.W.H. Mar. 31, 1872."

26 *Works,* III, 328.

27 *Ibid.,* III, 319.

28 *Ibid.,* III, 107, 106.

29 Mar. 27, 30, 1871, Morse, II, **14**.

30 Mar. 30, 1871, *ibid.,* II, 15.

31 *Works,* III, 262.

32 Mar. 30, 1871, Morse, II, 15.

33 Holmes, Notebook for the *Poet at the Breakfast-Table,* 1871-2, p. (12), ms., HC.

34 *Ibid.,* p. (18).

35 *Works,* III, 6.

36 *Ibid.,* III, 174-**182.**

37 *Ibid.,* III, 183.

38 *Ibid.,* III, 307.

39 *Ibid.,* III, 306, **268.**

40 *Ibid.,* III, 303-4.

41 *Ibid.,* III, 136.

42 *Ibid.,* III, 65-66 and 62. The first dramatizes the ms. notebook entry "intelligence at a premium as against narrow expertism," p. (20).

43 Motley, *Correspondence,* II, 335-6.

44 A.ll., spring, 1872, Dr. J. C. Dalton to Holmes re anatomical models, HC.

45 July 16, 1872, to Caroline Kellogg, Morse, I, **330-1.**

46 A.l., Sept. 30, 1872, privately owned.

CHAPTER 21. *SEPTUAGENARIAN*

1 Motley, *Correspondence,* II, 358.

2 Jan. 24, 1873, typed copy of letter, Duke University Library. A.l., Dec. 1872, Tennyson to Holmes, LC.

3 Nov. 16, 1872, Morse, II, 196-9.

4 Aug. 28, 1872, *ibid.,* II, 195.

5 Emerson, *Journals,* typescript *OP Gulistan,* p. 4; ms. pp. 6-7, HUh. Emerson goes on to comment on Holmes's "tertility and aptness of illustration," a passage which appears in *The Early Years of the Saturday Club,* p. 151.

6 Morse, II, 179, 123.

7 Annie Fields, *op. cit.,* p. 132.

8 Letter, Jan. 24, 1873, see n. 2.

9 Holmes, Review of *Parthenia* by Eliza Buckminster Lee, *AM*, 1 (Feb. 1858), 509. Late in the '70's Holmes contributed a review and an article to a magazine edited by his wife's nephew, John T. Morse, Jr., his future biographer. See Morse, I, 219; II, 11, 257-8.

10 Holmes, Review of *Sex in Education, AM*, 32. (Dec. 1873), 738. Clarke was Holmes's brother-in-law as well as colleague.

11 *BET*, Oct. 26, 1872.

12 His ms. notes for the lecture begin in the notebook for *The Poet* and run over into a second notebook. Nearly all the notes are technical, exercises in scansion for the most part. The clinical emphasis in the lecture is obvious; the notes include references to an article on hallucinations in childhood in the *Transactions of the Connecticut Medical Society* and to Winslow's *Brain and . . . Mind* about "insane persons versifying." "The Physiology of Verse" is in *Works* VIII, 315-321; it first appeared in *BMSJ*, 92 (Jan. 7, 1875), 6-9.

13 A.l., Aug. 3, 1880, LC.

14 April 14, 1873, to John Collins Warren, Morse, I, 349-350. A letter to Longfellow (Dec. 1, 1875, Craigie House), is amusing here. Holmes was surprised that Longfellow could believe in homeopathic infinitesimals and not believe the verifiable facts of microphotography, which Holmes proceeded to explain to the poet. He concluded by remarking that his strictures on homeopathists did not extend to their "unfortunate patients who if they are honest are not competent to weigh medical evidence."

15 Thomas Dwight, *op. cit.*, p. 127.

16 *AM*, 45 (Feb. 1880), Supplement, 11.

17 Dwight, *op. cit.*, p. 125.

18 Henry James, *Charles William Eliot* (Boston, 1930), I, 276.

19 Dwight, *op. cit.*, p. 125.

20 Holmes, "The Medical School," *Harvard Book*, I, 249.

21 *BDA*, July 1, 1880, report of commencement dinner, June 30.

22 A.l., July 8, 1879, HUh. An exchange of letters between Holmes and Howells is revealing for both men. On May 12, 1876, Holmes wrote: "I have learned to trust a great deal to your critical taste and judgment." (A.l., HUh.) On the 13th, Howells answered: "What will you think of my taste, I wonder, when I tell you that I think Mark Twain's last one his very best?" (A.l., LC.)

23 May 18, 1874, to Motley, Morse, II, 207. A.ll., June 7, 1878, July 2, 1882, to Lowell, HUh.

24 *Works*, III, 44-5.

25 A.l. [Spring, 1875] to Holmes, HUh.

26 June 14, 1876, Henry Adams, *Letters . . . 1858-1891*, ed., C. Worthington Ford, (Boston, 1930), p. 288.

27 *BDA*, June 1, 1877, report of Holmes's speech of May 31.

28 A.l., May 26, 1875, L.BK. 81.

29 May 18, 1874, Morse, II, 206.

30 Motley, *Correspondence*, II, 361.

31 July 26, 1874, Morse, II, 210.

32 *Works,* VIII, 324. He received the book in January (a.l., Jan. 9, 1875, to Henry Bellows, MHS), discussed the Irish prison system with Martin Brimmer at the Saturday Club on Jan. 30, and wrote a long letter to Sanborn on the 31st (privately owned).

33 *Works,* VIII, 326.

34 *Poems,* pp. 251-2.

35 *Poems,* p. 251. See also Morse I, 236-9, and *Proceedings of the Harvard Club of New York City* (New York, 1878), pp. 16-17.

36 Mar. 6, 1878, Morse, I, 239.

37 A.ll., Feb. 21, Mar. 10, Aug. 22, 1871, BPL. Holmes later in the year performed the same service for H. H. Brownell; Henry Jacob Bigelow being ill, Holmes secured for his friends his former demonstrator, the surgeon Richard Hodges.

38 June 17, 1877, to Lady Harcourt, Mildmay, *op. cit.* pp. 305-6.

39 *Poems,* pp. 138-9.

40 A.l., June 7, 1878, HUh.

41 A.l., June 19, 1876, LC.

42 A.l., Apr. 22, 1878, HC.

43 Sept. 22, 1878, Morse, II, 120.

44 A.l. [Aug. 29, 1879], HUh.

45 A.l., May 5 [1879], Augusta Astor to Holmes, HC.

46 *AM,* 45 [Feb. 1880], Supplement. The Party was held on Dec. 3.

47 *Works,* IX, 416-7.

48 Holmes, Speech, *Parks for the People,* Proceedings of a Public Meeting held in Faneuil Hill, June 7, 1876, pp. 20-5.

49 Holmes, *An Address Delivered at the Annual Meeting of the Boston Microscopical Society* (Cambridge, 1877).

50 "Introductory . . . 1879," MS.BK., p. 197.

51 *Ibid.,* p. 185.

52 *Ibid.,* p. 189. Another introductory lecture, apparently given several times by request, is on the general subject of the course of medical history; it appeared in print finally (1882) as *Medical Highways and Byways.* An ms. in BML entitled "Some Stepping Stones and Stumbling Blocks" is misdated 1880 by Holmes; it is an 1881 version of the 1882 essay. MS.BK., pp. 233-375, has an ms., entitled "Introductory Lecture—Oct. 1881," and a number of scattered fragments which appear to be preliminary drafts, one on p. 445 being labeled, "first notes my lecture on medicine, 1881," and those on pp. 457-463, "this will do better for my medical essay."

53 Henry J. Bigelow, ms. notes, HUm, and College Records, XIII, 131-2.

54 Morse, II, 49-50.

CHAPTER 22. *MAN OF LETTERS*

1 A.l., Oct. 29, 1883, Aldrich to Holmes, LC.

2 *Proceedings at the Dinner Given by the Medical Profession of . . . New York* (New York, 1883), pp. 58-9.

3 *Poems*, pp. 68-71.

4 A.l., Winthrop to Holmes, May 12, 1883, HC. Holmes's interrupted notes are in HC; other notes and the final manuscript are in MS.BK. pp. 531-561, 567-9 and 293-357.

5 See newspaper accounts of the hearings and the official report; Massachusetts General Court, House . . . no. 300, Boston, 1883.

6 A.ll., v.d., to Holmes, HC. Holmes's address appears in *The New Century and the New Building of the Harvard Medical School* (Cambridge, 1884), pp. (3)-35. His appeal for funds is at pp. (51)-55.

As early as 1849 (Apr. 5) Holmes had written to John K. Mitchell, author of *The Cryptogamous Origin of Fevers,* to declare himself a believer in the organic origins of disease.

7 Holmes, "Address," *op. cit.,* pp. 18-19, and Thomas Dwight, *op. cit.,* pp. 126-7.

8 "Address," pp. 23-24.

9 *Ibid.,* p. 27.

10 *Ibid.,* pp. 28-31.

11 *Ibid.,* p. 34.

12 *Works,* IX, 438.

13 Feb. 24, 1883, Morse, I, 244.

14 *Poems*, pp. 269-271.

15 Henry I. Bowditch, "Did Mr. Emerson Sympathize with the Abolitionists?" a letter to the *Index,* Nov. 19, 1885, No. 17 in Vol. II of *Monographs, Chiefly Medical,* arranged for the Library of the Class of 1828, v.p., v.d., bound 1887, HUa.

Bowditch's letter was written after Holmes's book was published; he was—rather to his own surprise apparently—defending Holmes's picture of Emerson as a mild abolitionist. Bowditch himself had been a militant one, an active worker in the underground railway and participant in demonstrations against the fugitive slave bill.

16 Emerson, *Journals,* typescript *OP Gulistan,* p. 5; ms. p. 8, HUh. Emerson here remarks that Holmes defended Whitman, apparently referring to some Saturday Club conversation. Annie Fields reports a conversation in which Holmes, after explaining that he read too carelessly to be a good critic, remarked that the right thing had not been said about Whitman. "His books sell largely, and there is a large audience of friends in Washington who praise and listen. Emerson believes in him; Lowell not at all; Longfellow finds some good in his 'yaup'; but the truth is, he is in an amorphous condition." (Annie Fields, *op. cit.,* p. 133.) See Chap. 24, n. 11, p. 437.

17 *Works*, XIV, 133.

18 Hayakawa and Jones, *op. cit.,* p. lx. Part of the tone of the biography as a whole may be due to the restraints he had to impose upon himself as much as to his feeling of insecurity about his subject; he is just as "dull" in his memoir of Motley, an intimate friend, whose personal confidences he enjoyed and whom he certainly understood. Moreover the biography called for more labor, both in collecting and organizing the material,

than Holmes was good for; he was not in the habit of *planning* his books, as his ms. notebooks show; the ms. notes for the Emerson, however, indicate that he tried hard here.

Holmes is certainly more at ease in his short "Tribute to Emerson," *Tributes to Longfellow and Emerson by the Massachusetts Historical Society* (Boston, 1882), pp. 39-50.

19 *Works,* XIV, 234-5.

20 Bowditch, *Monographs,* Vol. II, No. 17. See n. 15.

21 A.l., Jan. 27, 1885. HC.

22 *Henry Adams and His Friends,* ed., Harold Dean Cater (Boston, 1947), pp. 134-5.

Another letter is of some interest. S. Weir Mitchell wrote: "I wish that queer creature Walt Whitman could tell you as he did me of a walk on the Common with Emerson and of their discussion on poetical forms and license. I carried away one phrase—'that to read Emerson was like a cool plunge in some pure mountain lake—a shock and a wholesome freshness.' " (A.l., Dec. 21, 1884, HC.)

23 *New York Herald,* Apr. 18, 1883.

24 A.l., Jan. 16, 1885, to George Bancroft, Bancroft papers, MHS. The sudden death of his younger son, Edward Jackson Holmes, on June 17, 1884, was an unexpected shock that probably contributed to his feeling of weariness.

25 Lowell, *Letters,* II, 282. Holmes himself, thanking one of his correspondents, wrote: "almost any account of such a man must be good reading, especially if the memoir was made up largely of extracts from his writings in prose and verse." (A.l., Sept. 15, 1885, privately owned.)

26 N.d., Morse, II, 63.

27 *Works,* VII, 4.

28 *Ibid.,* VII, 21.

29 Aug. 31, 1884, *Critic,* 5 (Sept. 6, 1884), 109.

30 *Works,* VII, 23, 27.

31 *Ibid.,* VII, 28.

32 A.l., Sept. 3, 1885, to Gosse, privately owned.

33 Holmes, Notebook for *A Mortal Antipathy,* p. (17), ms., HC. The novel was originally called *A Tutor's Antipathy.*

34 *Works,* VII, 32.

35 *AM,* 57 (Jan. 1886), 91-98.

36 Edward Jackson Holmes.

37 Aug. 31, 1879, Morse, II, 258.

38 A.l., Mar. 13, 1886, privately owned.

39 *Works,* X, 14-15.

CHAPTER 23. *CELEBRITY IN ENGLAND*

1 *Critic,* 5 (May 15, 1886), 245.

2 *Works,* X, 18-19. This chapter is not documented in detail; besides *Our Hundred Days in Europe,* the chief sources are the mss. in

HC which provide dates and names not in the book. The mss. include two notebooks, a weather diary, several fragments, passport, and Amelia Sargent's Diary and Engagement Book.

3 *Works,* X, 19-22.

4 *Ibid.,* X, 22.

5 A.l., May 13, 1886, to Lowell, privately owned.

6 *Works,* X, 24.

7 *Ibid.,* X, 25.

8 *Ibid.,* X, 45.

9 A.ll., May 19, 22, 1886, J. E. Pfeiffer to Holmes, HC, identify Lady Harberton. Lady Stanley, described *Works,* X, 26, is identified in Holmes's ms. notebook.

10 *Works,* X, 193.

11 Holmes, Notebook for *Our Hundred Days in Europe,* ms., HC.

12 *Works,* X, 31-37, 39.

13 *Ibid.,* X, 63-65.

14 *Ibid.,* X, 50-52.

15 *Ibid.,* X, 199-200.

16 Holmes's passport is in HC. The description reads:
"Forehead—medium

Chin—narrow	Eyes—Blue	Nose—Small
Complexion—light	Hair—Gray	Mouth—Small
	Face—oval."	

17 *Works,* X, 102-3.

18 *Ibid.,* X, 110-1.

19 "The Broken Circle," *Poems,* p. 147.

20 *Works,* X, 167.

21 *Ibid.,* X, 171-2.

22 A.l., Aug. 30, 1886, HC.

CHAPTER 24. *LAST LEAF*

1 Christopher Cranch, *Life and Letters,* ed., Leonora Scott Cranch (Boston, 1917), p. 355; *Princeton Alumni Weekly* (Feb. 16, 1940), *Harvard Alumni Bulletin* (Mar. 3, 1940). See Scudder, *op. cit.,* II, 337-342, for story of Lowell's address.

2 *Poems,* p. 282.

3 A.l., May 29, 1887, to Julia Dorr, Middlebury College Library. See also May 4, 1888, Morse, II, 261-2.

4 *Poems,* p. 30.

5 *Works,* IV, 272-3.

6 Dec. 1887, Morse, II, 74.

7 A.l., Apr. 6, 1888, to Lowell, HUh.

8 *BMSJ,* 120 (Feb. 7, 1889), 129-130.

9 Emerson, *Journals,* X, 335. For the verses see *Poems,* p. 293. For

a good comment on Holmes as a poet for public occasions, see Hayakawa and Jones, *op. cit.*, pp. lxxxviii-xcv and Mr. Hayakawa's unpublished dissertation on Holmes, University of Wisconsin.

10 A.l., Feb. 25, 1889, HC.

11 *Poems*, p. 294. See Chap. 22, n. 16, p. 434. Other notes on Whitman are in Holmes's notebooks for *The Poet* and for *Over the Teacups*. In the first, p. (15), Holmes has written: "Walt Whitman—mush-bag." In the second, p. (29), he calls Whitman's poetry literature "camping out." See *Works*, IV, 234-5, for his printed observations on Whitman.

12 Scudder, *op. cit.* II, 334.

13 *Poems*, p. 295.

14 A.l., Mar. 13, 1889, John Holmes to Mary Lee Ware, HUh.

15 Apr. 13, 1889, Morse, II, 263-4.

16 Sept. 2, 1889, *ibid.*, II, 82.

17 *N.d.* [1891?], *ibid.*, II, 316.

18 *Works*, IV, 11.

19 *Ibid.*, IV, 187.

20 Emerson, *Journals*, Typescript *OP Gulistan*, p. 5; ms. p. 9.

21 *Works*, IV, 16-17.

22 *Ibid.*, IV, 163.

23 *Ibid.*, IV, 56-63.

24 A.l., Aug. 29, 1885, Holmes to his son, Harvard Law School.

25 A.l., June 27, 1885, to his son, Harvard Law School. See Holmes, *Speeches*, pp. 1-15, for the addresses to which Dr. Holmes refers.

26 A.l., Jan. 21 (1881) to his son, Harvard Law School. The doctor was being facetiously meek as he asked permission to attend a dinner for his son (as junior judge of the Supreme Judicial Court of Massachusetts).

27 *Works*, IV, 179, 182-185.

28 *Ibid.*, IV, 193-9.

29 *Poems*, pp. 301-4.

30 Jan. 15, 1891, Morse, II, 70.

31 A.l., Oct. 31, 1890, Lowell to Holmes, LC.

32 A.l., Aug. 18, 1890, to Lowell, HUh.

33 A.l., Jan. 15, 1891, to Julia Dorr, Middlebury College. Holmes's admiration for Arnold is expressed in a letter which he wrote after hearing the Englishman lecture in 1883. He defended Arnold against the criticisms of an English correspondent, observing: ". . . he recites his verses as if he lived them . . . he believes in himself which is what gives one vigor and enthusiasm . . ." (A.l., Nov. 29, 1883, NYPL; see also *Works*, XIV, *passim*.)

34 N.d. [1891?], Morse, II, 316.

35 A.l., July 11, 1889, to May, HUh.

36 Horace E. Scudder, Notebook for *AM*, ms.

37 A.l., Oct. 14, 1891, to Julia Dorr, Middlebury College. His admission probably accounts for his reference to "Emma" Dickinson, whose poetry interests him.

38 Holmes, ms., n.d. (Jan. or Feb. 1892), Parkman papers, HUh.

39 Miriam R. Small, *op. cit.*, p. 419.

40 A.l., Oct. 15, 1894, John Holmes to Mary Lee Ware, HUh.

41 *BET*, May 22, 1928, letter to editor from Ellen B. Stebbins.

42 A.l., Sept. 28, 1894, Francis J. Garrison to May, Class of '29 papers.

43 A.l., Oct. 8, 1894, Class Bk. p. 398.

44 Class Bk. p. 585.

45 *Works*, III, 337.

46 *Ibid.*, III, 105-6.

47 Black notebook, p. 103, and elsewhere in ms. notebooks; he refers several times to the observation.

48 Black notebook, pp. 90-110. See also "Pillow-Smoothing Authors," *AM*, 51 (April, 1883) 452-464.

49 Black notebook, p. 103. The entry reads: "Chapt. on Books very delightful."

LYCEUM LECTURES

CHRONOLOGICAL LIST

In the following list of Holmes's lyceum lectures, the dates in the first column indicate the seasons in which the lectures were first given. The breaks in the chronology indicate intervals when Holmes did not lecture.*

In the second column all known titles are recorded. The two titles in parentheses have been assigned to their dates by conjecture. To two different lectures, Holmes gave the same title, "English Versification." "The Americanized European" (1854-5) was first offered as a pair of lectures; the second was given only once. Titles of series of lectures are followed by arabic numerals indicating the number of lectures in the series.

In the third column, the sources of the fullest reports are given. For other reports see text and notes as indicated in the index. Blanks in the third column signify that no reports have been located. *CC* abbreviates *Cambridge Chronicle;* and B., Boston.

1837-38	English Versification	
1838-39	(Cities)	
1839-40	(Medicine, Past and Present)	
	National Prejudices	*BET*, 12/11/39.
1840-41	Natural Diet of Man	*B. Courier*, 12/12/40.
	unidentified series (3)	

* It is possible that Holmes lectured in 1844 and 1845. In his "Memoranda" (ms. notebook, HC), he lists towns, agents, and fees, but a check in the newspapers, and in printed and ms. lyceum records for four of the seven towns listed reveals no sign that Holmes accepted the invitations.

1841-42	Physical History of Mankind (3)	
	Scientific Mysticism (3)	
	1. Astrology and Alchemy	*MS.BK.*, pp. 77-125.
	2. Medical Delusions	*Works*, IX, 1-102.
	3. Homeopathy	*Works*, IX, 1-102.
1846-47	Urania	*Poems*, pp. 43-54.
1848-49	History of Medicine	*B. Post*, 12/7/48.
1849-50	Races	
1850-51	Love of Nature	*CC*, 1/24/52.
1851-52	Lectures and Lecturing	*CC*, 12/18/52.
1852-53	The Audience	*CC*, 12/10/53.
	The English Poets (12)	
	1. Rogers. . . .	*B. Traveller*, 3/23/53.
	2. Byron & Moore	*N. Y. Post*, 11/12/53.
	3. Scott & Macaulay	*N. Y. Post*, 11/26/53.
	4. Coleridge	*B. Traveller*, 4/2/53.
	5. Southey & Landor	*B. Traveller*, 4/6/53.
	6. Keats	*N. Y. Post*, 11/19/53.
	7. Shelley	*B. Traveller*, 4/13/53.
	8. Wordsworth	*N. Y. Herald*, 10/30/53.
	9. Tennyson & Browning	*N. Y. Post*, 12/3/53.
	10. Religious Poets	*N. Y. Post*, 11/5/53.
	11. Female Poets	*B. Traveller*, 4/28/53.
	12. Conclusion . . .	*B. Traveller*, 5/2/53.
1853-54	Literary Tribunals	*B. Journal*, 2/16/54.
1854-55	Americanized European I	*MS.BK.*, pp. 13-75.
	Americanized European II	*CC*, 11/11/54.
1855-56	Heart's Own Secret	Private Printing, HC.
1856-57	Lyrical Passion	*B. Journal*, 1/16/57.
1857-58	Our Second Selves	*B. Journal*, 12/24/57.
1858-59	Chief End of Man	*CC*, 12/4/58.
1863-64	The Weaning of Young America	Private Printing, HC.
1864-65	New England's Master-Key	Private Printing, HC.
1865-66	Poetry of the War	Private Printing, Huntington Library .
1872-	English Versification	Ms. notebooks, HC, and *Works*, VIII, 315-21.

REPRESENTATIVE ITINERARY
1851-52

The following itinerary for the season of 1851-52 is representative for the years 1850-56, when Holmes was most actively engaged in lecturing. Although he lectured in Baltimore in 1841 and in Cincinnati and Louisville in 1855, his orbit was ordinarily the one represented here, with the trips to central New York and to Maine coming after the close of the medical school session. His repertoire ordinarily included three lectures, occasionally four, at least one being new for the season.

The lectures for 1851-52 were "History of Medicine" (1848), "Love of Nature" (1850), and "Lectures and Lecturing" (1851); these are abbreviated below as Med., Nat., and Lec., respectively.

The itinerary is constructed from the lecture schedule in MS. BK., pp. 1055-6, the interleaved *Old Farmer's Almanac* for 1852, and the newspapers. The dates in parentheses are conjectural.

Med.	Amesbury, Mass.	(Nov.) 1851
Med.	North Bridgewater, Mass.	(Nov.)
Med.	Manchester, N. H.	(Nov.)
Med.	Great Falls, N. H.	(Nov.)
Med.	Randolph, N. H.	(Nov.)
Med.	Brooklyn, N. Y.	Dec. 8
Nat.	New York, N. Y.	Dec. 9
Nat.	Springfield, Mass.	(Dec. 10)
Nat.	Hartford, Conn.	Dec. 12
Nat.	Plymouth, Mass.	(Dec.)
Nat.	Portsmouth, N. H.	(Dec.)
Nat.	Beverly, Mass.	(Dec.)
Nat.	Whitinsville, Mass.	(Dec.)
Nat.	Stoughton, Mass.	(Dec.)
Nat.	Woburn, Mass.	(Dec.)
Nat.	Concord, (N. H.?)	(Dec.)
Nat.	South Reading, Mass.	(Dec.)
Nat.	Taunton, Mass.	(Dec.)
Nat.	Brighton, Mass.	(Dec.)
Nat.	Boston, Mass.	Dec. 31
Nat.	Salem, Mass.	Jan. 1, 1852
Nat.	Norwich, Conn.	Jan. 7
Nat.	Providence, R. I.	Jan. 8
Nat.	Woonsocket, R. I.	Jan. 9
Nat.	Lawrence, Mass.	Jan. 14
Nat.	Dorchester, Mass.	Jan. 16
Nat.	Cambridgeport, Mass.	Jan. 20
Nat.	North Brookfield, Mass.	Jan. 21
Nat.	Hopkinton, Mass.	Jan. 22

Med.	Woonsocket, R. I.	Jan.	23
Nat.	West Cambridge, Mass.	Jan.	26
Nat.	New Haven, Conn.	Jan.	29
Nat.	Medford, Mass.	Jan.	30
Nat.	East Boston, Mass.	Feb.	2
Nat.	North Bedford, Mass.	Feb.	3
Nat.	Millers Village, Mass.	Feb.	4
Nat.	Winchester, Mass.	Feb.	5
Nat.	Great Falls, N. H.	Feb.	6
Nat.	West Andover, Mass.	Feb.	9
Nat.	Newton Corners, Mass.	Feb.	10
Nat.	Milford, Mass.	Feb.	11
Nat.	Franklin, Mass.	Feb.	12
Nat.	Marblehead,-Mass.	Feb.	16
Nat.	Dover, N. H.	Feb.	17
Nat.	Lowell, Mass.	Feb.	18
Lec.	Boston, Mass.	Feb.	19
Lec.	Dorchester, Mass.	Feb.	20
Lec.	Waltham, Mass.	Feb.	21
Lec.	Boston, Mass.	Feb.	23
Lec.	Newton Lower Falls, Mass.	Feb.	24
Med.	Boston, Mass.	Feb.	25
Nat.	Hingham, Mass.	Feb.	26
Lec.	Portsmouth, N. H.	Mar.	1
Lec.	Danvers, Mass.	Mar.	3
Lec.	Roxbury, Mass.	Mar.	4
Lec.	Buffalo, N. Y.	Mar.	8
Lec.	Rochester, N. Y.	Mar.	9
Lec.	Troy, N. Y.	Mar.	11
Lec.	Saco, Me.	Mar.	16
Lec.	Portland, Me.	(Mar.	17)
Lec.	Augusta, Me.	Mar.	18
Lec.	Newburyport, Mass.	Mar.	19
Nat.	Neponset, Mass.	Mar.	22
Lec.	Charlestown, Mass.	Mar.	23
Lec.	Northampton, Mass.	Mar.	25
Lec.	Greenfield, Mass.	Mar.	26
Lec.	West Amesbury, Mass.	Mar.	29
Lec.	Whitinsville, Mass.	Mar.	30
Lec.	Ipswich, Mass.	Mar.	31
Lec.	East Bridgewater, Mass.	Apr.	1
Nat.	Charlestown, Mass.	Apr.	6

Index

443